Edited and designed
by David Dew

Contributors

Richard Birch
James Burn
Tom Collins
Richard Forristal
Ian Greensill
Dylan Hill
Paul Kealy

Lawrie Kelsey
Andrew King
Justin O'Hanlon
Brian Sheerin
James Stevens
Craig Thake
Nick Watts

Cover artwork by Duncan Olner
Inside artwork by Stefan Searle

Published in 2020 by Pitch Publishing on behalf of Racing Post, A2 Yeoman Gate, Yeoman Way, Worthing, Sussex, BN13 3QZ.

ISBN: 978-1785318320

Printed by Pureprint Group

LOWDOWN FROM THE TRAINERS

RACING POST EXPERTS

THIS SEASON'S KEY HORSES

HENRY DE BROMHEAD

Huge firepower hints at best season so far

IN A land in which Willie Mullins and Gordon Elliott have been so dominant over the past number of years, being the third-biggest jumps trainer is not a bad place to be and is where Henry de Bromhead has been for the last three or four seasons. Numbers are up this time though and quality is up too, so much so that the Knockeen trainer has never had so much ammunition at the very highest level going into the winter.

It seems appropriate to start with the

stable star, Kenny Alexander's unbeaten mare **Honeysuckle**. Already approaching stardom at the beginning of last season, she came out of it with her record unblemished and three more Grade 1s to her credit.

An impressive performance in the Hatton's Grace Hurdle was followed by a less convincing victory in the Irish Champion Hurdle. It showed two things. One was how

she battled back to win, and the other seemed to expose that her jumping probably was not slick enough for her to be competitive in the Champion Hurdle. But she went on to produce possibly a career-best in getting the better of the brilliant Willie Mullins-trained mare Benie Des Dieux in a vintage running of the Close Brothers Mares' Hurdle.

De Bromhead says of her: "She's summered really well and has come back in looking brilliant – she's working well. We'll aim initially for the Hatton's Grace Hurdle at Fairyhouse and go from there. We'll look for a similar campaign as last year and go for the Irish Champion Hurdle, and from there we'll see how things are unfolding.

"It was a close call last year between the

Henry de Bromhead and his superstar mare Honeysuckle

■ From four runners at Kempton, De Bromhead has saddled two winners and a third

5

Champion Hurdle and the Mares' Hurdle and it probably will be again."

You would imagine that Honeysuckle will be given her every chance to prove she could go to the Champion Hurdle with a genuine chance. She doesn't have to improve that much to be a factor.

Going for gold

In no division is De Bromhead more stacked than among the three-mile chasers, with potentially at least two genuine Gold Cup hopefuls.

Although **Monalee** failed to score last season in three outings, it was the season when he seemed to come of age. An unlucky defeat to Delta Work in the Savills Chase at Leopardstown when Rachael Blackmore lost an iron did not do a whole lot to convince about him staying the 3m2f Gold Cup trip, and it seemed the wise course of action would be to go for the Ryanair Chase.

However, the decision to go for the Gold Cup was fully justified as he saw out every yard of the trip in being beaten less than two lengths in fourth place behind Al Boum Photo – and he might well have been third but for meeting some interference at the top of the hill.

"He ran a blinder in the Gold Cup and we'll be plotting a similar campaign this year. He stayed really well, which was in some doubt, and it was unfortunate the way he was hampered and lost his place a little at the top of the hill. It possibly cost him a place.

"We're thinking of starting him off in a Listed 2m6f chase at Thurles in mid-November. It looks an ideal race and I don't think he'll have a penalty. We'll see how things go there and we might even have a crack at the King George at Christmas," says the trainer.

Also potentially in the mix for top staying chase honours is second-season chaser **Minella Indo** owned like Monalee by Barry Maloney.

The 2019 Albert Bartlett Novices' Hurdle winner had a relatively quiet campaign last

Minella Indo: his trainer describes him as "very exciting"

season which his trainer described as being totally concentrated on the RSA Chase, and it would have worked out perfectly but for the extraordinary finishing effort of Barry Geraghty on Champ. But it did demonstrate once again how well Minella Indo operates around Cheltenham.

De Bromhead says: " He always takes a run or two so it's important we get him out. Last year we took the decision to focus strongly on Cheltenham – this year we're going to focus up to Christmas and then see how we're going. The RSA Chase was just such an extraordinary race last season with where Champ came from to beat us. We lost very little in defeat I thought. He ran really well and he is a very exciting horse I think."

Going for gold

The target for **Chris's Dream** remains a little more uncertain. The Robcour-owned gelding enjoyed a lucrative if very light campaign last season. A convincing victory in the valuable Troytown Handicap Chase over 3m at Navan was followed by dropping back to 2m4f successfully in the Red Mills Chase at Gowran in February.

It was a run the team had to get into him as he had been taken out of the Irish Gold Cup two weeks previously due to the ground being too quick.

At Cheltenham in the Gold Cup, he travelled beautifully into the race under Aidan Coleman before fading in the straight as his stamina seemingly gave out.

De Bromhead says: "We're aiming him for the Champion Chase at Down Royal initially, but I'm not so sure whether we'll train him as a Gold Cup horse. He seems to travel effortlessly up to three miles so we might end up dropping him back in trip.

"He's a hard horse to judge. I wouldn't like to discount the Gold Cup because he's always looked like a staying horse, but the first impression from last season's race was that he didn't stay. We'll pick our races for him after Down Royal."

More to come from Kettle

At the end of last season, De Bromhead arguably had the best pair of two-mile novice chasers in his care, headed by Arkle winner **Put The Kettle On**, a mare whose love for Cheltenham became very apparent as the season progressed, and it is a venue she will be returning to.

The difference between last season and this is already very apparent. She had come through quite a busy summer campaign last year, winning around the likes of Kilbeggan and Downpatrick, before winning a Grade 2 at Cheltenham in November.

Whether by design or circumstance, she didn't appear again until the festival in March when she pulled out all the stops up the hill under Aidan Coleman to see off Fakir D'oudairies.

Her trainer says: "We had her in the Grade 2 at Gowran but the ground was a

Connections of Put The Kettle On celebrate Arkle victory at Cheltenham last season

little better than I would ideally have wanted, so we decided to go straight for the Shloer Chase at Cheltenham next month. She showed last season how much she loves Cheltenham.

"She came out of the blue a little when winning there last November and she was probably the forgotten horse in the Arkle. She's still a young mare and we're hoping she can progress into a mare for a championship race."

Cheltenham hoodoo

While Put The Kettle On was coming to the boil on the sidelines, stable companion **Notebook** carried all before him in the 2m novice division as he reeled off four straight victories including a pair of sound-jumping and game successes in a pair of 2m1f Grade 1s at Leopardstown.

In that context, his poor performance at Cheltenham was inexplicable, although little went right in the preliminaries or during the race. His ability is not in question, but the concern is that he has performed poorly on both visits to Cheltenham, having been beaten 51 lengths in the Ballymore Novices' Hurdle in 2019.

"I was looking at the Grade 2 at Down Royal for him over two miles three furlongs and the Poplar Square Chase at Naas over two miles. He excelled over two miles last year and I'm not pushed about going out in trip with him, it's just that the Down Royal race is so suitable with it being for second season novices.

"He didn't run his race at Cheltenham but a couple of his wins were very impressive and I would certainly hope he'll be able to mix it with the best of the two-mile chasers," says De Bromhead.

More to come from Plus Tard

The interesting horse at around that trip could well be **A Plus Tard**, who put up a fine performance to beat Chacun Pour Soi in a Grade 1 over 2m1f at Leopardstown last Christmas. The Ryanair Chase was his

preferred target and he put up his best RPR of the season in finishing a close third to Min.

"We'll aim him at the Fortria Chase at Navan and see how that goes. He's fairly versatile as to trip but he won his Grade 1 over 2m1f at Leopardstown and that's the trip we'll start off at. His run in the Ryanair was probably his best run of last season, but he's still only six and still just a baby and we are really looking forward to getting him out," says De Bromhead.

Expect the stable to be strong in the novice chase divisions once more this season. The Robcour-owned filly **Zarkareva** has done well in a short space of time, and as a four-year-old she will enjoy some significant allowances for the rest of this year.

She looks set to go to Cheltenham in November to try to land the same Grade 2 novice chase won last season by Put The Kettle On.

'Jumping is his game'

A potentially exciting prospect as a staying novice chaser is **Cobbler's Way**. Winner of a Leopardstown maiden hurdle last Christmas, he put up his best performance when a staying-on runner-up to Latest Exhibition in a 2m6f Grade 1 novice hurdle at the Dublin Racing Festival. A disappointing effort in the Albert Bartlett put a bit of a dampener on the season, but chasing was always going to be his game.

His trainer says: "He'll go for a beginners' chase in the next few weeks. He's won his point-to-point and he jumps well, it looks to be his game."

There was excitement about **Captain Guinness** before he flopped on his chasing debut at Tipperary in October when he was pulled up early and found to be clinically abnormal. His novice hurdle form from last season, particularly when so unluckily brought down two out in the Supreme Novices' Hurdle at Cheltenham led to high hopes he would make the grade as a novice chaser this season and perhaps he still can.

Notable as a staying novice hurdle prospect is **Royal Thief**. He might well have exceeded expectations last year by winning a maiden and a staying novice hurdle, and did enough to land a beginners' chase on his debut over fences at Kilbeggan in October.

A dour stayer, he could well develop enough to be an Irish Grand National horse in the spring. De Bromhead says: "He's a real staying type who is taking to fences really well. We will see how he progresses but he's a real out-and-out stayer."

There is a good team of young horses in the yard for novice hurdling, and one who looks particularly exciting is the once-raced **Bob Olinger**.

A point-to-point winner for Pat Doyle, he came to a point-to-point bumper at Gowran Park in March with a reputation and it proved well founded as he quickened like a good horse to win a traditionally well-contested contest by ten lengths.

He should make his mark in novice hurdles at 2m to 2m4f.

"We like him and he works well. He'll go for a maiden hurdle in the next few weeks and we'll take it from there," says De Bromhead.
Interview by Justin O'Hanlon

Three De Bromhead beauties (from top): Notebook, A Plus Tard and Royal Thief

HENRY DE BROMHEAD
KNOCKEEN, COUNTY WATERFORD

RECORD AROUND THE COURSES

	Total W-R	Per cent	Non-hcp Hdle	Non-hcp Chase	Hcp Hdle	Hcp Chase	N.H. Flat	£1 level stake
Punchestown	54-417	12.9	14-124	30-134	2-57	6-67	2-35	-155.07
Clonmel	40-245	16.3	25-128	8-49	6-42	1-14	0-12	+5.78
Kilbeggan	35-188	18.6	12-67	12-42	3-24	6-44	2-11	-11.42
Limerick	35-210	16.7	13-85	13-56	4-23	3-32	2-14	-25.88
Tramore	35-258	13.6	11-104	11-73	7-51	4-20	2-10	-100.90
Killarney	32-192	16.7	7-40	14-64	2-27	5-45	4-16	-17.02
Fairyhouse	32-249	12.9	19-90	6-57	2-43	1-31	4-28	-36.93
Tipperary	29-153	19.0	13-61	11-40	0-21	5-24	0-7	-20.36
Leopardstown	29-248	11.7	14-65	9-66	3-62	3-47	0-8	-39.12
Gowran Park	28-173	16.2	7-72	13-45	4-26	1-17	3-13	-42.78
Thurles	28-186	15.1	16-83	8-46	4-21	0-9	0-27	-80.74
Navan	23-155	14.8	8-57	9-50	2-16	3-20	1-12	-36.15
Galway	23-162	14.2	1-29	13-43	3-29	6-54	0-7	+0.10
Cork	22-175	12.6	11-72	5-29	2-31	1-25	3-18	-66.75
Down Royal	21-87	24.1	12-41	4-19	0-6	4-15	1-6	+37.05
Naas	21-130	16.2	5-54	13-40	1-12	2-16	0-8	-8.87
Listowel	20-117	17.1	5-32	8-28	0-15	7-36	0-6	-13.57
Wexford	20-129	15.5	7-58	8-33	1-20	4-16	0-2	-30.99
Roscommon	16-86	18.6	10-33	5-28	0-5	1-12	0-8	-20.02
Downpatrick	13-73	17.8	6-39	2-12	5-17	0-5	0-0	-3.51
Wexford (rh)	8-59	13.6	2-22	1-11	4-11	1-9	0-6	-8.92
Ballinrobe	6-56	10.7	0-17	5-20	1-9	0-8	0-2	-30.98
Bellewstown	5-35	14.3	4-20	0-0	1-15	0-0	0-0	-3.20
Sligo	2-13	15.4	0-4	1-4	0-1	1-4	0-0	-4.7
Cheltenham	13-145	9.0	4-33	6-64	1-16	2-30	0-2	-4.75
Aintree	6-48	12.5	1-9	3-15	0-1	2-22	0-1	+21.00
Kempton	2-4	50.0	0-0	2-4	0-0	0-0	0-0	+3.73
Sandown	2-13	15.4	0-2	2-10	0-0	0-1	0-0	-6.63
Newton Abbot	1-1	100.0	0-0	1-1	0-0	0-0	0-0	+0.44
Newcastle	1-2	50.0	1-2	0-0	0-0	0-0	0-0	+5.00
Uttoxeter	1-3	33.3	0-0	0-0	0-0	1-3	0-0	+2.00
Ffos Las	0-1	0.0	0-0	0-0	0-0	0-1	0-0	-1.00
Ascot	0-4	0.0	0-0	0-2	0-0	0-2	0-0	-4.00

GORDON ELLIOTT

The perfect blend of youth and experience for best season so far

First light on the gallops at Gordon Elliott's Longwood Stables in County Meath

WINNERS IN LAST FOUR SEASONS 193, 210, 177, 156

THE premature end to the 2019-20 jumps season denied racing fans what was shaping up to be another almighty scrap for the trainers' championship in Ireland.

Willie Mullins led Gordon Elliott by just shy of €160,000 when racing ground to a halt in March and the Fairyhouse and Punchestown festivals were lost due to the coronavirus pandemic.

Elliott has made no secret about the fact that winning a trainers' championship is up there with his greatest ambitions in racing and there is little doubt he is best placed to do so this season.

A shot at rewriting history with **Tiger Roll** has to be high up on the priority list as well. Last season did not go to plan for Elliott's star inmate, who finished second in the Glenfarclas Cross Country Chase after arriving at Cheltenham off the back of a less than ideal prep, and the trainer admits the Aintree Grand National being cancelled was a blessing in disguise for the most popular horse in training.

Elliott says: "The plan is to go back for the cross-country at Cheltenham and then all the talk will be about Aintree, but we'll be training him for Cheltenham first and foremost.

"We made no secret of the fact he had a less than ideal prep for Cheltenham and then the ground turned up soft on the day when he was second to a very good horse. It was going to be a bit of a rush to build him back up for the Grand National and, in hindsight, what happened with the race may have been

a blessing in disguise as far as he was concerned."

Elliott reports Tiger Roll to have come out of his pipe-opener on the level at Navan in top shape and revealed he will be charting a path towards the November meeting at Cheltenham next.

The trainer says: "He gave away a lot of ground at Navan but came home well and that will leave him spot on. We have lots of options but I'd say we'll go to Cheltenham for the cross-country at the November meeting next. He's a different horse now to this time last year. He's absolutely bouncing."

If the stars align and Tiger Roll makes it back to Aintree to try to win the Grand National for an unprecedented third time in a row, he could be joined by **Alpha Des Obeaux** and **Ravenhill**.

Elliott says: "I was really looking forward to running Alpha Des Obeaux in the race last year and I think he'll have a big chance again this year. I've always felt he has the right attributes for a race like the National. Ravenhill could also run well especially if it's nice ground. We might put him away and aim him at that."

Strong Gold Cup challenge

New recruit **Presenting Percy** will also have the Aintree Grand National on his agenda but will chart a path towards the Gold Cup at Cheltenham alongside **Delta Work** beforehand. Both horses are in line to return in the Ladbrokes Champion Chase at Down Royal.

Elliott says: "I've always liked Presenting Percy. He has to improve 6lb or 7lb to be in with a chance of winning a Gold Cup but we're hopeful he can and we're very happy with what he's showing us at home. I can't wait to start him off at Down Royal and hopefully he has a big season ahead of him.

"If you look back at last season's Gold Cup, there's no reason to say he wouldn't have been in the money if he hadn't fallen. They went no gallop and he was coming from off the pace, which wouldn't have

suited, but he was coming with a good run when he came down two out. We're very glad to have him. The plan is very much the Gold Cup but we'll also give ourselves the option of the Grand National. I think he could run very well in that."

Of Delta Work, Elliott says: "We've learned a bit more about him every year and we know he always comes on from his first run, so we'd be expecting him to take a good step forward from whatever he does in the Ladbrokes Champion Chase at Down Royal.

"He's still a young horse and we think there could be more improvement with another summer under his belt. He was beaten only six or seven lengths in the Gold Cup despite the fact he didn't jump well on the day – he just never got into a rhythm for whatever reason at Cheltenham – so I wouldn't be writing him off at all.

"Jack [Kennedy] seems to get a tune out of him that nobody else can, so hopefully he'll be back in time to ride him at Down Royal. He'll take the exact same path to the Gold Cup this season and I still believe in him."

Ryanair plan for Samcro

Samcro will have the Ryanair as his main target this season while Elliott believes there's a lot more fun to be had with **Chosen Mate** and **Battleoverdoyen**, who will be campaigned over shorter distances.

Elliott says: "Samcro will head for the second-season novice chase at Down Royal and then you'd love to aim him back at something like the Ryanair at Cheltenham. We could go for the John Durkan at Punchestown and maybe something like the Kinloch Brae at Thurles before Cheltenham.

"I'm not going to do what I did last season in running him on bottomless ground during the winter. Everyone was saying how good a training performance it was getting him back to win the Marsh but I'd argue it was one of the worst training decisions I've ever made when I ran him on heavy ground at Limerick last winter. I won't make that mistake again with him and he could get a

Get closer to the racing.

RACE REPLAYS
Watch unlimited video race replays from all 86 British and Irish racecourses

DIGITAL NEWSPAPER
Get tomorrow's Racing Post paper digitally and in full every day at 9pm

EXPERT ANALYSIS
Study the form alongside our experts with in-running comments and post-race analysis.

Join now at racingpost.com/membersclub

For The Must-Have Racing Info
RACING POST

little break during the winter as he's just not the same horse on deep ground."

He adds: "We could bring Battleoverdoyen back in trip and may even start him off in the Fortria Chase over two miles at Navan. He didn't do a whole pile wrong last year but maybe his form just tapered off a little bit.

Chosen Mate won the Grand Annual at Cheltenham last season and will be competitive in all of those conditions chases over two miles. He could pick up a lot of prize-money."

Envoi's Marsh aim

The Marsh Novices' Chase will be the long-term plan for the unbeaten Champion Bumper and Ballymore winner **Envoi Allen** (*streaking home at Cheltenham, above*) who, like most of Elliott's best horses, will start back at Down Royal.

Elliott is convinced Envoi Allen will make an even better chaser and, while the RSA Chase would appear unlikely at this early stage, he is not ruling out running the young star over three miles in Ireland at some point.

He says: "We can't wait to send him over a fence as this is what he was bought to do. It's no secret that I like to start off my best horses at Down Royal and the beginners' chase that Samcro won last year looks the right place for him to go. He can come up and down in trip in Ireland, like he did last season in his novice hurdles, but if I was to put my hand on my heart about what race he'll run in at Cheltenham I'd have to say it would be the Marsh."

Elliott adds: "Easywork chased home Envoi Allen in the Ballymore last season and that's good form. We're looking forward to seeing what he can do over fences and he stays well."

Grade 1-winning novice hurdler **Felix Desjy** is the opposite to Envoi Allen and Easywork in that he's all speed and he'll be bidding to prove he's a genuine Arkle contender when he takes on Darver Star in the Craddockstown Novice Chase at Punchestown.

Elliott says: "He'll go for the

Craddockstown. He'll come on a lot for Killarney and he's a nice horse to have for the two-mile novice chasing sphere. The Arkle will be on his agenda but you'd have to say he's more effective on a flat track, where he can put other horses under pressure, and he could be hard to beat at Aintree. He won a Grade 1 over hurdles there as a novice a couple of seasons back, so we know he likes it there."

On the rest of his novice chase squad, Elliott says: "**Column Of Fire** looked as though he was delivering a winning challenge when falling at the last in the Martin Pipe last season. He was very sore afterwards, but thankfully we have him for this season and we'll go over fences. He's a classy horse.

"**Commander Of Fleet** is a Grade 1 winner. He got a leg last year but he's back and looks great. He's an exciting horse to go chasing with. I'm going to give **Galvin** a break and aim him at the National Hunt Chase at Cheltenham. I think he's made for that race.

"There could be a nice handicap in **Run Wild Fred**, while **Daylight Katie** is an exciting mare to go chasing with. **Andy Dufresne** is there as well and I think he can be better over fences."

Champion Hurdle material

When Gigginstown's Eddie O'Leary went to the sales, the brief was simple; buy big, good-looking staying chasers that would hopefully develop into Gold Cup horses.

Abacadabras is the exception to the rule and would appear a major contender for the Champion Hurdle, a race the powerful owners, along with Elliott, have unfinished business in following the disappointing effort of Apple's Jade a couple of seasons back.

Elliott says: "He'll start off at Down Royal in the Grade 3 WKD Hurdle and we'll go down the Champion Hurdle route with him. He's always shown us loads of pace and you could say he was a bit unlucky not to win the Supreme last season. He was left in front a bit too soon and it didn't suit but he ran a huge race to finish second. We're hoping he's up to the standard needed to win a Champion Hurdle."

Elliott has added **Petit Mouchoir** to his team and has the Morgiana Hurdle at Punchestown pencilled in as a possible target for the 2017 winner of the Irish Champion Hurdle.

He says: "Petit Mouchoir is a great horse as he can run in all of the big hurdle races in Ireland and hopefully pick up a cheque each time provided he stays sound. How many horses can you buy for £70,000 and know that he will win at least half of that if he stays sound? Not many.

"He's classy and we thought he was worth taking a chance on. We'll keep him over hurdles for the time being but I wouldn't rule out going back over fences with him. The Morgiana Hurdle might be a nice starting point for him."

The weakness of the staying hurdle division has tempted Elliott to keep last

season's Albert Bartlett third **Fury Road** over the smaller obstacles for another season while **Sire Du Berlais**, winner of the past two Pertemps Finals at the festival, will tackle open company.

Elliott says: "Fury Road is going to stay over hurdles this season and there's a nice second-season novice race over 2m6f at Navan for him to start off in. You'd be hoping he can develop into a horse who would be competitive in the Stayers' Hurdle. That division looks quite open and that's why we kept him to hurdles this year."

He adds: "Sire Du Berlais will have to improve if he's to step up into open company but hopefully he can. We don't really have any other option but to go down that route, so hopefully he's up to it."

Looking forward to Fantasio

Gigginstown might be exiting the stage, but there are a couple of chapters yet to be written and, judging by the strength in depth in the arsenal of the powerful owner's novice

Petit Mouchoir has joined Gordon Elliott and is set to start off over hurdles but could also switch back to fences at some stage

hurdles team, they are set to be around for a good while longer.

On the best of the Gigginstown youngsters, Elliott says: "**Fantasio D'alene** should develop into a good staying novice this year and is one we're really looking forward to. He could end up being an Albert Bartlett horse.

"**Farouk D'alene** won two bumpers for us and is a tough horse who jumps and gallops well. He could be a real good staying novice hurdler. The Ballymore could be the race for him. **Wide Receiver** probably should have won at Punchestown but should come on from that. We like him a lot and there should be more to come."

Ballyadam can take high rank

Cheveley Park Stud has become an increasingly important cog in the wheel of Elliott's juggernaut operation. Finding another Envoi Allen is going to be a tall order but, in **Ballyadam**, the trainer believes the owners have another classy novice hurdler to go to war with this season.

He says: "Ballyadam is a smart horse. The plan will be to start him off in a maiden hurdle at Down Royal and I'd be disappointed if he's not a Graded horse over hurdles this season."

Speaking about other novice hurdlers to note, Elliott says: "**Homme D'un Soir** could be a bit of a dark horse this season. **Eskylane** will come on a lot from his win at Punchestown and will go to Navan next for the For Auction Novice Hurdle. Then there's **Queens Brook**, a mare I really like because she wants to win and I just love that in horses. She'll go to Down Royal next for the Grade 3 mares' novice that Daylight Katie won last year and, depending on how that goes, I wouldn't be afraid of taking on the boys at some stage with her before Cheltenham where you'd be hoping she'd run well in a mares' novice hurdle."

Malone Road is a horse who promised the world as a bumper horse but has endured hardship off the track with injuries and

■ Elliott doesn't have many runners in claiming races but take the hint when he does – he has a 50% record

Malone Road cruises home in his bumper days; (right, from top): Indigo Breeze, Fantasio D'alene, Weseekhimhere, Eskylane and Queens Brook

Elliott raised doubts about the youngster ever fulfilling his massive potential.

Elliott says: "Malone Road came home from his run in Listowel very sore and he's on the easy list, so we probably won't see him until Christmas. He looks like he'll need stepping up in trip but you'd have to say it's unlikely he'll ever be the horse he promised to be as a bumper horse, which is unfortunate. He just doesn't seem to be the same since he came back from his injury."

Best bunch of bumper horses

You can talk until the cows come home about your Delta Works and your Tiger Rolls but the stars of the future excite Elliott just as much. He has any amount of potential top-notchers to run in bumpers this season.

He says: "We have a lot of horses who have won bumpers and most of them will be aimed at a winners' bumper next rather than going hurdling. We think **Chemical Energy** is very good. He was impressive at Roscommon and the plan is to go for a winners' race at Down Royal and take things from there. **Dark Spark**, **Weseekhimhere** and **Indigo Breeze** are others we'll aim at winners' bumpers in the coming weeks."

Elliott adds: "There is some serious talent there and I pinch myself some mornings watching them go up the gallop.

"**Sir Gerhard** is a point-to-point winner and he's doing everything right at home. He should be ready to start soon.

"**Fiston Des Issards** came highly recommended out of Colin Bowe's after he won his point and he's one we're looking forward to as well but he's a big staying chaser for the future.

"**Gars De Sceaux** is another point winner we're excited about and **Gerri Colombe** is also nice.

"**Magic Tricks** is a brother to Abacadabras and he also goes well. He's like his brother in that he's speedy. I've made no secret about the fact I like **Hollow Games**, who wants soft ground and there's a lovely horse called **Glenglass**, who did exceptionally well to win a point at four, because he's massive and he's one for the future.

Ginto won a point for us last month and, to be honest, we'd have been shocked if he was beaten because he's a horse Jamie Codd has been very excited about for a while now. If Jamie is right about him, and hopefully he is, I'd say he's a horse we'll be hearing plenty more about."

Interview by Brian Sheerin

GORDON ELLIOTT
LONGWOOD, COUNTY MEATH

RECORD AROUND THE COURSES

	Total W-R	Per cent	Non-hcp Hdle	Non-hcp Chase	Hcp Hdle	Hcp Chase	N.H. Flat	£1 level stake
Fairyhouse	131-877	14.9	56-306	29-163	10-166	14-133	22-109	-312.32
Punchestown	128-870	14.7	50-306	30-175	12-159	11-117	25-113	-113.78
Downpatrick	113-550	20.5	55-235	7-52	20-137	10-47	21-79	-47.72
Navan	110-675	16.3	49-271	14-91	18-156	8-89	21-68	-166.59
Down Royal	98-497	19.7	40-200	26-97	9-94	5-46	18-60	-107.63
Limerick	61-405	15.1	27-161	15-86	8-73	3-37	8-48	-119.26
Thurles	56-275	20.4	21-120	18-69	7-41	1-7	9-38	-37.56
Kilbeggan	52-393	13.2	18-116	13-76	6-83	6-80	9-38	-168.20
Clonmel	50-280	17.9	17-126	11-58	12-57	1-7	9-32	-46.12
Leopardstown	49-465	10.5	19-168	10-73	7-98	7-78	6-48	-109.19
Cork	46-271	17.0	23-128	6-36	6-50	4-30	7-27	-63.05
Tramore	38-279	13.6	10-95	13-73	7-60	4-18	4-33	-61.35
Naas	38-291	13.1	20-126	6-50	2-46	1-32	9-37	-114.01
Gowran Park	38-317	12.0	19-126	6-54	3-60	2-52	8-25	-123.77
Galway	38-330	11.5	12-76	13-68	2-91	5-58	6-37	-139.78
Ballinrobe	35-264	13.3	15-98	6-26	7-85	0-16	7-39	-58.01
Roscommon	34-170	20.0	12-64	6-28	7-37	1-17	8-24	+2.50
Bellewstown	25-147	17.0	9-50	0-0	12-82	0-0	4-15	-32.99
Sligo	22-139	15.8	9-55	5-18	3-40	1-6	4-20	-38.03
Wexford	22-165	13.3	9-57	8-44	1-25	0-14	4-25	-87.12
Killarney	19-150	12.7	7-36	8-48	1-37	3-19	0-10	-70.49
Listowel	17-135	12.6	8-32	2-22	2-36	3-33	2-12	-35.82
Tipperary	16-130	12.3	3-44	5-26	2-35	0-7	6-18	-68.29
Wexford (rh)	4-50	8.0	2-20	1-9	1-14	0-3	0-4	-36.00
Perth	149-528	28.2	60-138	6-37	46-181	28-134	9-38	-34.80
Cheltenham	44-311	14.1	9-61	15-61	12-112	6-67	2-10	+76.54
Ayr	16-80	20.0	7-27	0-5	4-21	2-13	3-14	-28.93
Sedgefield	12-37	32.4	8-17	1-4	3-9	0-5	0-2	-5.85
Cartmel	11-44	25.0	5-12	0-5	3-16	3-11	0-0	-7.56
Aintree	11-88	12.5	1-12	2-14	4-15	3-43	1-4	+8.00
Uttoxeter	8-23	34.8	3-7	1-1	3-8	0-4	1-3	+0.80
Hexham	7-26	26.9	0-7	0-2	3-7	2-6	2-4	+1.09
Musselburgh	6-14	42.9	4-8	0-0	0-2	1-1	1-3	-0.51
Ludlow	4-14	28.6	2-6	0-4	1-3	1-1	0-0	+7.37
Southwell	3-5	60.0	3-4	0-0	0-1	0-0	0-0	-0.67
Bangor	3-11	27.3	0-2	0-1	3-5	0-2	0-1	-0.01
Worcester	3-14	21.4	2-6	0-2	0-2	0-1	1-3	-6.91
Carlisle	2-3	66.7	1-2	0-0	0-0	0-0	1-1	+10.00
Leicester	2-3	66.7	1-2	0-0	1-1	0-0	0-0	+7.25
Newton Abbot	2-3	66.7	1-1	0-1	1-1	0-0	0-0	+0.37
Ffos Las	2-7	28.6	2-3	0-0	0-1	0-3	0-0	-1.89
Kelso	2-8	25.0	0-2	0-1	0-1	2-2	0-2	-1.38
Ascot	2-9	22.2	0-1	0-1	2-6	0-0	0-1	+32.00
Wetherby	2-14	14.3	2-8	0-2	0-3	0-1	0-0	-11.00
Stratford	2-18	11.1	2-10	0-1	0-4	0-2	0-1	-9.88
Exeter	1-1	100.0	1-1	0-0	0-0	0-0	0-0	+0.33
Taunton	1-2	50.0	1-1	0-0	0-1	0-0	0-0	-0.27
Towcester	1-2	50.0	1-2	0-0	0-0	0-0	0-0	-0.82
Fakenham	1-3	33.3	0-1	0-0	0-1	1-1	0-0	+2.50
Huntingdon	1-3	33.3	1-1	0-1	0-0	0-0	0-1	+0.00
Hereford	1-4	25.0	0-2	1-1	0-1	0-0	0-0	-2.00
Haydock	1-6	16.7	1-1	0-2	0-3	0-0	0-0	-2.25
Newcastle	1-6	16.7	0-2	0-0	0-0	1-3	0-1	-4.33
Doncaster	0-1	0.0	0-1	0-0	0-0	0-0	0-0	-1.00
Plumpton	0-1	0.0	0-0	0-1	0-0	0-0	0-0	-1.00
Chepstow	0-2	0.0	0-0	0-0	0-1	0-1	0-0	-2.00
Market Rasen	0-2	0.0	0-0	0-0	0-1	0-1	0-0	-2.00
Catterick	0-3	0.0	0-1	0-1	0-0	0-0	0-1	-3.00
Sandown	0-4	0.0	0-1	0-0	0-2	0-0	0-1	-4.00
Kempton	0-5	0.0	0-2	0-2	0-1	0-0	0-0	-5.00
Newbury	0-5	0.0	0-1	0-0	0-3	0-1	0-0	-5.00
Warwick	0-8	0.0	0-2	0-1	0-4	0-0	0-1	-8.00

WARREN GREATREX

High hopes Bague can sign off on a high note

THERE'S still a big race waiting to be won by stable favourite **La Bague Au Roi** in what will be the mare's swansong season.

That is the opinion of Warren Greatrex, the master of Uplands stable in Upper Lambourn.

And a small wind operation after a seasonal opening fourth at Perth in late September gives connections hope of giving the mare a huge send-off.

La Bague Au Roi: tough mare will bow out this season

WINNERS IN LAST FOUR SEASONS **58, 52, 38, 18**

The successful operation shortly after the Scottish trip came on the advice of former champion jockey Richard Johnson, who survived a final-fence blunder which cost his mount second place behind race-fit Perth specialist Amalfi Doug.

"Dickie [Johnson] said she felt as if she had all her old enthusiasm and galloped from fence to fence, although she was getting tired when she made her mistake at the last.

■ Greatrex does particularly well in bumpers. He has a 21% five-year strike-rate and a profit of £45.20

"He thought we might want to get her wind checked. These soft-palate operations can make a big difference," says Greatrex, who has La Bague Au Roi pencilled in for the Grade 2 Charlie Hall Chase over three miles at Wetherby on the last weekend of October.

It was a race in which she made her reappearance last season but was pulled up before four out after never travelling with her usual zest.

"The plan is to go for the Charlie Hall again as long as the ground isn't as soft as it was last year. I made a mistake in running her and I think it left a mark on her," says Greatrex.

"I think it's fair to say the rest of the season wasn't as good as the previous season, when she won four times [including the Grade 1 Kauto Star Novices' Chase at Kempton and the Grade 1 Flogas Novice Chase at Leopardstown]."

La Bague Au Roi was already fit before the operation, so getting her ready for the Charlie Hall should pose no problems. Whatever the Wetherby outcome, Greatrex is also considering the Grade 3 Ladbrokes Trophy Chase over 3m2f at Newbury in late November, a track where she has won three times from three runs.

"We don't want to overface her but we wouldn't be surprised if she still had a big race in her," adds Greatrex. "If all goes well, we'd like to enter her for the King George at Kempton and the new Grade 2 mares' chase over 2m4f at the Cheltenham Festival. That would be a great way to end her career."

Emitom to do well over fences

Another stable favourite is **Emitom**, a high-class hurdler rated 155 who was fourth in the Stayers' Hurdle at the Cheltenham Festival this year.

He was made odds-on favourite to win his first venture over fences in early October at Uttoxeter but was caught on the line.

"We know he will improve and he has bigger targets. What pleased me was the way he jumped and measured his fences."

He was made favourite for a three-runner novice chase at Ffos Las in mid-October but after leading until before three out, he weakened and was eased before the line.

"He's only six years old and I've always thought he would be a better chaser than hurdler – and I think I'll be proved right."

Audacity has talent but "is a bit of a monkey to put it politely", is Greatrex's colourful description of the four-year-old.

He contrasted a Listed bumper victory at Cheltenham on New Year's Day with the gelding's first attempt over hurdles at Fontwell in early October when he was eighth of 12.

"He was ridden aggressively from the front in the Listed bumper but was ridden with way too much restraint at Fontwell and I think he sulked.

"We can put a line through that race and next time we will be more positive with him over two and a half miles. He'll possibly get further in time."

That was the plan in a maiden 2m3½f hurdle at Lingfield three weeks later and Audacity duly made the running, but he weakened rapidly before two out, perhaps leaving Greatrex to tweak tactics.

Mahler's Aintree aim

The amusingly named **Bob Mahler** had a fine season last term, winning the Edinburgh National Chase over 4m1f at Musselburgh in the dying strides, then going on to finish third in the Kim Muir at the Cheltenham Festival.

"If the jockey had ridden him differently [at Cheltenham] it would have been a different story and he would have been very hard to beat. He was a strong staying-on third," says Greatrex.

"His main target is the Grand National but he's rated 142, so he needs to go up 4lb to definitely get a run."

"He's developed every year and is now a big, strong, chasing type. He's taken time to come to hand and we're now reaping the rewards. He's the ideal type for the National."

Bob Mahler was pulled up in a 3m1f handicap chase at Cheltenham in late October.

Keeper Hill was being lined up for a crack at the American National at Far Hills, New Jersey, but that plan was altered and a crack at the Charlie Hall Chase at Wetherby has been pencilled in "as long as the ground isn't bottomless".

"If that doesn't work out the Peterborough Chase at Huntingdon is a possibility. He's a 152-rated, high-class horse who deserves to win a good race."

He had a fine season last term, winning a valuable graduation chase at Haydock, then finishing a close runner-up to Frodon in a Grade 2 at Kempton.

"He's summered well and there's every chance he can build on last season, but he's better in small fields."

'He has a touch of class'

Greatrex has high hopes for Aintree Grade 2 bumper winner **Portrush Ted**, who won a novice hurdle in the summer of 2018, then returned from a 519-day break to land a handicap hurdle at Ayr in January.

He was fancied to book his place in the Pertemps Hurdle Final at the festival in a qualifier at Haydock, but fell at the last flight when in contention, so missed out on Cheltenham.

"We all thought he would have won. He has a mark of 139 but he's better than that. You have to be on the right side of the handicapper and I think Portrush Ted has a seriously good chance this season.

"He's coming along well. He loves soft ground and we'll start him off in a valuable three-mile hurdle on Betfair Chase day at Haydock in November. It wouldn't surprise me if he won.

"He has a touch of class and will make a good staying horse. He hasn't had many races and this could be his season."

'Big handicaps in him'

Mahlervous is a second-season chaser who has taken time to warm to the discipline after winning three times over hurdles, but big things are expected of him.

"If we can get a full season into him, he'll be a proper staying chaser. He'll definitely have some big handicaps in him."

Mahlervous finished a promising ninth of 18 on his handicapping debut.

"**Martha Brae** is a mare I really like. For a horse who doesn't show a lot at home, she

Potential winners from the Greatrex yard: Portrush Ted (main) and (from top) Mahlervous, Keeper Hill, Printing Dollars and Young Lieutenant

WARREN GREATREX
UPLANDS, UPPER LAMBOURN

RECORD AROUND THE COURSES

	Total W-R	Per cent	Non-hcp Hdle	Non-hcp Chase	Hcp Hdle	Hcp Chase	N.H. Flat	£1 level stake
Stratford	29-96	30.2	13-35	5-9	3-22	3-14	5-16	+26.34
Uttoxeter	24-114	21.1	5-28	0-7	4-31	4-21	11-27	-9.67
Wetherby	23-85	27.1	11-36	2-7	5-20	2-8	3-14	+1.47
Bangor	18-72	25.0	6-27	0-6	2-13	2-6	8-20	+21.71
Newbury	18-126	14.3	4-54	4-7	4-25	4-25	2-15	-27.89
Fontwell	16-75	21.3	8-36	0-1	6-23	1-8	1-7	+19.52
Ffos Las	16-82	19.5	7-29	0-9	4-15	1-15	4-14	-23.34
Plumpton	15-82	18.3	8-41	0-2	3-22	2-7	2-10	-9.11
Exeter	12-71	16.9	3-30	2-6	6-21	0-9	1-5	-23.51
Warwick	12-85	14.1	1-27	0-2	4-24	1-8	6-24	+4.33
Chepstow	12-88	13.6	6-33	0-2	3-22	3-20	0-11	-24.05
Lingfield	11-36	30.6	7-20	2-4	2-6	0-6	0-0	+3.58
Wincanton	11-80	13.7	3-25	0-3	5-37	2-6	1-9	-32.38
Hereford	10-42	23.8	4-15	1-3	3-11	0-4	2-9	-5.62
Cheltenham	10-124	8.1	3-34	1-13	2-37	2-23	2-17	-41.38
Doncaster	9-53	17.0	1-19	4-11	1-9	2-8	1-6	-15.98
Market Rasen	9-55	16.4	5-25	0-0	3-20	0-3	1-7	-23.64
Worcester	9-60	15.0	2-18	1-6	2-18	0-7	4-11	-18.93
Huntingdon	9-85	10.6	4-39	0-3	1-18	2-8	2-17	-52.48
Taunton	8-43	18.6	2-12	0-0	3-17	0-3	3-11	-7.79
Newton Abbot	8-44	18.2	0-10	0-1	4-20	0-3	4-10	-13.86
Kempton	8-74	10.8	2-27	2-7	3-28	1-10	0-2	-22.50
Towcester	7-33	21.2	4-14	1-1	1-8	0-4	1-6	-10.12
Southwell	7-54	13.0	3-14	0-2	0-17	1-6	3-15	-8.25
Kempton (AW)	5-30	16.7	0-0	0-0	0-0	0-0	5-30	+12.50
Haydock	5-33	15.2	2-13	1-1	0-13	2-6	0-0	+7.82
Perth	4-11	36.4	1-3	0-0	3-4	0-4	0-0	+4.55
Fakenham	4-24	16.7	0-4	0-3	0-5	1-4	3-8	-4.00
Sandown	4-62	6.5	1-12	0-1	0-25	0-12	3-12	-40.75
Kelso	3-6	50.0	1-2	1-2	1-1	0-1	0-0	+0.78
Lingfield (AW)	3-13	23.1	0-0	0-0	0-0	0-0	3-13	+4.01
Newcastle	3-13	23.1	2-5	0-2	0-1	0-3	1-2	-7.65
Sedgefield	3-24	12.5	1-4	0-1	1-7	0-6	1-6	-10.35
Ayr	3-26	11.5	0-3	0-0	3-15	0-5	0-3	-8.63
Aintree	3-51	5.9	0-12	0-4	1-14	0-11	2-10	-17.00
Ascot	3-52	5.8	1-14	0-4	0-12	0-7	2-15	-37.27
Cartmel	2-4	50.0	1-2	0-0	0-1	1-1	0-0	+3.50
Musselburgh	2-7	28.6	0-0	0-3	0-1	2-3	0-0	+5.00
Southwell (AW)	2-10	20.0	0-0	0-0	0-0	0-0	2-10	-0.75
Catterick	2-19	10.5	0-7	1-4	0-4	0-3	1-1	-15.65
Carlisle	2-22	9.1	1-5	1-1	0-6	0-6	0-4	-17.43
Ludlow	2-40	5.0	0-19	1-2	1-10	0-2	0-7	-29.00
Leicester	1-19	5.3	1-9	0-3	0-1	0-6	0-0	-18.00
Wolverhampton (AW)	0-3	0.0	0-0	0-0	0-0	0-0	0-3	-3.00
Hexham	0-6	0.0	0-2	0-0	0-2	0-0	0-2	-6.00

does well on the track. She's improved over the summer, is tough and jumps very nicely."

She has won once and been runner-up three times in her last four mares' novice hurdles and Greatrex expects her to pay her way this season when she goes handicap hurdling, despite finishing eighth of 13 at Uttoxeter on her seasonal debut.

Young Lieutenant was placed in three hurdle races earlier this year, then had a wind operation. After a 211-day break he reappeared at Sedgefield to land his seasonal opener over hurdles.

"The operation made a big difference. He'll improve a lot for the run and will probably go chasing now. I've been waiting to go down that route with him. He'll stay three miles and I think he's an exciting prospect."

Another horse Greatrex is looking forward to is **Dhowin**, bought at the Trevor Hemmings dispersal sale in mid-September.

Winner of a Hereford novice hurdle when trained by Jonjo O'Neill last year, Greatrex says Dhowin "looks a typical Hemmings horse – a big, staying, chasing type".

Nevertheless, he will be started off down the hurdling route some time in November before going over fences.

Wind op could do the trick

Printing Dollars hasn't won since February 2019 and had a particularly poor season last term, but Greatrex is hoping a wind operation has rectified her breathing problems and she can begin to improve.

Her poor form has meant her mark has tumbled to 121, which Greatrex thinks she can win off. "She's also a good jumper, so we could go over fences with her," he says.

A wind op could also turn around the fortunes of **Kemble's Cascade**, who has had only three runs in bumpers over the last 18 months, but Greatrex remains optimistic.

"Physically, he has done very well and his homework has shown us he could make a very nice horse."

He opened his season at Huntingdon in mid-October when he finished down the field in a novice hurdle.

Full Spes ran in two junior bumpers last season and was still quite weak, but has strengthened over the summer and has shown he can jump well.

"He has a very good attitude and I think he can develop into a nice novice hurdler," says Greatrex, who began his season in a Huntingdon bumper in mid-October when he finished down the field.

Greatrex also talks up the chances of **Calvario**, fourth in a Newbury bumper in January.

"He's had his problems but he's a good jumper and if we can just bring him along slowly he could be a really nice horse in time. He's mentally slow and still a big baby."

He opened his season in mid-October in a novice hurdle at Uttoxeter where he led until three out before weakening into eighth.

Take careful note of **Go Pharisee Flyer**, who turned in a confident display on his first time on a racecourse to finish fourth in a Fontwell bumper in early October.

"He showed a really good attitude, especially since he was being harried all the way round. He deserved a lot of credit and it was very encouraging," says Greatrex. "He'll run in another bumper and could go hurdling."

Another for the notebook is the unraced **Silver And Gold**, described by Greatrex as "a really lovely horse with a great attitude, a very bright future, and who moves well and covers a lot of ground".

'She has a very bright future'

Finally, do not miss the trainer's dark horse – **Lucy In The Sky**, a four-year-old bay filly by Milan.

"She was a bit weak last year and we didn't manage to get her on to the track, but she's summered well.

"We haven't asked her any questions but every morning she catches my eye. I think she has a very bright future and she should be out in mid- to late November in a bumper."

Interview by Lawrie Kelsey

PHILIP HOBBS

Defi leads strong pack for the master trainer

PHILIP HOBBS is one of a tiny group of trainers, jumps or Flat, to have entered racing with a degree – a BSc from Reading University.

Not surprisingly, he has become known among jump racing's cognoscenti as the thinking man's trainer, one whose cerebral approach has brought him to within striking distance of 3,000 winners.

By late October his 2,806 winners over jumps had put him fifth in the all-time list behind Martin Pipe, Nicky Henderson, Paul Nicholls and Arthur Scotland Yates, who rode more than 700 winners in the 19th century before turning to training.

Stable star Defi Du Seuil at home and in action on the track

WINNERS IN LAST FOUR SEASONS 111, 63, 106, 75

Hobbs has also saddled 37 on the Flat, including the Cesarewitch with Detroit City in 2006 and Big Easy in 2014, which, added to his jumps tally, means he could hit the 3,000 mark late next year.

At the start of each season Hobbs's stated aim is to train more than 100 winners and earn £1 million prize-money.

Reasonable aspirations from a trainer who has been in the top six over the last two decades, but that will be difficult in the year of the coronavirus pandemic when the jumping programme has been affected and a second wave of Covid-19 infections could hit it even harder if there is another lockdown.

"I think 100 winners will be unachievable because we missed May and June, and July, August and September were slow. As for £1m, we don't know what's going to happen with prize-money, but we have a good mixture of horses and we're hopeful."

Defi Champion plan

Hobbs's Sandhill stable six miles from Minehead in Somerset and 22 miles from Taunton racecourse houses around 110 horses and spearheading the string is **Defi Du Seuil**, winner of £616,000 prize-money, including earnings from seven Grade 1 races.

He had an outstanding 2019-20 season which brought victories in the Grade 1 Tingle Creek and Clarence House Chases, as well as the Grade 2 Shloer Chase.

After those wins Defi Du Seuil was made 2-5 favourite for the Queen Mother Chase at the festival but flopped inexplicably, never travelling with his usual zest.

The Sandhill superstar finished fourth of five and to this day Hobbs can offer no reason for such a mysteriously lacklustre performance.

"He was very disappointing and we still don't know why. He didn't seem himself in the preliminaries and Barry [Geraghty] said he felt flat from the start, but he was absolutely fine the day after," says Hobbs.

The stable star was given a long break in Ireland over the summer and is expected to be aimed at the same races as last season, which means the opening Sandhill salvo will be aimed at the Shloer Chase at Cheltenham in November.

The Champion Chase is still on the agenda "if all goes to plan", but Defi Du Seuil has shown he stays two and a half miles after landing the Scilly Isles and JLT novice chases, and three-mile targets are a possibility if it's found the gelding's speed has been blunted.

"He won the Triumph Hurdle in 2017 and nearly all Triumph winners stay three miles, so that's an option," says Hobbs.

Thyme Hill is another who had a fine season last year. He won three times over hurdles, including Grade 2s at Chepstow and Cheltenham, and the Grade 1 Challow Hurdle at Newbury, before finishing fourth in the Albert Bartlett at the festival.

He has impressed in schooling sessions over fences but Hobbs plans to keep Thyme Hill over hurdles to aim him at the top staying races. As he points out, with the exception of Emma Lavelle's Paisley Park, the staying division looks wide open.

"He'll go for the Stayers' Hurdle at Cheltenham and with a bit of luck he could become top of the division," says Hobbs, who intends to make the initial target Wetherby's Grade 2 West Yorkshire Hurdle at the end of October.

Chepstow Christmas aim

The Welsh Grand National has been won once before by Hobbs, in 2009 with Dream Alliance, and this season he hopes **Deise Aba** can repeat the feat.

The seven-year-old is a progressive young chaser who has won twice over fences, a two-horse affair at Catterick on New Year's Day, then a fine performance at Sandown in February.

That earned him a crack at the Kim Muir at the Cheltenham Festival, but he couldn't trouble the leaders late on and finished fifth.

"He's still lightly raced and has been extremely green, but hopefully there's plenty of room for improvement," says Hobbs, who plans to get one run into Deise Aba before the Welsh National at Chepstow on December 27.

"He stays well and doesn't mind soft ground, which you always get at Chepstow [at that time of year], and if he does well the Aintree Grand National is an option."

Hobbs has never won the Aintree spectacular, although he has had two seconds and a third.

Deise Aba's owner Trevor Hemmings, who has cut back his large string because of the effect Covid-19 has had on him personally and professionally, is different. He's won the Grand National three times with Hedgehunter (2005), Ballabriggs (2011) and Many Clouds (2015).

Could the Isle of Man-based owner of Preston North End FC – whose famous colours of emerald green and yellow quarters, white sleeves and cap will still be seen on about 25 horses spread around the country – change Hobbs's Aintree luck and win him promotion to an exclusive division of trainers?

Hemmings' gelding could get the adrenaline flowing for Team Hobbs and so too could **Everglow**, described by the trainer as "an exciting prospect".

He acquitted himself well in two bumpers last season. He was beaten a neck into second on debut at Chepstow and finished third on his next start in a Listed bumper at Cheltenham. Hobbs purposely missed the festival to aim Everglow at the Goffs sales race at Newbury in March, only to see that plan thwarted by lockdown.

"It was very frustrating," says Hobbs, who started Everglow off in the Grade 2 Persian War Hurdle over two and a half miles with a view to going three miles later on.

It was a similar path taken last season by Thyme Hill, who made his hurdles debut in the Persian War. Unlike his highly rated stablemate, however, Everglow was a disappointing fifth of seven.

"He was green in a very hot race and will

improve for the experience," says Hobbs.

Jatiluwih performed very well last season for leading amateur owner/rider David Maxwell, who won three times over hurdles on his soft-ground-loving six-year-old before finishing a creditable eighth of 24 in the Pertemps final at the Cheltenham Festival.

This season's plan is to go for the Cheltenham Foxhunter Chase, qualifying him either via point-to-points or hunter chases in the new year.

Dolphin on the up

Maxwell also has **Dolphin Square** to look forward to. He won three novice hurdles on him last year at Exeter, Newton Abbot and Wincanton, then landed a handicap hurdle at Ludlow in January before finishing second at Newbury.

"He's a lovely horse who stays well, has a very good attitude and is improving," says Hobbs.

Dolphin Square has winning Irish point-to-point form, so the team knows he can jump fences and the plan is to go novice chasing this autumn.

Another likely to go novice chasing is **Kalooki**, winner twice over hurdles at Ludlow and Wetherby before a creditable second in a Grade 2 at Haydock in heavy ground.

"He's a big, strong horse who stays three miles and copes with soft ground. I would imagine he'll have to go over fences. I don't think he is up to Graded races over hurdles," reckons Hobbs.

Jerrysback was being readied for a tilt at the Irish Grand National until Covid-19 restrictions intervened, which points to the high regard connections have of him.

He was runner-up in a couple of Grade 2 chases at Ascot and Haydock, then finished third in the National Hunt Challenge Cup at the Cheltenham Festival last year in soft

Early morning mist on the gallops at Philip Hobbs's Sandhill stables

Facing page (from top): Deise Aba, Jatiluwih and Kalooki

ground, and third in a valuable Listed chase at Ascot in December.

He's been knocking at the door but finding it's not been opening wide enough for him, although Hobbs feels Jerrysback is capable of winning "a big one".

"He's a very decent horse but it's very difficult to find a race for him. He needs to go right-handed over three to three and a quarter miles, but long distances are a doubt."

Legacy could be well treated

Masters Legacy looked to be a quickly improving novice hurdler last season after three runs at Hobbs's local Taunton track.

After finishing runner-up on his debut over two miles, the five-year-old won over the same distance a month later. A week into the new year he won again, this time over three furlongs further to earn a rating of 136.

"It was a shame the season ended early because he's a progressive but green horse who needs more experience," says Hobbs. "He's maybe reasonably well handicapped and we're hoping he can step up to two and a half miles and win a decent handicap."

Musical Slave was another improver when switched to chasing after winning three times over hurdles in the spring last year, including a big-field, 2m5f handicap at the Punchestown Festival for owner JP McManus.

"He did well last season and progressed with each race, winning at Exeter. He's a big, strong, set of a horse and we're hoping he'll be able to pick up a decent handicap. I'm sure he'll stay three miles."

Off The Planet, a promising fifth of 12 in a Worcester bumper in October last year, running on and looking as if he would fare better over a longer trip.

The form of the Worcester race is working out well with three horses coming out and winning again, including in a Listed bumper, so stable hopes are high.

He should be followed when switched to hurdles, although Hobbs could opt to start his season in another bumper before sending him over timber.

After two easy novice hurdle victories in January **Pileon** carried a saddleful of stable hope in the Martin Pipe Conditional Jockeys' Handicap Hurdle at the Cheltenham Festival, and his backers piled on, pushing the gelding's starting price into single figures.

Pileon led between the last two flights and was left three lengths clear at the last after strong Irish fancy Column Of Fire fell when challenging.

Victory looked certain halfway up the run-in until Rex Dingle conjured a flying finish along the stands' rail on the mare Indefatigable, who lived up to her name by pipping Ben Jones in a bobbing finish.

"He ran a very good race and was unlucky not to win," says Hobbs, who began Pileon's chasing career in a hot little four-runner novice chase at Cheltenham towards the end of October.

But he fluffed his lines. He made a mistake at the first fence, seemed to lose confidence and was a well-beaten last. There will be other days.

Venture one to follow

It's worth making a note of **Potters Venture**, winner of a Chepstow maiden hurdle last November, who has recovered well from a tendon injury and is back in work.

"His time off looks to have done him good and hopefully he could be progressive and well handicapped when he appears in November or December," says Hobbs.

And **Orbys Legend**, second in an Irish point-to-point in February and bought at the Cheltenham sales three weeks later, is also one to watch when he makes his bow in novice hurdles from the autumn onwards after this comment from Hobbs: "I've been well pleased with everything he's done at home."

The same take-note comment applies to the promising **Truckers Pass**, owned by Brocade Racing, whose Native River won the 2018 Cheltenham Gold Cup.

After finishing a photo-finish runner-up in an Irish point-to-point, he was unlucky

not to win a Warwick bumper first time out for Hobbs last October.

On the strength of that performance he was made a hot favourite to land an Exeter bumper on New Year's Day, but again found one too good.

He made his novice hurdle debut at Ffos Las in early October and would probably have won but for jumping out to his left at the final flight.

"He'll come on for the run and should have a good chance next time out," says Hobbs.

Another Brocade-owned runner to watch is **Tidal Flow**, an improving 148-rated chaser who won two of his four races last season and was second and third in the other two. He could excel in small fields over two and a half miles.

"He has a very good attitude and is one who will improve," says Hobbs, who started off Tidal Flow against three rivals in a 2m5f chase at Newton Abbot where he weakened gradually from three out to finish a well-beaten third.

"He probably needs softer ground and a longer trip next time," says Hobbs.

Dual hurdles winner **St Barts** will go novice chasing over three miles with the stable confident he'll jump well after landing a point-to-point in March last year.

Interview by Lawrie Kelsey

■ Following Hobbs during November would have resulted in profit for two of the last three years

On the schooling grounds and (below) up close at home with Thyme Hill

PHILIP HOBBS
WITHYCOMBE, SOMERSET

RECORD AROUND THE COURSES (last ten years)

	Total W-R	Per cent	Non-hcp Hdle	Non-hcp Chase	Hcp Hdle	Hcp Chase	N.H. Flat	£1 level stake
Exeter	87-454	19.2	40-147	12-54	15-105	12-113	8-35	-126.57
Chepstow	62-311	19.9	23-91	7-21	11-71	15-92	6-36	-3.08
Cheltenham	59-499	11.8	9-61	15-70	12-162	19-178	4-28	-144.59
Newton Abbot	51-307	16.6	16-72	3-21	12-91	15-104	5-19	-68.17
Worcester	50-209	23.9	16-63	5-14	14-53	11-61	4-18	+57.13
Ludlow	45-220	20.5	13-82	7-20	12-35	12-67	1-16	-25.20
Newbury	44-278	15.8	13-55	3-13	11-87	16-110	1-13	+121.05
Wincanton	44-345	12.8	8-96	5-16	14-91	11-99	6-43	-102.27
Taunton	41-278	14.7	16-101	1-6	9-91	11-54	4-26	-114.90
Warwick	40-200	20.0	10-50	5-13	7-48	10-50	8-39	-21.57
Uttoxeter	34-206	16.5	15-61	5-17	7-60	3-51	4-17	-62.88
Fontwell	31-128	24.2	11-39	1-3	7-42	10-35	2-9	-18.84
Stratford	29-153	19.0	6-28	3-13	3-30	17-75	0-7	-1.86
Sandown	28-183	15.3	5-22	6-17	7-59	9-75	1-10	-44.76
Ascot	27-184	14.7	6-30	5-24	8-49	5-66	3-15	-43.55
Kempton	26-206	12.6	10-47	5-23	3-61	7-58	1-17	-101.39
Ffos Las	20-123	16.3	7-33	2-7	3-29	5-34	3-20	-33.62
Aintree	20-172	11.6	5-21	2-19	4-61	7-57	2-14	-51.56
Market Rasen	16-72	22.2	6-19	1-3	6-25	1-19	2-6	-2.38
Bangor	16-78	20.5	4-20	3-7	6-21	3-20	0-10	+50.61
Wetherby	15-61	24.6	8-21	2-12	2-10	3-18	0-0	-6.32
Huntingdon	15-107	14.0	7-44	3-12	1-19	0-16	4-16	-45.09
Leicester	14-39	35.9	4-15	1-2	5-9	4-13	0-0	+6.40
Haydock	13-122	10.7	0-14	0-9	8-56	4-36	1-7	-44.25
Southwell	11-56	19.6	4-18	1-4	4-17	1-9	1-8	-22.88
Hereford	11-56	19.6	6-24	2-7	1-10	1-10	1-5	-23.64
Doncaster	10-59	16.9	2-14	0-9	5-18	3-18	0-0	-0.99
Perth	8-31	25.8	3-8	0-2	2-4	3-17	0-0	-5.13
Towcester	7-32	21.9	4-16	1-6	2-5	0-2	0-3	-5.34
Hexham	6-11	54.5	2-4	3-3	0-0	0-2	1-2	+3.22
Lingfield	6-21	28.6	3-11	1-1	0-4	2-5	0-0	-5.20
Plumpton	6-35	17.1	5-15	0-2	1-10	0-6	0-2	-22.60
Catterick	5-11	45.5	2-4	3-4	0-1	0-1	0-1	-3.50
Musselburgh	4-7	57.1	1-2	0-0	1-2	2-3	0-0	+1.93
Sedgefield	3-10	30.0	3-5	0-1	0-1	0-3	0-0	-4.78
Fakenham	2-6	33.3	0-0	1-1	0-1	0-2	1-2	-2.44
Cartmel	2-8	25.0	0-0	0-0	1-3	1-5	0-0	-2.13
Kelso	1-4	25.0	1-2	0-1	0-0	0-1	0-0	-2.33
Carlisle	1-9	11.1	0-3	1-1	0-3	0-1	0-1	-7.17
Ayr	1-23	4.3	0-0	0-0	1-12	0-11	0-0	-12.00
Lingfield (AW)	0-1	0.0	0-0	0-0	0-0	0-0	0-1	-1.00
Newcastle	0-5	0.0	0-1	0-0	0-1	0-2	0-1	-5.00

NEIL MULHOLLAND

Soup on the up for stable going places

SOUPY SOUPS could be served up as a main course for the Grand National if his season pans out as connections hope.

The nine-year-old is rated 139 after the handicapper raised him 7lb for winning the Perth Gold Cup *(right)* at the end of August, so he might have to go up a few pounds to make the line-up.

Before the Aintree spectacular becomes a reality rather than a mere dream, however, Soupy Soups will have to add a little piquancy to his CV.

His record could be spiced up in the Listed Badger Beers Silver Trophy at Wincanton in early November, a race in which he just failed to catch Give Me A Copper last year.

He was staying on strongly over the 3m1f trip on good to soft ground and gave the impression staying further would pose no problems.

In March he found the Ultima Handicap at the Cheltenham Festival a little too hot and was pulled up, but after a couple of warm-up races in July he went to Perth fully wound up and won cosily.

WINNERS IN LAST FOUR SEASONS **108, 59, 49, 50**

■ Back runners between 2m7f and 3m2½f. Their five-year strike-rate might be only 14% but the profit is £21.79

"We had originally targeted the Kerry National [a week earlier at Listowel] but that didn't work out because of the coronavirus, so we took him to Scotland," says Mulholland.

"He won well at Perth and has come out of the race well. He's been freshened up and we'll have a crack at the Badger Ales at Wincanton again. He was just beaten in it last year.

"Long term the Grand National is a possibility but he'd have to do a bit more before we think about that. There are a few bridges to cross before Aintree, but we know he jumps and stays."

Kalondra to return

Like his stablemate Soupy Soups, **Kalondra** was also pulled up at the festival after travelling well to before two out in the Grade 3 Brown Advisory & Merriebelle Chase.

"He slipped a tendon from his hind hock. It's taken time but he's recovered well," says Mulholland, who plans to take a softly-softly approach to his gelding's recovery programme so his confidence can return.

"We'll start him off over hurdles on ground that isn't too soft and see what the handicapper does to him. We'll nurse him back.

"Whether he sticks to chasing or goes back over hurdles, we'll have to wait and see, but I would like to think he could be a Lanzarote Hurdle [Listed 2m5f at Kempton in January] horse. I think he's entitled to be mentioned in those races."

Milkwood is a hurdler whom Mulholland is hoping can make his name at a higher level.

After winning a Fontwell bumper in April last year the six-year-old has made a smooth transition to hurdling, winning once and finishing second and third in two other races last autumn.

On his seasonal reappearance in early October he cruised home at Ffos Las in ultra-smooth style, never coming off the bridle, and the Welsh Champion Hurdle was considered a natural fit for him over course and distance.

Although he didn't win, he didn't disappoint in finishing fourth, a little under six lengths behind some more seasoned hurdlers.

"He's progressing very nicely. He ran very well in the Welsh Champion Hurdle; he wouldn't have had as much experience as the other horses, so I was very happy with him.

"He's come out of the race well and will go for some of those nicer two-mile hurdle races now," says Mulholland.

The trainer certainly won't be letting the grass grow under Milkwood. He has pencilled him in for the Grade 3 Greatwood Hurdle at Cheltenham's meeting in mid-November, as well as the Grade 3 Betfair Hurdle at Newbury in February.

"You would have to like him for what he's done; in fact, he's done very little wrong. He's only six and is still learning the tricks of the trade. He won't go novice chasing until next season."

Decent ground key to Switch

Fingerontheswitch is one of the most consistent horses at Mulholland's Conkwell Grange yard four miles south-east of Bath and before he was pulled up in the Kim Muir at the festival in March, the ten-year-old had not been out of the first three in his previous six outings, including winning a Kempton chase and finishing runner-up in Doncaster's Sky Bet Chase.

"He runs off a light weight, is consistent and pays his way. He should be ready to run by November and might go to Cheltenham, Wincanton for the Badger Beer or Ascot for the Sodexo Gold Cup. He needs nice ground."

There's plenty of stable confidence behind **Solwara One**, whose only appearance on the track was runner-up in a Wetherby bumper in February to the well-regarded hat-trick scorer Ask A Honey Bee, who was not disgraced in the Champion Bumper at the Cheltenham Festival meeting in his next outing.

The form of the Wetherby race is working out well with the winner successful on his seasonal return and the third and fourth horses coming out to win, while others have been placed.

"He'll start off in a bumper, then he'll go novice hurdling. Whatever he does in bumpers or over hurdles, he's a nice, big chaser in the making," says Mulholland.

Doing Fine might have reached the veteran stage of his career at the age of 12, but he keeps living up to his name by winning.

Neil Mulholland (left) can taste further success with Fingerontheswitch (main), Kalondra (top left) and Doing Fine

On the day he turned 12 he won at Cheltenham and repeated the feat at Uttoxeter in August.

"He's been placed in some good races and is a very solid and genuine horse," says Mulholland.

And that's just what he proved by finishing a respectable sixth of 12 in the Durham National at Sedgefield in mid-October.

Any News's only appearance on the racecourse until this season was when he fell in an Irish point-to-point a year ago, but since the five-year-old moved to England Mulholland has always felt he had the makings of a decent horse – and he was spot on when the gelding made his debut under rules in early October.

He opened his career with a seven-length demolition of his rivals in an Exeter bumper and looks to have a bright future.

Mulholland says: "We'd always treated him like a nice horse and he won very well; we're very happy. He'll stay further and handle softer going. He'll now go novice hurdling."

After finishing runner-up in a Stratford novice chase shortly after jumping's resumption in July, **Scardura** was made hot favourite to win a similar race at Perth but didn't get further than the first fence before unshipping his rider.

He made no mistake at Newton Abbot at the end of September for which he went up 7lb to 134.

"I like him. He's done very little wrong,

but I don't want him to run in novice chases off that rating, so I'll be looking at more valuable pots."

That plan backfired when Scardura unseated Sam Twiston-Davies at Cheltenham in a hot Class 2 handicap.

Keep faith with Charges

No Hidden Charges has some decent form, notably a couple of pointing successes, 11 of 17 in the Betway Hurdle at Kempton in

February, then a fifth of 20 in the Paddy Power Silver Plate Handicap Hurdle at Kempton three weeks later.

He had his first outing over fences at Market Rasen just after jumping's resumption in July when he was upsides the winner at the last but was just run out of it in the last 100 yards and finished second.

He went to Cartmel a month later and led until the final fence before weakening and eased to finish last of four.

NEIL MULHOLLAND
LIMPLEY STOKE, WILTSHIRE

RECORD AROUND THE COURSES

	Total W-R	Per cent	Non-hcp Hdle	Non-hcp Chase	Hcp Hdle	Hcp Chase	N.H. Flat	£1 level stake
Fontwell	63-324	19.4	10-65	5-16	28-126	13-88	7-29	+46.87
Worcester	33-252	13.1	9-54	4-12	13-104	7-67	0-15	-85.45
Sedgefield	23-56	41.1	6-16	1-1	6-19	9-18	1-2	+15.33
Wincanton	23-271	8.5	5-92	0-6	9-87	8-69	1-17	-111.82
Uttoxeter	22-216	10.2	5-54	0-1	10-101	7-49	0-11	-73.97
Fakenham	20-74	27.0	4-16	0-0	14-35	2-21	0-2	+12.25
Newton Abbot	20-222	9.0	6-53	0-9	6-96	8-56	0-8	-78.56
Chepstow	19-154	12.3	2-48	1-5	9-41	6-49	1-11	-26.55
Cheltenham	18-132	13.6	2-21	4-16	1-33	11-59	0-3	-21.35
Southwell	18-148	12.2	2-21	2-5	6-64	7-48	1-10	-31.13
Taunton	18-180	10.0	3-45	1-4	10-86	4-31	0-14	-33.64
Plumpton	17-146	11.6	3-44	0-3	7-55	6-35	1-9	-47.71
Stratford	16-118	13.6	5-33	1-4	7-43	2-33	1-5	+13.24
Ffos Las	15-134	11.2	2-31	1-3	5-38	5-44	2-18	-3.26
Wetherby	13-50	26.0	3-13	2-4	3-14	4-13	1-6	+1.31
Warwick	13-76	17.1	2-16	2-5	4-30	4-20	1-5	-10.59
Huntingdon	13-86	15.1	2-14	2-3	4-39	5-24	0-6	-33.91
Market Rasen	11-76	14.5	1-7	1-3	3-30	4-32	2-4	-31.09
Perth	10-46	21.7	3-8	0-0	4-17	3-21	0-0	+10.63
Ludlow	10-66	15.2	4-16	0-0	4-24	2-17	0-9	+20.99
Towcester	9-41	22.0	2-7	1-3	3-14	2-13	1-4	-12.20
Exeter	9-138	6.5	1-64	1-4	4-49	2-17	1-4	-93.25
Newbury	8-58	13.8	0-10	0-0	5-17	3-29	0-2	+2.12
Cartmel	7-36	19.4	2-8	1-2	3-13	1-13	0-0	-10.06
Doncaster	7-52	13.5	1-14	1-3	5-22	0-12	0-1	-10.50
Hereford	7-52	13.5	2-11	0-0	2-22	1-12	2-7	-23.47
Kempton	7-73	9.6	2-16	0-3	1-27	4-25	0-2	+19.00
Bangor	6-83	7.2	2-22	1-4	3-29	0-22	0-6	-52.77
Sandown	5-48	10.4	0-3	0-1	1-16	4-28	0-0	-17.00
Catterick	4-15	26.7	4-7	0-2	0-2	0-3	0-1	+6.74
Lingfield	4-37	10.8	1-8	0-1	1-12	2-16	0-0	+17.00
Aintree	3-30	10.0	1-2	0-2	1-9	1-13	0-4	+5.00
Ascot	3-39	7.7	0-6	0-0	1-13	2-17	0-3	-24.75
Kelso	2-8	25.0	0-1	0-0	0-0	2-6	0-1	-3.20
Hexham	2-8	25.0	0-1	1-1	0-3	0-2	1-1	-3.27
Newcastle	2-13	15.4	0-2	0-0	0-1	1-9	1-1	-5.75
Wolverhampton (AW)	1-3	33.3	0-0	0-0	0-0	0-0	1-3	+8.00
Musselburgh	1-6	16.7	0-3	0-0	1-1	0-2	0-0	-2.00
Lingfield (AW)	1-10	10.0	0-0	0-0	0-0	0-0	1-10	-6.75
Carlisle	1-17	5.9	1-6	0-2	0-1	0-4	0-4	-15.75
Leicester	1-18	5.6	0-6	0-0	1-6	0-6	0-0	-5.00
Folkestone	0-4	0.0	0-1	0-0	0-2	0-1	0-0	-4.00
Kempton (AW)	0-4	0.0	0-0	0-0	0-0	0-0	0-4	-4.00
Ayr	0-8	0.0	0-0	0-0	0-2	0-6	0-0	-8.00
Haydock	0-23	0.0	0-2	0-2	0-11	0-8	0-0	-23.00

Mulholland has not lost faith, however, and reckons the seven-year-old can still "make his presence felt" over fences.

"He jumps well and is a nice horse, so we'll see how he goes next time."

Rookie Trainer finished a decent runner-up in a Fontwell maiden hurdle in soft ground in January on his first run for Mulholland after switching stables from Kayley Woollacott.

It was a performance full of promise and as if to confirm that potential the six-year-old began looking good at home, but he's a horse who probably needs decent ground, so his programme will be chosen carefully.

"Hopefully, he can make his presence felt as he gets stronger. We'll take each day as it comes and pick races to suit him," says Mulholland.

Rookie Trainer, who pipped the well-regarded Truckers Pass in an Irish point-to-point almost two years ago, looks to have a bright future and proved that by winning first time out at Fontwell on testing ground.

Viking has more to give

Hurdler **Viking Ruby** may be exposed but she is consistent and genuine. After winning on her seasonal reappearance at Uttoxeter, she lost second place in the dying strides at Market Rasen before finishing runner-up back at Uttoxeter after being upsides the winner at the last flight.

She ran another brave race at Plumpton, leading at the last flight but weakened on the run-in to finish third.

"She's tough and is always there or thereabouts. She just puts her head down and gallops away.

"She's well enough weighted and can win again, but she likes good ground."

Chinwag has earned figures of 1, 2, 3 in his last three races and still has improvement in him. "He's a nice chaser in the making and can give his owners a lot of fun," says his trainer, who also suggests following **Cesar Et Rosalie**.

"His form was a bit hit and miss last season because of the wet winter, but if you look at his race at Wincanton in the Silver Buck handicap, he was beaten only eight lengths. I think that's good enough for him to run well in handicap chases."

His mark is down to 120, only 2lb above his rating when he last won at Uttoxeter, so he could be weighted to win again.

Express to deliver as chaser

Exelerator Express has finished first and second in his last two runs over hurdles and had the speed to finish runner-up in two bumpers, but his future lies over fences.

"He'll be going chasing sooner rather than later. He jumps well but we'll be starting off low key with him. We like him and he could turn into a nice chaser. Although he's won in the soft, I think he'll like good ground."

Full Of Surprises won a mares' novice hurdle first time on a racecourse at Catterick in December, but finished down the field in the mares' novice hurdle at the Cheltenham Festival.

"Her form was a bit hit and miss and she was a little disappointing at Cheltenham, but she's just back in training and hopefully after a long break under her belt she can carry on where she left off last year [at Catterick].

"It'll be nice to get her back on track on good ground."

Lord Accord is two from two under rules after winning his bumper smoothly first time out at Fontwell in early September, then cruising home by 13 lengths at the same track on his hurdles debut towards the end of October.

The half-brother to smart hurdler Monksland looks to have a very bright future judged on his runs to date, a view underlined by Mulholland.

"He has a good attitude, jumps well and can make his presence felt over hurdles. He's ground dependent and wouldn't want it bottomless."

Interview by Lawrie Kelsey

JONNY - ROCKS®
Chauffeurs

LONDON:
luxurychauffeurhirelondon.co.uk

BRISTOL & BATH:
luxurychauffeurhirebristol.co.uk

BERKSHIRE:
luxurychauffeurhirereading.co.uk

BIRMINGHAM:
luxurychauffeurhirebirmingham.co.uk

BUCKINGHAMSHIRE:
luxurychauffeurhiremarlow.co.uk

**CARDIFF:
SOUTH WALES**
luxurychauffeurhirecardiff.co.uk

HEREFORDSHIRE:
luxurychauffeurhirehereford.co.uk

GLOUCESTERSHIRE:
jonnyrockschauffeurs.co.uk

OXFORDSHIRE:
luxurychauffeurhireoxford.co.uk

WILTSHIRE:
chauffeurhireswindon.co.uk

WORCESTERSHIRE:
luxurychauffeurhireworcester.co.uk

WARWICKSHIRE:
luxurychauffeurhirewarwick.co.uk

Equine and human talent in abundance

AS IF to show the rest of Britain's jumping firmament that he is one of its brightest young stars, Olly Murphy grabbed a four-timer on the opening day of racing resumption after lockdown – and has hardly stopped firing in the winners since that Southwell spectacular.

After taking out a licence in the summer of 2017, the former assistant to Irish maestro Gordon Elliott has been saddling winners at the rate of almost one every five runners.

But for lockdown, Murphy would have gone close to topping his best score of 82 winners, as well as improving the prize-money haul of £663,000 he amassed in his second season – he was only £50,000 down when jumping was halted.

Add to those stats 22 winners on the Flat and it's easy to see why owners are beating a path to his Warren Chase winner factory four miles north-west of Stratford-upon-Avon.

The son of former trainer Anabel Murphy and bloodstock agent Aiden Murphy says: "I'm young and hungry with a young and hungry team behind me, and I want to be the best at what I do," which loosely translates as he wants to become champion trainer.

One horse who could help improve Murphy's upward trajectory is **Itchy Feet**, the

horse "with a big engine" who gave him a first success at the top level when he landed the Grade 1 Scilly Isles Novices' Chase at Sandown in February this year.

Murphy started him off in the Grade 2 Old Roan Chase at Aintree over 2m4f this season to see how he fared before mapping out races for later in the season.

It is a race with a list of winners that includes Monet's Garden three times and Kauto Star. So Itchy Feet had some big footprints in which to scratch his trainer's ambitions.

He finished third, two and a half lengths behind the winner Nuts Well, and appeared to need the race, but Murphy was far from despondent.

"It was a very tactical race," he says. "He needs a trip and it turned into a sprint, which didn't suit him. But it was a nice starting point and he jumped really well. I was very happy with him. He definitely needs further.

"We might look at the BetVictor Gold at Cheltenham. That's over two miles five – and likely soft ground to slow down the other horses."

Another horse almost guaranteed to boost the yard's coffers is **Brewin'upastorm**, a 148-rated hurdler who finished fourth in the Ballymore Novices; Hurdle at Cheltenham, and transferred that talent over fences to land a couple of novice chases after a summer wind op, persuading the team to go for the Arkle. He was made joint third favourite but blundered four out and unseated Richard Johnson.

"He'd looked a good horse until that point," says Murphy. "We'll stick to two and a half miles and he'll probably run in a Graded race at Carlisle in November.

"If he does well we might think of the Ryanair for him, but that's a long way off just yet."

Hunters Call is also a candidate for the shortlist of certain winners this season. He

Murphy's runners in maidens last season had a strike-rate of 22% and a profit of £5.67

helped rocket Murphy's name into the headlines when winning the Racing Welfare Handicap Hurdle at Ascot in December 2017, the old Ladbroke Hurdle, a mere five months after the trainer launched his career. Three lengths away in second was Silver Streak, who went on to finish third in the following season's Champion Hurdle.

He was off the track for 921 days with "a couple of niggly injuries" before returning to become one of Murphy's quartet of Southwell winners on July 1, which was a prep race for an ambitious trip to Ireland for the

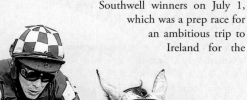

Linelee King: dual winner under rules can progress further

Galway Hurdle at the end of July.

Hunters Call didn't win but he put up a mighty effort to finish fourth behind the Willie Mullins-trained Aramon with several well-fancied Irish beasts in his wake.

"Nothing went right for him at Galway and making the running didn't help, but he ran with plenty of credit," says Murphy.

"He'll run over two to two and a half miles in handicap hurdles with the Greatwood Hurdle at Cheltenham in November his early target. If he wins we'll put him in one of those Graded races."

World Hurdle aim for Darby

The yard has high hopes for **Thomas Darby**, second in the 2019 Supreme Novices' Hurdle at Cheltenham, where stablemate Itchy Feet was half a length away in third, and winner of a Grade 3 handicap hurdle at Ascot in January.

"He stays over hurdles and could go for a conditions race at Aintree. He's strengthened up over the break and he's a horse we're looking forward to," says the trainer.

"He has a big engine and could stay three miles. If he does, the Stayers' Hurdle at the festival could become a possibility."

After winning a Pertemps qualifier at Aintree in November, then following up with victory in a Cheltenham handicap hurdle in January, **Skandiburg** was made third favourite for the Pertemps final at the festival, but the six-year-old could never land a blow and trailed in 15th of 24.

"In time he could be a really nice chaser. He wants soft ground," says Murphy.

He finished a staying-on last of four in a four-runner novice chase at Fakenham, one of the tightest jumps tracks in the land.

"We sent him to the wrong track," admits Murphy candidly. "He'll go back to a big galloping track next time, but at least he's experienced now."

It's always a good idea to study the opposition using your own runners as a yardstick, so when odds-on **Linelee King** went down by half a length to Plenty In The

Tank in a Chepstow bumper last October, Murphy made a mental note of the winner, knowing how much his team had fancied their horse.

When **Plenty In The Tank** came up for sale a little over two weeks later at the Cheltenham Tattersalls sale, Murphy snapped him up for £75,000 for Linelee King's owner, Diana Whateley, whose famous light and dark blue colours have been carried by the likes of Menorah, Wishfull Thinking, Rock The Kasbah and Captain Chris.

"Plenty In The Tank was a very impressive winner of that bumper," says Murphy. "His work since then has been very good and he'll start out in a novice hurdle. He'll handle soft ground very well and I think he'll be a well-above average horse.

"Linelee King is better than that bumper form. He wants ease in the ground and is another horse to look forward to."

Linelee King proved Murphy was spot on by winning a Sedgefield bumper impressively in January.

He was strongly fancied to make a winning seasonal return over hurdles at Kelso in early October, and did not disappoint, cruising home by five lengths, and looks to have a bright future.

"We'll now step him up in trip and look for something where he can carry a penalty," said a delighted Murphy.

Cottage one to watch for

Punters should take note of the trainer's comments about £200,000 former Irish pointer **Grandads Cottage**.

"He was unlucky not to win a bumper at Stratford in March. After being hampered on the home turn, he lost by a head. He won his only point-to-point, so jumps well. He is a lovely horse who will make a cracking staying chaser in time."

He was evens favourite on his seasonal reappearance over hurdles at Carlisle but was disappointing, weakening from three out to finish fifth.

Hunters Call: fourth in the Galway Hurdle and has the Greatwood Hurdle on his agenda

The Gerry Feilden Hurdle at Newbury's late November meeting is the early major target for **Nickolson**, a winner of two of his three races before this season and a horse for whom his trainer has a soft spot.

"He's had a few niggles and hasn't a lot of experience, but he's a horse I've always highly regarded," he says.

Nickolson, whose rating of 135 is exploitable, according to Murphy, started off in an intermediate hurdle at Carlisle where he was a five-length second of four in

RACING POST SHOP

NEW for 2021

RACING POST 2021 Desk Calendar

RACING POST 2021 CALENDAR
INCLUDING DAY-BY-DAY BRITISH AND IRISH FIXTURES

Racing Post Annual 2021
Nick Pulford
PB £14.99
9781785318337

100 Winners
Jumpers to Follow 2020-21
James de Wesselow
PB £5.99
9781785318313

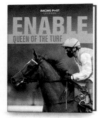

Enable
Queen of the Turf
Andrew Pennington
HB £19.99
9781785318375

2021 Pocket Diary
Racing Post
£11.99
9781785318368

2021 Desk Calendar
David Dew
£11.99
9781785318351

2021 Wall Calendar
David Dew
£11.99
9781785318344

Face Masks

£11.99

⭐ 25% OFF AND FREE P&P*

When you buy three or more of the following books

WHILE STOCKS LAST!

Beyond the Frame Great Racing Photographs
Edward Whitaker
⭐ HB £30.00
9781908216601

A Year in the Frame
Edward Whitaker
⭐ HB £30.00
9781910497784

McCoy In the Frame
Edward Whitaker
⭐ HB £20.00
9781909471702

Her Majesty's Pleasure
How Horseracing Enthrals the Queen
Julian Muscat
⭐ HB £20.00
9781905156863

Queens of the Turf
Andrew Pennington
⭐ HB £18.99
9781910497456

Churchill at the Gallop
Winston's Life in the Saddle
Brough Scott
⭐ PB £16.99
978-1910497364

Henderson's Heroes
The Story of an Unbelievable Season
Nicky Henderson
⭐ HB £20.00
9781909471184

In Search of the Winning System
Peter May
⭐ PB £14.99
9781908216953

No Easy Money
A Gambler's Diary
Dave Nevison and David Ashforth
⭐ HB £16.99
9781905156481

⭐ Only books featuring the star are available in the **25% OFF** offer.

Value Seeker
The Betting System
Anthony Gibson

⭐ PB £7.99

9781909471962

Cue Card
The People's Champion
*Lee Mottershead and
Andrew Pennington*

⭐ HB £20.00

9781910497814

Tommo
Too Busy to Die
*Derek Thompson with
Lee Mottershead*

⭐ PB £9.99

9781909471412

Down the Bookies
The First 50 Years of
Betting Shops
John Samuels

⭐ HB £18.99

9781908216175

Taking My Time
George Baker,
My Autobiography
*George Baker
and Tom Peacock*

⭐ HB £20.00

9781910497890

Beckhampton
The Men and Horses of
a Great Racing Stable
Paul Mathieu

⭐ HB £25.00

9781910498293

Fifty Shades of Hay
The Extraordinary World
of Racehorse Names
David Ashforth

⭐ PB £12.99

9781910497715

Off Track
Magic Memories
from Racing Greats

⭐ PB £9.99

9781910497470

Dorothy Paget
The Eccentric Queen of
the Sport of Kings
*Graham Sharpe and
Declan Colley*

⭐ HB £25.00

9781910497357

**The Druid's Lodge
Confederacy**
The Gamblers Who
Made Racing Pay
Paul Mathieu

⭐ PB £12.99

9781910498118

**The Definitive Guide
to Betting on Sport**
Bruce Millington

⭐ PB £9.99

9781904317364

**The Definitive
Guide to Betting
on Football**
Kevin Pullein

⭐ PB £9.99

9781905153657

ORDER NOW www.racingpost.com/shop
OR CALL 01933 304858

*FREE P&P WITH ALL ORDERS OVER £40.00 £2.99 P&P FOR ALL OTHER ORDERS

Racing Through Life
A Jump Jockey's Tale
Sam Morshead

⭐ HB £20.00

9781910498903

Blown
The Incredible Story of
John Goldsmith, Racehorse
Trainer, Gambler and
Wartime Secret Agent
Jamie Reid

⭐ HB £20.00

9781910498064

Starting From Scratch
Inspired to be a
Jump Jockey
Henrietta Knight

⭐ HB £20.00

9781839500305

Moments in the Sun
Tales from the
Punter's Pal
Claude Duval

⭐ HB £20.00

9781910497418

Strictly Classified
Insights into the
Trainer's Mind
Marten Julian

⭐ HB £20.00

9781909471535

The Scudamores
Three of a Kind
*Michael Scudamore,
Peter Scudamore,
Tom Scudamore,
and Chris Cook*

⭐ HB £25.00

9781910497722

Kauto Star
A Steeplechasing
Legend
Racing Post

⭐ HB £14.99

9781909471023

Henry Cecil
Trainer of Genius
Brough Scott

⭐ PB £10.99

9781909471405

Hurricane Fly
The Ultimate Hurdler
Andrew Pennington

⭐ PB £14.99

9781910498699

Racing Post A5 Notepad
A5 Racing Post notebook,
featuring an elasticated
enclosure to keep the
notebook shut when not
in use.

⭐ £9.99

Being A.P.
Being A.P. celebrates an
incredible man who became
the greatest jump jockey the
world has ever seen.

⭐ £14.99

Blu-ray

Warrior
The Real War Horse
The story of 'Galloper'
Jack Seely and his
horse Warrior, true
heroes of WW1.

⭐ £14.99

DVD

preparation for the Newbury race, won last season by Epatante.

'A great chaser in time'

The same sentiments hold for the quaintly named **The Butcher Said**, who is being lined up for a Graded novice chase at the Paddy Power meeting at Cheltenham in November.

Big things were expected of him after finishing a close second in a 23-strong field of bumpers in Ireland in April 2017, and in the spring of last year he came good, rattling up a four-timer over hurdles to earn a rating of 139.

He had a wind operation last December, returned to the track in March and ran well to be runner-up in a 20-runner handicap hurdle at Kempton.

After lockdown he came out and won a bloodless three-runner novice chase over an extended three miles at Southwell in mid-August, then ran a creditable race to be a close second in a 2m4f novice chase at Uttoxeter in early September, beaten only three-quarters of a length after being hampered at the last fence.

Three weeks later he ran in a novice chase over three miles at Bangor and clung on to get the verdict in a photo finish after a last-fence mistake.

"He was a very progressive horse over hurdles and could make a great chaser in time," says the trainer.

"He ran a bit flat at Uttoxeter but he's better than he showed and held on well at Bangor next time and has come out of the race well."

Presence of Mind made his seasonal bow in a handicap hurdle at Uttoxeter where he finished down the field.

"He was very disappointing but he's better than that. He was an easy winner of his only Irish point-to-point and won two of his first three starts under rules after being a half-length second in the other," says Murphy. "He's a nice progressive type, but he won't want it too soft."

The Wolf, who won twice over hurdles and finished seventh in the Albert Bartlett at the festival in March, is expected to make a decent novice chaser but opened his season in a two-runner intermediate hurdle at Bangor at the end of September.

He couldn't quite get to the winner and went down by three-quarters of a length.

After a wind op and a 200-day break Murphy wasn't too disappointed, saying: "He could be a smart chaser eventually."

I K Brunel, who was a decent 140-rated hurdler, made a fine start to his chasing career when beaten on the nod in a driving finish to a novice chase at Fontwell at the beginning of October.

"He'll be a different horse next time out. He'll make a lovely chaser and will stay very well," says Murphy.

River a promising hurdler

He also likes the look of **Sangha River**, who was very impressive in his first run over hurdles, winning by over nine lengths before finishing a respectable third in a hot Listed hurdle at Kempton.

The five-year-old **Fearless** made his seasonal debut in a novice hurdle at Fontwell at the beginning of October and was second of nine.

"I was pleased with him and he'll come on for the run. He could be a good horse in time," says Murphy, who is keen to make special mention of Fontwell bumper winner **Blazer's Mill**.

He was sent to Scotland for his seasonal opener where he made a smooth winning debut over hurdles at Perth, and he looks as though he will add to that success.

"He won well and looks above average. He'll go chasing sooner rather than later," reports Murphy, who picks out a further trio of horses he feels are poised to make their marks and ideal for punters' notebooks.

In the short time he has been training Murphy has built an enviable record in bumpers, racking up a winner with every fourth runner.

That strike-rate hasn't been hit so far this season, but **Restandbethankful** set the ball rolling in the first week of September when he made a 730-mile round trip to Perth pay off by holding on in a photo finish.

Murphy is confident of more bumper winners and **No Risk Des Flos** (third on debut at Carlisle) and **Ewood Park** (fourth on debut at Newton Abbot), bolstered that belief with encouraging first runs.

"Both ran lovely races and both look above average. All being well they'll run in maiden hurdles soon," he says.

Joining them over hurdles will be **Lord Of Kerak**, who cost €240,000 as a three-year-old. He ran a cracker to be second to hotpot Wilde About Oscar at Uttoxeter in mid-October and looked a certain winner.

"Lord of Kerak ran a lovely race, never having seen a racetrack before. He's a gorgeous horse who is well above average," says Murphy.

He nominates a further four bumper horses to follow – **Fletch**, **Doctor Ken**, **Italian Spirit** and **Moore Margaux**.

"I have a big team of four- and five-year-old bumper horses for the season who are showing me plenty at home to say they'll be winning races somewhere," he says confidently.

Interview by Lawrie Kelsey

OLLY MURPHY
WILMCOTE, WARWICKSHIRE

Three to follow (from top): The Butcher Said, I K Brunel and The Wolf

RECORD AROUND THE COURSES

	Total W-R	Per cent	Non-hcp Hdle	Non-hcp Chase	Hcp Hdle	Hcp Chase	N.H. Flat	£1 level stake
Market Rasen	30-151	19.9	14-51	1-2	12-67	2-20	1-11	-32.74
Fakenham	29-120	24.2	13-50	0-2	11-42	4-18	1-8	-7.28
Southwell	14-80	17.5	9-29	1-3	3-34	1-10	0-4	-40.77
Stratford	14-92	15.2	7-38	0-0	2-34	3-12	2-8	-44.40
Uttoxeter	13-77	16.9	5-28	1-3	4-29	1-9	2-8	-10.74
Huntingdon	11-41	26.8	5-15	0-0	1-13	1-6	4-7	-11.25
Fontwell	10-42	23.8	4-14	0-2	2-15	2-6	2-5	-2.29
Newton Abbot	9-23	39.1	4-7	0-0	2-10	2-2	1-4	+22.05
Bangor	8-57	14.0	3-21	1-2	1-16	3-12	0-6	-35.64
Ayr	6-20	30.0	2-6	1-2	0-5	0-3	3-4	+0.49
Warwick	6-65	9.2	4-32	0-3	0-14	0-6	2-10	-2.33
Musselburgh	5-10	50.0	1-2	0-0	1-1	2-5	1-2	+6.85
Leicester	5-13	38.5	4-6	1-1	0-3	0-3	0-0	+26.20
Newcastle	4-12	33.3	3-6	0-0	0-3	0-0	1-3	-1.66
Carlisle	4-14	28.6	2-6	1-3	0-2	0-0	1-3	-3.06
Wincanton	4-16	25.0	3-10	0-0	0-4	1-2	0-0	-2.27
Kelso	4-17	23.5	1-6	0-0	2-6	1-5	0-0	-4.21
Perth	4-18	22.2	2-6	0-0	1-6	0-4	1-2	-0.88
Sedgefield	4-18	22.2	0-3	0-1	1-3	0-5	3-6	-7.94
Worcester	4-24	16.7	2-7	0-0	2-13	0-2	0-1	-11.30
Ffos Las	3-11	27.3	0-2	1-1	0-3	1-2	1-3	+3.37
Chepstow	3-19	15.8	1-9	0-2	1-2	0-2	1-4	+1.00
Taunton	3-25	12.0	1-16	1-1	0-5	1-2	0-1	-19.40
Ludlow	3-32	9.4	2-11	0-2	1-11	0-4	0-4	-25.53
Ascot	2-5	40.0	0-2	0-0	2-3	0-0	0-0	+14.00
Lingfield	2-7	28.6	0-1	1-1	1-4	0-1	0-0	+7.00
Doncaster	2-7	28.6	0-0	1-2	0-2	0-1	1-2	-4.03
Catterick	2-10	20.0	1-5	0-1	1-4	0-0	0-0	-2.75
Aintree	2-12	16.7	0-3	0-0	2-7	0-2	0-0	-1.67
Hereford	2-14	14.3	0-5	0-1	1-4	0-1	1-3	-7.50
Cheltenham	2-29	6.9	1-10	0-0	1-13	0-2	0-2	-18.50
Hexham	1-5	20.0	0-2	1-1	0-2	0-0	0-0	-2.90
Haydock	1-7	14.3	0-4	0-0	1-2	0-1	0-0	-5.33
Sandown	1-9	11.1	0-4	1-1	0-4	0-0	0-0	-1.00
Plumpton	1-12	8.3	0-3	0-0	1-6	0-3	0-0	-1.00
Kempton	1-13	7.7	1-6	0-2	0-5	0-0	0-0	-9.50
Cartmel	1-14	7.1	1-5	0-0	0-7	0-2	0-0	-11.25
Wetherby	1-20	5.0	0-13	0-2	0-2	1-2	0-1	-17.50
Newcastle (AW)	0-2	0.0	0-0	0-0	0-0	0-0	0-2	-2.00
Exeter	0-4	0.0	0-1	0-0	0-1	0-1	0-1	-4.00
Lingfield (AW)	0-8	0.0	0-0	0-0	0-0	0-0	0-8	-8.00
Towcester	0-10	0.0	0-1	0-2	0-6	0-1	0-0	-10.00
Newbury	0-13	0.0	0-8	0-0	0-2	0-1	0-2	-13.00

GALLOP

WITH CONFIDENCE

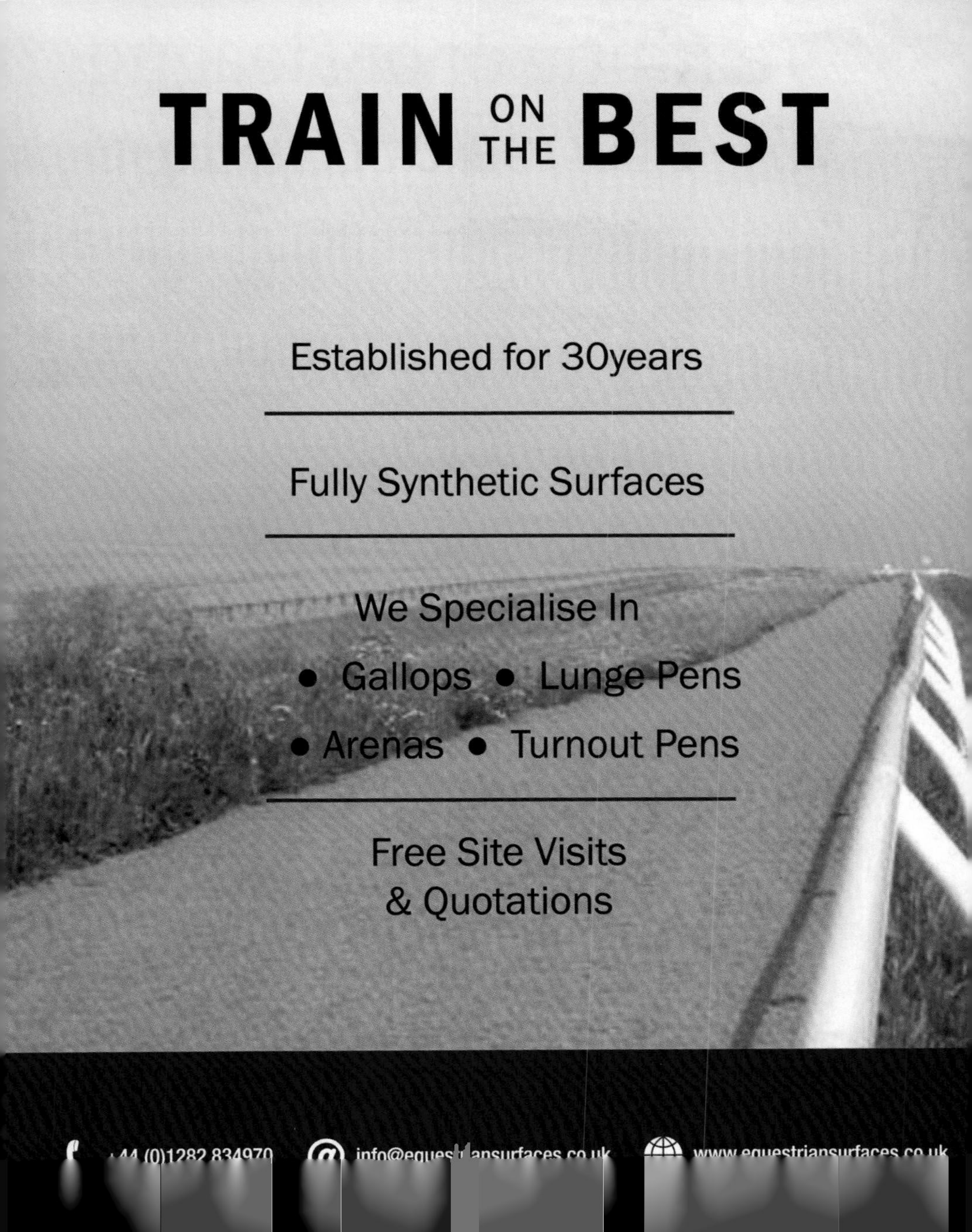

TRAIN ON THE BEST

Established for 30years

Fully Synthetic Surfaces

We Specialise In
- Gallops ● Lunge Pens
- Arenas ● Turnout Pens

Free Site Visits
& Quotations

RICHARD NEWLAND

Dreaming of big league with French ace Al Roc

SIX years after astonishing the world of National Hunt racing by winning the Grand National with Pineau De Re, racing's most famous doctor is hoping history can repeat itself.

Former GP Richard Newland has bought **Al Roc**, a nine-year-old French-bred who has won seven races for Maisons-Laffitte trainer Yannick Fouin and prize-money of £350,000.

"He has an English rating of 158, so he should at least get in, but first we have to qualify him by finishing in the first four of a three-mile chase to prove he stays," says Newland, who has kept a leg for himself and sold the other three to cousin Chris Stedman, and friends Mark Albon and Mike Tudor.

"It's an exciting thing for us and I'm hoping we can have some fun with him," says Newland.

"He's been racing over two miles six furlongs in France where they have very few staying chases, but generally he's been finishing his races well. So he has to prove he stays. He's unexposed over three miles but he's been threatening to stay further.

"It's early days yet but he's sound as a pound, although a bit buzzy. So we'll have to teach him to settle."

What gives Newland extra hope his new purchase will turn into a staying chaser is Al Roc's dam Al Cov is a half-sister to Al Co,

WINNERS IN LAST FOUR SEASONS 35, 43, 53, 60

who won the Scottish Grand National in 2014 on good to soft ground over four miles.

Coincidentally, that was the year Newland saddled Pineau De Re to win the Aintree Grand National. Could that be an omen?

Al Roc's first test will be the Grade 2 Many Clouds Chase over 3m1f at Aintree in early December, won by talented horses such as Native River, Definitly Red and Many Clouds.

Newland has shown repeatedly that his unusual "free range" method of training – where he turns his horses out into paddocks after training to graze naturally like other herd animals – is a winning formula.

His 65-horsepower operation in Worcestershire accommodates his system on 60 acres at his old Linacres yard and another 120 acres at his new Urloxhey stable about eight miles away.

Already this season Newland's strike-rate is around the 20 per cent mark, and his 150-rated hurdler **Le Patriote**, who was bang there two out in the Champion Hurdle

Richard Newland and team celebrate success in the 2014 Grand National with Pineau De Re

■ Newland has a five-year 36% strike-rate in bumpers and a profit of £10.88 during that time

last spring until fading, is helping to maintain the rate.

He couldn't live with the best of the British and Irish hurdlers but he could be a force now switched to chasing.

And he showed Newland that's just what he could be on his first outing over fences at Market Rasen in the middle of October when he impressed in beating two decent rivals to earn quotes of 33-1 for the Arkle at the Cheltenham Festival.

Newland could now aim him at the 2m novice chase at the three-day Cheltenham meeting in mid-November, the Grade 2 Arkle Challenge Trophy Trial.

"He was Cinderella level over hurdles, probably not quite top grade, but we deliberately kept him away from novice chasing last year so we could have a clear run this season with his racing programme. We just wanted to get his head in front in a good handicap, and he's done that.

"The year before he won the Swinton off top weight, so he's a good horse and he's still got plenty of ability; it's exciting.

"He's quite old to be starting a proper chasing career, but he schooled beautifully and he's been training really well."

'Absolute star' in great form

Caid Du Lin could be difficult to place this season off his chasing mark of 146 after running over two miles, so Newland could consider longer distances for him.

"He was an absolute star for us the season before last. He's in great form at home and ready to run soon, but he's not easy to place now off 146."

He prefers right-handed courses like Ludlow, where he won last December over two miles, and could go back there for his season opener, possibly over further.

Cat can pounce again

Big things are expected from **Captain Tom Cat**, who was a successful novice hurdler this summer with two wins and a second from three runs over two miles.

After a break of 76 days the five-year-old raised hopes even higher by coming out and hammering a decent field in a hot handicap at Cheltenham, under Cillin Leonard.

Newland says: "Cillin did ever so well because I thought we'd hang on a bit longer, but he pressed the button and took his advantage. It was a very good ride and a super performance from the horse.

"He looks a really nice, big galloping type. He's only five and looks a good prospect as a chaser for the future.

"He'll probably run next in the 2m5f handicap hurdle at the Paddy Power Cheltenham meeting in November."

Marine One earned a crack at the Welsh Champion Hurdle at Ffos Las after three victories in three runs, including a Listed handicap hurdle at Market Rasen, after being bought out of Denis Hogan's Irish stable, but he found the opposition too hot and finished down the field.

"He's by Frankel but we got him relatively cheaply. He's been a revelation and is still progressing," says Newland.

There's little doubt **Benson** has talent but it's allied to an eccentric nature, which could pose problems down the line. He landed a

Market Rasen bumper last November and looked as if he would have gone close to winning a Listed Sandown hurdle in February but for unseating his rider two out.

"He's had a wind op and is one of our better types to go novice hurdling, but he is a quirky talent. He would have been second at Sandown but he planted himself," says Newland.

"We'll stay low with him and get his confidence high. I'd like to think he can win a novice hurdle, then switch him to decent handicaps."

That comment was borne out when Benson justified odds-on favouritism at Hereford in mid-October after Lee Edwards urged his mount in front on the run-in.

"He was very green and tricky to ride but has a good engine," said Newland, who aims to find another small race as the confidence-boosting plan grows. "He needs to mature."

Billy to come good

Billy Bronco is a recent recruit from Evan Williams and has been pleasing Newland since his arrival.

"He wasn't an expensive buy and we're pleased to have him. He lost his form last year and I'm hopeful we can turn that round. Infections might have been holding him back. He's a big stuffy horse and it's taken time to get him right."

Mr Muldoon is described by Newland as "one of our better novice chase prospects".

"He has been an excellent horse for us. He's won three times and was never out of the first three in five outings over hurdles since joining us in September last year.

Newland started his season off in a 2m3½f beginners' chase at Sedgefield in late October when he stayed on gamely to win going away.

"He should improve for a step up in trip and we're hoping he can progress to become a decent staying chaser."

Roman to rock

Roman Rock joined Newland recently from Mouse Morris in Ireland. He's by Presenting and is a half-brother to Go Native, a 164-rated hurdler at his best who won the Supreme Novices' Hurdle at the Cheltenham Festival for Noel Meade, the Grade 1 Fighting Fifth Hurdle at Newcastle and the Grade 1 Christmas Hurdle at Kempton.

Roman Rock failed to win in five outings over hurdles but has shown promise over fences, finishing third in a beginners' chase at Cork, a career described by Newland as "chequered".

"He's only six and I've bought him as a chaser. I'm taking a chance with him but I think he's quite a nice prospect."

Rose Sea Has won once in five outings over fences since coming over from France at the beginning of last year but Newland feels there is much more to come from him.

"He was a tearaway in France and we're having to make him learn to relax and settle. He's training well and I'm confident we can

Six of Newland's promising squad (top to bottom starting opposite page): Marine One, Captain Tom Cat scooting home at Cheltenham, Caid Du Lin, Billy Bronco, Mr Muldoon and Rose Sea Has

get a lump of improvement out of him. His best distance is two and a half miles-plus, but he's been running like a two-miler."

He ran a race full of promise when settled out the back in a 2m5½f Market Rasen handicap chase, only to fall two out when moving up to dispute fourth place.

Saquon is a half-brother to Classic Escape, who is also trained by Newland.

"He's had two runs in point-to-points. He's only four but he's training well and looks quite a nice horse. He'll have his first run for us in a bumper, then we'll send him hurdling. He's a chaser down the line."

Charlie can improve

Tango Echo Charlie is another recruit from Ireland where he was a promising third in a bumper at Thurles in March.

"This summer he's been placed three times in novice hurdles for us, the last time he was third in a three-way photo finish at Uttoxeter.

"He's a trier and a reasonably well-handicapped hurdler on 112. Soft ground will suit him well. He looks a nice chaser in the making and I'm hoping there will be improvement next year."

After a break of 59 days he ran in a 2m4f handicap hurdle at Carlisle in mid-October when he was in with a chance two out before weakening to finish sixth of 17.

"He ran well but needs softer ground. He'll have a couple more runs before a break," says Newland.

Doubleubee won two Irish point-to-points and finished third in another. He's by Yeats and is a half-brother to 141-rated chaser Stilletto.

"He's an incredible doer and is a nice horse to look forward to. He'll go novice hurdling and will be a three-miles chaser down the line."

Wigglesworth is a five-year-old bought at the Doncaster sales in September.

"He's by Doyen and looks a very nice horse. I was impressed with his last run when he was a very good second on his debut in a maiden hurdle. He's training nicely and will be out in a novice hurdle in November."

Enqarde, bought from France, looks as though he could be "quite well handicapped" over hurdles with a mark of 115, particularly on soft ground.

"**I'm So Busy** is a lovely horse from Jessie Harrington. He was second in a Down Royal maiden hurdle at the end of August, is lightly raced and looks a nice type for a maiden hurdle on soft ground off a mark of 115.

"**Makka Pakka** is a lovely big type who will go chasing sooner rather than later. He had a suspensory injury but recovered and ran well for a long way in a maiden hurdle on his debut for us in early October after a break of 522 days."

First Soldier is another recruit from France, where he "hadn't cut the mustard", despite showing flashes of ability.

"He looks a very nice horse and is capable of winning races. He'll go hurdling in November.

"**Minella Encore** was a top-class bumper horse for Willie Mullins and one of the last generation of King's Theatre. He joined us in September and won a maiden hurdle nicely over 2m4f at Uttoxeter shortly after."

He ran against five rivals in a three-mile novice hurdle at Cheltenham in late October and led at the last flight before weakening up the hill to finish a gutsy second.

"**Little Rory Mac** came to us from Henry Oliver in February. He seems to want to do everything in a rush, so he's got to learn to settle. He has plenty of ability but needs to channel it.

"The original plan was to go novice chasing, but we'll keep him to hurdling to see if we can unlock some improvement. He handles soft ground."

Fox relishing new lease of life

Clever As A Fox had been bedevilled by gastric ulcers, but was cured and returned from a 283-day layoff to win a Uttoxeter handicap hurdle over two and a half miles during the first week after racing resumed from lockdown on July 1.

He followed up with victory at Perth, then

ran in a similar two-and-a-half-mile handicap at Aintree, where he finished tailed off.

"He likes a flat track and will stay handicap hurdling this year to reassure him. I'm happy with his progress. He's working really well and I'm hopeful he can be competitive before going chasing next year."

On The Wild Side has had issues and benefited from being sidelined during lockdown. After a break of 259 days he went to Hexham and won a novice hurdle impressively. "We were thrilled with his win because I thought he might need the race and the opposition was quite decent. He's not a horse to run frequently and he'll run next with a penalty. He's a chaser in the making."

On The Wild Side returned to Hexham two weeks later for a carbon-copy victory over course and distance.

Interview by Lawrie Kelsey

Bright prospects (from top): Clever As A Fox, On The Wild Side, Minella Encore and Makka Pakka

RICHARD NEWLAND
CLAINES, WORCESTERSHIRE

RECORD AROUND THE COURSES

	Total W-R	Per cent	Non-hcp Hdle	Non-hcp Chase	Hcp Hdle	Hcp Chase	N.H. Flat	£1 level stake
Uttoxeter	47-163	28.8	19-53	1-4	18-66	8-38	1-2	+14.64
Worcester	40-154	26.0	18-48	4-17	10-61	8-27	0-1	-26.28
Market Rasen	36-152	23.7	8-27	2-9	11-58	13-56	2-2	+18.68
Stratford	26-98	26.5	10-29	1-7	7-31	8-31	0-0	-23.25
Southwell	20-75	26.7	11-30	0-2	5-30	4-12	0-1	-19.59
Fontwell	18-69	26.1	5-15	0-3	7-32	6-17	0-2	-12.43
Newton Abbot	17-65	26.2	5-15	2-6	6-28	4-16	0-0	+1.49
Sedgefield	14-36	38.9	4-14	1-2	3-5	5-14	1-1	+13.44
Wetherby	13-46	28.3	2-11	2-4	1-15	8-16	0-0	+5.95
Huntingdon	13-50	26.0	3-12	0-3	6-23	4-11	0-1	+11.05
Ffos Las	12-46	26.1	1-6	0-0	8-26	3-14	0-0	+3.68
Perth	10-26	38.5	2-4	1-1	3-10	4-11	0-0	+7.22
Fakenham	9-28	32.1	5-13	1-2	1-6	2-6	0-1	+10.06
Ascot	9-50	18.0	0-4	0-3	6-20	3-21	0-2	+25.25
Bangor	8-45	17.8	2-16	0-3	2-11	3-14	1-1	+0.83
Ludlow	8-52	15.4	4-14	0-3	2-20	2-15	0-0	-10.77
Carlisle	6-13	46.2	3-3	0-0	2-8	1-2	0-0	+6.67
Kelso	6-19	31.6	2-4	0-1	0-1	4-13	0-0	+3.67
Cheltenham	6-96	6.2	0-9	0-3	4-52	2-32	0-0	-38.50
Leicester	5-23	21.7	1-8	2-3	1-4	1-8	0-0	-8.13
Exeter	5-25	20.0	0-3	1-3	1-12	3-7	0-0	-3.00
Taunton	5-25	20.0	1-4	0-0	3-12	1-9	0-0	-6.25
Warwick	5-36	13.9	0-7	0-0	3-13	2-16	0-0	+0.25
Aintree	5-61	8.2	0-2	0-4	4-23	1-32	0-0	-8.88
Lingfield	4-11	36.4	1-2	0-0	1-2	2-7	0-0	-1.05
Hexham	4-14	28.6	3-7	0-0	0-3	1-4	0-0	+0.25
Towcester	4-14	28.6	1-3	0-0	2-9	1-2	0-0	-0.34
Kempton	4-30	13.3	2-5	0-2	0-12	2-11	0-0	-13.74
Wincanton	4-30	13.3	2-5	1-2	1-13	0-9	0-1	-17.50
Chepstow	4-32	12.5	1-4	0-0	3-16	0-12	0-0	-20.84
Sandown	4-63	6.3	0-8	0-2	1-30	3-23	0-0	-4.00
Ayr	3-12	25.0	1-1	0-0	1-5	1-6	0-0	-1.25
Hereford	3-16	18.7	1-5	0-2	1-1	1-7	0-1	-4.33
Plumpton	3-17	17.6	0-2	0-0	1-11	2-4	0-0	-10.44
Doncaster	3-29	10.3	0-4	0-1	1-8	2-16	0-0	-15.00
Haydock	3-31	9.7	0-2	1-2	1-12	1-15	0-0	+5.10
Newcastle	2-11	18.2	1-4	0-0	1-3	0-4	0-0	-6.55
Cartmel	2-20	10.0	2-3	0-0	0-13	0-4	0-0	-16.36
Newbury	2-30	6.7	1-5	0-1	1-9	0-13	0-2	-15.50
Musselburgh	1-2	50.0	0-0	0-0	0-1	1-1	0-0	+0.62
Catterick	1-12	8.3	0-4	0-0	1-3	0-4	0-1	-10.71
Kempton (AW)	0-2	0.0	0-0	0-0	0-0	0-0	0-2	-2.00

COLIN TIZZARD

Lostintranslation tops huge line-up of talent

*Colin Tizzard with
Lostintranslation (left)
and 2018 Gold Cup
winner Native River*

WINNERS IN LAST FOUR SEASONS 57, 79, 77, 61

AFTER sharing farming duties with training for the last 25 years and saddling festival winners since Cue Card became his first big winner in 2010, Colin Tizzard's Venn Farm yard in Dorset has been one of jumping's leading operations.

The stable has sent out winners of the Gold Cup, two King Georges and the Stayers' Hurdle, to name a mere handful,

and this season's team is teeming with talent, including expensive point-to-point purchases Rose Of Arcadia, Amarillo Sky and Shirocco's Dream.

Despite the stable's talent, however,

challenging for the trainers' title could be beyond Team Tizzard.

Although they have a leading hand in almost every division, they lack numbers to challenge Nicky Henderson and Paul Nicholls.

Finishing third and hitting the million-pound mark in prize-money for a sixth successive season, however, would be a more than acceptable consolation for the team, which includes son Joe, who could end up with dual licences after their introduction this year.

"He's a young mind and is confident," says dad. "I think there's a very good chance Joe's name will be on the licence sooner rather than later."

Leading the charge from Venn Farm will be **Lostintranslation**, third in last season's Gold Cup, and out to emulate Native River's success in 2018.

He was up beside the winner Al Boum Photo in March but was just run out of it on the gruelling uphill climb to the line.

"He had a huge chance jumping the last and travelled as well as anything coming down the hill," says Tizzard with pride.

"Our horses were a bit quiet at the festival

■ Backing Tizzard's runners at 3m3f+ yields a five-year profit of £45.25 (14% strike-rate)

but the way he ran compared to everything else was massive.

"We're aiming him at the Betfair Chase, which he won last season, for his first run but we'll try to have a gallop somewhere to get him ready.

"After Haydock we'll give him another crack at the King George and then his third run will be the Gold Cup, all being well.

"We're beginning to ramp up his work with Haydock in our minds. With any sort of natural progression, a bit of luck and having him in peak form, there's no reason why he won't be jumping the last in the Gold Cup upsides again.

"Further ahead, he's a Grade 1 winner at Aintree, so we'll look to save a bit of petrol for the Bowl and hopefully Punchestown after that. His owners are keen to go for all of

Native River leads up the gallops at Venn Farm

those big-race targets and it's no surprise that they're loving life with him."

Also in the Venn van will be **Native River**, who will join his stablemate in the Gold Cup if all goes according to plan.

"We had one of the wettest winters and the wettest February on record but when Native River ran at Newbury in the Denman Chase the ground was quick," recalls Tizzard.

"We thought about pulling him out of the race but felt we had to run – and he won – but he picked up a small injury that eventually forced him out of the Gold Cup.

"It was a big shame because he was in brilliant form. He's not finished at all and he's in great form again.

"We want to give him two runs before the Gold Cup, and if it's soft ground there it will help him. There aren't too many races before then for him anyway as he'd be carrying a stone more if we went back to something like the Welsh National, so we'll look to go back to the Many Clouds at Aintree, which he won last year.

"The Grand National isn't on the owners' agenda – everything is geared up to getting him to the Gold Cup. He's forgotten about a bit but he's a brilliant stayer – not many horses have finished first, third and fourth in a Gold Cup."

Breakaway has big future

Many eyes this year will be on **The Big Breakaway**, who looks the most likely to be the next three-mile chasing sensation from Venn Farm.

"He's class. He was the best British-trained runner in the Ballymore and the three horses who finished ahead of him were a year older.

"We consider him a very nice prospect over fences and we'll start off at Newbury in a 2m6½f novice chase Lostintranslation started in two years ago.

"The track and trip look as if they would be perfect for him. After that I'd hope we'd go back to Newbury for the Grade 2 John Francome [November 28] and target the Grade 1 Kauto Star Novices' Chase a month later on Boxing Day.

"He's been taught how to jump before, as he won a point-to-point, so schooling him was basically just a reminder and he does everything lovely.

"We hope he'll be a Gold Cup horse one day, which is why we're going chasing now. His novice form is rock solid and, while he's got to go and improve, potentially he's as good as any chaser we've had."

Old favourite back for more

Many racing fans will be waiting to see how former favourite **Thistlecrack** fares. He won the 2016 Ryanair and the King George the same year. He may be a veteran now at the age of 12, but Tizzard reckons the old boy is not ready to retire yet.

"Remember he'd only run three times before he was seven – so we'll have one more season with him.

"He looked so well in the field and we've tweaked the back of his knee, which we've done with a few horses in the past, including Native River.

"If we could get a clear run with him – have about three or four starts – he could still be as good as anything. If it turns out that he isn't, then we'll stop as he doesn't owe us anything.

"It's not impossible for him to win and we still think he's a Grade 1 horse. The Long Distance Hurdle at Newbury, which he was second in to Paisley Park last year, would be on his radar."

The stable has yet to win the Grand National but in **Elegant Escape** the Tizzards think they may have a decent chance this season.

"The National is his big target. We might look at running him over hurdles first but it's difficult to place him without giving him a hard race.

"We're looking at getting him ready for the Becher Chase in the first week of December as we want to give him a good spin over the big fences and hopefully then have a real good crack at the Grand National. He'd then have one run before Aintree," says Tizzard.

Seven-year-old **Mister Malarky** could also turn into a National contender, although perhaps not this season.

"We'll aim for the Ladbrokes Trophy again as he didn't run too badly in it last year [sixth to De Rasher Counter beaten just over 11 lengths].

"There's also the Sodexo Gold Cup which we could look at first. He deserves to be in all those good staying handicap chases.

"He was a better horse after Christmas and looked really impressive when he won a big race at Kempton. There's no doubt he'll have his day again and he could turn into a Grand National type."

Christmas In April is another chaser whom Tizzard thinks could end up in one of the Nationals.

"He's a lovely prospect for big staying handicaps but he won't be ready for about a month. He looks an ideal Welsh National horse as the trip, track and ground are perfect for him.

"We think we'll try to start him off in a little race over three miles as a pipe-opener before going to Chepstow. He progressed all through last season and it was a case of the further he went the better he was.

"You can forgive him his last run in the Midlands National as some of ours weren't right at the time. He's a big, strong horse and he could be a Grand National horse for us later in the season — one more win and he'd get in."

Fiddlerontheroof won the two-mile Tolworth Hurdle in heavy ground at Sandown in January and ran well for a long way in the Supreme Novices' Hurdle at the festival in March before weakening to finish 11th, but as yet Tizzard is uncertain which distance will suit the six-year-old.

"We're not sure what direction we're going to go with him in terms of trip but we think he's a two-and-a-half-miler.

"He's strong and is a Tolworth winner on heavy ground, which he seems to handle

Mister Malarky: looks a long-term Grand National contender

really well. He could stay three miles in time.

"We were really pleased with his run at Ffos Las behind If The Cap Fits. He jumped beautifully, travelled well and it was a good performance behind a horse who was once rated 166.

"I think he'd be out again in a month, which gives us the option of going to Cheltenham for the November meeting or to Newbury a fortnight later for the Berkshire Novices' Chase or the John Francome."

Slate House: options open for last season's Kauto Star Novices' Chase winner

Arkle plan for Eldorado

When a trainer points out his best-in-division, it's worth taking careful note, which is what Tizzard has done with **Eldorado Allen**.

"He's our best two-mile novice chaser by a long streak and you'd like to think he'll end up in the Arkle," is his bold prediction.

"He looked really impressive when he won at Newton Abbot [in October]. He jumped like a stag and was foot-perfect all the way apart from missing the last.

"He had us very excited two years ago after he bolted up at Sandown but then he got an injury in a freak accident at Aintree.

"Last season he started off very well again but then didn't quite go on real heavy ground and was behind at Cheltenham.

"When he came back this year I hardly recognised him as he's developed into a huge, strong horse, and he was working on one of our gallops and beating everything without breaking sweat.

"He's a class animal and I'm sure he'll be going to the Grade 1 tracks. I think we'll look at the November meeting at Cheltenham, then the Henry VIII going back to Sandown."

The fragile **Fox Norton**, who had a brilliant season in 2016-17 when he won at Aintree and Punchestown and was second in the Champion Chase, could be aimed at the Tingle Creek.

"He's just cantering at the moment but he's about to have his work stepped up. He's been in all of the best races and, despite the fact he's not getting any younger, he's had some real decent form.

"I'd imagine we'll look to start him off in the Tingle Creek or the Grade 2 Chanelle Pharma Chase at Ascot in November. We haven't got a lot of options, but he's flexible in terms of trip and he hasn't got too many miles under his belt in the last couple of years.

"We want to get him racing again, although we expect him to improve for his first run. On his day he's a very talented horse."

That description certainly applies to **Slate House**, who won the Grade 1 Kauto Star at Kempton last Christmas.

"We're not totally sure which way we'll go this season. We could go to the BetVictor Gold Cup, in which he fell last year, but we're also considering the Ladbrokes Trophy, although he's not guaranteed to get three and a quarter miles."

Master can step it up

The Champion Hurdle is the target this season for **Master Debonair** after he landed a Grade 2 novice hurdle at Ascot just before Christmas.

"We toyed with the idea of a prep race on the Flat at Ascot but the meeting got called off. His bumper form was decent and he's had four good runs over hurdles but we still think he's totally unexposed.

"He's a fast, slick hurdler and we're looking forward to seeing if he can take that next step now. He'll need to find a bit on ratings, but he's just coming out of his novice hurdling season, he's in good nick at home and there's no reason why he can't improve again."

Point-to-point recruits

Some expensive sales purchases packed with potential are worth noting, starting with **Amarillo Sky**, who cost £280,000 at the Cheltenham Festival sale in March, 11 days after winning a Borris House point-to-point.

"We've got some nice point-to-pointers in this year and they've all worked well but we know we'll find out a lot more about them when they run. This one was impressive in his maiden with Colin Bowe. He's a nice one to look forward to."

Rose Of Arcadia cost £170,000 at last December's Cheltenham sale five days after an impressive point-to-point win in Ireland.

She won a bumper in heavy ground at Taunton in March on her first run under rules, but disappointed over hurdles at Ffos Las in mid-October.

"She ran with her choke out for the first mile last time and was a bit guessy with her hurdling – eventually she paid the price for it.

"She'll improve no end for that run but she

needs to settle a bit better. We may try to drop her in next time and teach her a bit more but we'll give her a little bit of time off before we look for another mares' novice hurdle.

"I'm sure she'll take a lot of beating wherever that is. We definitely think she's better than that Ffos Las run as she works very well at home and looked pretty good in her point-to-point and bumper, so hopefully she can translate that to novice hurdles.

"The mares' novice hurdle at the Cheltenham Festival is her big target but we've got to get her there first – she needs to learn to race and step up on that first run."

Second in Rose Of Arcadia's Irish point-to-point was **Shirocco's Dream**, who won her next point. That point was not lost on buyers at the Cheltenham Festival sale in March this year when she cost £260,000.

"We weren't the only ones at the sale who thought she was potentially quite good – that's always a positive. She's a nice horse and we're looking at starting her off in a mares' novice hurdle at Newbury. She was a bit big when she came in but has really tightened up now and looks the part."

The fourth of Tizzard's pricey pointing purchases is **Royal Crown**, who was second at Lisronagh and bought for £110,000 at the Aintree sales in April last year.

"We like him. We thought he was promising in three runs over hurdles last season and we think he's got a real nice mark.

"He'll go novice handicap chasing this season as he jumps a fence really well at home. He should be ideal for those handicaps and two and a half miles will be fine for him. We hope he can climb the ladder."

'He's a gorgeous, big horse'

Bold Conduct has been chosen by Tizzard as "an exciting dark horse" this season.

"He won his only point-to-point but hasn't raced for us yet as he had a bit of leg trouble when he came here, so we were careful with him. I don't imagine he'll be out until we get proper winter soft ground.

"He's a gorgeous, big horse and he's

exciting – he could be the dark horse of our lot. He seems to be training right and his homework is exciting, so we'll look for a good novice hurdle and we'll try to get a few runs in. He'll make a nice chaser in the future."

The four-year-old French import **Road Senam**, who was never out of the first four in six outings under rules, is another name to note when he goes hurdling.

"He's got some cracking form in France, including a second in a Grade 2 chase behind a horse who then won at the top level.

"He's only just come over to us and we've taken our time with him, but we're really looking forward to seeing what he can do.

"We schooled him for the first time with Daryl Jacob on and he went well. He's a nice, athletic horse and he'll be ready in about a month. I'm not quite sure where we'll start him off but it will be over hurdles."

Switch to fences will be key

Born In Borris could have masses of improvement in her when she switches from hurdles to fences, predicts Tizzard.

"She ran well at Chepstow at the start of October and I think after one more hurdle run we might go chasing. She jumps ever so well and is a big mare. She's rated 128, but we'd like to think she can improve another 10lb or more when we switch to fences."

Tizzard is aiming high again with his 156-rated chaser **Copperhead**, whose first big target will be the Ladbrokes Trophy over 3m2f at Newbury in late November.

"He fits the profile for it. We think we'll need a run before that, so we might go to Carlisle for the Colin Parker Memorial, which we won with Lostintranslation last year. That's back at two and a half miles but he's not slow and the four-week gap between Carlisle and Newbury is ideal for him.

"He's a big, smart horse who improved loads last season, going from moderate form in bumpers and over hurdles to become an impressive Grade 2 novice chase winner, and he seems a bit stronger again.

"He's 20lb away from becoming a Gold

Cup horse – and every horse has their ceiling – but he's still only a six-year-old and he did look very good last season."

A well-handicapped chaser looks to be **Darlac**, who was second at Hereford on his seasonal reappearance.

"We'll have some fun with him this season at those small tracks. He's nicely handicapped and I think he's best over three miles to something up to 3m5f. He could stay a bit further and we may have a look at some of those West Country regional Nationals."

Another promising novice chaser is **Ofalltheginjoints**, a big, heavy horse who doesn't want quick going. He was third on his fencing debut at Aintree towards the end of October.

"He ran a cracker at Aintree when travelling well until the lack of a recent run took its toll going to the last.

"We rate him as quite a nice novice chaser for the season. He was still a bit of a big baby last year but he won at Chepstow and went on to run at Graded level, although his last run at Kempton in February was a bit disappointing.

"He did have a penalty to carry that day and we thought he was slightly out of form."
Interview by James Stevens and Lawrie Kelsey

Three to follow (from top): Copperhead, Darlac and Master Debonair

COLIN TIZZARD
MILBORNE PORT, SHERBORNE, DORSET

RECORD AROUND THE COURSES

	Total W-R	Per cent	Non-hcp Hdle	Non-hcp Chase	Hcp Hdle	Hcp Chase	N.H. Flat	£1 level stake
Wincanton	66-475	13.9	13-98	2-19	14-130	33-181	4-47	-67.64
Exeter	50-332	15.1	11-79	14-39	11-84	14-106	0-24	-107.88
Newton Abbot	48-325	14.8	5-63	7-26	17-91	18-133	1-12	-45.77
Fontwell	37-208	17.8	8-41	2-10	6-53	18-81	3-23	-67.13
Chepstow	37-324	11.4	13-84	6-18	2-55	15-133	1-34	-127.47
Cheltenham	36-404	8.9	13-90	13-95	0-56	9-140	1-23	-121.05
Taunton	32-255	12.5	6-54	2-10	12-83	10-88	2-20	-58.49
Newbury	30-218	13.8	6-48	7-29	3-30	13-87	1-24	-43.82
Plumpton	23-144	16.0	7-50	1-6	5-26	10-54	0-8	-54.16
Aintree	18-104	17.3	6-27	6-15	0-12	6-48	0-2	+98.32
Kempton	18-136	13.2	5-25	6-31	2-24	3-45	2-11	-8.93
Ascot	15-118	12.7	5-23	4-26	1-17	4-43	1-9	-28.76
Uttoxeter	14-92	15.2	0-9	4-12	4-23	6-46	0-2	+0.74
Ffos Las	12-73	16.4	2-13	3-10	3-16	4-24	0-10	+7.23
Sandown	12-117	10.3	7-23	1-18	1-23	3-53	0-0	-69.96
Haydock	11-59	18.6	0-8	5-16	1-11	5-24	0-0	-0.47
Warwick	9-92	9.8	2-17	1-11	2-24	3-28	1-12	-18.75
Ludlow	8-57	14.0	3-9	0-2	2-11	2-29	1-6	+1.01
Hereford	7-49	14.3	1-7	0-1	1-14	5-22	0-5	-20.25
Huntingdon	6-26	23.1	0-2	1-3	2-7	3-10	0-4	+1.17
Newcastle	5-11	45.5	2-6	0-0	0-0	3-5	0-0	+29.50
Worcester	5-70	7.1	0-6	0-7	0-16	4-38	1-3	-45.75
Wetherby	4-19	21.1	1-2	1-7	1-1	1-9	0-0	+4.98
Lingfield	4-33	12.1	0-7	0-0	1-8	3-18	0-0	-19.50
Stratford	4-56	7.1	2-7	0-3	0-8	2-32	0-6	-26.50
Carlisle	3-12	25.0	0-1	2-5	0-1	1-5	0-0	-2.00
Southwell	3-15	20.0	0-2	0-1	2-5	1-6	0-1	+5.00
Market Rasen	2-11	18.2	1-2	0-1	1-3	0-4	0-1	-3.00
Bangor	2-21	9.5	1-4	0-2	0-3	0-8	1-4	-7.09
Sedgefield	1-2	50.0	0-1	0-0	0-0	0-0	1-1	-0.09
Fakenham	1-6	16.7	0-1	0-1	0-1	1-3	0-0	-2.75
Towcester	1-6	16.7	1-3	0-0	0-0	0-0	0-2	-4.47
Kelso	0-1	0.0	0-0	0-1	0-0	0-0	0-0	-1.00
Lingfield (AW)	0-1	0.0	0-0	0-0	0-0	0-0	0-1	-1.00
Perth	0-2	0.0	0-0	0-0	0-0	0-1	0-0	-2.00
Cartmel	0-2	0.0	0-0	0-0	0-1	0-1	0-0	-2.00
Kempton (AW)	0-2	0.0	0-0	0-0	0-0	0-0	0-2	-2.00
Leicester	0-5	0.0	0-0	0-1	0-0	0-4	0-0	-5.00
Doncaster	0-7	0.0	0-0	0-1	0-2	0-3	0-1	-7.00
Ayr	0-16	0.0	0-0	0-0	0-3	0-12	0-1	-16.00

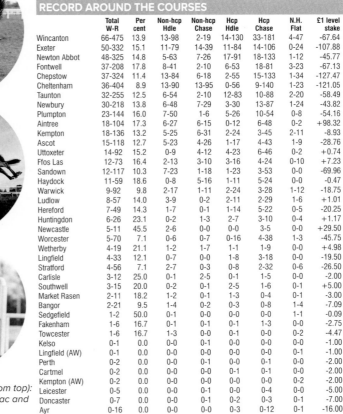

HARRY WHITTINGTON

Awesome Rouge tops squad full of promise

ATTRACTING big owners willing to invest in equine talent can give a huge boost to a yard and, in Kate and Andrew Brooks, trainer Harry Whittington has the ideal backer.

Among the ten or so horses they have at Whittington's Hill Barn stables on the highest point of the Berkshire Downs overlooking Lambourn is a trio who could set the Cheltenham Festival alight in Brooks's now familiar red, white and blue colours.

Leading the way is **Rouge Vif**, who earned a 20-1 quote for the two-mile Betway Queen Mother Champion Chase after demolishing his opponents over course and distance towards the end of October.

It was a performance Whittington was moved to describe as "awesome", adding: "They couldn't go his gallop and he was in his comfort zone out there; it was lovely to watch. To do it like that in a handicap off a rating of 156 is impressive, so he has slightly surprised me.

"Good to soft is his best ground, although he was third in the Arkle on soft. He's a warrior who'd run through a brick wall. I don't think undulations are a problem as he's got good form on most courses, but he was impressive in the Kingmaker at Warwick on a flat track."

The same Cheltenham race won by Rouge Vif was won last season by **Saint Calvados**, a horse Whittington had described as "super exciting" well before he came within a nose of upsetting Irish hotpot Min in last year's Ryanair Chase with Henry de Bromhead's A Plus Tard one and a half lengths further back.

Whittington's classy seven-year-old, already a winner of £282,000 in prize-money, could become Gold Cup material this season if connections want to aim that high.

Then there's **Simply The Betts**, who won the Brown Advisory & Merriebelle Plate at the festival last season, now rated 157 and winner of four of his five chases.

He could be aimed at the Paddy Power Gold Cup at the three-day November Cheltenham meeting.

"He got beaten at Kempton on Boxing Day when he couldn't jump and I drove away thinking, 'Why haven't I sent him to [eventer] Laura Collett?'.

"She had him as a youngster and it helped enormously, so he went each week from Kempton until Trials day at Cheltenham and just got better and better.

"He loved it so much we sent him on the way on Trials day and maybe it gave him an edge. As he won, we thought we'd better not change for the festival and he duly won there.

"He's in good form and I think two and a half miles is his trip for the moment, although Gavin [Sheehan, jockey] has always felt he's got the speed for two, probably on very soft, and would also stay three."

The Brooks factor helped Whittington to a record personal best in winners [30] and prize-money [£455,000] last season.

"It's a season I'll remember forever and it works in waves, so it might be hard to follow up, but we do have some very smart horses and promising youngsters."

Sholokhov has big future

Whittington also attracted top owners Simon Munir and Isaac Souede, who have a couple of horses in the yard, including **Sir Sholokhov**.

"They're top owners who are great to deal with. This fella is huge and won his only point. He's an out-and-out chaser, but we'll tip away over hurdles over two and a half to three miles this term. He's a fine, big horse who moves great and covers lots of ground. He'll want soft conditions."

Already in Whittington's mind for his festival team is another Brooks' horse, **Jammy George**, who could develop into a National Hunt Chase type.

He followed two solid runner-up performances over fences last winter with a promising effort at Aintree in October when beaten six lengths in a 3m1f handicap chase, showing he can jump and compete.

"He had an operation on his back and is still a novice over fences, which is probably a blessing in disguise," says Whittington.

"He needed that operation and his work is much better, so we're looking forward to seeing if he can improve on the track."

Bigmartre should be noted when he

■ Side with Whittington's runners in maidens — his strike-rate of 17% has produced has a profit of £24.98

73

runs on "proper good to soft ground" after returning jarred up from a Ludlow run on quick ground.

"I was pleased with him at Ludlow recently [fourth of eight], but the ground was too quick. I think with his aches and pains he probably just wants a touch of cut now.

"We'll look for sharp tracks over 2m5f or 2m6f as I don't think he gets three miles. Jamie Neild, our 10lb claimer, has a good bond with him and hopefully they can win soon because Bigmartre is well handicapped."

Another to have had an operation on his back this summer is **Breaking Waves**, who is new to the yard.

"He's a great big chasing type and I see him at galloping tracks over three miles on soft ground – he's got some good form [wins at bumper, hurdles and chasing level]."

Captain Tommy produced a good performance when second on his penultimate start at Bangor, but was disappointing in his last race at Wincanton where he hated the quick ground. "I'm sure he'll bounce back on softer ground next time. He's economical over his fences," says Whittington.

Bright future on the cards

The yard is excited about **Dargiannini**, who was impressive in winning a Sedgefield bumper by 20 lengths in mid-October after his homework had been "well above average".

"We expected him to win, although not quite in that manner! He's a very good jumper and has got a fantastic pedigree being a half-brother to the talented Keeper Hill.

"As he's five, I imagine he'll be novice hurdling this season."

Another who is getting the adrenaline flowing at Hill Barn is **Docpickedme**, an Irish point-to-point winner on his only start, who came across with a big reputation.

"He jumps very well and seems to have speed, so might start in a bumper before hurdling. He'll want soft ground."

Yet another horse Whittington and his team can't wait to see on the racecourse is **Emerging Force**, who is back after three

years off – two of them spent in the field.

"He was exciting, so I'm looking forward to his return," says Whittington. "He's had an operation on his back, but his work suggests he retains ability and his brother, Barel Of Laughs, had a long layoff in the middle of his career and was still winning as a 12-year-old. We'll aim him at veterans' chases."

Flash De Clerval will go novice chasing after proving well above average jumping fences. "I'm hoping he's nicely handicapped. He appreciates some soft ground."

'He jumps unbelievably well'

The massive **Franigane** [he stands about 17 hands] finished second in an Irish point a year ago and was fourth of seven in a Wetherby bumper in March.

"I'd given him time through the winter and he came there to win [at Wetherby] but was a bit weak," says Whittington.

"He's transformed over the summer and will start in novice hurdles and might end up over three miles at the end of the season. He jumps unbelievably well for a novice."

Medalla De Oro was runner-up in three novice hurdles, in one of which he ran "a belter" against Enemy Coast Ahead at Southwell, then he came up against another useful rival in Brian Ellison's well-regarded Cormier at Fakenham in mid-October.

"He's a novice over hurdles until the end of November. He's in very good form, though, and should win a novice hurdle soon. He wants a sharp track and two miles," was Whittington's advice.

Numberoneson was a winner on the Flat for Joseph O'Brien at Leopardstown and could have a bright future.

"He looks as if he's got class, speed and an ability to stay well, being by Camelot. He's been at [eventer] Laura Collett's for some schooling and jumps well," says Whittington.

Another speedy sort is French import **Qualismart**. "He would appreciate soft ground and a flat track. He's been pleasing us and I think he'll go straight hurdling because he jumps so well having come from France."

See The Eagle Fly failed to win in eight outings on the Flat in Ireland but obliged at the first attempt for Whittington in a Fontwell juvenile hurdle.

"She showed gears on her first start for us. The Listed race for juvenile fillies at Aintree in December could be an option and she's got a great attitude."

Despite winning twice over hurdles last season **Shantou Vow** has been backward mentally, according to the trainer, but that's because he's from a good family who need time.

"He ran a cracker to finish second at Wetherby, so he obviously improved for the three-mile trip. I see him as a chaser, but he's not ready – physically or mentally – yet."

Sirobbie loves Uttoxeter. He's run in eight races at the track, won five of them and been runner-up once. The six-year-old was far from disgraced in finishing fourth of 17 to runaway winner Honest Vic in a Pertemps qualifier at the Cheltenham October meeting.

"We can switch him back to fences at any point, but it didn't work out on his handicap

Rouge Vif (left),
Simply The
Betts, Saint
Calvados and
Jammy George

HARRY WHITTINGTON
SPARSHOLT, OXFORDSHIRE

RECORD AROUND THE COURSES

	Total W-R	Per cent	Non-hcp Hdle	Non-hcp Chase	Hcp Hdle	Hcp Chase	N.H. Flat	£1 level stake
Southwell	14-56	25.0	10-20	0-0	1-12	1-7	2-17	+44.08
Chepstow	9-36	25.0	4-16	0-0	1-6	3-9	1-5	-2.46
Uttoxeter	8-46	17.4	3-15	0-3	5-15	0-9	0-4	+16.00
Huntingdon	7-37	18.9	0-9	1-3	2-12	1-4	3-9	-2.77
Newbury	7-40	17.5	1-10	0-0	0-11	4-13	2-6	+47.25
Sedgefield	6-13	46.2	2-4	0-0	2-3	1-4	1-2	+5.11
Ffos Las	6-30	20.0	2-7	0-2	1-5	1-9	2-7	+5.23
Fontwell	6-33	18.2	5-16	0-0	0-4	0-6	1-7	+5.55
Wetherby	5-22	22.7	2-6	0-0	2-6	0-3	1-7	-8.15
Warwick	5-30	16.7	1-7	2-3	1-7	1-7	0-6	-14.26
Ludlow	5-36	13.9	2-13	0-0	0-7	2-6	1-10	+5.06
Plumpton	4-22	18.2	2-12	0-0	1-7	1-2	0-1	-8.77
Kempton	4-25	16.0	1-9	0-2	2-9	1-5	0-0	+2.50
Taunton	4-27	14.8	1-8	0-0	3-14	0-4	0-1	-7.84
Market Rasen	4-37	10.8	1-11	1-2	0-14	1-5	1-5	-22.68
Newcastle	3-10	30.0	2-4	0-0	0-1	1-4	0-1	-4.03
Doncaster	3-16	18.7	1-5	0-1	2-8	0-2	0-0	-3.60
Wincanton	3-17	17.6	2-5	0-0	1-7	0-4	0-1	+2.50
Worcester	3-23	13.0	1-8	0-0	2-10	0-1	0-4	-7.00
Cheltenham	3-26	11.5	0-3	0-9	0-4	3-6	0-4	-11.67
Hexham	2-5	40.0	2-3	0-0	0-1	0-0	0-1	-0.90
Perth	2-8	25.0	0-2	0-0	1-4	1-2	0-0	+2.50
Aintree	2-15	13.3	1-2	1-2	0-4	0-5	0-2	-6.25
Exeter	2-17	11.8	0-2	1-1	0-6	1-6	0-2	-9.97
Fakenham	2-18	11.1	1-10	0-0	0-5	1-1	0-2	-12.75
Hereford	2-19	10.5	1-10	1-1	0-5	0-2	0-1	-15.27
Newton Abbot	2-22	9.1	0-4	0-2	1-9	1-5	0-2	-9.50
Lingfield (a.W)	1-2	50.0	0-0	0-0	0-0	0-0	1-2	+9.00
Kelso	1-2	50.0	1-1	0-0	0-0	0-1	0-0	+2.50
Wolverhampton (a.W)	1-2	50.0	0-0	0-0	0-0	0-0	1-2	+1.50
Cartmel	1-3	33.3	0-1	0-0	0-0	1-2	0-0	-0.50
Musselburgh	1-5	20.0	0-1	0-0	1-1	0-1	0-2	-2.00
Ayr	1-6	16.7	0-1	1-1	0-1	0-1	0-2	-1.00
Leicester	1-6	16.7	1-4	0-0	0-2	0-0	0-0	-4.67
Ascot	1-9	11.1	1-2	0-0	0-4	0-2	0-1	-2.50
Haydock	1-9	11.1	1-2	0-0	0-6	0-1	0-0	-5.75
Bangor-On-Dee	1-18	5.6	0-3	0-0	0-5	1-7	0-3	-16.13
Sandown	1-19	5.3	0-2	0-1	1-11	0-4	0-1	-16.00
Stratford	1-21	4.8	0-4	0-0	0-7	1-8	0-2	-17.75
Southwell (a.W)	0-1	0.0	0-0	0-0	0-0	0-0	0-1	-1.00
Lingfield	0-4	0.0	0-0	0-1	0-0	0-3	0-0	-4.00
Carlisle	0-4	0.0	0-0	0-0	0-0	0-1	0-3	-4.00
Catterick	0-9	0.0	0-5	0-0	0-2	0-1	0-1	-9.00
Towcester	0-15	0.0	0-6	0-1	0-3	0-1	0-4	-15.00

chase debut, so we'll keep him to hurdles for the foreseeable future," says Whittington.

Torigni won impressively in France last year. He will start over two miles in handicap hurdles, while **Warranty** has been singled out for special mention.

"This one looks the part. He won at Beverley in July, beating Frankenstella, who has since won three. He appears to have a bit of class and I like him."

Young Bull, a bumper winner who won three times over hurdles last winter, ran well on his first time over fences to finish third of 18 at Uttoxeter in mid-October and could develop into "some sort of National type in time", says the trainer.

"He ran an absolute belter to finish third on his novice handicap chase debut. The ground wasn't quite soft enough, but it was an ideal introduction and he'll improve for softer ground and a step up to three miles.

"I've been looking forward to him going chasing."

Interview by James Burn and Lawrie Kelsey

EVAN WILLIAMS

Dreaming Silver can lift top hurdling prize

FINGERS are crossed at Fingerpost Farm that Silver Streak can land the Grade 1 prize Evan Williams is convinced his star hurdler deserves.

It almost came last season in Newcastle's Fighting Fifth Hurdle but deep, heavy ground blunted Silver Streak's speed and he had to settle for third behind Cornerstone Lad and Buveur D'Air.

After an impressive six-length victory in a Listed two-miler at Kempton in mid-October, Williams' grey marvel will head back to Newcastle in late November for another crack at the Fighting Fifth, no doubt hoping the track doesn't feature the same piles of snow heaped by the side of the track.

"The meeting was borderline [being called off] last year; it was very deep," says Williams. "He likes a sound surface – he'll handle other surfaces because he's tough, but he's better on better ground."

Whatever happens at Newcastle, Silver Streak will again go for the Grade 1 Christmas Hurdle at Kempton on Boxing Day, a race in which he was beaten by eventual Champion Hurdle winner Epatante last season.

"He ran a smashing race last year. It was a joy to see; he blew me away. But there's no point kidding ourselves. As I see it, all the aces in the hurdling division are held by Nicky Henderson and by a multitude of the Irish boys.

"So if I could make him a Grade 1 winner, it would be brilliant for the horse; he deserves it. It would be fantastic if he got there, but they don't give away Grade 1 prizes in Christmas crackers; you have to earn them."

After Kempton, most thoughts will turn to Cheltenham and the Champion Hurdle, but Williams aims to keep an open mind.

"We mustn't be blinded by Cheltenham; the festival isn't the be all and end all. We'll look at other Grade 1 races."

Whatever happens this season, the horse who was third in the 2019 Champion Hurdle and sixth in this year's race, definitely won't go chasing next season.

"We've schooled him over fences and chasing won't happen. He'll stay hurdling. Let's hope the horse is lucky."

Williams' 80-horsepower yard in the Vale of Glamorgan reached the landmark figure of 1,000 winners in January this year when **Annsam** won at Catterick.

He was a well-backed 9-4 shot to overturn an odds-on favourite and did it comfortably, landing his third victory in a modest handicap hurdle over 2m3½f.

No matter how modest, they all count, and Annsam is expected to add to the Fingerpost fortunes this season, although not over hurdles. His route forward will be over fences.

"He's built to jump a fence," says Williams. "He's a strong physical type with scope for chasing and I imagine that's the route we'll take. He's a progressive horse, nice and strong."

Joining Silver Streak at the Cheltenham Festival last spring was **Esprit Du Large**, who fell two out in the Arkle Chase when beaten. He'd had a good season until that point, winning a beginners' chase at Exeter before landing the Henry VIII Novices' Chase at Sandown.

"He ran really well [in the Arkle] for a horse who'd had very few runs over fences," says Williams.

"We'll see how we go with him but we could start him off in a graduation chase at somewhere like Carlisle to get his confidence back before deeper waters, then go for something like the Haldon Gold Cup at Exeter in November."

Cody's Cheltenham mission

Coole Cody is being aimed at the Grade 3 BetVictor Gold Cup at Cheltenham in mid-November after a fine run in a hot four-runner novice chase over course and distance in late October.

He finished second, beaten only a length and a half off level weights by the higher

First light at Fingerpost Farm in the Vale of Glamorgan, home of Evan Williams, whose stable star Silver Streak (left) will be trained once again for the Champion Hurdle

Coole Cody:
Paddy Power
Gold Cup aim

rated Southfield Stone, but looked as though he might win two out.

"He ran a cracker, although these small fields can sometimes throw up unusual results. But I thought it was a genuinely good run."

His participation at the big meeting, however, depends how the handicapper treats Coole Cody. If he keeps the nine-year-old's 137 rating the same, as Williams thinks he ought to, it will be all systems go. If not,

and the handicapper raises Coole Cody's mark, plans may have to change.

"Can the handicapper raise him? My way of thinking is, he can't. My reading of the rules is that he has to keep Coole Cody on the same mark. If that's the case, then we'll go for the BetVictor Gold Cup with a great chance."

Ballinsker is described by his handler as "a lovely horse" and can be followed this season.

■ Watch out for Williams' runners in claimers. A five-year strike-rate of 24% turns up a profit of £20.63

After being bought at the sales, the Irish point-to-point winner impressed in landing a Ludlow novice hurdle first time out by six lengths in October last year.

So Williams took a chance a month later by stepping Ballinsker up to Listed hurdle level at Haydock, and the gelding was far from disgraced when finishing fourth of seven.

"We'll have to study the form book to see where he'll go next," says Williams after the gelding earned a rating of 130 for his second at Ffos Las on his seasonal debut. "He could run in a good handicap hurdle somewhere in early autumn."

Bold Plan is another for the shortlist. He put in a fine performance to win a handicap hurdle at Haydock in November, then fell [third fence] in a Grade 3 handicap hurdle at Ascot in January.

Two weeks later he was pulled up in another Grade 3 race at Sandown. Both failures were in heavy ground and perhaps better ground would be more suitable.

"He's a tricky horse to get spot on and it's a fine line to draw," says Williams. "He has a nice bounce to him, so I would say we'll go over fences with him."

Quoi all set for chasing

The trainer is quite effusive in his praise for **Quoi De Neuf**, a six-year-old for whom he has high hopes.

"He's a smashing horse. He was second in a handicap hurdle at Chepstow before finishing a superb fourth in the Greatwood Hurdle at Cheltenham.

"We ran him in the Betfair Exchange Trophy at Ascot just before Christmas when he got wiped out at the fourth and was brought down. He then ran in the Betfair Hurdle at Newbury in February when he finished tenth, beaten less than ten lengths.

"He's a nice horse to go chasing with and will probably be out from November onwards."

Mack The Man is expected to pay his way. "He was very progressive last year and is a nice horse with plenty to offer," says Williams.

He won a handicap hurdle at Warwick in November and followed up in a Listed handicap hurdle at Sandown a month later. He was brought down at the last flight when close up in the Betfair Hurdle at Newbury in February.

"He did well to get up from that fall but he's a strong horse. He has plenty to offer and in the short term we'll stick to hurdles, but he has the scope and physique to jump a fence and is a horse who ticks all the right boxes."

Another to follow is **Olympic Honour**, who was made favourite first time out

Quoi De Neuf (left): smart hurdler set to embark on novice chasing this season

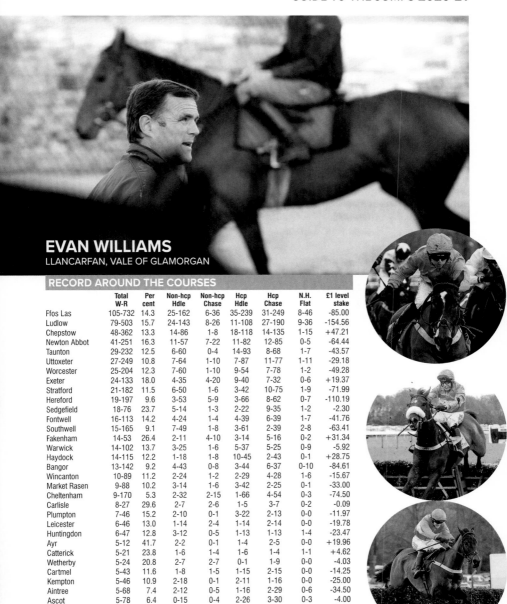

EVAN WILLIAMS
LLANCARFAN, VALE OF GLAMORGAN

RECORD AROUND THE COURSES

	Total W-R	Per cent	Non-hcp Hdle	Non-hcp Chase	Hcp Hdle	Hcp Chase	N.H. Flat	£1 level stake
Ffos Las	105-732	14.3	25-162	6-36	35-239	31-249	8-46	-85.00
Ludlow	79-503	15.7	24-143	8-26	11-108	27-190	9-36	-154.56
Chepstow	48-362	13.3	14-86	1-8	18-118	14-135	1-15	+47.21
Newton Abbot	41-251	16.3	11-57	7-22	11-82	12-85	0-5	-64.44
Taunton	29-232	12.5	6-60	0-4	14-93	8-68	1-7	-43.57
Uttoxeter	27-249	10.8	7-64	1-10	7-87	11-77	1-11	-29.18
Worcester	25-204	12.3	7-60	1-10	9-54	7-78	1-2	-49.28
Exeter	24-133	18.0	4-35	4-20	9-40	7-32	0-6	+19.37
Stratford	21-182	11.5	6-50	1-6	3-42	10-75	1-9	-71.99
Hereford	19-197	9.6	3-53	5-9	3-66	8-62	0-7	-110.19
Sedgefield	18-76	23.7	5-14	1-3	2-22	9-35	1-2	-2.30
Fontwell	16-113	14.2	4-24	1-4	4-39	6-39	1-7	-41.76
Southwell	15-165	9.1	7-49	1-8	3-61	2-39	2-8	-63.41
Fakenham	14-53	26.4	2-11	4-10	3-14	5-16	0-2	+31.34
Warwick	14-102	13.7	3-25	1-6	5-37	5-25	0-9	-5.92
Haydock	14-115	12.2	1-18	1-8	10-45	2-43	0-1	+28.75
Bangor	13-142	9.2	4-43	0-8	3-44	6-37	0-10	-84.61
Wincanton	10-89	11.2	2-24	1-2	2-29	4-28	1-6	-15.67
Market Rasen	9-88	10.2	3-14	1-6	3-42	2-25	0-1	-33.00
Cheltenham	9-170	5.3	2-32	2-15	1-66	4-54	0-3	-74.50
Carlisle	8-27	29.6	2-7	2-6	1-5	3-7	0-2	-0.09
Plumpton	7-46	15.2	2-10	0-1	3-22	2-13	0-0	-11.97
Leicester	6-46	13.0	1-14	2-4	1-14	2-14	0-0	-19.78
Huntingdon	6-47	12.8	3-12	0-5	1-13	1-13	1-4	-23.47
Ayr	5-12	41.7	2-2	0-1	1-4	2-5	0-0	+19.96
Catterick	5-21	23.8	1-6	1-4	1-6	1-4	1-1	+4.62
Wetherby	5-24	20.8	2-7	2-7	0-1	1-9	0-0	-4.03
Cartmel	5-43	11.6	1-8	1-5	1-15	2-15	0-0	-14.25
Kempton	5-46	10.9	2-18	0-1	2-11	1-16	0-0	-25.00
Aintree	5-68	7.4	2-12	0-5	1-16	2-29	0-6	-34.50
Ascot	5-78	6.4	0-15	0-4	2-26	3-30	0-3	-4.00
Sandown	5-89	5.6	0-13	1-9	1-36	3-30	0-1	-41.00
Perth	4-17	23.5	1-1	1-2	1-3	1-11	0-0	+6.00
Lingfield	4-30	13.3	0-9	0-1	1-9	3-11	0-0	-12.00
Newbury	4-78	5.1	2-14	0-3	2-21	0-30	0-10	-40.01
Towcester	3-20	15.0	0-9	0-0	3-8	0-3	0-0	+11.50
Doncaster	3-24	12.5	1-5	0-3	1-4	1-11	0-1	-8.25
Musselburgh	2-3	66.7	0-0	1-1	1-1	0-1	0-0	+3.60
Hexham	2-6	33.3	2-2	0-1	0-2	0-1	0-0	-1.14
Lingfield (AW)	0-1	0.0	0-0	0-0	0-0	0-0	0-1	-1.00
Kelso	0-3	0.0	0-2	0-1	0-0	0-0	0-0	-3.00
Newcastle	0-9	0.0	0-1	0-1	0-3	0-4	0-0	-9.00

Likely winners (from top): Mack The Man, Bold Plan and Esprit Du Large

83

at Ludlow in a maiden hurdle but unseated his rider when badly hampered halfway round.

He was made odds-on for a similar race at Uttoxeter nine days later but was beaten into second. However, he made amends in a handicap hurdle at Fakenham in December, partnered by Williams' 7lb claiming daughter Isabel.

He had a pipe-opener on the Flat at Ripon at the end of August when down the field, and was again unplaced in his opener over hurdles at Chepstow.

"He's a tough, genuine, bonny little horse who wants good ground. He's a smashing ride for a claimer," was Williams' summation.

The Last Day is expected to step up on what he achieved last season. He was very impressive in winning a two-mile chase easily at Aintree last November and two weeks later demolished a fence at Ascot, performing a miracle to finish fourth.

"He had no right to finish fourth; it was quite remarkable," says Williams.

"There'll be no rush with him this season, although he'll be out before Christmas. There are plenty of handicap chases for him at the likes of Ascot, Aintree and Haydock.

'Fences will be making of him'

The progressive **Holly James** is a name to remember. Although he's a young, immature, gangly type, he had the ability to win a novice hurdle at Ffos Las, then had a bad fall at Chepstow in December.

After that he was down the field in a Hereford handicap hurdle before running second at Warwick, where he blundered at the last and was beaten only three-quarters of a length.

"Fences will be the making of him," says Williams. "He was a little sloppy over hurdles and needs a fence to wake him up. He should have a good, solid season."

Coconut Splash is "an honest young horse" who seems to have been bedevilled by bad luck. On his debut in late October at

Aintree he was beaten a nose after leading on the run-in. A month later he ran at Newbury and was again out of luck when falling at the last when in contention.

He was taken to Wetherby for a maiden hurdle where he was odds-on, his backers realising what an unlucky horse he had been. He didn't disappoint and won well.

"He's a tough horse and that was a lovely performance. He's benefited from the coronavirus lockdown by having an enforced holiday, which has probably been a blessing for him," says his trainer.

Confidence the key to Court

Court Royale has been slow to come to hand over fences. He had a pipe-opener at Stratford a week after the resumption of jumps racing when he was down the field over 2m5f, which was probably a little too far, then came out 13 days later and won over 2m1f at the same track after travelling strongly throughout.

He ran at Cartmel towards the end of August when he was never travelling and was pulled up. He was then third at Uttoxeter at the beginning of October.

"He's one of those horses who, if he gets it right, is good. It's a matter of confidence with him. He's a great horse to have around free-draining tracks like Taunton and Ludlow."

Ex-Irish pointer **Fado Des Brosses** won his only point-to-point and is expected to progress through the ranks.

He was beaten under seven lengths in fifth on his hurdling debut at Chepstow, then went to Ffos Las a month later when he was second, less than two lengths behind a horse who came out to win again.

In January he was taken back to Chepstow where he got up in the dying strides to win over 2m3½f.

"He's a tough horse with a great attitude and needs plenty of cut in the ground. He could go over fences. We'll have to wait and see," says Williams.

Interview by Lawrie Kelsey

FOR-RECOVERY

THE
EXPERTS

Al Boum and Tiger can provide cheer during tricky times

ON THE back of a season that didn't even run to its scheduled conclusion, the prospect of jump racing's marquee names returning to light up the gloomy winter months is a welcome distraction from the prevailing Covid-19 stupor.

Mercifully, while we're loath to speak too soon given the pandemic's ever-evolving nature, it looks like the sport will continue unabated this time.

And if the balls bounce favourably, we have the prospect of Tiger Roll bidding to emulate Red Rum and plunder an historic third Grand National, shortly after Al Boum Photo's attempt to become the first horse since Best Mate to win three Gold Cups.

Those are utterly tantalising possibilities, and also reminders of how last term petered out so abruptly. On the afternoon Al Boum Photo plundered his second Gold Cup, it felt like the last days of Rome in the Cotswolds. Cheltenham got mired in the eye of the swelling coronavirus storm, and there hasn't been a mass gathering grace a sporting event in this part of the world since. Three days later, although racing still continued, the Grand National was unceremoniously cancelled.

With that, the dream of Gordon Elliott and Gigginstown Stud's pint-sized sensation completing the first uninterrupted hat-trick in the Aintree showpiece died. Exactly a month had passed since it was confirmed unequivocally that he would be allowed to take part in the National following Eddie and Michael O'Leary's customary assault on the handicapping process, so it was a short-lived countdown. This time, all being well, the opposite will be the case.

Elliott has suggested that, given the injury Tiger Roll picked up in November 2019, what unfolded in the spring might have been a blessing in disguise. His four-time Cheltenham Festival hero – runner-up to Easysland in 2020 – dusted off the cobwebs with a spin on the Flat at Navan in October, and all roads now lead back to Prestbury Park for a stab at a third cross-country triumph before attention turns to Aintree.

Two days after the cross-country race, Al Boum Photo will hopefully be on the verge of an even more illustrious treble under Paul Townend. Chances are we won't see Willie Mullins's totem until New Year's Day at Tramore, as the intention is to not divert from a programme that brought an end to the perennial champion trainer's Gold Cup jinx.

Given that Al Boum Photo didn't get a run after Cheltenham last spring, his 2021 Gold Cup appearance could be just his seventh in three seasons, which would make Best Mate's campaigning look positively aggressive. We'd all love to see a bit more of him but there'll be few complaining if he stands triumphant in the hallowed turf of Prestbury Park's winner's enclosure come March 19.

It would be nice to think he could return

to a trademark Cotswolds reception, but that really does seem like an impossible dream. We got to witness him up close by the skin of our teeth in 2020, so we'll settle for the race taking place this time and him getting the job done – again.

SENIOR CHASERS

Needless to say, **Al Boum Photo** stands alone atop this division. To some extent, it's still not easy to get a handle on just how good he is or might be, but the manner in which he bossed the Gold Cup when sent about his business early by Paul Townend was striking.

Sure, Santini came with a late flourish to get within a neck, but Townend's mount had put the race to bed after the last fence when seeing off Lostintranslation. Santini eventually got his second wind, but he didn't have the toe to live with the winner in the championship quarter of the race.

Likely challengers from home soil maybe aren't plentiful. **Delta Work**, a slightly claustrophobic sort that seems to have a distinct preference for daylight in his races, is better than his Gold Cup fifth suggests, as he was covered up from the get-go and duly made a raft of mistakes.

There are still Grade 1 chases to be won with him, although whether he can improve enough to win a Gold Cup is another matter. The likes of **Kemboy**, **Monalee** and **Presenting Percy** are of a certain level, while, for all that their respective narratives have been utterly invigorating, **Faugheen** and **Samcro** could hardly be considered genuine Gold Cup contenders at this stage.

They may yet prove more effective over intermediate trips. **Minella Indo**, such a galling second to Champ in the RSA, is

Top chasers: Delta Work (main) and (from left) Presenting Percy, Monalee and Kemboy

another second season chaser with the profile to step up, while his Henry de Bromhead-trained stablemate **A Plus Tard** also has the capacity to progress, potentially significantly if he stays further. The redoubtable Arkle Chase heroine **Put The Kettle On** is another from De Bromhead's all-conquering Knockeen stable with marquee potential, probably within the two to two-and-a-half-mile range.

Min has emerged as something of a mid-distance stalwart, last March relishing Cheltenham's 2m 4f Grade 1 showpiece that past stars like Native Upmanship or Merry Gale would have thrived on. He is relatively lightly raced and will doubtless still have a big impact again, while his fellow Rich Ricci-owned **Chacun Pour Soi** remains a precocious but injury-prone two-miler. An 11th hour Queen Mother Champion Chase withdrawal, he has had just eight

starts in his life, so there is little mileage on the clock despite the fact that he is rising nine years of age.

Chacun Pour Soi is a worthy ante-post favourite to give Mullins a breakthrough Champion Chase victory, but, given his track record, getting him there could be the hard part. **Douvan**, likewise, has become a little fragile at this stage, while **Melon**, who has finished second in a Supreme Novices' Hurdle, two Champion Hurdles and split Samcro and Faugheen in the 2020 Marsh Novices' Chase, seems to save his best for Cheltenham in March. It would be rather apt if he and his trainer ended their respective hoodoos in the Champion Chase.

SENIOR HURDLERS

There is a wealth of top-class two-mile hurdlers in Ireland, but the real championship hopes probably rest with two up-and-coming horses.

While Gigginstown's **Abacadabras** just got worried out of it by Shishkin in the Supreme, his only other defeat in five starts as a novice came when he was no match for his exceptional fellow Elliott-trained youngster **Envoi Allen**. He has the makings of a proper two-mile hurdler, as does **Saint Roi**.

Mullins' JP McManus-owned five-year-old sluiced up off a mark of 137 in the County Hurdle, when he swatted away Aramon, a Grade 1-winning novice who went on to deliver one of the most stunning handicap hurdle weight-carrying performances of modern times at Galway.

Saint Roi returned with a bloodless success at Tipperary and looks the prime candidate to deliver his trainer a fifth Champion Hurdle. Aramon is sidelined for the remainder of the campaign, but **Sharjah** and **Saldier** are others who will pay their way.

Honeysuckle and **Benie Des Dieux** are also heavyweight players, albeit the latter could yet revert to chasing now that the mares' race has been added to the Cheltenham Festival programme. If Honeysuckle keeps improving at the rate she did last term, the debate about whether she should swerve the mares' hurdle for a tilt at the Champion Hurdle will rage once again.

NOVICES

As has become the norm, this is a realm in which Irish handlers are well stocked. Over flights, the Champion Bumper 1-2-3 winner **Ferny Hollow**, **Appreciate It** and **Queens Brook** set a tall standard, while the fifth, **Eskylane**, looks pretty useful as well. **Ballyadam** is another cracking Elliott prospect, while his Cheveley Park Stud colours will also be sported by Envoi Allen.

Unbeaten in eight track starts, plus a point-to-point, the emphatic Ballymore Novices' Hurdle winner is up there with the most exciting novice chasing candidates in recent times.

He seems to have the size, scope and constitution for the job, so the sky is his limit, with the Marsh seemingly the primary target as Elliott plots a route to the 2022 Gold Cup. Right now, he is the precocious epitome of what it is about jump racing that so enthrals us.

Others with the capacity to improve for fences are the Mullins quartet of **The Big Getaway**, **Elixir D'ainay**, **Klassical Dream** and **Asterion Forlonge**. Each has the physique of an embryonic chaser.

ANTE-POST ANALYSIS NICK WATTS

Goshen and Defi look early value

CHAMPION HURDLE

Katchit was the last horse to do the Triumph Hurdle-Champion Hurdle double back in 2008 and that statistic is unlikely to be troubled in 2021 with Burning Victory having no more than an outside chance of victory.

However, the 2020 Triumph may still have some bearing on what happens next year as trainer Gary Moore's

Defi Du Seuil: 14-1 for the Champion Chase looks tempting

Goshen would have won that race without coming off the bridle but for tipping up at the last with the race at his mercy.

His dominance up until his unfortunate departure was quite staggering and there has to be a chance he can make an impact despite it being his difficult second season.

Epatante won the Champion last year but was it a great race? She beat Sharjah and Darver Star – good but not great hurdlers – and this is a new year with different horses to have to think about.

Goshen will have his whole season geared around Cheltenham and it will be interesting to see what route Moore plots on his way there. He did have a couple of pipe-openers on the Flat recently, and while beaten in both the most recent was over 1m4f – way short of his best. It will have served to blow away the cobwebs though before he heads to Wincanton for the Elite Hurdle. Let's hope he is as good as he looked last season then we will be in for a treat.

CHAMPION CHASE

The Champion Chase is a tricky one. Chacun Pour Soi is currently market leader and many view him as the second coming. But he is seldom seen so isn't easy to train, and for all his equine riches, it is a race Willie Mullins has yet to win.

Politologue, a horse whose form figures at Cheltenham prior to winning this race last season were U04422, is surely opposable so there simply has to be something at a bigger price to get stuck into.

Defi Du Seuil catches the eye at a top price of 14-1. He was 2-5 to win this year and ran inexplicably badly. However, he was brilliant prior to that in winning the Tingle Creek and Clarence House, plus he had an impeccable festival record going into the race.

If you are of a forgiving persuasion – and it was his first bad run since his chase debut behind Lalor in November 2018 – then that is a big price.

It's always possible he could go out in trip,

but it wasn't the distance that got him beat this year – he was simply never going at any stage.

If there is one to come out of nowhere, it's not impossible that Gordon Elliott's Chosen Mate makes the transition from smart handicapper – he won the Grand Annual in a canter last season – to Grade 1 performer. He is young enough to do so and the way he won at the festival was deeply impressive. At 28-1 he represents reasonable value.

STAYERS' HURDLE

Richard Johnson won the Stayers' Hurdle way back in 1999 on Anzum, and he may have a good chance of making it two some 21 years later with Thyme Hill.

Philip Hobbs's hurdler had a good first campaign over obstacles, winning the Grade 1 Challow, and he was slightly unlucky to finish only fourth in his big seasonal aim, the Albert Bartlett.

He was squeezed out approaching the last yet was still only beaten a length and a half at the line by Monkfish.

He had enjoyed a perfect record up to that point, and this strong stayer can make an impact in this division, with Paisley Park having questions to answer and Lisnagar Oscar having come out of the blue to win last season.

With him not being the biggest, it would make sense for him to stay hurdling this season and see where it takes him – hopefully it will be to the Stayers' next March and a generally available 12-1 isn't a bad price if he hits the ground running as he did last year.

GOLD CUP

In the Gold Cup, the question is whether Al Boum Photo can do a Best Mate and win three in a row. His unusual preparation of one run at Tramore prior to his big day seems to work well for him and his jumping is generally secure now.

He didn't have much to spare last season

over Santini though, and there are some different horses who take him on this season, including Champ and Topofthegame.

Champ showed a remarkable burst to win the RSA last season, but he will need to brush up on his jumping at this level, and the loss of Barry Geraghty could be important for him.

Topofthegame has no such worries with his jumping, and the RSA he won where he saw off Santini and Delta Work quite readily looks a fantastic piece of form now.

Injury robbed us of his presence last season, but all is well again now and the 16-1 being offered by bet365 is quite a carrot.

Even if you base his chance solely on his RSA win – that puts him right there with the horses half his current price.

GRAND NATIONAL

It is a bit too far out to be thinking about the Grand National at present, but if Gordon Elliott decides to aim **Presenting Percy** at the race then 33-1 is huge. His Gold Cup ship has probably sailed, but he is a classy handicapper on his day, having won a Pertemps Final over hurdles and a big handicap at Punchestown over 3m5f over fences.

He has class, staying power and jumps well normally, while the drop down to handicaps, having contested Graded races for the last couple of seasons, may suit him nicely.

Long-range fancy: Presenting Percy could be huge value for the Grand National at 33-1

GETTING AN EDGE RICHARD BIRCH

Surefire winners away from the big meetings

CHELTENHAM may be the pinnacle of the jumps season, but it's only four afternoons in March. Let's not forget all the other fixtures during the 2020-21 campaign which provide countless punting opportunities. Here are 12 horses with the potential to win at least two handicaps in non-festival events over the next six months.

ANNSAM

The apple of my eye, and just the type to land a valuable 2m4f handicap hurdle or two at Grade 1 tracks. The fact he won a Catterick 0-130 on the bridle despite pulling fiercely in the early stages is testament to his natural ability. He was trained like a good horse last season and remains thoroughly unexposed after just four runs in handicaps. He starts off on 127 and could develop into a 140-plus horse. I'm not saying he's another Silver Streak, who started handicapping off 96, but he could be.

ART OF DIPLOMACY

Three quick runs in novice events he simply couldn't win, including the Grade 1 Finale Juvenile Hurdle at Chepstow, has meant this lightly raced four-year-old qualifies for handicap hurdles off an eyecatching mark of 102. A big horse, who is probably only just strengthening into his frame, he won a Hamilton soft-ground handicap on the Flat off 65 last September, and I'll be surprised if he doesn't rattle off a sequence this winter.

BURN BABY BYRNE

Anything this multiple point-to-point scorer achieved over hurdles was always going to prove an added extra in the 2018-19 season. She duly landed two handicaps at Ludlow and promises to be even better when switched to fences if returning from a year on the sidelines.

CATHAL'S STAR

A big chasing sort who made a huge impression when powering clear of 0-110 opposition in a Sedgefield handicap hurdle in September. Clearly in a totally different league to that calibre of rival, he was still hard on the bridle at the top of the hill, with all the others under maximum pressure. This seven-year-old looks just the type to improve further when switched to fences and is emphatically one to keep on your side. His trainer Nicky Richards places this sort of horse particularly well.

DING DING

Plumpton specialist who begins this season attractively treated after registering a rare blank last term having won twice the previous seoason. She acts on soft ground, but is more effective on good going and there will be plenty of opportunities to add to her six Plumpton victories. Mares' only handicaps at the Sussex venue are likely to be the focus of attention.

RoR
Retraining of Racehorses

Racing to a new career at ror.org.uk

Source a Horse

sourceahorse.ror.org.uk

A new website for selling or loaning a horse directly out of a trainer's yard and for all former racehorses.

Owner/Trainer Helpline

A dedicated helpline to assist in the placement of horses coming out of training.

Rehoming Direct

RoR has compiled a checklist to safeguard your horse's future when moved directly into the sport horse market.

Retrainers

RoR has a list of retrainers recommended by trainers who can start the retraining process and assess each horse.

Visit
ror.org.uk
for rehoming options and advice

Equine Charities

Retrain former racehorses for a donation, as well as care for vulnerable horses with the help of RoR funding.

RoR is British horseracing's official charity for the welfare of horses retired from racing.

T: 01488 648998

DONTDELAY

This ten-year-old comes alive in Hexham four-mile chases when the mud is flying. He boasts course form figures of 1171 at the Northumberland track, and his trainer will prime him for the days when stamina is at a premium. There are two 4m handicaps at Hexham during the course of the season which are obvious targets, including the one on the Thursday of the Cheltenham Festival.

KLOUD GATE

Looked a hurdler going places in the 2018-19 season until suffering a serious injury in the Lanzarote at Kempton in January. He was sent off 7-2 favourite for that contest and looks a strong candidate to land a similar sort of race over 2m4f-plus if returning as good as ever this term. He has been given plenty of time to get over that setback and could resume where he left off.

MR MEDIC

Fought a losing battle with the handicapper after soaring from 134 to 143 following his impressive Ascot chase victory over 2m4f in November 2018. However, he's back down to 130 now and appeals strongly as one who could win a couple of valuable handicaps at the southern tracks. He's at his best in strongly run races on good ground and goes really well at Ascot. When fully on-song his jumping is a joy to watch.

OUR MERLIN

The handicapper looked to have his measure when he signed off his hurdles career, but the manner of Our Merlin's chase debut success at Taunton suggests the eight-year-old could take his form to another level over fences. He had less than no chance in the Arkle, but can exploit a mark of 132 in his trademark bold, front-running style in a more suitable race. The softer the ground the better for him.

ROSY WORLD

In common with several of her stablemates in the Suzy Smith yard last season, Rosy World didn't fulfil expectations after leaving a lasting impression with a five-length Plumpton win in March 2019. It could be, of course, that she was highly tried in good-class handicaps at Aintree and Ascot, but the suspicion remains that the daughter of Shirocco is capable of much better than she showed on those two occasions. Her dam developed into a 149-rated performer, and there is plenty of scope for Rosy World off a current hurdles mark of 117.

SEABORN

On paper he looked potentially the best handicapped hurdler in training after racing's resumption in June, and this 79-rated Flat performer duly hacked up off hurdle marks of 87 and 100 at Stratford and Fontwell (both at around 2m) during the summer. The handicapper responded by raising him 17lb after that last success, but I expect connections will have the last laugh as Seaborn could develop into a 125-plus horse when he steps up in trip. The 2m5f Lanzarote Hurdle, which his trainer Gary Moore often targets, looks ideal for him in January. He jumps well, and possibly wouldn't want the ground too soft.

SOME CAN DANCE

His first season over fences rather petered out after a fluent Ffos Las success in December. However, he gained valuable experience in subsequent starts at Exeter and Cheltenham (pulled up behind Ravenhill in the Grade 2 National Hunt Chase over 3m6f), and starts the new season off a workable mark of 122. He showed a particular affinity for Carlisle during his hurdle days and there ought to be several good opportunities for him at that track over 3m2f. He possesses a good cruising speed for a stayer and loves the mud.

RACING POST

UPPING THE ANTE

SPONSORED BY **bet365**

Expert advice to help you pick the best ante-post bets for Cheltenham.

Watch every week between now and the Festival.

The perfect match – McCain and Bangor

ONE of the most commonly used cliches in racing is horses for courses. The truism has plenty of legs, especially at idiosyncratic and unique venues like Southwell and Chepstow, but in the majority of races at these one-of-a-kind tracks, punters get presented with a convoluted problem as numerous former course-and-distance winners face off.

What factor a horse appreciates in a track varies. It could be the regular occurrence of deep or rattling fast ground; a steep incline or decline to the finish; the galloping or tight turns or a mixture of them all – but once they prove they're best at one venue, that is often where they ply their trade.

That decision is made by the trainer and owners. Veering off to the Flat scene, the likes of Scott Dixon, who now trains his

horses on the iconic Fibresand at Southwell, might have spotted an edge. A tried and tested horse is better than one who is encountering conditions for the first time, right? Dixon certainly thinks so.

The trainer has been a regular customer at the Nottinghamshire venue over the years, proved by the fact that he sent out 41 per cent of his runners (134 out of 327) at Southwell in 2018. That strike-rate remained the same last year, but instead of 41 per cent of his runners racing at Southwell, Dixon upped it to 58 per cent (138-236).

That technique could and should be used to great effect over the jumps and, while it would be inaccurate to say that Donald McCain trains on track at Bangor like Dixon does at Southwell – I'm sure he would if he could – McCain is starting to implement that tactic at his local venue.

Situated 12 miles away at Bankhouse Stables in the beautiful Cholmondeley Castle Estate, McCain not only targets every meeting at his beloved circuit, but he sponsors an impressive amount of races too – if you're winning the contests, you might as well get your name in the race titles and win your own money back!

Given the amount of runners in his yard and the small number of fixtures allocated to Bangor, it would be ludicrous to see the same

Donald McCain (above) has a superb record at Bangor (main picture)

kind of runner-to-track percentage as earlier stated for Dixon, but in the last five years, McCain has made Bangor his home.

A total of 288 Bangor runners for McCain have amassed prize-money of just over £385,000 and rewarded loyal punters with an impressive £1 level-stake profit of +£80.95. Those figures are trumped by McCain's whopping 22 per cent strike-rate, which is courtesy of 64 winners. A further 116 have finished second, third and fourth combined.

McCain, who has won a substantial number of Graded races since taking over from his father Ginger, is also known to send his prized possessions to Bangor. Take dual Grade 1-winner Peddlers Cross, for example.

The £100,000 purchase was always considered top class by his astute handler, but McCain didn't just stick to the major track with the subsequent Neptune Novices' Hurdle and Fighting Fifth winner – Peddlers Cross also ran three times at Bangor. Most notably, two of those came on his hurdles and chase debuts.

The Cheshire trainer is, as an American football announcer would say about a highly talented quarterback, 'money' at his favourite hunting ground and will continue to be so. He hasn't lost a trainer's title here since Warren Greatrex sent out eight winners from 11 runners in the 2016-17 season and will be long odds-on to continue his domination.

Instead of targeting a track, some trainers aim to plunder significant types of races and that can prove a real money-spinning ploy for stable and punters alike. It would be folly to go through a piece like this without mentioning the names of Nicky Henderson and Paul Nicholls, and that duo are key to this section.

Henderson, who has an embarrassment of riches at his Seven Barrows stables, is sure to win race after race throughout the season due to the quality of his string. However, watching out for his novice hurdlers at Newbury and Sandown has proved noticeably interesting and profitable.

Although he went to other venues with

Altior, Henderson ran dual Champion Hurdle winner Buveur D'Air in a maiden hurdle there in November 2015, in which he unsurprisingly scooted home by 11 lengths, while another of the stable's leading lights Santini also made his debut over hurdles at Newbury in 2017.

Statistically, Newbury comes out on top for Henderson's novice hurdlers with a mighty 30 per cent strike-rate (34-114) and it's not just a case of farming these races with all types of racehorse. He tends to send his top echelon future stars to the track, so

Trainers for tracks: Nicky Henderson (top left) does particularly well at Newbury, where he introduced Gold Cup second Santini (above) in 2017, while Paul Nicholls has an astonishing record at Fontwell and Wincanton

make note when you see Henderson's name next to an exciting, young horse.

The same can be said for Nicholls with his chasers at Fontwell and Wincanton. It's no secret he does well at both of those tracks, but strike-rates of 49 and 33 per cent respectively in that sphere over the last five years is breathtaking.

Capitalising on weak events could certainly be argued in this case, but if that is the answer then Nicholls' race placing has to be greatly admired. He is operating well above anything that could be considered

average and although the level-stake profits indicate a fair few of his runners go off at short prices, he is still on the plus side of the scales at both courses.

The cliche horses for courses might have to be joined by trainers for tracks should the three maestros continue to churn out strikes at their local venues.

A dozen big guns to follow on main stage

ABACADABRAS

I think the front two in the Supreme Novices' Hurdle are going to make big waves in different divisions this season and it's Abacadabras who could be back for a crack at the Champion Hurdle in March. Okay, it's hardly original picking the first two from one of the Cheltenham Grade 1 novice hurdles, but the Supreme looked well up to scratch and this pair pulled 11 lengths clear of the rest. Time may tell Abacadabras was unlucky to run into a horse as good as Shishkin in the Supreme and unlucky to find the ground as soft as it was on the day. He is a really strong traveller who is going to be well suited by the cut and thrust of a Champion Hurdle and if all goes well it's easy to see him lining up in March with a serious chance.

ALLAHO

There's a fair chance this Willie Mullins inmate will be underestimated this season, but I fancy him to have a really good year. He hasn't put up that massive winning performance that gets jumps fans drooling, but in a short career he has run to a very high level and I'm sure he has far more potential than the two who finished ahead of him in the RSA: Champ, who will be nine next year, and Minella Indo, who is going to need extreme trips. I'm not convinced it's an advantage to be an out-and-out stayer at such a young age and those who reckon Allaho won't get the Gold Cup trip with

another summer on his back could be in for a surprise. He has, after all, finished placed in three 3m Grade 1s at the age of six. I think he'll win one this year, and if not, he could always prove top class at shorter.

GREANETEEN

Greaneteen is another who finished fourth at the festival, but if he'd had any luck in running he'd have been at least a couple of places better. The Paul Nicholls-trained six-year-old was thrown into the deep end there, having won only three novices yet earned a mark of 150, but he jumped fast and accurately until being short-sighted and blundering at the second-last, and in the circumstances he did well to get as close as he did. There is going to be room at the top in the two-mile division, and if there is a horse capable of stepping up from handicap company to the top level it could well be this one. He couldn't be in better hands given Nicholls has won six Champion Chases and an incredible ten Tingle Creeks.

IMPERIAL ALCAZAR

Having shown serious ability without winning in bumpers in the 2018-19 season, Imperial Alcazar was described as still a big baby after getting his head in front in a maiden hurdle on his seasonal return, and it was a case of a learning process for him over hurdles after that. Imperial Alcazar ran perfectly respectable races in defeat on his next two starts, finishing second each time,

Shishkin and Abacadabras – first and second in the Supreme Novices' must be followed

and it's fair to say he didn't have much to beat when last seen in January. He remains a very promising horse, though, and a handicap mark of 140 will surely underestimate him if he stays over hurdles. It looks like he'll make a chaser, though, so it remains to be seen what Fergal O'Brien's plans are for him. The trainer could not have made a better start to the season, and is clearly going to have a cracking campaign.

LOSTINTRANSLATION

He was just about my number one horse to follow last season and, although things did not go entirely according to plan, I'm not going to moan about a Betfair Chase win and a Gold Cup third. Having thrashed RSA winner Topofthegame (who should make a comeback this term) at Aintree at the end of his novice season, plenty was expected of Lostintranslation and he delivered early on, winning in comfortable fashion in a weak race at Carlisle on his return and then beating Bristol De Mai in his own backyard in the Betfair Chase at Haydock. He was always travelling well there and won with a bit in hand, but then it went pear-shaped in the King George at Kempton, where he was never travelling, made mistakes and was pulled up at the first in the home straight. Whether he simply didn't like running right-handed at the top level, that run was too bad to be true and Lostintranslation was not seen again until the Gold Cup, having had wind surgery in the meantime. He ran a cracker there, just being run out of it by Al Boum Photo and Santini despite his yard being under something of a cloud, and he should not be ruled out of challenging for the big one again. A more straightforward campaign would certainly give connections cause for encouragement, as Lostintranslation clearly handles Cheltenham very well.

MAIRE BANRIGH

Dan Skelton's mare looked like failing to live up to her hefty price tag when well beaten on her first two starts over hurdles, but a wind operation in January 2018 turned her around and she ran up a sequence of six wins over the next two seasons. Switched to fences last term, she won four in a row and jumped like an old hand, so it was a little surprising she was an unconsidered 16-1 shot in the Arkle at Cheltenham. Surprisingly for one who had jumped so assuredly, it was her jumping which let her down as she fell four out, but she was going as well as anything at the time and, given she stays a good deal further than two miles, she would surely have played a hand in the finish. She may be approaching nine, but has run only nine times under rules, and there is more to come. She could easily run up a sequence in mares' company, but is more than capable of holding her own in better class and early shows of 40-1 for her to win the new mares' chase at the festival are an insult.

McFABULOUS

Having shown red-hot form in bumpers the season before last, McFabulous was a bitter disappointment on his first two hurdles starts last term, being beaten at odds of 3-10 on his debut at Chepstow and then finishing last of four in a Grade 2 at Ascot. However, it was evidently just a learning process as he is unbeaten in three starts since and has been hugely impressive on the last two of them. The first was in a Grade 3 handicap at Kempton just after Cheltenham, in which he blew his rivals away by six and a half lengths, and then he returned to canter home by three lengths in the Persian War at Chepstow. Handicaps look out of the question now and, while trainer Paul Nicholls says he may be a Gold Cup horse one day, the plan is to stay over hurdles for the time being to see if he is up to Stayers' Hurdle standard. He travels very nicely in his races, but is certainly bred for three miles and could go right to the top in the staying division.

*Maire Banrigh:
smart chaser who
could easily run
up a sequence in
mares' races*

MONKFISH

The Albert Bartlett was a bad race for me in 2020 as I thought Monkfish was typical of the slow-maturing type who was stepping up in class too soon for a race at the festival and I got against him wherever I could. I can't hold that against him, though, as he did enough wrong in the contest, racing keenly and almost knocking a hurdle out of the ground at one stage, but still stuck his head down and fought all the way to the line to win by a neck from Latest Exhibition and Fury Road. I'm now firmly in his camp and, given his size, you would be surprised if he didn't take to fences like a duck to water. All

roads will doubtless lead back to the RSA, but Monkfish, who seems to handle any ground, will surely rack up a sequence en route.

SAINT ROI

It's not that often these days that bookmakers are caught on the hop by a JP McManus-owned horse at Cheltenham, but Saint Roi was barely even considered in the betting for the County Hurdle on the eve of the festival, but come race time had been punted into 11-2 favourite and won like a horse with a huge amount in hand. He had run in only two maiden hurdles for Willie Mullins (having been beaten on both starts in France), winning the second of them at lowly Tramore in January, but the connections sure knew what they had and Saint Roi, given a patient ride, quickened really nicely to settle issues in a matter of strides after the last. That was off a mark of just 137, and Saint Roi didn't really need to improve when coasting home at Tipperary in a weak Grade 3 on his return (second was rated just 131), but this is a five-year-old of immense potential and he is going to hold his own in Grade 1 company.

SAINT SONNET

Paul Nicholls doesn't normally rush his horses into top company without reason, so the fact he allowed Saint Sonnet to take his chance at odds of 33-1 in the Marsh at Cheltenham should not be underestimated. The five-year-old had a typically busy time of things as a younger horse in France, running eight times in all and winning four. He made it five career wins when scoring at odds of

1-5 in a five-runner chase at Catterick on his debut for Nicholls in February, so he really was going into the deep end little over two weeks later in the Marsh. The record will show he finished only seventh, but he shaped really well against a bunch of horses with festival experience and, like a lot of Nicholls chasers, he certainly knows how to jump.

Lostintranslation (right) alongside (from left) Footpad, Cyrname and Clan Des Obeaux at the start of last season's King George

Don't be surprised if he lands a big handicap or two before going back into Graded company this season.

SHISHKIN

This is about as unoriginal as you can get, but Shishkin really does look a potential superstar and has done since he put up an impressive time performance when slamming 13 rivals to get off the mark at Newbury in January. He needed every bit of that speed to get out of trouble in a really messy Supreme and to be able to pull 11 lengths clear with the runner-up after that marks him down as something special. Having seen nowhere near enough daylight on the inside in the early stages, Nico de Boinville moved him out wide approaching the third-last, but that was just when leader Asterion Forlonge decided to start jumping sideways, and he was remarkably lucky not to be brought down two out. Hopefully he will prove just as nimble when it comes to tackling a fence, and if that's the case he must have a good chance of emulating stablemate Altior, who won the Supreme and Arkle in successive years.

THE BIG BREAKAWAY

A heavy defeat at the Cheltenham Festival as a novice should not be held against any horse, and The Big Breakaway ran really well despite being beaten 14 lengths by Envoi Allen in the Ballymore anyway. This half-brother to Kildisart, who has twice finished in the first four at the festival over fences, didn't have much in the way of experience heading into the Ballymore as all he'd done was destroy much inferior rivals in two novice events, so that fourth place was the first time he'd been asked to properly race, and came at a time when Colin Tizzard's runners were not going particularly well. He is going to be better than that, especially when presented with a fence, and his best days, plenty of them, are surely ahead of him.

109

THIS SEASON'S KEY HORSES

By Dylan Hill

A Plus Tard (Fr)

6 b g Kapgarde - Turboka (Kahyasi)

Henry de Bromhead (Ire) — Cheveley Park Stud

PLACINGS: 12231/2121/3213- — RPR **171**c

Starts	1st	2nd	3rd	4th	Win & Pl
13	5	5	3	-	£246,349

	12/19	Leop	2m1f Gd1 Ch soft	£66,441
144	3/19	Chel	2m4f Cls1 Nov List 138-145 Ch Hcap soft	£39,389
	12/18	Naas	2m3f Ch yield	£7,904
0	4/18	Autl	2m2f List Hdl 4yo Hcap heavy	£39,823
	10/17	Sbri	2m2f Hdl 3yo gd-sft	£6,974

Stepped up to Grade I level with distinction last season, notably beating Chacun Pour Soi (lacked race fitness) at Leopardstown; stepped back up to 2m4½f at Cheltenham for the Ryanair Chase but beaten into third behind Min and Saint Calvados.

A Wave Of The Sea (Ire)

4 b g Born To Sea - Je T'Adore (Montjeu)

Joseph O'Brien (Ire) — John P McManus

PLACINGS: 2112317-0413 — RPR **140**+h

Starts	1st	2nd	3rd	4th	Win & Pl
11	4	2	2	1	£113,130

9/20	Kbgn	2m4f Ch yield	£5,500
2/20	Leop	2m Gd1 Hdl 4yo yield	£75,000
11/19	DRoy	2m¹/₂f Hdl 3yo soft	£7,986
10/19	Punc	2m Hdl 3yo gd-yld	£8,253

Did well during a busy juvenile campaign last season; won the Grade I Spring Juvenile Hurdle at Leopardstown, albeit flattered after Aspire Tower fell at the last; beaten just over six lengths when seventh in the Triumph Hurdle at Cheltenham.

Abacadabras (Fr)

6 b g Davidoff - Cadoubelle Des As (Cadoudal)

Gordon Elliott (Ire) — Gigginstown House Stud

PLACINGS: 104/211212- — RPR **160**+h

Starts	1st	2nd	3rd	4th	Win & Pl
9	4	3	-	1	£146,330

12/19	Leop	2m Nov Gd1 Hdl soft	£53,153
11/19	Navn	2m Nov Gd3 Hdl sft-hvy	£17,275
10/19	Gowr	2m Mdn Hdl gd-yld	£7,454
10/18	Gway	2m¹/₂f NHF 4yo yield	£5,451

Top-class novice hurdler last season, winning three times and beaten only by Envoi Allen and Shishkin; narrow defeat to the latter in the Supreme came when tanking to the front and just getting overhauled by a stronger stayer; leading Champion Hurdle contender.

Acapella Bourgeois (Fr)

10 ch g Network - Jasmine (Valanjou I)

Willie Mullins (Ire) — Slaneyville Syndicate

PLACINGS: 41165/F2P/013/00261- — RPR **164**+c

Starts	1st	2nd	3rd	4th	Win & Pl
27	8	3	3	2	£180,050

2/20	Fair	3m1f Gd3 Ch heavy	£21,250
3/19	Clon	2m4f Ch good	£9,712
2/17	Navn	3m Nov Gd2 Ch sft-hvy	£21,432
1/17	Navn	2m4f Ch soft	£6,833
3/16	Fair	2m4f Nov Gd2 Hdl yield	£19,522
2/16	Thur	2m4f Nov Gd2 Hdl soft	£19,522
12/15	Leop	2m Mdn Hdl heavy	£6,953
10/14	Rcpp	1m4f NHF 4-5yo gd-sft	£4,167

As good as ever last season and produced a terrific performance to win the Bobbyjo Chase by 15 lengths on his final run; ideally suited by heavy ground that day, relishing a stiff test of stamina; had been on course for the Aintree or Irish National (third in the latter in 2019).

Al Boum Photo (Fr)

8 b g Buck's Boum - Al Gane (Dom Alco)

Willie Mullins (Ire) — Mrs J Donnelly

PLACINGS: /3115/1F2F10/11:211- — RPR **176**+c

Starts	1st	2nd	3rd	4th	Win & Pl
16	8	2	1	-	£898,384

3/20	Chel	3m2¹/₂f Cls1 Gd1 Ch gd-sft	£351,688
1/20	Tram	2m5¹/₂f Gd3 Ch soft	£20,000
3/19	Chel	3m2¹/₂f Cls1 Gd1 Ch gd-sft	£351,688
1/19	Tram	2m5¹/₂f List Ch soft	£16,622
4/18	Fair	2m4f Nov Gd1 Ch sft-hvy	£52,212
11/17	Navn	2m1f Ch sft-hvy	£8,950
4/17	Fair	2m4f Nov Gd2 Hdl sft-hvy	£21,432
1/17	Thur	2m Mdn Hdl 4-5yo yld-sft	£5,256

Has won the Cheltenham Gold Cup for the last two seasons, holding off Santini to retain his crown in March; has used the same New Year's Day chase at Tramore for his sole prep run both times; sure to have his campaign geared solely around a third Gold Cup win.

Alfa Mix

5 b g Fair Mix - Alora Money (Alflora)

Gavin Cromwell (Ire) — John P McManus

PLACINGS: F/096415127- — RPR **142**+h

Starts	1st	2nd	3rd	4th	Win & Pl
9	2	1		1	£42,039

127	12/19	Navn	2m4f 120-148 Hdl Hcap soft	£26,577
	10/19	Tram	2m Mdn Hdl sft-hvy	£5,857

Very much a work in progress as a novice hurdler

Follow us @RacingPost

last season, taking a big step forward once sent handicapping and stepped up in trip to win over 2m4f at Navan; improved again when second off 9lb higher next time and far from disgraced when seventh in the Coral Cup.

Allaho (Fr)

6 b g No Risk At All - Idaho Falls (Turgeon)

Willie Mullins (Ire)   Cheveley Park Stud

PLACINGS: 2/413/2213-   RPR **164**+c

Starts	1st	2nd	3rd	4th	Win & Pl
8	2	3	2	1	£94,299
1/20	Fair	2m5¹/₂f Ch yld-sft.................................. £7,012			
2/19	Clon	3m Nov Gd3 Hdl gd-yld £21,261			

Excellent third in last season's RSA Chase, matching his position in the 2019 Albert Bartlett; had been expected to do even better in the RSA

(sent off favourite) after a wide-margin win in a beginners' chase; still very lightly raced and open to significant improvement.

Allart (Ire)

6 b g Shantou - The Adare Woman (Oscar)

Nicky Henderson   R A Bartlett

PLACINGS: 3/F115-   RPR **144**h

Starts	1st	2nd	3rd	4th	Win & Pl
5	2	-	1	-	£11,699
2/20	Donc	2m¹/₂f Cls4 Nov Hdl soft...................... £3,769			
1/20	Ludl	2m Cls4 Nov Hdl soft.......................... £4,224			

Quickly proved a very useful novice hurdler last season, winning twice in the new year (both at odds-on) and finishing fifth when taking a big step up in class for the Supreme; entitled to leave that form behind and bred to get further.

Allmankind: third in last season's Triumph Hurdle and very exciting

Allmankind

4 b g Sea The Moon - Wemyss Bay (Sadler's Wells)

Dan Skelton   W J & T C O Gredley

PLACINGS: 1113-				RPR **143**+h

Starts	1st	2nd	3rd	4th	Win & Pl
4	3		1	-	£73,649
	12/19	Chep	2m Cls1 Gd1 Hdl 3yo heavy		£37,018
	11/19	Chel	2m¹/₂f Cls1 Gd2 Hdl 3yo soft		£18,224
	11/19	Wwck	2m Cls4 Hdl 3yo gd-sft		£4,549

Exciting front-running hurdler who was hugely impressive when winning first three starts over hurdles last season, including the Finale Hurdle at Chepstow by nine lengths; outclassed by the unlucky Goshen in the Triumph Hurdle but stuck on well for a brave third.

Altior (Ire)

10 b g High Chaparral - Monte Solaro (Key Of Luck)

Nicky Henderson   Mrs Patricia Pugh

PLACINGS: 111111/111/11111/21-				RPR **177**c

Starts	1st	2nd	3rd	4th	Win & Pl
24	21	1	1	-	£1,278,319
	2/20	Newb	2m¹/₂f Cls1 Cls1 Ch good		£28,609
	4/19	Sand	1m7¹/₂f Cls1 Gd1 Ch good		£85,425
	3/19	Chel	2m Cls1 Gd1 Ch soft		£225,080
	1/19	Asct	2m1f Cls1 Gd1 Ch gd-sft		£85,425
	12/18	Kemp	2m Cls1 Gd2 Ch gd-sft		£56,950
	12/18	Sand	1m7¹/₂f Cls1 Gd1 Ch soft		£84,405
	4/18	Sand	1m7¹/₂f Cls1 Gd1 Ch gd-sft		£74,383
	3/18	Chel	2m Cls1 Gd1 Ch soft		£228,872
	2/18	Newb	2m¹/₂f Cls1 Gd1 Ch soft		£28,475
	4/17	Sand	1m7¹/₂f Cls1 Gd1 Ch good		£71,188
	3/17	Chel	2m Cls1 Nov Gd1 Ch gd-sft		£99,663
	2/17	Newb	2m¹/₂f Cls1 Gd2 Ch soft		£28,475
	12/16	Kemp	2m Cls1 Nov Gd2 Ch good		£22,780
	12/16	Sand	1m7¹/₂f Cls1 Nov Gd1 Ch gd-sft		£25,628
	11/16	Kemp	2m2f Cls4 Nov Ch soft		£4,549
	3/16	Chel	2m¹/₂f Cls1 Nov Gd1 Hdl gd-sft		£68,340
	12/15	Kemp	2m¹/₂f Cls1 Nov Hdl gd-sft		£11,696
	11/15	Chel	2m¹/₂f Cls1 Nov Gd2 Hdl gd-sft		£17,286
	10/15	Asct	1m7¹/₂f Cls3 Nov Hdl good		£7,798
	10/15	Chep	2m Cls4 Nov Hdl good		£3,899
	5/14	MRas	2m¹/₂f Cls6 NHF 4-6yo good		£1,560

Legendary chaser who won a jumps-record 19 successive races from 2015 to 2019; beaten for the first time over jumps when second to Cyrname last term on first run beyond 2m2f, though could return to longer trips again; denied crack at a third Champion Chase through injury.

Andy Dufresne (Ire)

6 b g Doyen - Daytona Lily (Beneficial)

Gordon Elliott (Ire)   John P McManus

PLACINGS: 1/1/1213-				RPR **150**+h

Starts	1st	2nd	3rd	4th	Win & Pl
5	3	1	1	-	£45,808
	1/20	Punc	2m¹/₂f Nov Gd2 Hdl soft		£22,250
	11/19	Navn	2m4f Mdn Hdl sft-hvy		£7,188
	1/19	DRoy	2m NHF 5-7yo yield		£5,550

Sky-high reputation took a bit of a hit last season when beaten twice at short prices in novice hurdles, though he still won twice including a Grade 2; had won his point-to-point impressively enough to fetch £330,000 at the sales and could do better over fences.

Annamix (Fr)

7 gr g Martaline - Tashtiyana (Doyoun)

Willie Mullins (Ire)   Mrs S Ricci

PLACINGS: 2/21/41-				RPR **154**+c

Starts	1st	2nd	3rd	4th	Win & Pl
5	2	2	-	1	£21,142
	1/20	Fair	2m1f Ch soft		£8,514
	3/19	Clon	2m Mdn Hdl gd-yld		£6,105

Massive talking horse in recent seasons but has proved massively fragile, running just four times since arrival at Closutton in 2017; slightly disappointing over hurdles but hacked up on his chasing debut at Fairyhouse in January before suffering latest setback.

Annie Mc (Ire)

6 b m Mahler - Classic Mari (Classic Cliche)

Jonjo O'Neill   Coral Champions Club

PLACINGS: 2/2324151/41119-				RPR **147**+c

Starts		1st	2nd	3rd	4th	Win & Pl
11		5	1	1	2	£54,506
	2/20	Bang	2m4¹/₂f Cls4 Nov Ch soft		£5,718
	1/20	Weth	2m3¹/₂f Cls4 Nov Ch soft		£4,606
	12/19	Winc	2m4f Cls3 Nov Ch heavy		£9,097
127	3/19	Newb	2m4¹/₂f Cls1 Nov 107-127 Hdl Hcap gd-sft		£24,760
118	1/19	Chep	2m3¹/₂f Cls3 117-129 Hdl Hcap gd-sft		£6,238

Won the EBF Mares' Final in 2019 and took to fences well last season, winning her first three chases, albeit all in small-field mares' races; tailed off when taking a big step up in class in the Marsh Novices' Chase at Cheltenham.

Another Crick

7 b g Arcadio - Suetsu (Toulon)

Noel Williams   David Sewell

PLACINGS: 4/564235/82211/				RPR **139**c

Starts		1st	2nd	3rd	4th	Win & Pl
12		2	3	1	2	£24,607
124	2/19	Kemp	2m4¹/₂f Cls3 109-132 Ch Hcap good		£8,447
117	12/18	Newb	2m¹/₂f Cls3 Nov 113-125 Ch Hcap gd-sft		£8,058

Missed last season through injury but had been a sharply progressive novice chaser in 2018-19, climbing 26lb in just four races and finishing with handicap wins at Newbury and Kempton (most impressive when stepped up to 2m4f); strong traveller and seen by trainer as the type to thrive in top handicaps.

Any Second Now (Ire)

8 b g Oscar - Pretty Neat (Topanoora)

Ted Walsh (Ire)   John P McManus

PLACINGS: /22238/52531F/62U31-				RPR **158**+c

Starts		1st	2nd	3rd	4th	Win & Pl
20		4	5	4	-	£152,698
	2/20	Naas	2m Gd3 Ch heavy		£23,250
143	3/19	Chel	3m2f Cls2 133-144 Am Ch Hcap gd-sft		£41,510
	1/17	Punc	2m Nov Gd2 Hdl soft		£22,440
	12/16	Navn	2m Mdn Hdl 4yo yld-sft		£5,426

Hugely impressive winner of the Kim Muir at Cheltenham in 2019 and shaped well throughout last season in preparation for the Grand National; looked better than ever when winning over an inadequate 2m at Naas in February; likely to be a leading National contender again.

Apple's Shakira (Fr)

6 b m Saddler Maker - Apple's For Ever (Nikos)

Nicky Henderson   John P McManus

PLACINGS: 111143/P6/   RPR **142**h

Starts	1st	2nd	3rd	4th	Win & Pl
8	4		1	1	£74,989
1/18	Chel	2m1f Cls1 Gd2 Hdl 4yo soft			£18,224
12/17	Chel	2m1f Cls2 Hdl 3yo soft			£12,512
11/17	Chel	2m¹/₂f Cls1 Gd2 Hdl 3yo soft			£17,085
5/17	Vich	2m¹/₂f Hdl 3yo v soft			£8,615

Has run just twice since exciting juvenile campaign in 2017-18 when she won first four races and went off 6-5 for the Triumph Hurdle only to finish fourth; finished a close sixth in the Coral Cup in 2019 but then missed last season through injury.

Appreciate It (Ire)

6 b g Jeremy - Sainte Baronne (Saint Des Saints)

Willie Mullins (Ire)   Miss M A Masterson

PLACINGS: 31/3112-   RPR **138**+b

Starts	1st	2nd	3rd	4th	Win & Pl
4	2	1	1		£73,150
2/20	Leop	2m Gd2 NHF 4-7yo yield			£50,000
12/19	Leop	2m4f NHF 4-7yo soft			£6,389

Warm favourite for last season's Champion Bumper at Cheltenham and ran well despite losing out to Ferny Hollow, travelling strongly to the front on the bridle; had run away with a strong Grade 2 bumper at Leopardstown on quicker ground; top prospect for novice hurdles.

Aramax (Ger)

4 b g Maxios - Aramina (In The Wings)

Gordon Elliott (Ire)   John P McManus

PLACINGS: 31F311-08   RPR **138**+

Starts	1st	2nd	3rd	4th	Win & Pl
138	3		2	-	£65,682
3/20	Chel	2m¹/₂f Cls1 Gd3 129-140 Hdl 4yo Hcap soft			£45,016
2/20	Naas	2m Nov Hdl 4yo gd-yld			£9,250
7/19	Vitt	2m¹/₂f Hdl 3yo gd-sft			£7,351

French hurdles winner who got better and better with every run for new connections last season, winning twice more including the Fred Winter at Cheltenham; still looks a work in progress and could have another big handicap in him.

Ask Ben (Ire)

7 b g Ask - Decheekymonkey (Presenting)

Graeme McPherson   Mrs Liz Prowting

PLACINGS: 52/1V120/42P-   RPR **141**+h

Starts	1st	2nd	3rd	4th	Win & Pl
8	2	2	-	1	£29,910
1/19	Ayr	3m¹/₂f Cls4 Nov Hdl gd-sft			£4,744
12/18	Newc	2m6f Cls2 Nov Hdl soft			£9,384

Very useful novice hurdler during the 2018-19 season (won twice and second to Stayers' Hurdle winner Lisnagar Oscar in a Grade 2 at Haydock) and progressed again in good staying handicaps last season; pulled up when favourite for a valuable race at Sandown but later found to be lame.

Ask For Glory (Ire)

6 b g Fame And Glory - Ask Helen (Pistolet Bleu)

Paul Nicholls   Colm Donlon & Mrs P K Barber

PLACINGS: 119/41-   RPR **139**+h

Starts	1st	2nd	3rd	4th	Win & Pl
4	2	-	-	1	£8,599
2/20	Winc	2m5¹/₂f Cls4 Nov Hdl soft			£4,224
12/18	Chep	2m Cls4 NHF 4-6yo soft			£3,899

Smart bumper performer (sent off just 13-2 when ninth in the 2019 Champion Bumper) who missed much of last season but belatedly built on a promising hurdles debut to win easily at Wincanton, albeit in moderate company at 1-5; likely to go novice chasing.

Aso (Fr)

10 b/br g Goldneyev - Odyssee Du Cellier (Dear Doctor)

Venetia Williams   The Bellamy Partnership

PLACINGS: 4218434/5/1162/3547-   RPR **158**c

Starts	1st	2nd	3rd	4th	Win & Pl
33	9	6	5	4	£355,573
158	1/19	Chel	2m4¹/₂f Cls1 Gd3 133-158 Ch Hcap gd-sft			£42,285
150	11/18	Newb	2m4f Cls2 130-152 Ch Hcap gd-sft			£31,396
145	12/16	Chep	2m3¹/₂f Cls2 127-149 Ch Hcap soft			£25,320
	4/16	NAbb	2m5f Cls3 Nov Ch soft			£7,280
	1/16	MRas	2m5¹/₂f Cls4 Ch soft			£12,777
	1/15	Hayd	2m Cls1 Nov Gd2 Hdl heavy			£15,661
	12/14	Tntn	2m3f Cls4 Nov Hdl soft			£3,574
	11/14	Wwck	2m Cls4 Nov Hdl soft			£3,899
	7/13	Gran	1m4f NHF 3yo gd-fm			£4,065

Out of sorts last season, doing best when third in the Charlie Hall and a distant fourth in the King George; failed to build on breakthrough 2018-19 campaign when second in the Ryanair at Cheltenham; dropped back to last winning mark (158 at Cheltenham in January 2019).

Aspire Tower (Ire)

4 b g Born To Sea - Red Planet (Pivotal)

Henry de Bromhead (Ire)   Brendan McNeill & Jonathan Maloney

PLACINGS: 11F2-   RPR **145**h

Starts	1st	2nd	3rd	4th	Win & Pl
4	2	1	-	-	£61,191
12/19	Leop	2m Gd2 Hdl 3yo soft			£26,577
11/19	Punc	2m¹/₂f Mdn Hdl 3yo soft			£6,922

Quickly proved a very smart juvenile hurdler, winning first two starts by wide margins; didn't quite live up to expectations in two runs at Grade 1 level, though still held every chance when falling at the last at Leopardstown and fought hard to take second in the Triumph Hurdle.

Assemble

6 b g Getaway - Annaghbrack (Rudimentary)

Joseph O'Brien (Ire)   Gigginstown House Stud

PLACINGS: 23/44/1163-   RPR **144+**h

Starts	1st	2nd	3rd	4th	Win & Pl
7	2	-	2	2	£19,412
12/19	Limk	2m4f Mdn Hdl heavy			£7,188
11/19	Fair	2m NHF 5-7yo heavy			£5,591

Won a bumper and a maiden hurdle last season before a couple of useful efforts in defeat, finishing a ten-length sixth in a 2m6f Grade 1 at Leopardstown and third in a Grade 3 at Thurles; likely to be sent over fences and looks a fine chasing type.

Asterion Forlonge (Fr)

6 gr g Coastal Path - Belle Du Brizais (Turgeon)

Willie Mullins (Ire)   Mrs J Donnelly

PLACINGS: 1/1114-   RPR **156+**h

Starts	1st	2nd	3rd	4th	Win & Pl
4	3	-	-	1	£95,202
2/20	Leop	2m Nov Gd1 Hdl yield			£75,000
1/20	Naas	2m Mdn Hdl gd-yld			£7,986
11/19	Thur	2m NHF 5-7yo soft			£5,591

Much better than he showed when fourth in

last season's Supreme Novices' Hurdle, going too fast in front and jumping wildly to his right; had been sent off favourite for that race after thrashing subsequent Ballymore runner-up Easywork in a Grade 1 at Leopardstown.

Bacardys (Fr)

9 b/br g Coastal Path - Oasice (Robin Des Champs)

Willie Mullins (Ire)   Shanakiel Racing Syndicate

PLACINGS: 11P1/3FF0/7F6/21243-   RPR **159**h

Starts	1st	2nd	3rd	4th	Win & Pl
21	6	2	4	1	£282,981
11/19	Navn	2m4f Gd2 Hdl sft-hvy			£22,590
4/17	Punc	2m4f Nov Gd1 Hdl gd-yld			£50,427
2/17	Leop	2m2f Nov Gd1 Hdl soft			£45,385
12/16	Leop	2m Mdn Hdl yield			£6,331
4/16	Aint	2m1f Cls1 Gd2 NHF 4-6yo soft			£22,508
12/15	Leop	2m NHF 4yo heavy			£5,349

Benefited from being kept to hurdles last season after previous two campaigns had seen him fall over fences; placed three times at Grade 1 level since latest failed chasing attempt, including in the Stayers' Hurdle at Cheltenham, and gained overdue win in the Lismullen Hurdle.

Bacardys: consistent performer in Graded hurdles in Ireland

Bachasson (Fr)

9 gr g Voix Du Nord - Belledonne I (Shafoun)

Willie Mullins (Ire)   Edward O'Connell

PLACINGS: 128U/F21/11F/14/361-   RPR **160**+c

Starts	1st	2nd	3rd	4th	Win & Pl
21	11	2	1	1	£129,249
	3/20	Clon	2m4f Ch soft		£9,004
	12/18	Punc	2m4f Hdl good		£10,903
	1/18	Tram	2m5f List Ch heavy		£16,327
	11/17	Thur	2m6f List Ch sft-hvy		£14,981
	2/17	Gowr	2m4f Ch heavy		£7,371
	10/15	Tipp	2m Nov Gd3 Hdl good		£15,116
	9/15	Gway	2m2f Nov Hdl good		£9,093
	7/15	Gway	2m Nov Hdl 4yo yield		£10,078
	7/15	Slig	2m Mdn Hdl 4yo good		£5,616
	9/14	Stra	1m4f NHF 3yo v soft		£5,000
	7/14	Vitt	1m4f NHF 3yo gd-sft		£4,583

Very lightly raced in recent seasons, especially over fences, yet has won four chases in a row when completing; thrashed Death Duty at Clonmel in March on first run over fences since falling in the 2018 Cheltenham Gold Cup; yet to win beyond 2m6f but promises to get further.

Baddesley Knight (Ire)

7 b g Doyen - Grangeclare Rhythm (Lord America)

Chris Gordon   Richard & Mrs Carol Cheshire

PLACINGS: 321/4513/212-6   RPR **140**+c

Starts	1st	2nd	3rd	4th	Win & Pl
11	3	3	2		£23,087
131	11/19	Winc	1m7¹/₂f Cls3 Nov 115-133 Ch Hcap good	£9,747
	1/19	Plum	2m Cls4 Nov Hdl good	£4,094
	4/18	Plum	2m1¹/₂f Cls5 NHF 4-6yo gd-sft	£2,274

Looked a smart novice chaser early last season, winning a novice handicap at Wincanton after finishing second to Rouge Vif first time out; well-beaten second to Maire Banrigh when favourite at Doncaster on final run but subsequently found to have broken a blood vessel.

Ballyandy

9 b g Kayf Tara - Megalex (Karinga Bay)

Nigel Twiston-Davies   Options O Syndicate

PLACINGS: 4/14P/3P4133/642318-   RPR **154**h

Starts	1st	2nd	3rd	4th	Win & Pl
26	8	4	5	5	£305,239
	1/20	Hayd	1m7¹/₂f Cls1 Gd2 Hdl heavy	£42,713
142	1/19	Uttx	2m4f Cls2 116-142 Hdl Hcap soft	£9,384
	9/17	Prth	2m4f Cls3 Nov Ch heavy	£7,507
135	2/17	Newb	2m1¹/₂f Cls1 Gd3 126-146 Hdl Hcap soft	£88,273
	3/16	Chel	2m1¹/₂f Cls1 Gd1 NHF 4-6yo good	£39,865
	2/16	Newb	2m1¹/₂f Cls1 List NHF 4-6yo heavy	£11,390
	11/15	Chel	2m1¹/₂f Cls1 List NHF 4-6yo gd-sft	£11,390
	10/15	Worc	2m Cls6 NHF 3-5yo gd-sft	£1,560

Took a long time to build on 2017 Betfair Hurdle win but benefited from return to 2m last season, running consistently well in good races and winning the Champion Hurdle Trial at Haydock; came up short against the very best, including when eighth in the Champion Hurdle.

Ballyoptic (Ire)

10 b g Old Vic - Lambourne Lace (Un Desperado)

Nigel Twiston-Davies — Mills & Mason Partnership

PLACINGS: /5124142/F6PF/11401- — RPR **167**c

Starts		1st	2nd	3rd	4th	Win & Pl
27		9	3	-	4	£342,390
157	2/20	Asct	3m Cls1 List 139-157 Ch Hcap soft			£42,713
	11/19	Weth	3m Cls1 Gd2 Ch soft			£57,218
152	10/19	Chep	2m7¹/₂f Cls2 135-152 Ch Hcap soft			£17,408
	2/18	Weth	3m Cls1 Nov Gd2 Ch heavy			£20,284
	11/17	Extr	3m Cls2 Nov Ch soft			£14,206
148	10/16	Chep	2m3¹/₂f Cls1 Gd3 131-148 Hdl Hcap good			£28,475
	4/16	Aint	3m¹/₂f Cls1 Nov Gd1 Hdl soft			£56,270
	3/16	Uttx	2m4f Cls4 Nov Hdl soft			£5,064
	2/16	Ffos	2m4f Cls4 Nov Hdl 4-7yo heavy			£4,549

Smart stayer who produced career-best form last season, winning three times including the Charlie Hall Chase; was being aimed at the Grand National but has fallen twice over those fences and ran poorly in the Becher Chase last season.

Band Of Outlaws (Ire)

5 b g Fast Company - Band Of Colour (Spectrum)

Joseph O'Brien (Ire) — John P McManus

PLACINGS: 31115/23- — RPR **147**h

Starts		1st	2nd	3rd	4th	Win & Pl
7		3	1	1		£103,526
139	3/19	Chel	2m1¹/₂f Cls1 Gd3 129-141 Hdl 4yo Hcap soft			£45,016
	2/19	Naas	2m Nov Hdl 4yo good			£10,267
	12/18	Limk	2m Mdn Hdl 3yo sft-hvy			£7,359

Landed a big gamble when winning the Fred Winter Hurdle at Cheltenham in 2019; didn't quite build on that subsequently, finishing only fifth at Aintree, but ran well enough when third in the Galway Hurdle; missed the rest of last season but set to return from injury.

Bapaume (Fr)

7 b g Turtle Bowl - Brouhaha (American Post)

Willie Mullins (Ire) — Mrs S Ricci

PLACINGS: 83P5/214324/3427168- — RPR **147**c

Starts		1st	2nd	3rd	4th	Win & Pl
26		5	6	5	3	£444,393
	12/19	Naas	2m3f Ch soft			£7,720
	6/18	Autl	2m3¹/₂f Gd2 Hdl v soft			£69,690
	4/17	Punc	2m Gd1 Hdl 4yo gd-yld			£50,427
	12/16	Leop	2m Gd2 Hdl 3yo yield			£19,522
	4/16	Fntb	1m7f Hdl 3yo v soft			£7,059

High-class hurdler (Grade 1 winner as a juvenile and fourth in the Stayers' Hurdle in 2019) but didn't quite cut the mustard as a novice chaser last season; won a strong beginners' chase but last of six in a Grade 1 at Leopardstown and only eighth in the Marsh at Cheltenham.

Baron Alco (Fr)

9 ch g Dom Alco - Paula (Network)

Gary Moore — John Stone

PLACINGS: 86/11120/312122/214/ — RPR **157**c

Starts		1st	2nd	3rd	4th	Win & Pl
21		7	6	2	2	£204,630
146	11/18	Chel	2m4f Cls1 Gd3 135-161 Ch Hcap good			£90,299
	1/17	Plum	2m1f Cls3 Nov Ch soft			£7,988
	11/16	Plum	2m3¹/₂f Cls3 Nov Ch good			£6,657
127	12/15	Kemp	2m5f Cls3 118-135 Hdl Hcap gd-sft			£9,747
123	11/15	Font	2m1¹/₂f Cls3 110-124 Hdl Hcap soft			£6,330
116	10/15	Strf	2m2¹/₂f Cls3 107-129 Hdl Hcap soft			£6,330
	11/14	Sand	2m Cls3 Hdl 3yo soft			£6,497

Has been plagued by injuries, running just three times since March 2017, but confirmed himself a very smart chaser in 2018 when winning the BetVictor Gold Cup; returned sore after finishing fourth in the Caspian Caviar Gold Cup the following month and hasn't run since.

Battleoverdoyen (Ire)

7 b g Doyen - Battle Over (Sillery)

Gordon Elliott (Ire) — Gigginstown House Stud

PLACINGS: 1/111P/111F4- — RPR **158+**c

Starts		1st	2nd	3rd	4th	Win & Pl
9		6	-	-	1	£157,108
	12/19	Leop	3m Nov Gd1 Ch good			£53,153
	11/19	Punc	2m6¹/₂f Nov Gd2 Ch soft			£23,653
	10/19	Gway	2m6¹/₂f Ch soft			£10,116
	1/19	Naas	2m4f Nov Gd1 Hdl good			£46,991
	12/18	Navn	2m Mdn Hdl yield			£8,177
	11/18	Punc	2m NHF 4-7yo good			£5,451

Grade 1 winner over hurdles and fences, most recently in a three-runner novice chase at Leopardstown last season; beaten three times in stronger races in that grade, including for the second time at the Cheltenham Festival when fourth in last season's RSA.

Beacon Edge (Ire)

6 b g Doyen - Laurel Gift (Presenting)

Noel Meade (Ire) — Gigginstown House Stud

PLACINGS: 14/3122-1 — RPR **145+**h

Starts		1st	2nd	3rd	4th	Win & Pl
7		3	2	1	1	£38,122
	10/20	Dpat	2m3f Hdl yield			£5,750
	10/19	Punc	2m Mdn Hdl yield			£6,922
	10/18	Ayr	2m Cls5 NHF 4-6yo good			£2,274

Did well during a light campaign in novice hurdles last season, twice going close in good races after a debut win; beaten by a nose in a Grade 2 at Naas and failed by a neck to justify favouritism in a Listed race back there next time; should stay further.

Battleoverdoyen: top operator over hurdles and now as a chaser

Beakstown (Ire)

7 b g Stowaway - Midnight Reel (Accordion)

Dan Skelton   Bryan Drew

PLACINGS: 12/121P/2435-					RPR **142**c
Starts	1st	2nd	3rd	4th	Win & Pl
9	2	3	1	1	£32,730
	1/19	Wwck	2m5f Cls1 Nov Gd2 Hdl good		£19,933
	11/18	Uttx	2m4f Cls5 Mdn Hdl good		£3,119

Grade 2 novice hurdle winner in January 2019 but failed to win when switched to fences last season, albeit always keeping good company; promising fifth in the novice handicap at the Cheltenham Festival (closest to well-handicapped first two until the run-in).

Benie Des Dieux (Fr)

9 b m Great Pretender - Cana (Robin Des Champs)

Willie Mullins (Ire)   Mrs S Ricci

PLACINGS: 1/633/1/1111/F/1112-					RPR **162+**h
Starts	1st	2nd	3rd	4th	Win & Pl
16	10	1	2	1	£472,643
	1/20	Gowr	3m Gd2 Hdl sft-hvy		£22,500
	5/19	Autl	3m1¹/₂f Gd1 Hdl v soft		£141,892
	5/19	Punc	2m4f Gd1 Hdl gd-yld		£53,153
	4/18	Punc	2m4f Gd1 Hdl yld-sft		£52,212
	3/18	Chel	2m4f Cls1 Gd1 Hdl heavy		£67,582
	2/18	Naas	2m List Ch heavy		£17,688
	12/17	Carl	2m4f Cls1 List Ch soft		£17,286
	12/16	Limk	2m3¹/₂f Ch sft-hvy		£6,105
	4/15	Autl	2m2f Hdl 4-5yo v soft		£22,326
	10/14	Autl	2m2f Hdl 3yo heavy		£22,000

Outstanding mare who has been beaten just once in nine completed starts for Willie Mullins, finishing second to Honeysuckle in last season's Mares' Hurdle (also fell at the last when set to win that race in 2019); had won the Galmoy Hurdle to underline effectiveness over 3m.

Bennys King (Ire)

9 b g Beneficial - Hellofafaithful (Oscar)

Dan Skelton   Mezzone Family

PLACINGS: 622/22104/P/11/6152-					RPR **154+**c
Starts	1st	2nd	3rd	4th	Win & Pl
15	4	5	-	1	£68,044
134	11/19	Newb	2m6¹/₂f Cls2 124-145 Ch Hcap gd-sft	£25,024
126	12/18	MRas	2m5¹/₂f Cls3 Nov 106-126 Ch Hcap soft	£7,798
120	12/18	Chep	2m3¹/₂f Cls4 97-120 Ch Hcap heavy	£4,938
122	12/16	Uttx	2m4f Cls3 103-129 Hdl Hcap soft	£9,097

Lightly raced for his age and highly progressive over fences during the last two seasons, winning three times in six races and improving again when a neck second at Ascot on final run last season (made serious mid-race blunder); hadn't stayed 3m previously.

Beware The Bear (Ire)

10 b g Shantou - Native Bid (Be My Native)

Nicky Henderson   G B Barlow

PLACINGS: /11174/1P4P/411P/48-					RPR **165**c
Starts	1st	2nd	3rd	4th	Win & Pl
19	7	1	1	5	£174,236
151	3/19	Chel	3m1f Cls1 Gd3 140-155 Ch Hcap soft	£61,897
146	1/19	Chel	3m2¹/₂f Cls2 121-146 Ch Hcap gd-sft	£15,475
145	12/17	Newc	2m7¹/₂f Cls1 List 126-150 Ch Hcap soft	£40,053
136	12/16	Newb	2m7¹/₂f Cls3 Nov 116-136 Ch Hcap gd-sft	£6,498
130	11/16	Asct	3m Cls3 Nov 122-135 Ch Hcap gd-sft	£7,148
	5/16	Sthl	3m Cls4 Nov Hdl good	£3,899
	4/16	Bang	2m7f Cls5 Mdn Hdl heavy	£3,139

Much improved two seasons ago when helped by a wind operation and sharpened up by headgear, winning two good handicaps at Cheltenham including the Ultima; restricted to just two runs last term but ran another cracker when a close fourth in the Ladbrokes Trophy.

Billingsley (Ire)

8 b g Millenary - Retain That Magic (Presenting)

Alastair Ralph — Walters Plant Hire & Potter Group

PLACINGS: 34/011/504/U111- — RPR **142+**c

Starts		1st	2nd	3rd	4th	Win & Pl
12		5	-	1	2	£30,799
129	2/20	Newb	2m¹/₂f Cls3 120-131 Ch Hcap soft			£7,018
122	1/20	Hayd	2m¹/₂f Cls3 116-129 Ch Hcap heavy			£9,747
117	12/19	Hrfd	2m Cls4 Nov 109-120 Ch Hcap heavy			£4,289
	4/18	Chep	2m Cls4 Nov Hdl heavy			£4,094
	2/18	Chep	2m Cls4 Nov Hdl 4-7yo heavy			£4,094

Unbeaten when completing over fences after notching a hat-trick at the end of last season (had been beaten when unseating first time out); has also won his last five at around 2m, including twice over hurdles, all on soft or heavy ground; tends to jump to his right.

Birchdale (Ire)

6 b g Jeremy - Onewayortheother (Presenting)

Nicky Henderson — John P McManus

PLACINGS: 1/11P/38- — RPR **141**h

Starts		1st	2nd	3rd	4th	Win & Pl
5		2		1		£24,576
	1/19	Chel	2m4¹/₂f Cls1 Nov Gd2 Hdl gd-sft			£18,219
	12/18	Wwck	2m5f Cls4 Mdn Hdl gd-sft			£4,549

Lightly raced youngster who won twice in 2018-19, including a Grade 2 at Cheltenham, but fluffed his lines on chase debut last season and managed only eighth on only subsequent run in the Coral Cup; raw chasing type and likely to get another chance over fences.

Black Corton (Fr)

9 br g Laverock - Pour Le Meilleur (Video Rock)

Paul Nicholls — The Brooks Family & J Kyle

PLACINGS: 121154/2P2221/23242- — RPR **166**c

Starts		1st	2nd	3rd	4th	Win & Pl
35		14	11	5	3	£391,194
	4/19	Sand	2m6¹/₂f Cls1 Gd2 Ch good			£31,323
	2/18	Asct	3m Cls1 Nov Gd2 Ch soft			£22,780
	12/17	Kemp	3m Cls1 Nov Gd1 Ch soft			£43,466
	11/17	Chel	3m¹/₂f Cls2 Nov Ch soft			£15,640
	10/17	Chel	3m¹/₂f Cls2 Nov Ch good			£16,218
	10/17	NAbb	2m5f Cls2 Ch good			£18,705
	8/17	Font	2m5¹/₂f Cls4 Nov Ch gd-fm			£3,899
	7/17	Worc	2m7f Cls4 Nov Ch good			£3,899
	6/17	Font	2m1¹/₂f Cls4 Nov Ch gd-sft			£3,899
135	4/17	Tntn	2m3f Cls3 124-135 Hdl Hcap good			£7,280
	10/16	Kemp	2m Cls1 Nov List Hdl good			£11,390
	10/16	NAbb	2m2¹/₂f Cls4 Nov Hdl 4-6yo good			£4,549
	4/16	Extr	2m1f Cls5 Mdn Hdl good			£2,599
	5/15	Pina	1m7f NHF 4yo gd-sft			£5,426

Has found it hard to win since stepping out of

novice company two seasons ago but remains a model of consistency; gained sole win in a Grade 2 at Sandown in April 2019 and largely kept to big handicaps since then, finishing second in the Galway Plate and Betway Chase.

Billingsley: loves the mud and is a smart performer at around 2m

Black Op (Ire)

9 br g Sandmason - Afar Story (Desert Story)

Tom George | R S Brookhouse

PLACINGS: /19/41221/33304/122- RPR **156**c

Starts	1st	2nd	3rd	4th	Win & Pl
15	4	4	3	2	£147,121
	10/19	Strf	2m5f Cls4 Ch soft		£5,458
	4/18	Aint	2m4f Cls1 Nov Gd1 Hdl soft		£56,141
	1/18	Donc	2m5f Cls5 Mdn Hdl soft		£3,119
	2/17	Donc	2m¹/₂f Cls6 NHF 4-6yo good		£1,949

Grade 1 novice hurdle winner in 2018 who has been slowly getting the hang of jumping since going chasing; benefited from step up to 3m when second to Slate House in a Grade 1 at Kempton last Christmas, not helped by a bad mistake two out.

Black Tears

6 b m Jeremy - Our Girl Salley (Carroll House)

Gordon Elliott (Ire) | Mrs Caren Walsh & John Lightfoot

PLACINGS: 2122/22145/63P23122- RPR **147**h

Starts	1st	2nd	3rd	4th	Win & Pl
17	3	8	2	1	£135,528
133	2/20	Leop	2m2f 111-140 Hdl Hcap yield		£50,000
	2/19	Fair	2m Mdn Hdl good		£6,382
	3/18	Cork	2m NHF 4-7yo sft-hvy		£5,451

Took form to a new level in a couple of big-field handicaps last season, winning at Leopardstown before finishing second in the Coral Cup at Cheltenham; yet to prove as effective in smaller fields, though still placed three times in Grade 3/Listed mares' races last season.

Blackbow (Ire)

7 b g Stowaway - Rinnce Moll (Accordion)

Willie Mullins (Ire) | Roaringwater Syndicate

PLACINGS: 1/1152/2F42- RPR **139**+h

Starts	1st	2nd	3rd	4th	Win & Pl
8	2	3		1	£68,735
	2/18	Leop	2m Gd2 NHF 4-7yo soft		£39,159
	12/17	Leop	2m NHF 4yo yield		£5,528

Beaten at odds-on in four maiden hurdles last season but fell at the last when in command at Navan and beaten a short head at the same track; had been a high-class bumper performer in 2017-18 (second in a Grade 1 at Punchestown) and could get back on track over fences.

Blacko (Fr)

4 gr g Balko - Ascella (Astair)

Alan King | Apple Tree Stud

PLACINGS: 5211P-5 RPR **128**h

Starts	1st	2nd	3rd	4th	Win & Pl
6	2	1	-	-	£15,142
	1/20	Wwck	2m Cls4 Hdl 4yo soft		£4,549
	12/19	Tntn	2m¹/₂f Cls4 Hdl 3yo soft		£5,458

Won first two races in Britain after being bought from France and was a big gamble for the Fred Winter Hurdle at Cheltenham (sent off joint-favourite) only to be pulled up; likely to be aimed at more big handicap hurdles and looks open to improvement.

Blue Sari (Fr)

5 b g Saddex - Blue Aster (Astarabad)

Willie Mullins (Ire) | John P McManus

PLACINGS: 12/14P- RPR **122**+h

Starts	1st	2nd	3rd	4th	Win & Pl
5	2	1	-	1	£32,518
	11/19	Punc	2m4f Mdn Hdl 4yo soft		£7,188
	1/19	Gowr	2m NHF 4yo soft		£5,827

Came closer than any horse to beating Envoi Allen when a close second in the Champion Bumper at Cheltenham in 2019; made a winning start over hurdles last season but ran as if something amiss twice subsequently, stopping quickly both times.

Bob Mahler (Ire)

8 b g Mahler - Cooladurragh (Topanoora)

Warren Greatrex | Bolingbroke, Bunch, Howard & Sutton

PLACINGS: 32212/823811/PP3213- RPR **147**c

Starts	1st	2nd	3rd	4th	Win & Pl
23	4	5	7	4	£77,316
135	2/20	Muss	4m1f Cls2 119-140 Ch Hcap gd-sft		£28,152
132	4/19	Chel	3m1¹/₂f Cls3 Nov 114-133 Ch Hcap good		£10,840
128	3/19	Newb	2m7¹/₂f Cls3 Nov 114-136 Ch Hcap gd-sft		£7,343
	3/18	Weth	3m Cls4 Nov Hdl soft		£4,484

Appreciated stepping up significantly in trip when winning last season's Edinburgh National at Musselburgh, needing every yard of 4m1f to get up on the line; confirmed progressive profile with a fine third in the Kim Muir at Cheltenham; still unexposed over marathon distances.

Bob Mahler leaps his way to a marathon victory at Musselburgh

Boldmere

7 b g Multiplex - Pugnacious Lady (Hernando)

Caroline Bailey · W J Odell

PLACINGS: 5/96192/P11F-4					RPR **151**+c

Starts	1st	2nd	3rd	4th	Win & Pl
11	3	1	-	1	£23,983
133	12/19	Donc	3m Cls3 122-137 Ch Hcap gd-sft £7,018
123	12/19	Leic	2m4f Cls3 122-126 Ch Hcap gd-sft.................. £8,058
	2/19	MRas	2m4¹/₂f Cls3 Nov Hdl 4-7yo gd-sft.................. £6,498

Shot up the ratings when switched to fences last season, winning handicaps at Leicester and Doncaster by wide margins; fell at the last when set to add the Towton Novices' Chase at Wetherby on soft ground (felt to prefer quicker and withdrawn on heavy subsequently).

Boss Man Fred (Ire)

6 ch g Dubai Destination - Aboo Lala (Aboo Horn)

Dan Skelton · Masomo

PLACINGS: 1/1114-3					RPR **134**c

Starts	1st	2nd	3rd	4th	Win & Pl
5	3	-	1		£16,497
124	12/19	Donc	3m¹/₂f Cls3 122-132 Hdl Hcap gd-sft £5,913
	12/19	Sthl	3m Cls4 Nov Hdl soft £3,861
	11/19	Kemp	2m5f Cls4 Nov Hdl good £4,094

Won first three races over hurdles last season, most notably when hacking up by nine lengths on handicap debut at Doncaster; joint-favourite for a Grade 2 novice hurdle back there next time

but ran well below par in fourth; won sole point-to-point and likely to go novice chasing.

Botox Has (Fr)

4 b g Dream Well - Bournie (Kahyasi)

Gary Moore · John Stone

PLACINGS: 2/121-					RPR **129**+h

Starts	1st	2nd	3rd	4th	Win & Pl
4	2	2	-	-	£39,312
	12/19	Chel	2m1f Cls2 Hdl 3yo soft £15,640
	10/19	Font	2m1¹/₂f Cls4 Hdl 3yo good............................... £3,861

Won two out of three in juvenile hurdles last season, most notably at Cheltenham in December after finishing second behind Allmankind at the track previously; missed the Triumph Hurdle with trainer keen to mind him for the future; should stay well beyond 2m.

Breaken (Fr)

6 b g Sunday Break - Kendoretta (Kendor)

Willie Mullins (Ire) · Mrs J Donnelly

PLACINGS: 2/1/4F-					RPR **142**+c

Starts	1st	2nd	3rd	4th	Win & Pl
4	1	1		1	£17,961
	3/19	Limk	2m Mdn Hdl good.. £7,214

French recruit who won by 17 lengths on first run for Willie Mullins in March 2019 and looked an exciting prospect on chase debut last term

when set to win easily until falling three out; missed the rest of the season but set to return.

Brelan D'As (Fr)

9 b g Crillon - Las De La Croix (Grand Tresor)

Paul Nicholls   John P McManus

PLACINGS: 1/33500/2215135/U28-   RPR **147**c

Starts		1st	2nd	3rd	4th	Win & Pl
20		5	3	3	1	£102,858
	2/19	Fknm	2m1/2f Cls3 Nov Ch good			£8,058
	12/18	Hayd	1m7¹/₂f Cls3 Nov Ch heavy			£9,615
130	11/16	Winc	2m4f Cls3 115-135 Hdl Hcap good			£5,848
	10/15	Sabl	2m1f Hdl 4yo gd-sft			£8,558
	8/15	Gran	1m7f NHF 4-5yo gd-sft			£3,876

Slow learner over fences and still let down by jumping errors last season but has proved himself a very smart handicapper on his day, finishing second in the BetVictor Gold Cup; might well have had a say in the Caspian Caviar Gold Cup but for a bad mistake three out.

Brewin'upastorm (Ire)

7 b g Milan - Daraheen Diamond (Husyan)

Olly Murphy   Mrs Barbara Hester

PLACINGS: 1/14/14F42/11U-   RPR **158+**c

Starts		1st	2nd	3rd	4th	Win & Pl
10		4	1	-	3	£53,385
	11/19	Tntn	2m2f Cls4 Nov Ch good			£6,590
	10/19	Carl	2m Cls3 Ch gd-sft			£7,473
	12/18	Hntg	2m Cls4 Nov Hdl gd-sft			£5,523
	1/18	Hrfd	2m Cls5 Am NHF 4-6yo soft			£2,599

Just below the best as a novice hurdler two seasons ago but looked potentially better over fences last term, winning twice in small fields before unseating four out in the Racing Post Arkle; yet to win beyond 2m2f but solid hurdles form up to 2m5f (fourth in the Ballymore).

Bright Forecast (Ire)

6 b g Arcadio - Check The Forecast (Shernazar)

Ben Pauling   The Aldaniti Partnership

PLACINGS: 3/1123/   RPR **150**h

Starts		1st	2nd	3rd	4th	Win & Pl
4		2	1	1	-	£33,189
	12/18	Leic	1m7¹/₂f Cls3 Nov Hdl good			£6,758
	11/18	Newb	2m1¹/₂f Cls3 Mdn Hdl soft			£6,758

Missed last season through injury but ran a huge race when last seen in the Ballymore at Cheltenham in 2019, finishing third behind City Island and Champ; had shown smart form at 2m prior to that but stayed on strongly over 2m5f and likely to get further; could go novice chasing.

Bristol De Mai (Fr)

9 gr g Saddler Maker - La Bole Night (April Night)

Nigel Twiston-Davies   Simon Munir & Isaac Souede

PLACINGS: 1375/11632/1F34/229-   RPR **174**c

Starts		1st	2nd	3rd	4th	Win & Pl
33		10	10	5	2	£708,386
	11/18	Hayd	3m1¹/₂f Cls1 Gd1 Ch good			£112,540
	11/17	Hayd	3m1¹/₂f Cls1 Gd1 Ch heavy			£113,072
	11/17	Weth	3m Cls1 Gd2 Ch soft			£57,218
154	1/17	Hayd	3m Cls1 Gd2 142-162 Ch Hcap soft			£28,475
	2/16	Sand	2m4f Cls1 Nov Gd1 Ch gd-sft			£25,628
	1/16	Hayd	2m4f Cls1 Nov Gd2 Ch heavy			£18,438
	12/15	Leic	2m4f Cls3 Nov Ch soft			£6,330
	11/15	Wwck	2m Cls3 Nov Ch 4-5yo gd-sft			£9,384
	12/14	Chep	2m Cls1 Gd1 Hdl 3yo heavy			£19,933
	9/14	Autl	2m2f Hdl 3yo v soft			£19,200

Dual winner of the Betfair Chase at Haydock and again ran a cracker in that race last season when second to Lostintranslation; yet to win a big race elsewhere but finished third in the 2019 Cheltenham Gold Cup and was second to Santini in last season's Cotswold Chase.

Bun Doran (Ire)

9 b g Shantou - Village Queen (King's Theatre)

Tom George   Crossed Fingers Partnership

PLACINGS: 1P63/2335/122/521F3-   RPR **163**c

Starts		1st	2nd	3rd	4th	Win & Pl
22		5	4	6	1	£206,389
	12/19	Kemp	2m Cls1 Gd2 Ch soft			£56,950
138	11/18	Chel	2m Cls2 122-140 Ch Hcap good			£27,855
134	12/16	Newc	2m4f Cls3 109-135 Ch Hcap soft			£9,747
	1/16	Hayd	2m3f Cls4 Nov Hdl 4-7yo heavy			£3,899
	11/15	Chep	2m Cls6 NHF 4-6yo soft			£1,560

Steadily progressive over the last two seasons despite winning only twice; finished second in three good 2m handicaps, including the 2019 Grand Annual, before winning the Desert Orchid Chase on step up in class; good third in the Champion Chase last time out.

Burning Victory (Fr)

4 br f Nathaniel - M'Oubliez Pas (El Corredor)

Willie Mullins (Ire)   Mrs Audrey Turley

PLACINGS: 11-   RPR **140+**h

Starts		1st	2nd	3rd	4th	Win & Pl
2		2	-	-	-	£89,755
	3/20	Chel	2m1f Cls1 Gd1 Hdl 4yo soft			£73,506
	2/20	Fair	2m Gd3 Hdl 4yo heavy			£16,250

Fortuitous winner of last season's Triumph Hurdle at Cheltenham, picking up the pieces after Goshen's exit at the last; still a fine achievement to win that race on just her second start over hurdles (had won on the Flat) and could improve again, most likely over further.

Injured Jockeys Fund

A range of unique
RACING GIFTS
for all...

NEW FOR 2020

Compassion • Care • Support

To view the full range of exclusive gifts visit our website
www.ijf.org.uk
To request a printed catalogue call Freephone 08080 453 453

Burrows Edge (Fr)

7 b g Martaline - La Vie De Boitron (Lavirco)

Nicky Henderson | Michael Buckley

PLACINGS: 32/241126/23/F10- | RPR **139+**

Starts	1st	2nd	3rd	4th	Win & Pl
11	3	3	1	1	£45,506
132	1/20	Kemp	2m5f Cls1 List 118-140 Hdl Hcap gd-sft £25,628
	3/18	Hrfd	2m3½f Cls4 Nov Hdl soft............................... £4,809
	2/18	MRas	2m4½f Cls3 Nov Hdl 4-7yo soft........................ £6,498

Lightly raced hurdler who proved a very useful handicapper when winning last season's Lanzarote Hurdle at Kempton, albeit fortunate to exploit a final-flight fall; had fallen four out when going well on chasing debut previously and could go back over fences.

Burrows Saint (Fr)

7 b g Saint Des Saints - La Bombonera (Mansonnien)

Willie Mullins (Ire) | Mrs S Ricci

PLACINGS: /2742/1203/4111/531- | RPR **153+h**

Starts	1st	2nd	3rd	4th	Win & Pl
17	5	4	2	2	£368,347
144	12/19	Punc	2m3½f Hdl gd-yld............................... £10,649
	4/19	Fair	3m5f 135-157 Ch Hcap gd-yld......... £243,243
	3/19	Limk	3m½f Nov Gd3 Ch good................... £22,590
	3/19	Gowr	2m4f Ch soft................................... £8,047
	11/17	Punc	2m4f Mdn Hdl 4yo sft-hvy.................. £7,108

Hugely impressive winner of the Irish Grand National in 2019 on just fourth run over fences; has also proved effective over much shorter trips, albeit perhaps flattered by victory over hurdles at Punchestown last season (gifted an easy lead); likely Grand National contender.

Buveur D'Air (Fr)

9 b g Crillon - History (Alesso)

Nicky Henderson | John P McManus

PLACINGS: 11111/1111/121F2/12- | RPR **160+h**

Starts	1st	2nd	3rd	4th	Win & Pl
24	17	4		1	£1,210,095
	5/19	Punc	2m Gd1 Hdl gd-yld............................. £159,459
	2/19	Sand	2m Cls1 List Hdl soft........................ £17,286
	12/18	Newc	2m Cls1 Gd1 Hdl soft........................ £62,629
	3/18	Chel	2m1½f Cls1 Gd1 Hdl heavy £266,384
	2/18	Sand	2m Cls1 List Hdl soft........................ £17,085
	12/17	Kemp	2m Cls1 Gd1 Hdl soft........................ £68,340
	12/17	Newc	2m Cls1 Gd1 Hdl soft........................ £61,897
	4/17	Aint	2m4f Cls1 Gd1 Hdl good.................. £112,260
	3/17	Chel	2m1½f Cls1 Gd1 Hdl gd-sft............. £227,800
	2/17	Sand	2m Cls1 List Hdl heavy..................... £14,238
	12/16	Wwck	2m Cls4 Nov Ch soft......................... £5,198
	12/16	Hayd	1m7½f Cls2 Nov Ch soft................... £11,574
	4/16	Aint	2m1½f Cls1 Nov Gd1 Hdl soft........... £42,203
	1/16	Hntg	2m Cls4 Nov Hdl gd-sft..................... £3,249
	11/15	Newb	2m1½f Cls3 Mdn Hdl soft................... £6,498
	10/14	Nant	1m4f NHF 3yo gd-sft........................ £6,250
	8/14	Sjdm	1m5f NHF 3yo soft............................ £4,167

Champion Hurdle winner in 2017 and 2018 but lost aura of invincibility the following season when beaten twice either side of a fall at

Cheltenham; got back on track with a Grade 1 win at Punchestown but injured when second in the Fighting Fifth and missed the rest of last season.

Buzz (Fr)

6 gr g Motivator - Tiysha (Araafa)

Nicky Henderson · Thurloe For Royal Marsden Cancer Charity

PLACINGS: 114- · RPR **138**+h

Starts	1st	2nd	3rd	4th	Win & Pl
3	2	-	-	1	£10,501
	2/20	Donc	2m¹/₂f Cls4 Nov Hdl good		£3,769
	1/20	Tntn	2m¹/₂f Cls4 Mdn Hdl soft		£5,133

Won first two starts over hurdles last season, neither above Class 4 level but beating a solid yardstick for second win at Doncaster (pair clear); sent off just 6-4 for a Grade 2 at Kempton after that only to run a flat race in fourth; still a smart prospect.

Cabaret Queen

8 b m King's Theatre - La Dame Brune (Mansonnien)

Willie Mullins (Ire) · Syndicates.Racing

PLACINGS: /411P5P74/F21PF00-31 · RPR **148**c

Starts	1st	2nd	3rd	4th	Win & Pl
21	5	2	3	2	£170,181
142	9/20	List	3m 131-153 Ch Hcap soft		£75,000
126	10/19	Limk	3m 125-147 Ch Hcap heavy		£53,153
123	6/18	Worc	2m7f Cls3 119-133 Ch Hcap good		£7,408
116	6/18	Uttx	3m Cls4 Nov 108-116 Ch Hcap good		£4,614
	10/17	MRas	2m4¹/₂f Cls4 Nov Hdl good		£3,899

Narrow winner of the Kerry National at Listowel this summer, adding to Munster National victory in 2019; gained those victories on soft and heavy

ground so should be suited by winter conditions, though form had tailed off last winter.

Cadmium (Fr)

8 b g Early March - Mirquille (Passing Sale)

Willie Mullins (Ire) · In Our Element Syndicate

PLACINGS: 141/1521344121/5743- · RPR **151**c

Starts	1st	2nd	3rd	4th	Win & Pl
21	7	2	3	5	£214,627
152	4/19	Aint	2m5f Cls1 Gd3 136-162 Ch Hcap soft		£78,582
	2/19	Naas	2m Gd3 Ch good		£24,716
	10/18	Punc	2m2¹/₂f Nov Gd3 Ch good		£17,688
	6/18	Rosc	2m Nov Ch good		£7,632
133	4/18	Punc	2m 122-150 Ch Hcap yld-sft		£33,938
	2/18	Fair	2m1¹/₂f Ch soft		£9,267
	12/16	Limk	2m3f Mdn Hdl yield		£4,522

Disappointing in four runs last season, all in small-field conditions races (twice at Grade 1 level); has a much better record in big-field handicaps from limited opportunities, most recently when hacking up over the Grand National fences in the Topham in 2019.

Caid Du Lin (Fr)

8 gr g Della Francesca - Asia Du Lin (Agent Bleu)

Dr Richard Newland · Foxtrot Racing

PLACINGS: 0P2/12P21027/24P15U- · RPR **149**+c

Starts	1st	2nd	3rd	4th	Win & Pl
31	5	9	3	1	£167,792
144	12/19	Ludl	2m Cls2 127-144 Ch Hcap soft		£16,458
139	11/18	Asct	2m1f Cls2 135-154 Ch Hcap gd-sft		£78,200
	9/18	Worc	2m¹/₂f Cls4 Nov Ch good		£4,614
127	10/17	Font	2m1¹/₂f Cls3 105-127 Hdl Hcap good		£5,848
	10/16	Nior	2m3f Hdl 4yo gd-sft		£7,059

Couldn't quite build on promising novice campaign when winning just once last season in

Cadmium: proved adept over the Grand National fences when winning the 2019 Topham Chase at Aintree

a modest handicap chase at Ludlow; had five of six runs on soft ground and trainer has stated he prefers quicker (career-best run on good when a head second at Ascot in March 2019).

Call Me Lord (Fr)

7 b/br g Slickly - Sosa (Cape Cross)

Nicky Henderson — Simon Munir & Isaac Souede

PLACINGS: 5111/31321/73/2120- RPR **158**h

Starts		1st	2nd	3rd	4th	Win & Pl
15		6	3	3	-	£249,862
	12/19	Chel	2m1f Cls1 Gd2 Hdl soft			£78,778
	4/18	Sand	2m5¹/₂f Cls1 Gd2 Hdl gd-sft			£31,323
143	1/18	Sand	2m Cls2 117-143 Hdl Hcap heavy			£15,640
135	4/17	Sand	2m Cls2 109-135 Hdl 4yo Hcap good			£31,280
	3/17	Comp	2m2f Hdl 4yo heavy			£19,692
	12/16	Cagn	2m¹/₂f Hdl 3yo soft			£11,294

High-class hurdler who gained a second Grade 2 win in last season's International Hurdle at Cheltenham, disproving trainer's previous conviction that he needed a right-handed track; beaten at odds-on at Sandown next time before disappointing in the Champion Hurdle.

Capeland (Fr)

8 b g Poliglote - Neiland (Cyborg)

Paul Nicholls — Mrs Kathy Stuart

PLACINGS: 2/22211212284/5d1450- RPR **162**+c

Starts		1st	2nd	3rd	4th	Win & Pl
25		7	10	-	3	£178,631
143	11/19	Asct	2m1f Cls2 132-156 Ch Hcap soft			£78,200
133	12/18	Ludl	2m Cls2 120-147 Ch Hcap soft			£16,458
130	11/18	Winc	1m7¹/₂f Cls3 Nov 112-130 Ch Hcap gd-fm			£10,397
127	11/18	Winc	2m4f Cls3 105-127 Cond Ch Hcap good			£10,072
	10/16	NAbb	2m2¹/₂f Cls4 Nov Hdl heavy			£4,549
	1/16	Chel	1m6f Cls1 Nov Hdl 4yo heavy			£11,888
	5/15	Le L	1m3¹/₂f NHF 3yo heavy			£5,814

Big improver in two runs at Ascot early last season, winning a valuable handicap by 12 lengths to make up for an unlucky defeat three weeks earlier; came up just short in Grade 2 company next time and disappointed in a couple of runs in the new year.

Captain Chaos (Ire)

9 ch g Golan - Times Have Changed (Safety Catch)

Dan Skelton — Mike & Eileen Newbould

PLACINGS: 11415/008226/6P2P21- RPR **147**+c

Starts		1st	2nd	3rd	4th	Win & Pl
27		7	6	1	2	£148,622
134	2/20	Donc	3m2f Cls2 122-144 Ch Hcap heavy			£35,891
	2/18	MRas	3m Cls3 Nov Ch soft			£7,988
	11/17	Weth	3m Cls4 Nov Ch soft			£3,994
	11/17	Aint	3m1f Cls3 Nov Ch soft			£7,820
	2/16	Extr	2m2¹/₂f Cls4 Nov Hdl heavy			£3,249
	11/15	Uttx	2m Cls4 Nov Hdl soft			£3,925
	1/15	Newc	2m Cls6 NHF 4-6yo soft			£1,560

Ended a run of near misses in good staying handicaps when running away with last season's Grimthorpe Chase at Doncaster; had finished second in the Rehearsal Chase for a second successive year and the Classic Chase at Warwick, proving stamina for marathon trips.

Captain Cj (Ire)

9 b g Westerner - She's So Dainty (Great Commotion)

Dermot McLoughlin (Ire) — Mrs Fidelma Toole

PLACINGS: 311/1F33/241/223F21- RPR **151**+c

Starts		1st	2nd	3rd	4th	Win & Pl
11		2	4	3	1	£38,197
	2/20	Navn	3m Nov Gd2 Ch heavy			£21,250
	3/19	Hexm	2m7¹/₂f Cls4 Nov Hdl gd-sft			£4,809

Three-time point winner who quickly proved a very useful novice chaser last season despite needing six attempts to win; finished placed behind several classy opponents before winning a Grade 2 at Navan; strong stayer and a likely contender for good staying handicaps.

Captain Drake (Ire)

7 b g Getaway - Julika (Nebos)

Harry Fry — Gary Stevens, Brian & Sandy Lambert

PLACINGS: 21/35112/07U1U2-1 RPR **143**+c

Starts		1st	2nd	3rd	4th	Win & Pl
13		5	2	1	-	£73,221
137	10/20	Uttx	2m7¹/₂f Cls2 111-137 Hdl Hcap gd-sft			£9,384
127	1/20	Extr	3m Cls3 110-132 Ch Hcap soft			£11,696
121	3/19	Sthl	3m Cls3 115-126 Hdl Hcap good			£5,525
	12/18	Uttx	2m4f Cls5 Mdn Hdl heavy			£3,119
	3/18	Towc	1m7¹/₂f Cls5 Am Mdn NHF 4-6yo heavy			£3,119

Progressive novice chaser last season; took a big step forward when winning at Exeter and improved again when second in the Midlands National (would have finished close but for bad mistake at the last); relishes testing conditions and unexposed over marathon trips.

Captain Guinness (Ire)

5 b g Arakan - Presenting D'Azy (Presenting)

Henry De Bromhead (Ire) — Declan Landy

PLACINGS: 12B- RPR **150**+h

Starts		1st	2nd	3rd	4th	Win & Pl
3		1	1	-	-	£15,151
	12/19	Navn	2m Mdn Hdl soft			£7,986

Pitched straight into competitive novice hurdles last season and kept outrunning his odds, including when brought down two out in the Supreme (was going well); had won at 20-1 on his debut before running Andy Dufresne close in a Grade 2 at Punchestown.

Carefully Selected (Ire)

8 b g Well Chosen - Knockamullen Girl (Alderbrook)

Willie Mullins (Ire) — Miss M A Masterson

PLACINGS: 21/1123/1/3111U- RPR **154**+c

Starts		1st	2nd	3rd	4th	Win & Pl
10		6	1	2	-	£104,189
	1/20	Naas	3m Nov Gd3 Ch soft			£22,500
	1/20	Punc	2m4f Nov Gd3 Ch soft			£21,250
	11/19	Fair	2m5f Ch soft			£7,720
	3/19	Limk	2m NHF 4-7yo heavy			£7,214
	2/18	Naas	2m NHF 4-7yo soft			£7,087
	12/17	Leop	2m4f NHF 4-7yo soft			£6,318

Top-class bumper performer (neck second in

the 2018 Champion Bumper) who showed his big engine over fences last season, winning his first three chases despite jumping errors; found out when odds-on for the National Hunt Chase, departing at the last when booked for third.

Caribean Boy (Fr)

6 gr g Myboycharlie - Caribena (Linamix)

Nicky Henderson — Simon Munir & Isaac Souede

PLACINGS: F7515692/31- — RPR **143+c**

Starts	1st	2nd	3rd	4th	Win & Pl
10	2	1	1		£53,329
	2/20 Hayd	2m4f Cls3 Nov 127-138 Ch Hcap heavy............£9,747
	10/17 Autl	2m1¹/₂f Hdl 3yo v soft................................£19,692

Looked a useful recruit when winning a novice handicap chase at Haydock on his final run last season, improving massively on his debut third for current connections; had been off for nearly two years prior to that run after finishing second in a Listed hurdle in France.

Cash Back (Fr)

8 b g Linda's Lad - Holding (Useful)

Willie Mullins (Ire) — Watch This Space Syndicate

PLACINGS: 82677/22/12/5112F- — RPR **157c**

Starts	1st	2nd	3rd	4th	Win & Pl
14	3	5	-	-	£81,965
	1/20 Naas	2m Nov Ch yield....................................£11,162
	11/19 Navn	2m1f Ch soft...£9,051
	3/19 Thur	2m Mdn Hdl gd-yld................................£6,105

Hugely impressive on first two runs over fences last season, making all to beat subsequent Grade 3 winner Zero Ten by 12 lengths at Naas, and pushed Notebook close at Leopardstown; big disappointment in the Racing Post Arkle (well beaten when falling two out).

Castlebawn West (Ire)

7 b g Westerner - Cooksgrove Lady (Anshan)

Willie Mullins (Ire) — Mrs R Boyd, Mrs M J Armstrong & JB Anderson

PLACINGS: 41/21P4/6514U- — RPR **151+c**

Starts	1st	2nd	3rd	4th	Win & Pl
11	3	1	-	3	£30,606
	1/20 Fair	2m5f Ch yield.......................................£7,012
	12/18 Leop	2m4f Mdn Hdl gd-yld..............................£8,177
	3/18 Clon	2m NHF 5-7yo heavy..............................£5,451

Has won only a maiden hurdle and beginners' chase but gained his chase win in fine style last season and has been very highly tried after both those successes; best of four efforts at Grade 1 level came when fourth behind Faugheen at Leopardstown in February.

Castlegrace Paddy (Ire)

9 b g Flemensfirth - Thunder Road (Mtoto)

Pat Fahy (Ire) — Clipper Logistics Group

PLACINGS: 42415/115/14F6/3451- — RPR **154c**

Starts	1st	2nd	3rd	4th	Win & Pl
16	5	1	1	4	£127,885
	3/20 Navn	2m Gd2 Ch heavy.................................£21,250
	12/18 Cork	2m1¹/₂f Gd2 Ch soft...............................£31,327
	3/18 Thur	2m2f Nov List Ch soft............................£16,327
	12/17 Fair	2m Ch heavy.......................................£7,897
	3/17 Gowr	2m Mdn Hdl sft-hvy..............................£6,844

Very smart 2m chaser who has won four out of five races over fences below Grade 1 level, including a second Grade 2 at Navan in March when beating Ornua; yet to threaten in the top grade and had sights lowered after distant fourth behind Chacun Pour Soi at Leopardstown.

Cat Tiger (Fr)

6 b g Diamond Boy - Miss Canon (Cadoudal)

Paul Nicholls — David Maxwell Racing

PLACINGS: 7132/5131341/21211P- — RPR **144+h**

Starts	1st	2nd	3rd	4th	Win & Pl
19	7	4	3	1	£235,139
	1/20 Plum	2m4¹/₂f Cls4 Nov Hdl heavy.....................£4,094
	1/20 Plum	2m4¹/₂f Cls3 Nov Hdl 4-7yo soft................£6,498
	11/19 Extr	2m5¹/₂f Cls3 Nov Hdl soft........................£6,238
	11/18 Autl	2m6f Gd3 Ch 4yo heavy.........................£57,743
	9/18 Autl	2m6f Gd3 Ch 4yo soft...........................£57,743
0	5/18 Autl	2m1¹/₂f Ch 4yo Hcap heavy......................£22,301
	10/17 Madb	2m3f Ch 3yo soft.................................£5,333

French recruit who won three novice hurdles for new connections last season (up to Class 3 level) before being pulled up in the Albert Bartlett at Cheltenham; likely to switch back to fences having won four chases in France and finished fourth in a Grade 1.

Cepage (Fr)

8 b g Saddler Maker - Sience Fiction (Dom Alco)

Venetia Williams — The Bellamy Partnership

PLACINGS: 41F33/23414/2/24617- — RPR **161c**

Starts		1st	2nd	3rd	4th	Win & Pl
23		5	4	4	6	£171,622
154	1/20 Chel	2m4¹/₂f Cls1 Gd3 128-154 Ch Hcap soft.........£39,423
136	3/18 Kemp	2m4¹/₂f Cls2 152-139 Ch Hcap soft..............£25,024
119	12/16 Newb	2m¹/₂f Cls4 99-119 Ch Hcap gd-sft...............£4,549
	5/16 Lign	2m5¹/₂f Ch 4yo v soft..............................£4,588
	4/16 Pari	2m3f Hdl 4yo v soft...............................£7,412

Cheltenham specialist who ran consistently well in big handicap chases at the track last season, deservedly winning in January after making the frame in the Caspian Caviar Gold Cup for the second successive year; starts on a feasible mark after going up just 1lb for that win.

129

Cerberus

4 ch g Iffraaj - Miss You Too (Montjeu)

Joseph O'Brien (Ire)   John P McManus

PLACINGS: 211236-4   RPR **140**h

Starts	1st	2nd	3rd	4th	Win & Pl
7	2	2	1	1	£54,223
	12/19	Fair	2m Gd3 Hdl 3yo yld-sft		£17,275
	11/19	Fair	2m Mdn Hdl 3yo heavy		£5,857

Useful juvenile last season and unlucky not to win a Grade 1 at Leopardstown, idling when left in front at the last; reversed form with the winner in the Triumph Hurdle at Cheltenham, though still only sixth and had also been put in his place by Allmankind in a Grade 1 at Chepstow.

Ch'tibello (Fr)

9 b g Sageburg - Neicha (Neverneyev)

Dan Skelton   The Can't Say No Partnership

PLACINGS: 32/42280/569213/353-   RPR **156**h

Starts	1st	2nd	3rd	4th	Win & Pl
24	4	6	6	1	£317,297
146	3/19	Chel	2m1f Cls1 Gd3 127-153 Hdl Hcap gd-sft		£56,270
	11/16	Hayd	2m Cls2 Hdl heavy		£61,900
135	4/16	Ayr	2m Cls1 Gd2 133-147 Hdl Hcap gd-sft		£57,520
	4/15	Comp	2m1f Hdl 4yo heavy		£8,186

Only win since 2016 came in the County Hurdle two seasons ago but unlucky not to add to his haul last season, going close in the International and Kingwell Hurdles (best horse at the weights both times); has finished second or third seven times at Grade 1 or 2 level.

Chacun Pour Soi (Fr)

8 b g Policy Maker - Kruscyna (Ultimately Lucky)

Willie Mullins (Ire)   Mrs S Ricci

PLACINGS: 1253/1/121-   RPR **175+**c

Starts	1st	2nd	3rd	4th	Win & Pl
8	4	2	1	-	£191,129
	2/20	Leop	2m1f Gd1 Ch yield		£75,000
	5/19	Punc	2m Nov Gd1 Ch yield		£61,126
	3/19	Naas	2m Ch yld-sft		£8,047
	8/15	Diep	2m1f Hdl 3yo v soft		£8,558

Fragile but brilliant two-mile chaser who has been very lightly raced due to injury and was ruled out of the 2020 Champion Chase at the last minute due to latest setback; had looked right up to that level when beating Min at the Dublin Racing Festival in February.

Champ (Ire)

8 b g King's Theatre - China Sky (Definite Article)

Nicky Henderson   John P McManus

PLACINGS: 12/2/111121/11F1-   RPR **167+**c

Starts	1st	2nd	3rd	4th	Win & Pl
13	9	3	-	-	£276,491
	3/20	Chel	3m¹/₂f Cls1 Nov Gd1 Ch soft		£98,764
	11/19	Newb	2m4f Cls1 Nov Gd2 Ch gd-sft		£22,887
	11/19	Newb	2m6¹/₂f Cls3 Ch gd-sft		£7,018
	4/19	Aint	3m¹/₂f Cls1 Nov Gd1 Hdl soft		£56,130
	12/18	Newb	2m4¹/₂f Cls1 Nov Gd1 Hdl gd-sft		£25,628
139	12/18	Newb	2m4¹/₂f Cls2 120-145 Hdl Hcap soft		£25,992
	5/18	Wwck	2m5f Cls4 Nov Hdl gd-sft		£4,549
	5/18	Prth	2m4f Cls4 Mdn Hdl good		£4,224
	1/17	Sthl	1m7¹/₂f Cls6 Mdn NHF 4-6yo soft		£2,053

Remarkable winner of last season's RSA Chase at Cheltenham, coming from miles back to run down Minella Indo close home; strong suspicion the leaders did too much that day but still has the potential to become a Cheltenham Gold Cup horse if suspect jumping improves.

Chacun Pour Soi: top-class but lightly raced two-mile chaser

Champagne Platinum (Ire)

6 gr g Stowaway - Saffron Holly (Roselier)

Nicky Henderson | John P McManus

PLACINGS: 1/11/55437- | RPR **141**c

Starts	1st	2nd	3rd	4th	Win & Pl
7	2	-	1	1	£18,176
	12/18	Newb	2m¹/₂f Cls4 Hdl gd-sft............................£4,809
	12/18	Newc	2m Cls4 Mdn Hdl 4-6yo soft.....................£4,094

Disappointing when chasing last season but sent off joint-favourite for the Kim Muir at Cheltenham and travelled well before running out of stamina; had won first two novice hurdles in 2018 and still regarded as a high-class prospect.

Champagne Well (Ire)

7 b g Gold Well - Perkanod (Executive Perk)

Fergal O'Brien | The Bolly Champagne Crew

PLACINGS: 371/51321d36/1222P-3 | RPR **143**+h

Starts	1st	2nd	3rd	4th	Win & Pl
13	2	5	3	-	£48,895
	10/19	Chel	2m5f Cls2 Nov Hdl gd-sft.......................£12,512
	12/18	Sedg	2m1f Cls5 NHF 4-6yo soft........................£2,274

Has won just once in ten races over hurdles but has run well in several good novice events, finishing third in the EBF Final in 2019 and second in three successive Grade 2 races last season; third favourite for the Coral Cup but pulled up.

Chantry House (Ire)

6 br g Yeats - The Last Bank (Phardante)

Nicky Henderson | John P McManus

PLACINGS: U11/113- | RPR **148**h

Starts	1st	2nd	3rd	4th	Win & Pl
4	3	-	1		£32,003
	2/20	Newb	2m¹/₂f Cls3 Nov Hdl good........................£6,758
	12/19	Chel	2m1f Cls3 Nov Hdl 4-6yo gd-sft...............£9,384
	3/19	Wvck	2m Cls5 NHF 4-6yo soft...........................£2,599

Point-to-point and bumper winner who also justified odds-on favouritism in first two runs over hurdles at Cheltenham and Newbury last season before a fine third in the Supreme; stayed on well to suggest improvement likely over further; set to go novice chasing.

Chosen Mate (Ire)

7 br g Well Chosen - Norwich Star (Norwich)

Gordon Elliott (Ire) | The Northern Four Racing Partnership

PLACINGS: P/11215/P603411-04 | RPR **158**+c

Starts	1st	2nd	3rd	4th	Win & Pl
13	4	1	1	2	£113,415
147	3/20	Chel	2m¹/₂f Cls1 Gd3 140-155 Ch Hcap gd-sft..........£61,897
	1/20	Gowr	2m Ch sft-hvy.....................................£7,262
	2/19	Naas	2m Nov Gd2 Hdl good............................£24,716
	1/19	Fair	2m Mdn Hdl yield..................................£7,214

Made a mockery of an opening chase mark of 147 when hacking up in last season's Grand Annual at Cheltenham; had been slow to get the hang of fences until winning easily in a beginners' chase on his previous start; looks up to Graded level.

Chris's Dream (Ire)

8 b g Mahler - Janebailey (Silver Patriarch)

Henry De Bromhead (Ire) | Robcour

PLACINGS: 010/62119/1215/P110- | RPR **167**+c

Starts	1st	2nd	3rd	4th	Win & Pl
15	6	2	-		£154,079
	2/20	Gowr	2m4f Gd2 Ch heavy...............................£30,000
146	11/19	Navn	3m 121-149 Ch Hcap soft.......................£53,153
	2/19	Navn	3m Nov Gd2 Ch yield.............................£23,919
	12/18	Navn	2m4f Ch yield.......................................£7,904
	2/18	Navn	3m Nov Gd3 Hdl heavy...........................£20,409
	12/17	Limk	2m3f Mdn Hdl soft.................................£5,791

Massive improver last season, hacking up in the Troytown Chase at Navan before proving his versatility by coming back in trip in a smaller field to win the Red Mills Chase at Gowran Park; sent off 20-1 for the Cheltenham Gold Cup but faded into tenth.

Christmas In April (Fr)

8 b g Crillon - Similaresisoldofa (Kapgarde)

Colin Tizzard | Swallowfield Racing

PLACINGS: 5/34P/130053/21131P- | RPR **143**+c

Starts	1st	2nd	3rd	4th	Win & Pl
19	5	1	5	2	£54,072
129	2/20	Extr	3m6¹/₂f Cls3 119-135 Ch Hcap heavy..............£15,890
123	1/20	Plum	3m4¹/₂f Cls3 110-133 Ch Hcap soft...............£19,754
120	12/19	Font	3m2f Cls4 Nov 108-120 Ch Hcap soft.............£4,394
113	5/18	Wwck	2m5f Cls4 104-117 Hdl Hcap good................£4,549
	5/16	MRas	2m1¹/₂f Cls6 NHF 4-6yo good....................£1,560

Hugely progressive staying chaser last season; made it three wins out of four when an easy winner of the Devon National at Exeter, relishing step up to 3m6½f; subsequently sent off favourite for the Midlands National but well below best and pulled up.

Christopher Wood (Ire)

5 b g Fast Company - Surf The Web (Ela-Mana-Mou)

Paul Nicholls | Ms Sharon Kinsella

PLACINGS: 113/04910- | RPR **145**+h

Starts	1st	2nd	3rd	4th	Win & Pl
8	3	-	1	1	£28,730
135	2/20	Muss	1m7¹/₂f Cls3 115-135 Hdl Hcap soft.............£6,758
	3/19	Newb	2m1¹/₂f Cls4 Hdl 4yo gd-sft.....................£4,549
	2/19	Font	2m1¹/₂f Cls4 Hdl 4yo soft........................£3,249

Slow to build on promising juvenile campaign (won twice and third at Grade 1 level at Aintree) but bounced back after a wind operation midway through last season, hacking up by 11 lengths at Musselburgh; raised 10lb and well beaten in the County Hurdle.

Ciel De Neige (Fr)

5 b g Authorized - In Caso Di Neve (Country Reel)

Willie Mullins (Ire) | John P McManus

PLACINGS: 44/53/4220- | RPR **140**+h

Starts	1st	2nd	3rd	4th	Win & Pl
8	-	2	1	3	£54,376

Still a maiden over hurdles and even beaten at

1-4 at Limerick last season but has run well in some big handicaps; finished third on his debut for Willie Mullins in the Fred Winter at Cheltenham in 2019 and second in the Betfair Hurdle last season.

Cilaos Emery (Fr)

8 b g Califet - Queissa (Saint Preuil)

Willie Mullins (Ire)   Luke McMahon

PLACINGS: 11251/42/1/11F14-   RPR **166+**c

Starts	1st	2nd	3rd	4th	Win & Pl
13	7	2	-	2	£215,895

			Win & Pl
2/20	Gowr	2m Gd3 Hdl heavy	£30,000
12/19	Cork	2m½f Gd2 Ch soft	£45,180
11/19	Naas	2m Gd3 Ch sft-hvy	£17,275
1/19	Gowr	2m Ch soft	£8,047
4/17	Punc	2m½f Nov Gd1 Hdl gd-yld	£50,427
12/16	Navn	2m Mdn Hdl sft-hvy	£6,331
4/16	Punc	2m NHF 4yo gd-yld	£5,426

Finished fourth in last season's Champion Hurdle having spent the first half of the campaign emerging as a potential Champion Chase contender; reverted to hurdles after falling at Leopardstown in February but likely to prove best back over fences.

City Island (Ire)

7 b g Court Cave - Victorine (Un Desperado)

Martin Brassil (Ire)   Sean & Bernardine Mulryan

PLACINGS: 2/11d111/6P2P-   RPR **130**c

Starts	1st	2nd	3rd	4th	Win & Pl
10	4	2	-	-	£105,344

			Win & Pl
3/19	Chel	2m5f Cls1 Nov Gd1 Hdl soft	£70,338
2/19	Naas	2m3f Nov Hdl good	£11,099
12/18	Leop	2m Mdn Hdl gd-yld	£8,177
5/18	Punc	2m NHF 5-7yo good	£5,451

Beat Champ to win the Ballymore Novices' Hurdle at Cheltenham in 2019; bitterly disappointing in two runs over fences last season,

though a little better when a distant second behind Carefully Selected at Punchestown; pulled up back over hurdles in the Stayers' Hurdle.

Claimantakinforgan (Fr)

8 b g Great Pretender - Taquine D'Estrees (Take Risks)

Nicky Henderson   Grech & Parkin

PLACINGS: S1/16235/11352/13/   RPR **150**c

Starts		1st	2nd	3rd	4th	Win & Pl
12		4	2	3	-	£76,744
	11/18	Uttx	2m Cls3 Ch good			£7,408
	12/17	Asct	1m7¹/₂f Cls1 Nov Gd2 Hdl soft			£19,933
	11/17	Newb	2m¹/₂f Cls4 Nov Hdl gd-sft			£4,549
	11/16	Hayd	1m7¹/₂f Cls4 NHF 4-6yo heavy			£3,249

Hasn't raced since a distant third at Cheltenham in November 2018 but looked an exciting chase prospect prior to that; showed high-class form in bumpers and novice hurdles before an impressive win on chase debut at Uttoxeter.

Clan Des Obeaux (Fr)

8 b g Kapgarde - Nausicaa Des Obeaux (April Night)

Paul Nicholls   Mr & Mrs P K Barber, G Mason & Sir A Ferguson

PLACINGS: 2514/2123/41152/218-   RPR **178+**c

Starts		1st	2nd	3rd	4th	Win & Pl
22		8	6	1	3	£548,691
	12/19	Kemp	3m Cls1 Gd1 Ch soft			£144,050
	2/19	Asct	3m Cls1 Gd2 Ch gd-sft			£28,475
	12/18	Kemp	3m Cls1 Gd1 Ch gd-sft			£142,375
	11/17	Hayd	2m5¹/₂f Cls2 Ch heavy			£32,490
	3/17	Extr	2m3f Cls3 Nov Ch gd-sft			£7,148
	11/16	Newb	2m4f Cls1 Nov Gd2 Ch gd-sft			£19,933
	12/15	Newb	2m¹/₂f Cls4 Hdl 3yo soft			£3,249
	4/15	Lrsy	1m4f NHF 3yo gd-sft			£3,876

Has won the King George at Kempton for the last two seasons, hacking up by 21 lengths from Cyrname last term; has subsequently disappointed in the Gold Cup both times, taking Cheltenham record to 0-6, and trainer says he won't be asked to run there again.

Clondaw Anchor (Ire)

7 gr g Stowaway - Masiana (Daylami)

Dan Skelton   Highclere Thoroughbred Racing - Anchor

PLACINGS: 2/21348/212P-   RPR **145**c

Starts		1st	2nd	3rd	4th	Win & Pl
9		2	3	1	1	£18,575
127	11/19	Ling	2m7¹/₂f Cls3 115-128 Ch Hcap heavy			£7,018
	11/18	Carl	2m1f Cls4 Nov Hdl gd-sft			£4,549

Generally progressive when sent chasing last season, winning well at Lingfield and finishing a good second off 10lb higher at Chepstow; favourite for a stronger novice handicap on final

run at Uttoxeter but pulled up; could be one for good staying handicaps.

Clondaw Caitlin (Ire)

5 b m Court Cave - Kilmessan (Flemensfirth)

Ruth Jefferson   Drew & Ailsa Russell

PLACINGS: P/F271111-   RPR **135+**h

Starts		1st	2nd	3rd	4th	Win & Pl
5		4				£39,554
	2/20	Kels	2m2f Cls1 Nov Gd2 Hdl heavy			£28,475
	1/20	Newc	2m4¹/₂f Cls4 Nov Hdl soft			£3,769
	12/19	Weth	2m3¹/₂f Cls4 Nov Hdl soft			£4,224
	11/19	Weth	2m Cls5 NHF 4-6yo soft			£3,087

Exciting mare who won all three starts after going hurdling last season; twice won easily in mares' events before coping with a marked step up in class to score decisively in a Grade 2 novice hurdle at Kelso; should stay further.

Clondaw Castle (Ire)

8 b g Oscar - Lohort Castle (Presenting)

Tom George   J French, D McDermott, S Nelson & T Syder

PLACINGS: 118/1317/521144/291-   RPR **154+**c

Starts		1st	2nd	3rd	4th	Win & Pl
15		6	2	1	2	£91,114
143	2/20	Wwck	2m4f Cls2 130-148 Ch Hcap gd-sft			£31,280
134	2/19	Hntg	2m¹/₂f Cls3 Nov 119-134 Ch Hcap good			£9,653
	1/19	Leic	2m Cls3 Nov Ch gd-fm			£8,058
	1/18	Kels	2m Cls4 Nov Hdl soft			£4,159
	11/17	Hntg	2m Cls4 Mdn Hdl gd-sft			£3,249
	3/17	Strf	2m¹/₂f Cls4 Mdn NHF 4-6yo soft			£3,249

Progressive novice chaser in 2018-19 who improved again last season, winning well at Warwick on his final run after a close second in a valuable handicap at Ascot; best suited by good ground and had flopped on soft in between; expected to get 3m.

Cloudy Dream (Ire)

10 gr g Cloudings - Run Away Dream (Acceglio)

Donald McCain   Trevor Hemmings

PLACINGS: 12/1122221/222235/3/   RPR **162**c

Starts		1st	2nd	3rd	4th	Win & Pl
21		7	9	4	-	£258,344
	4/17	Ayr	2m4¹/₂f Cls1 Nov Gd2 Ch good			£26,283
	11/16	Hayd	2m¹/₂f Cls2 Ch soft			£12,996
	10/16	Carl	2m Cls4 Ch soft			£3,899
122	3/16	MRas	2m2¹/₂f Cls3 115-129 Hdl Hcap soft			£9,384
	11/15	Donc	2m3¹/₂f Cls4 Nov Hdl 4-6yo good			£3,899
	10/15	Carl	2m1f Cls6 NHF 4-6yo good			£1,560
	4/15	Hexm	2m Cls6 NHF 4-5yo good			£1,711

Hasn't run since finishing a close third in the Old Roan Chase at Aintree in 2018 on first start for Donald McCain; that extended long run of near misses having finished second in four successive

---

Clan Des Obeaux: dual winner of the King George Chase could be difficult to stop in his bid for a hat-trick this Christmas

Grade 2 races in 2017-18 as well as the Racing Post Arkle in 2017.

Cobbler's Way (Ire)

6 b g Oscar - Beeper's Leader (Supreme Leader)

Henry De Bromhead (Ire)   Gigginstown House Stud

PLACINGS: 2/1/212P-   RPR **147**h

Starts	1st	2nd	3rd	4th	Win & Pl
5	2	2	-	-	£40,185
12/19	Leop	2m4¹/₂f Mdn Hdl yield			£7,986
12/18	Limk	2m NHF 4-7yo soft			£5,724

Smart novice hurdler last season; won only a maiden hurdle at Leopardstown but went on to finish second behind Latest Exhibition back there in a 2m6f Grade 1; never a factor in the Albert Bartlett but suffered a rough race and was pulled up after losing his action.

Column Of Fire (Ire)

6 b g Robin Des Champs - Ghillie's Bay (King's Ride)

Gordon Elliott (Ire)   Gigginstown House Stud

PLACINGS: 2/13B2/32F13F-   RPR **146+**h

Starts	1st	2nd	3rd	4th	Win & Pl
11	2	3	3	-	£43,117
1/20	Punc	2m4f Mdn Hdl sft-hvy			£6,511
11/18	Navn	2m NHF 4-7yo good			£5,451

Developed into a very useful novice hurdler last season, especially when switched to handicaps; fell at the last when likely to go close in the Martin Pipe at Cheltenham having finished third in another valuable contest at Leopardstown.

Commanche Red (Ire)

7 ch g Mahler - Auntie Bob (Overbury)

Chris Gordon   Richard & Mrs Carol Cheshire

PLACINGS: 316/15731P/3313-   RPR **152+**c

Starts	1st	2nd	3rd	4th	Win & Pl
13	4	-	5	-	£39,365
137	12/19	Kemp	2m4¹/₂f Cls3 Nov 121-140 Ch Hcap soft	£16,245
127	3/19	Winc	1m7¹/₂f Cls3 Nov 103-130 Hdl Hcap good	£6,498
	10/18	Font	2m3f Cls4 Nov gd-sft	£4,094
	2/18	Kemp	2m Cls5 Mdn NHF 4-6yo soft	£2,859

Big improver when winning a novice handicap chase at Kempton on Boxing Day by nine lengths from subsequent Plate winner Simply The Betts (raised 13lb); below that form when a beaten favourite in a Grade 2 back there next time, possibly finding 2m4f too sharp on quicker ground.

Commander Of Fleet (Ire)

6 b g Fame And Glory - Coonagh Cross (Saddlers' Hall)

Gordon Elliott (Ire)   Gigginstown House Stud

PLACINGS: 11/1412/P-   RPR **152**h

Starts	1st	2nd	3rd	4th	Win & Pl
6	3	1	-	1	£156,892
2/19	Leop	2m6f Nov Gd1 Hdl gd-yld			£66,441
11/18	Punc	2m4¹/₂f Mdn Hdl 4yo good			£7,359
4/18	Punc	2m¹/₂f NHF 4-5yo yld-sft			£52,212

Missed last season through injury but had been a top-class staying novice hurdler in 2018-19, winning a Grade 1 at Leopardstown when stepped up to 2m6f and finishing second behind Minella Indo in the Albert Bartlett at Cheltenham; point-to-point and bumper winner who is set to go novice chasing.

Concertista (Fr)

6 ch m Nathaniel - Zagzig (Selkirk)

Willie Mullins (Ire)   Simon Munir & Isaac Souede

PLACINGS: 2/4331-   RPR **147+**h

Starts	1st	2nd	3rd	4th	Win & Pl
5	1	1	2	1	£78,986
3/20	Chel	2m1f Cls1 Nov Gd2 Hdl soft			£50,643

Tore apart a somewhat modest field in the mares' novice hurdle at the Cheltenham Festival last season, returning a much stronger mare 12 months after just getting touched off in the same race on her debut; largely disappointing in between but had got better all season.

Copperhead

6 ch g Sulamani - How's Business (Josr Algarhoud)

Colin Tizzard   Mrs G C Pritchard

PLACINGS: 779/03811/5111F-   RPR **158+**c

Starts	1st	2nd	3rd	4th	Win & Pl
13	5	-	1	1	£61,601
2/20	Asct	3m Cls1 Nov Gd2 Ch soft	£24,027
134	12/19	Newb	3m2f Cls3 118-135 Ch Hcap soft	£11,631
125	12/19	Winc	3m1f Cls3 101-127 Ch Hcap good	£16,245
116	2/19	Sand	2m4f Cls4 Nov 107-116 Hdl Hcap soft	£4,549
104	1/19	Extr	2m2¹/₂f Cls4 100-119 Hdl Hcap gd-sft	£4,094

Progressive young chaser who won Class 3 handicaps at Wincanton and Newbury last season before handling a sharp rise in class in the Reynoldstown at Ascot, staying on really strongly on soft ground; well beaten when falling at the last in the RSA Chase; no surprise to see him progress further this season.

> **FOR PULMONARY SUPPORT AND ELASTICITY**

Richard Hughes; "I have used Bronchix Pulmo syrup and Bronchix Pulmo syringes on two individual horses who have unfortunately been categorised as "bleeders". The product is simple and easy to use and we have had great success with it. We now would not do without it."

Cornerstone Lad

6 b g Delegator - Chapel Corner (Alhaarth)

Micky Hammond — Mrs B M Lofthouse

PLACINGS: 1312223/2131/113P- — RPR **159**h

Starts	1st	2nd	3rd	4th	Win & Pl
15	6	4	4	-	£111,409

	11/19	Newc	2m Cls1 Gd1 Hdl heavy	£61,897
142	11/19	Weth	2m Cls3 115-142 Hdl Hcap soft	£6,368
139	4/19	Newc	2m Cls3 113-139 Hdl Hcap gd-sft	£6,238
132	12/18	Hayd	1m7¹/₂f Cls3 118-137 Hdl Hcap heavy	£8,382
	1/18	Catt	1m7¹/₂f Cls4 Hdl 4yo soft	£4,809
	11/17	Hexm	2m Cls4 Hdl 3yo heavy	£3,249

Shock winner of last season's Fighting Fifth Hurdle from Buveur D'Air, benefiting from a soft lead and the runner-up's injury; had won his previous two starts in handicaps, though, and confirmed progressive profile with close third in Champion Hurdle Trial at Haydock.

Count Meribel

8 ch g Three Valleys - Bakhtawar (Lomitas)

Nigel Twiston-Davies — Charles C Walker

PLACINGS: 22/111265P/1147/26P- — RPR **151**c

Starts	1st	2nd	3rd	4th	Win & Pl
22	5	6	2	1	£69,868

	11/18	Chel	2m4f Cls2 Nov Ch good	£15,562
137	11/18	Carl	2m4f Cls3 Nov 115-137 Ch Hcap good	£8,123
	11/17	Asct	2m5¹/₂f Cls2 Nov Hdl gd-sft	£12,996
	11/17	Carl	2m4f Cls4 Nov Hdl soft	£4,224
	10/17	Carl	2m3¹/₂f Cls4 Nov Hdl soft	£4,224

Capable of smart form on his day but has struggled to maintain his level throughout a season; won his first two chases in November 2018 and bounced back with a good second behind Lostintranslation first time out last term; twice disappointed in top handicaps at Cheltenham.

Cracking Smart (Fr)

8 b g Great Pretender - Maya Du Frene (Le Pommier D'Or)

Gordon Elliott (Ire) — Gigginstown House Stud

PLACINGS: /1122/630/82F8P7514- — RPR **155**+h

Starts	1st	2nd	3rd	4th	Win & Pl
19	4	4	1	1	£92,074

	2/20	Navn	2m5f Gd2 Hdl heavy	£22,500
	11/17	Cork	3m Nov List Hdl soft	£20,171
	10/17	Punc	2m4f Mdn Hdl yld-sft	£7,108
	4/17	Fair	2m NHF 4-7yo gd-yld	£5,265

Hugely promising novice three seasons ago (favourite for the Albert Bartlett prior to injury) and finally back to that sort of form when winning the Boyne Hurdle and finishing fourth in the Coral Cup under a big weight last season; had lost his way over fences but retains novice status.

Crievehill (Ire)

8 b g Arcadio - Ma Douce (Mansonnien)

Nigel Twiston-Davies — Highclere T'Bred Racing

PLACINGS: 71324212/26644/1199- — RPR **160**+c

Starts	1st	2nd	3rd	4th	Win & Pl
24	5	5	2	4	£102,012

145	11/19	Hayd	3m1¹/₂f Cls2 130-145 Ch Hcap gd-sft	£31,280
138	10/19	Weth	2m3¹/₂f Cls3 129-138 Ch Hcap gd-sft	£8,187
129	3/18	Sand	2m4f Cls3 106-129 Ch Hcap soft	£9,419
127	11/17	Ling	2m Cls3 112-127 Ch Hcap soft	£12,660
122	1/17	Ling	2m Cls4 103-122 Hdl Hcap heavy	£3,249

Much improved in the first half of last season, easily winning handicap chases at Wetherby and Haydock; raised 17lb for those wins and couldn't land a blow in bigger races subsequently; trainer expects him to improve again with age and sees him as a Grand National hope.

Cyrname (Fr)

8 b g Nickname - Narquille (Passing Sale)

Paul Nicholls   Mrs Johnny De La Hey

PLACINGS: 56/7121214/3711/12F-					RPR **179**+c
Starts	1st	2nd	3rd	4th	Win & Pl
19	7	4	1	1	£320,738

	11/19	Asct	2m5f Cls1 Gd2 Ch soft	£39,865
	2/19	Asct	2m5f Cls1 Gd1 Ch gd-sft	£85,425
150	1/19	Asct	2m5f Cls2 135-152 Ch Hcap gd-sft	£46,920
	2/18	Kemp	2m4¹/₂f Cls1 Nov Gd2 Ch good	£18,224
	12/17	Kemp	2m Cls1 Nov Gd2 Ch soft	£23,491
130	11/17	Hntg	2m¹/₂f Cls3 Nov 123-131 Ch Hcap good	£7,798
	1/16	Pau	2m1¹/₂f Hdl 4yo v soft	£11,294

Highest-rated chaser in Britain and Ireland for the last two seasons on Racing Post Ratings; owes that status to three wide-margin wins at Ascot, most recently beating Altior last November; yet to prove as effective elsewhere and well beaten when second in last season's King George.

Dallas Des Pictons (Fr)

7 b g Spanish Moon - Nadia Des Pictons (Video Rock)

Gordon Elliott (Ire)   Gigginstown House Stud

PLACINGS: 41/1421120/153U4U-4					RPR **146**c
Starts	1st	2nd	3rd	4th	Win & Pl
16	5	2	1	4	£94,348

	10/19	Gowr	2m2f Ch soft	£7,454
130	2/19	Leop	3m 119-139 Hdl Hcap good	£46,509
	1/19	Punc	2m4f Mdn Hdl good	£7,214
	5/18	Pina	1m7¹/₂f NHF 4-5yo good	£5,973
	4/18	Loud	1m6f NHF 4-5yo heavy	£4,204

Controversially missed the Cheltenham Festival last season due to anger over British mark; showed little to justify rating over fences, doing best when a close fourth in a Grade 3 at Naas, but had looked much better over hurdles in 2018-19, finishing second in the Martin Pipe.

Dame De Compagnie (Fr)

7 b m Lucarno - Programmee (Kahyasi)

Nicky Henderson   John P McManus

PLACINGS: 1/322/1521/511-					RPR **147**+h
Starts	1st	2nd	3rd	4th	Win & Pl
11	5	3	1	-	£118,748

140	3/20	Chel	2m5f Cls1 Gd3 138-154 Hdl Hcap soft	£56,270
132	12/19	Chel	2m4¹/₂f Cls2 111-137 Hdl Hcap soft	£18,768
	4/18	Chel	2m4¹/₂f Cls1 Nov List Hdl good	£14,238
	11/17	Uttx	2m Cls4 Mdn Hdl good	£3,249
	4/16	Lrsy	1m4f NHF 3yo	£3,676

Missed more than 18 months after a promising novice campaign in 2017-18 and returned better than ever last season, winning two handicap hurdles at Cheltenham including the Coral Cup; raised another 8lb but still lightly raced and open to further improvement.

Cyrname: powerhouse chaser is something of a specialist at Ascot, where he is tough to master

Danny Kirwan (Ire)

7 b g Scorpion - Sainte Baronne (Saint Des Saints)

Paul Nicholls   Mrs Johnny De La Hey

PLACINGS: 110/22/6-   RPR **108**+h

Starts	1st	2nd	3rd	4th	Win & Pl
5	1	2	-	-	£11,800

2/18	Kemp	2m Cls5 NHF 4-6yo good		£3,119

Long held in high regard at home but has been plagued by injuries in the last two seasons; yet to score in three runs over hurdles in that time and suffered second odds-on defeat at Exeter on only run last term, though confirmed promise with second in a Grade 2 at Ascot in 2018.

Danny Whizzbang (Ire)

7 b g Getaway - Lakil Princess (Bering)

Paul Nicholls   Mrs Angela Tincknell

PLACINGS: P1/11/133-   RPR **148**+c

Starts	1st	2nd	3rd	4th	Win & Pl
5	3	-	2	-	£49,043

11/19	Newb	2m7½f Cls1 Nov Gd2 Ch gd-sft	£22,780
3/19	Extr	2m7f Cls4 Nov Hdl gd-sft	£4,224
11/18	Hrfd	3m1⅛f Cls4 Mdn Hdl gd-sft	£4,809

Very lightly raced gelding who won only two starts over hurdles before starting over fences with a Grade 2 win at Newbury last season; probably flattered by that (odds-on favourite Reserve Tank ran flat) and well beaten into third in stronger races subsequently.

Darasso (Fr)

7 br g Konig Turf - Nossora (Assessor)

Joseph O'Brien (Ire)   John P McManus

PLACINGS: 32/2121116/2511/420-   RPR **158**+h

Starts	1st	2nd	3rd	4th	Win & Pl
16	6	5	1	1	£243,657

3/19	Navn	2m Gd2 Ch soft	£23,919
2/19	Gowr	2m Gd3 Hdl yield	£31,892
3/18	Comp	2m3½f Ch 5yo heavy	£20,389
3/18	Comp	2m3½f Ch 5yo heavy	£22,088
0 11/17	Autl	2m3½f List Hdl 4yo Hcap v soft	£40,385
0 10/17	Autl	2m2f List Hdl 4yo Hcap v soft	£40,385

Disappointing in good 2m hurdles last season, finishing tenth in the Champion Hurdle having been last of four behind Ballyandy at Haydock and no match for Cilaos Emery at Gowran; could switch back to fences having thrashed Cadmium on only chase start in Ireland in March 2019.

Darver Star (Ire)

8 b g Kalanisi - Maggies Oscar (Oscar)

Gavin Cromwell (Ire)   SSP Number Twentytwo Syndicate

PLACINGS: 6594316/1111323-1   RPR **162**h

Starts	1st	2nd	3rd	4th	Win & Pl
15	6	1	3	1	£173,622

10/20	Punc	2m1f Ch yield	£6,250
10/19	Limk	2m5f Nov List Hdl heavy	£18,072
9/19	List	2m4f Nov Hdl yield	£11,959
133 8/19	Klny	2m1f 109-137 Hdl Hcap yld-sft	£26,577
8/19	Dpat	2m3f Hdl gd-yld	£10,649
106 4/19	Wxfd	2m4f 105-123 Hdl Hcap yield	£9,157

Remarkably progressive last season, finishing third behind Epatante in the Champion Hurdle less than a year after getting off the mark in a handicap at Wexford off 106; stays further having won a Listed novice over 2m5f; likely to go novice chasing.

Dashel Drasher

7 b g Passing Glance - So Long (Nomadic Way)

Jeremy Scott   Mrs B Tully & R Lock

PLACINGS: 106/3341111/2U1-   RPR **150**+c

Starts	1st	2nd	3rd	4th	Win & Pl
13	6	1	2	1	£57,702

12/19	Hayd	2m5½f Cls2 Nov Ch soft	£12,996
4/19	Chel	2m4½f Cls2 Nov Hdl good	£12,380
3/19	Newb	2m4½f Cls3 Nov Hdl gd-sft	£6,238
2/19	Asct	2m3½f Cls2 Nov Hdl gd-sft	£15,857
1/19	Chep	2m3½f Cls4 Nov Hdl gd-sft	£4,094
2/18	Winc	1m7½f Cls5 NHF 4-6yo heavy	£2,274

Won his last four races over hurdles and maintained his progress when switched to fences last season; second to Champ first time out and put an early exit next time behind him when winning well at Haydock; missed the rest of the season but set to return.

Daylight Katie (Fr)

7 b m Bonbon Rose - Sirani (Kapgarde)

Gordon Elliott (Ire)   Coldunell

PLACINGS: F/1/2313/211-   RPR **139**+h

Starts	1st	2nd	3rd	4th	Win & Pl
7	3	2	2	-	£47,994

11/19	DRoy	2m1f Nov Gd3 Hdl yld-sft	£19,955
10/19	Fair	2m Mdn Hdl yld-sft	£5,857
2/19	Gowr	2m1f NHF 4-7yo yield	£6,105

Missed much of last season after picking up an injury when winning a Grade 3 at Down Royal; struggled to land odds of 1-3 that day but looked

an exciting mare prior to that, hacking up on hurdling debut having been placed in Graded bumpers at Aintree and Punchestown.

De Rasher Counter

8 b g Yeats - Dedrunknmunky (Rashar)

Emma Lavelle — Makin' Bacon Partnership

PLACINGS: 521F72/3P7121/614P-2 — RPR **161+**c

Starts		1st	2nd	3rd	4th	Win & Pl
19		5	4	2	1	£203,662
149	11/19	Newb	3m2f Cls1 Gd3 135-160 Ch Hcap gd-sft			£142,375
140	3/19	Uttx	3m Cls2 Nov 118-140 Ch Hcap heavy			£25,024
133	12/18	Newb	2m6¹/₂f Cls3 Nov 129-148 Ch Hcap gd-sft			£7,343
124	1/18	Font	2m3f Cls3 105-127 Hdl Hcap heavy			£6,238
	3/17	Clon	2m NHF 5-7yo sft-hvy			£5,265

Won what looked a really strong Ladbrokes Trophy last season from subsequent Cheltenham Festival winner, capping a hugely progressive 12 months; disappointing fourth in the Cotswold Chase when stepped up in grade and pulled up in a gruelling Midlands National.

Defi Bleu (Fr)

7 b g Saddler Maker - Glycine Bleue (Le Nain Jaune)

Gordon Elliott (Ire) — Gigginstown House Stud

PLACINGS: 2/18/213203/P- — RPR **145**h

Starts		1st	2nd	3rd	4th	Win & Pl
9		2	2	2	-	£33,375
	11/18	Navn	2m4f Mdn Hdl good			£7,087
	12/17	Navn	2m NHF 4-7yo soft			£5,528

Missed last season through injury but had been a smart novice in 2018-19 despite winning only a maiden hurdle; twice placed at Grade 2 level, including a close second to Derrinross at Limerick, and finished third in the Martin Pipe at Cheltenham.

Defi Du Seuil (Fr)

7 b g Voix Du Nord - Quarvine Du Seuil (Lavirco)

Philip Hobbs — John P McManus

PLACINGS: 1111/47/51211/21114- — RPR **171+**c

Starts		1st	2nd	3rd	4th	Win & Pl
21		14	3	-	2	£616,112
	1/20	Asct	2m1f Cls1 Gd1 Ch heavy			£85,425
	12/19	Sand	1m7¹/₂f Cls1 Gd1 Ch soft			£84,405
	11/19	Chel	2m Cls1 Gd2 Ch soft			£42,203
	3/19	Chel	2m4f Cls1 Nov Gd1 Ch gd-sft			£88,209
	2/19	Sand	2m4f Cls1 Nov Gd1 Ch soft			£31,691
	12/18	Extr	2m3f Cls2 Nov Ch soft			£16,245
	4/17	Aint	2m1f Cls1 Gd1 Hdl 4yo good			£56,181
	3/17	Chel	2m1f Cls1 Gd1 Hdl 4yo good			£71,188
	1/17	Chel	2m1f Cls1 Gd2 Hdl 4yo soft			£17,085
	12/16	Chep	2m Cls1 Gd1 Hdl 3yo soft			£28,475
	12/16	Chel	2m1f Cls2 Hdl 3yo gd-sft			£12,512
	11/16	Chel	2m¹/₂f Cls1 Gd2 Hdl 3yo gd-sft			£17,165
	10/16	Ffos	2m Cls5 Mdn Hdl 3yo good			£2,599
	4/16	Pari	1m4f NHF 3yo v soft			£5,882

Seven-time Grade 1 winner who mopped up a string of top races at around 2m in Britain, beating Un De Sceaux in the Tingle Creek and Clarence House; below par when fourth in the Champion Chase; equally effective at 2m4f having won the JLT at Cheltenham in 2019.

Definitly Red (Ire)

11 ch g Definite Article - The Red Wench (Aahsaylad)

Brian Ellison — Phil & Julie Martin

PLACINGS: 1P/3116U/112B/54421- — RPR **164**c

Starts		1st	2nd	3rd	4th	Win & Pl
34		15	6	2	2	£456,034
	2/20	Kels	2m7¹/₂f Cls1 Ch heavy			£28,475
	12/18	Aint	3m1f Cls1 Gd2 Ch soft			£34,822
	11/18	Weth	3m Cls1 Gd2 Ch good			£58,727
	1/18	Chel	3m1¹/₂f Cls1 Gd2 Ch heavy			£56,950
	12/17	Aint	3m1f Cls1 Gd2 Ch heavy			£28,135
149	3/17	Donc	3m2f Cls2 137-161 Ch Hcap soft			£34,408
141	12/16	Weth	3m Cls1 Gd3 131-153 Ch Hcap soft			£22,780
140	10/16	Carl	2m4f Cls2 122-148 Hdl Hcap gd-sft			£12,512
137	4/16	Ayr	2m4¹/₂f Cls1 List 132-148 Ch Hcap soft			£25,628
	1/16	Catt	3m1f Cls4 Nov Ch soft			£7,148
	2/15	Hayd	2m4f Cls3 Nov Hdl gd-sft			£15,735
	1/15	Catt	2m3¹/₂f Cls4 Nov Hdl gd-sft			£4,874
	11/14	Chel	2m1¹/₂f Cls1 List NHF 4-6yo soft			£11,390
	2/14	Newb	2m1¹/₂f Cls1 List NHF 4-6yo heavy			£11,390
	12/13	Uttx	2m Cls6 Mdn NHF 4-6yo heavy			£1,949

Has a fine record just below the top level, winning four Grade 2 chases during his career; not quite at that level last season but ran well back in handicaps, notably when second in the Peter Marsh Chase, and got back to winning ways in a Listed chase at Kelso.

Delire D'Estruval (Fr)

7 b g Youmzain - Question D'Estruval (Phantom Breeze)

Ben Pauling — Simon Munir & Isaac Souede

PLACINGS: 2/413104/14921/7231- — RPR **149+**c

Starts		1st	2nd	3rd	4th	Win & Pl
22		6	4	4	3	£97,203
139	3/20	Kemp	2m4¹/₂f Cls2 121-140 Ch Hcap gd-sft			£25,024
134	3/19	Sand	2m4f Cls3 Nov 115-134 Ch Hcap soft			£7,535
	10/18	Carl	2m3f Cls3 Ch good			£7,473
	2/18	Towc	1m7¹/₂f Cls4 Nov Hdl soft			£4,549
	11/17	Hayd	1m7¹/₂f Cls1 Nov List Hdl heavy			£14,238
	8/16	Vitt	1m4f NHF 3yo gd-sft			£4,412

Steadily progressive over the last two seasons; beaten a head at Sandown in January and then bounced back from a rare below-par run back there next time to spring a 25-1 surprise at Kempton in March; has won last two races over 2m4f.

Delta Work (Fr)

7 br g Network - Robbe (Video Rock)

Gordon Elliott (Ire) — Gigginstown House Stud

PLACINGS: 13324312/1113/14115- — RPR **173+**c

Starts		1st	2nd	3rd	4th	Win & Pl
18		8	3	4	2	£512,992
	2/20	Leop	3m Gd1 Ch yield			£118,856
	12/19	Leop	3m Gd1 Ch good			£93,018
	4/19	Punc	3m1¹/₂f Nov Gd1 Ch yld-sft			£53,153
	12/18	Leop	3m Nov Gd1 Ch good			£52,212
	12/18	Fair	2m4f Nov Gd1 Ch good			£46,991
	11/18	DRoy	2m4f Nov Gd1 Ch good			£8,177
139	3/18	Chel	3m Cls1 Gd3 135-155 Hdl Hcap good			£56,950
	5/17	Punc	2m¹/₂f Mdn Hdl good			£6,844

Prolific Grade 1 winner since going chasing three seasons ago, adding last season's Savills Chase and Irish Gold Cup to three top-level victories as a novice; strong stayer and perhaps unsuited by relatively modest gallop when only fifth in the Cheltenham Gold Cup.

Deyrann De Carjac (Fr)

7 b g Balko - Queyrann (Sheyrann)

Alan King   J Law

PLACINGS: 0/332/12F225/11330-   RPR **148**c

Starts	1st	2nd	3rd	4th	Win & Pl
15	3	4	4	-	£35,880

11/19	Hntg	2m4f Cls3 Nov Ch good		£9,747
5/19	Ctml	2m5f Cls4 Nov Ch soft		£4,938
5/18	Wwck	2m Cls4 Mdn Hdl good		£4,549

Slightly disappointing over hurdles but soon proved much better as a novice chaser last season, winning twice and then not beaten far when twice third in Grade 2 races won by Champ and Midnight Shadow; finished lame when 14-1 on handicap debut in the Plate at Cheltenham.

Dickie Diver (Ire)

7 b g Gold Well - Merry Excuse (Flemensfirth)

Nicky Henderson   John P McManus

PLACINGS: 1/214/   RPR **145**h

Starts	1st	2nd	3rd	4th	Win & Pl
3	1			1	£11,699

2/19	Chep	2m3½f Cls4 Mdn Hdl gd-sft		£3,574

Missed last season through injury but had looked full of promise in three novice hurdles in 2018-19; just pipped by Stayers' Hurdle hero Lisnagar Oscar first time out and followed maiden win with an eyecatching fourth in the Albert Bartlett (finished well after not getting a clear run).

Diego Du Charmil (Fr)

8 b g Ballingarry - Daramour (Anabaa Blue)

Paul Nicholls   Mrs Johnny De La Hey

PLACINGS: 010/132F15/5235/122-   RPR **163**c

Starts	1st	2nd	3rd	4th	Win & Pl
23	6	6	3	1	£291,789

150	11/19	Asct	2m1f Cls1 List 129-150 Ch Hcap gd-sft	£34,170
	4/18	Aint	2m Cls1 Nov Gd1 Ch soft	£56,130
	9/17	NAbb	2m¹/₂f Cls3 Nov Ch gd-sft	£7,121
140	2/17	Muss	1m7¹/₂f Cls1 List 117-154 Hdl Hcap good	£28,475
138	10/16	Chep	2m Cls2 120-140 Hdl 4yo Hcap good	£12,996
133	3/16	Chel	2m¹/₂f Cls1 Gd3 128-142 Hdl 4yo Hcap good	£42,713

Former Grade 1 winner who benefited from some overdue help from the handicapper to win first time out at Ascot last season, albeit in fortuitous circumstances; well-beaten second off higher mark next time but came closer back over hurdles when second in the Kingwell.

Discorama (Fr)

7 b g Saddler Maker - Quentala (Lone Bid)

Paul Nolan (Ire)   Andrew Gemmell & Thomas Friel

PLACINGS: /123725/15F2/22833-2   RPR **154**+c

Starts	1st	2nd	3rd	4th	Win & Pl
17	2	7	3	-	£100,683

11/18	Naas	2m3f Ch yield		£7,904
12/17	Fair	2m2f Mdn Hdl soft		£7,108

Has won only once each over hurdles and fences

(on first run in each sphere) but has been placed at the last three Cheltenham Festivals; came closest in the 2019 National Hunt Chase before a fine third in last season's Ultima; should run well in more top handicaps.

Dolcita (Fr)

5 b m Saint Des Saints - Orcantara (Villez)

Paul Nicholls   Sullivan Bloodstock

PLACINGS: 32/132-   RPR **135**h

Starts	1st	2nd	3rd	4th	Win & Pl
5	1	2	2	-	£41,348

12/19	Tram	2m Mdn Hdl heavy		£5,857

Hugely impressive winner on Irish debut last season and ran well to be placed in good races subsequently, notably when second in the mares' novice hurdle at the Cheltenham Festival despite jumping errors; has since left Willie Mullins; open to significant improvement.

Dolos (Fr)

7 b g Kapgarde - Redowa (Trempolino)

Paul Nicholls   Mrs Johnny De La Hey

PLACINGS: 2013272/22315/12714-   RPR **166**+c

Starts	1st	2nd	3rd	4th	Win & Pl
26	6	8	6	1	£185,775

157	2/20	Sand	1m7¹/₂f Cls2 140-157 Ch Hcap soft	£19,577
154	5/19	Kemp	2m2f Cls2 128-154 Ch Hcap good	£14,389
149	5/18	Sand	1m7¹/₂f Cls2 128-154 Ch Hcap soft	£18,768
	11/17	Asct	2m3f Cls3 Ch gd-sft	£9,986
	4/17	Chep	2m Cls4 Nov Hdl good	£3,899
	10/16	Chep	2m Cls4 Hdl 3yo good	£3,899

Carefully campaigned in recent seasons when largely kept to small-field handicaps, notably winning off 157 at Sandown in February; disappointed when stepped up in class for the Tingle Creek but was being aimed at the Celebration Chase before the season ended early.

Domaine De L'Isle (Fr)

7 b g Network - Gratiene De L'Isle (Altayan)

Sean Curran   12 Oaks Racing & Ian Hutchins

PLACINGS: 232/11P5P4/361115-   RPR **148**+c

Starts	1st	2nd	3rd	4th	Win & Pl
15	5	2	2	1	£103,893

140	1/20	Asct	2m5f Cls2 127-153 Ch Hcap heavy	£46,920
130	1/20	Newc	2m7¹/₂f Cls3 122-132 Ch Hcap soft	£16,505
120	12/19	Chep	2m3¹/₂f Cls4 98-120 Ch Hcap soft	£4,289
	6/18	Clun	2m2f Ch good	£5,097
	5/18	Pmnl	2m4f Ch 5-6yo good	£5,522

Dual chase winner in France who proved well ahead of his mark when switched to Britain last season, rattling off a hat-trick of wins in handicap chases and going up 26lb in the weights; well below best when fifth at Ascot on only run off new mark.

Discorama: smart operator who looks likely to run well in top handicap chases

Douvan (Fr)

10 b g Walk In The Park - Star Face (Saint Des Saints)

Willie Mullins (Ire)   Mrs S Ricci

PLACINGS: 1/111111/11117/F2/1-   RPR **166** +c

Starts		1st	2nd	3rd	4th	Win & Pl
19		15	2	-	-	£609,834
	11/19 Clon	2m4¹/₂f Gd2 Ch sft-hvy				£39,865
	2/17 Punc	2m Gd2 Ch soft				£22,692
	12/16 Leop	2m1f Gd1 Ch yield				£43,382
	12/16 Cork	2m1f Gd2 Ch sft-hvy				£21,691
	4/16 Punc	2m Nov Gd1 Ch yield				£49,890
	4/16 Aint	2m Cls1 Nov Gd1 Ch gd-sft				£56,270
	3/16 Chel	2m Cls1 Gd1 Ch gd-sft				£85,827
	1/16 Leop	2m1f Nov Gd1 Ch soft				£39,706
	12/15 Leop	2m1f Nov Gd1 Ch heavy				£42,558
	11/15 Navn	2m1f Ch soft				£8,558
	4/15 Punc	2m Nov Gd1 Hdl gd-yld				£44,186
	3/15 Chel	2m¹/₂f Cls1 Nov Gd1 Hdl gd-sft				£68,340
	1/15 Punc	2m Nov Gd2 Hdl soft				£20,155
	11/14 Gowr	2m Nov Hdl 4yo heavy				£7,475
	6/14 Comp	2m1f Hdl 4yo v soft				£8,800

Outstanding chaser in his heyday, being sent off just 2-9 for the Champion Chase in 2017, but suffered a serious injury that day and has run just three times since; made a comfortable winning return at Clonmel last season only to suffer yet another setback.

Dragon D'Estruval (Fr)

7 b g Enrique - Rose D'Estruval (Lavirco)

Nicky Henderson   Simon Munir & Isaac Souede

PLACINGS: 2/214718/1730/35V1P-   RPR **151** +c

Starts		1st	2nd	3rd	4th	Win & Pl
23		6	3	4	1	£113,092
140	1/20 Ludl	3m1¹/₂f Cls3 114-140 Ch Hcap gd-sft				£7,018
	5/18 Ffos	2m6f Cls4 Nov Hdl good				£4,159
	11/17 Autl	2m6f Ch 4yo v soft				£23,795
	6/17 Autl	2m1¹/₂f Ch 4yo v soft				£21,744
	4/17 Fntb	2m2f Ch 4yo v soft				£9,846
	9/16 PLOR	1m3¹/₂f NHF 3yo gd-sft				£3,676

Three-time chase winner in France who has shown glimpses of potential for current connections, notably when winning at Ludlow last season; pulled up in a more competitive

handicap at Sandown having failed to stay 3m5f there in the voided London National.

Duc Des Genievres (Fr)

7 gr g Buck's Boum - Lobelie (Round Sovereign)

Paul Nicholls   Sullivan Bloodstock

PLACINGS: 132556/2311/3482F5-   RPR **164**c

Starts	1st	2nd	3rd	4th	Win & Pl
16	3	3	3	1	£192,740
	3/19	Chel	2m Cls1 Nov Gd1 Ch soft		£102,772
	2/19	Gowr	2m4f Ch yld-sft		£8,047
	5/17	Mlns	2m2f Hdl 4yo v soft		£7,385

Won what proved to be a weak Racing Post Arkle in 2019 and just found out in top company last season; came closest to winning when second in the Desert Orchid Chase at Kempton behind Bun Doran; fifth when stepped up in trip for the Ryanair Chase; has since left Willie Mullins.

Earlofthecotswolds (Fr)

6 bl g Axxos - Sissi Land (Grey Risk)

Nigel Twiston-Davies   Twiston-Davies, Mason, Greer & Kiely

PLACINGS: 3/16215121/2F310-6   RPR **146**c

Starts	1st	2nd	3rd	4th	Win & Pl
15	5	3	2	-	£54,426
	12/19	Extr	2m3f Cls2 Nov Ch soft		£14,945
129	4/19	MRas	2m4¹/₂f Cls3 105-129 Hdl Hcap good		£12,996
117	2/19	MRas	2m4¹/₂f Cls4 104-120 Hdl Hcap gd-sft		£6,498
	12/18	Carl	2m1f Cls4 Nov Hdl good		£4,549
	9/18	MRas	2m1¹/₂f Cls5 NHF 4-6yo good		£2,274

Progressive over hurdles in 2018-19 (won three times) and improved again when switched to fences last season, deservedly getting off the mark at Exeter in December; saved for the novice handicap chase at the Cheltenham Festival but well beaten.

Early Doors (Fr)

7 b g Soldier Of Fortune - Ymlaen (Desert Prince)

Joseph O'Brien (Ire)   John P McManus

PLACINGS: 3/112930/521/2262-01   RPR **148**+c

Starts	1st	2nd	3rd	4th	Win & Pl
17	5	5	2		£228,213
139	7/20	Gway	2m6¹/₂f 135-158 Ch Hcap gd-yld		£100,000
145	3/19	Chel	2m4¹/₂f Cls2 126-145 Cond Hdl Hcap gd-sft		£43,330
	11/17	Naas	2m Gd3 Hdl 4yo sft-hvy		£17,083
	10/17	Wxfd	2m Mdn Hdl 4yo good		£6,055
	2/17	Punc	2m1¹/₂f NHF 4yo heavy		£5,265

Finally got things right over fences when winning the Galway Plate in July after failing to win in four novice chases last season; capable of more handicap success on hurdles form having produced a high-class performance to win the Martin Pipe at Cheltenham in 2019.

Easy Game (Fr)

6 b g Barastraight - Rule Of The Game (Lavirco)

Willie Mullins (Ire)   Nicholas Peacock

PLACINGS: 4/11231183/7212F-011   RPR **166**+c

Starts	1st	2nd	3rd	4th	Win & Pl
17	7	3	2	1	£133,564
	10/20	Gowr	2m4f Gd2 Ch good		£17,500
	8/20	Tram	2m5¹/₂f Ch good		£6,250
	12/19	Leop	2m5f Ch yield		£9,318
	12/18	Navn	2m4f Nov Gd2 Hdl yield		£22,190
	11/18	Navn	2m4f Nov Gd3 Hdl good		£22,190
	7/18	Gway	2m1¹/₂f Nov Hdl 4yo good		£10,903
	7/18	Klny	2m4¹/₂f Mdn Hdl good		£6,269

Quickly proved himself a smart novice chaser last season, beating Allaho on his first run over fences before a close second to Faugheen in a Grade 1 at Leopardstown; faded out of contention late in the RSA before falling at the last (first run beyond 2m5f).

Easysland (Fr)

6 b g Gentlewave - Island Du Frene (Useful)

David Cottin (Fr)   John P McManus

PLACINGS: F317/651FFO11/11111-   RPR **171**+c

Starts	1st	2nd	3rd	4th	Win & Pl
17	9		1	-	£172,824
	3/20	Chel	3m6f Cls2 Ch soft		£40,235
	2/20	Pau	3m7¹/₂f List Ch v soft		£30,508
139	12/19	Chel	3m6f Cls2 122-148 Ch Hcap gd-sft		£21,896
	11/19	Comp	3m3f List Ch heavy		£20,757
	10/19	Comp	2m7¹/₂f Ch heavy		£9,081
	2/19	Pau	2m4¹/₂f Ch 5-6yo heavy		£11,243
	1/19	Pau	2m4¹/₂f Ch 5-6yo v soft		£12,108
	11/18	Drtl	2m5f Ch 4-5yo soft		£6,372
	2/18	Pau	2m1¹/₂f Hdl 4yo heavy		£13,593

Emerged as the dominant force in cross-country racing last season, winning five times including twice at Cheltenham, most notably a 17-length success over Tiger Roll in March; still only six and has the potential to develop into a top chaser over regulation fences.

Easywork (Fr)

6 b g Network - Rivabella De Saisy (Subotica)

Gordon Elliott (Ire)   Gigginstown House Stud

PLACINGS: 3/11122-   RPR **155**h

Starts	1st	2nd	3rd	4th	Win & Pl
6	3	2	1	-	£75,943
	12/19	Limk	2m4f Hdl heavy		£8,253
	11/19	Gowr	2m Mdn Hdl heavy		£7,986
	11/19	DRoy	2m1¹/₂f NHF 4-7yo soft		£7,986

Won first two novice hurdles on heavy ground last season and relished return to softer ground and a longer trip when second to Envoi Allen in the Ballymore at Cheltenham (beaten much more easily by Asterion Forlonge over 2m at Leopardstown); likely to stay further.

Eclair De Beaufeu (Fr)

6 b g Monitor Closely - Tenebreuse Gemm (Visionary)

Gordon Elliott (Ire)   Gigginstown House Stud

PLACINGS: 1/3233114U6/214312-   RPR **158+c**

Starts		1st	2nd	3rd	4th	Win & Pl
16		5	3	4	2	£119,335
140	2/20	Leop	2m1f 119-147 Ch Hcap yield..............			£50,000
	10/19	Wxfd	2m sft-hvy.......................			£6,655
	1/19	Fair	2m Hdl good.......................			£9,989
	12/18	Limk	2m Mdn Hdl 4yo soft..............			£7,359
	3/18	Porn	1m4f NHF 4yo stand..............			£5,310
	12/17	Seic	1m5½f NHF 3yo soft..............			£4,701

Big improver when switched to handicaps last season, winning a valuable chase at Leopardstown before finishing second in the Grand Annual; had twice disappointed in small-field Graded races, extending record to 0-3 (well beaten every time) in single-figure fields.

Edwardstone

6 b g Kayf Tara - Nothingtoloose (Luso)

Alan King   Robert Abrey & Ian Thurtle

PLACINGS: 222/1126-   RPR **142h**

Starts		1st	2nd	3rd	4th	Win & Pl
7		2	4	-	-	£24,398
	12/19	Aint	2m1f Cls3 Nov Hdl gd-sft...........			£7,798
	11/19	Winc	1m7½f Cls3 Nov Hdl 4-6yo good			£6,238

Very useful novice hurdler last season; beat subsequent Graded winners Fiddlerontheroof and Harry Senior in first two runs before a neck second at Haydock when stepped up to Grade 2 level himself; fair sixth in the Supreme at Cheltenham.

Eglantine Du Seuil (Fr)

6 b m Saddler Maker - Rixia Du Seuil (Ultimately Lucky)

Paul Nicholls   Sullivan Bloodstock

PLACINGS: 1/1313/33540-   RPR **148+h**

Starts		1st	2nd	3rd	4th	Win & Pl
10		3	-	4	1	£90,810
	3/19	Chel	2m1f Cls1 Nov Gd2 Hdl gd-sft.............			£50,643
	8/18	Slig	2m Mdn Hdl good............			£6,269
	10/17	Fntb	1m5f NHF 3yo soft............			£7,692

Won the mares' novice hurdle at the Cheltenham Festival in 2019 before twice finishing third in Grade 1 novice races; unable to win last season but ran well when penalised in good mares' races and again when fourth in a big 2m handicap at Leopardstown; has since left Willie Mullins.

Eldorado Allen (Fr)

6 gr g Khalkevi - Hesmeralda (Royal Charter)

Colin Tizzard   J P Romans & Terry Warner

PLACINGS: 23/31U/230-1   RPR **150+h**

Starts		1st	2nd	3rd	4th	Win & Pl
8		2	2	2	-	£29,843
	10/20	NAbb	2m1½f Cls3 Nov Ch gd-sft			£8,058
	11/18	Sand	2m Cls4 Mdn Hdl heavy............			£6,498

Made a huge impression on British debut

in November 2018 and still mentioned in Champion Hurdle terms when returning from a year out last season; just unable to defy top weight in a competitive handicap first time out but failed to build on that in two subsequent runs.

Elegant Escape (Ire)

8 b g Dubai Destination - Graineuaile (Orchestra)

Colin Tizzard   J P Romans

PLACINGS: 212133/121266/236P0-   RPR **167c**

Starts		1st	2nd	3rd	4th	Win & Pl
24		6	6	3	1	£347,277
151	12/18	Chep	3m5½f Cls1 Gd3 133-155 Ch Hcap soft ...			£85,425
	11/18	Sand	3m Cls1 List Ch soft.................			£17,085
	2/18	Extr	3m Cls2 Ch heavy.................			£12,512
	12/17	Newb	2m7½f Cls1 Nov Gd2 Ch gd-sft...........			£23,048
	11/16	Asct	2m5½f Cls2 Nov Hdl gd-sft..........			£12,512
	10/16	Chep	2m3½f Cls4 Mdn Hdl gd-sft..........			£3,899

Strong stayer who enjoyed his finest hour when winning the 2018 Welsh Grand National and ran well under a big weight again when third in the Ladbrokes Trophy last season; not quite as effective in conditions races and twice been well beaten in the Cheltenham Gold Cup.

Elfile (Fr)

6 b m Saint Des Saints - Rapide (Assessor)

Willie Mullins (Ire)   Kenneth Alexander

PLACINGS: 22121/162/11213-   RPR **149h**

Starts		1st	2nd	3rd	4th	Win & Pl
13		6	5	1	-	£115,671
	2/20	Punc	2m4f Gd3 Hdl heavy			£16,250
	11/19	Thur	2m Hdl soft............			£10,649
	5/19	Punc	2m Nov List Hdl gd-yld			£19,392
	1/19	Punc	2m4f Mdn Hdl good............			£7,214
	11/17	Ange	1m7f NHF 3yo soft............			£9,402
	9/17	Angl	1m5f NHF 3yo good............			£4,274

Developed into a very smart mare last season, winning a Grade 3 at Punchestown and finishing an excellent third behind Honeysuckle in the Mares' Hurdle at Cheltenham; should thrive beyond 2m4f; likely to go novice chasing.

Elimay (Fr)

6 gr m Montmartre - Hyde (Poliglote)

Willie Mullins (Ire)   John P McManus

PLACINGS: 4/13222/26/1111-   RPR **148+c**

Starts		1st	2nd	3rd	4th	Win & Pl
12		5	4	1	1	£187,736
	1/20	Thur	2m4½f Nov Gd2 Ch yield			£28,750
	12/19	Cork	2m½f Nov Gd3 Ch soft			£21,261
	5/19	Klny	2m1f List Hdl good			£16,622
	5/19	Punc	2m4f Hdl yield............			£13,851
	5/17	Autl	2m1½f Hdl 3yo v soft............			£19,692

Progressive mare who won her last two starts over hurdles before switching to fences last season and winning twice more, both in Graded mares' novice chases; finished strongly when stepped up to 2m4f on her final run and open to further improvement, perhaps over further.

Elixir D'ainay (Fr)

6 ch g Muhtathir - Perle Du Bocage (Agent Bleu)

Willie Mullins (Ire) — John P McManus

PLACINGS: 6/1/2/125F- RPR **151+h**

Starts	1st	2nd	3rd	4th	Win & Pl
7	2	2	-	-	£41,988
	11/19 Naas	2m3f Mdn Hdl sft-hvy			£7,188
	11/17 Pari	1m4f NHF 3yo soft			£14,530

Running a big race in last season's Supreme Novices' Hurdle at Cheltenham when badly hampered and falling two out; had been highly tried all season, finishing second behind Envoi Allen in a 2m4f Grade 1 but failing to stay further in another Grade 1 at Leopardstown.

Elixir De Nutz (Fr)

6 gr g Al Namix - Nutz (Turgeon)

Colin Tizzard — Terry Warner

PLACINGS: 16/F2111/77- RPR **147h**

Starts	1st	2nd	3rd	4th	Win & Pl
9	4	7	1	-	£66,713
	1/19 Sand	2m Cls1 Nov Gd1 Hdl soft			£28,475
	12/18 Chel	2m1f Cls3 Nov Hdl 4-6yo good			£9,285
	11/18 Chel	2m¹/₂f Cls1 Nov Gd2 Hdl good			£18,006
	10/17 Agtn	1m6f NHF 3yo gd-sft			£6,838

Bitterly disappointing last season after nearly a year off but had looked a top-class prospect prior to that, winning the Tolworth Hurdle in 2019; easily shaken off after making the running in the International Hurdle and beaten even more comprehensively in the Christmas Hurdle; could yet bounce back.

Elvis Mail (Fr)

6 gr g Great Pretender - Queenly Mail (Medaaly)

Nick Alexander — The Ladies Who

PLACINGS: 443/41231/181- RPR **141+h**

Starts	1st	2nd	3rd	4th	Win & Pl
11	4	1	2	3	£48,504
136	1/20 Kels	2m Cls2 118-142 Hdl Hcap heavy			£12,512
132	11/19 Ayr	2m Cls2 119-142 Hdl Hcap soft			£19,494
	4/19 Kels	2m2f Cls4 Nov Hdl gd-sft			£4,549
	12/18 Kels	2m Cls4 Nov Hdl good			£4,549

Progressive hurdler who has won three of his last four races, though was well beaten when facing his toughest test at Newbury behind Epatante; got back on track with a narrow victory at Kelso (heavy ground perhaps not ideal) and raised just 1lb.

Embittered (Ire)

6 b g Fame And Glory - Kilbarry Classic (Classic Cliche)

Joseph O'Brien (Ire) — Gigginstown House Stud

PLACINGS: U313/415363- RPR **152h**

Starts	1st	2nd	3rd	4th	Win & Pl
8	2	2	3	1	£46,019
	11/19 Naas	2m Mdn Hdl sft-hvy			£7,986
	12/18 Punc	2m NHF 4yo good			£5,724

Smart and progressive novice hurdler last season; just came up short in a couple of Grade 1 races (not beaten far by Envoi Allen in a red-hot Royal Bond) before improving when switched to handicaps, notably when third in the County Hurdle under a big weight.

Emitom (Ire)

6 b g Gold Well - Avenging Angel (Heron Island)

Warren Greatrex — The Spero Partnership

PLACINGS: 1/11112/614-2 RPR **157h**

Starts	1st	2nd	3rd	4th	Win & Pl
10	6	2		1	£83,966
	2/20 Hayd	3m1¹/₂f Cls1 Gd2 Hdl heavy			£22,887
	3/19 Newb	2m4¹/₂f Cls4 Nov Hdl gd-sft			£4,549
	1/19 Ling	2m Cls4 Nov Hdl gd-sft			£4,159
	11/18 Ffos	2m4f Cls4 Mdn Hdl soft			£4,159
	11/18 Asct	1m7¹/₂f Cls4 NHF 4-6yo good			£4,549
	4/18 Wwck	2m Cls5 NHF 4-6yo gd-sft			£2,599

Exciting young stayer who won five out of six in bumpers and novice hurdles before getting back on track with an easy win in a soft Rendlesham Hurdle last season; unlucky not to go close when fourth in the Stayers' Hurdle at Cheltenham (squeezed out when hitting the second-last).

Enrilo (Fr)

6 bl g Buck's Boum - Rock Treasure (Video Rock)

Paul Nicholls — Martin Broughton & Friends

PLACINGS: 141/1513-2 RPR **143+c**

Starts	1st	2nd	3rd	4th	Win & Pl
8	4	1	1	1	£36,452
	12/19 Sand	2m4f Cls1 Nov Gd2 Hdl soft			£17,085
	10/19 Winc	2m4f Cls4 Nov Hdl good			£5,198
	2/19 Kemp	2m Cls5 NHF 4-6yo good			£3,119
	10/18 Worc	2m Cls5 NHF 4-6yo good			£2,274

Rated a top long-term prospect over fences by his trainer but also paid his way over hurdles last season, winning a Grade 2 at Sandown before a well-beaten third behind Thyme Hill in the Challow; likely to go novice chasing.

Envoi Allen (Fr)

6 b g Muhtathir - Reaction (Saint Des Saints)

Gordon Elliott (Ire) — Cheveley Park Stud

PLACINGS: 1/1111/1111- RPR **161+h**

Starts	1st	2nd	3rd	4th	Win & Pl
8	8	-	-	-	£283,129
	3/20 Chel	2m5f Cls1 Nov Gd1 Hdl soft			£70,338
	1/20 Naas	2m4f Nov Gd1 Hdl gd-sft			£47,838
	12/19 Fair	2m Nov Gd1 Hdl yld-sft			£47,838
	11/19 DRoy	2m¹/₂f Mdn Hdl soft			£7,986
	3/19 Chel	2m1¹/₂f Cls1 Gd1 NHF 4-6yo soft			£42,203
	2/19 Leop	2m Gd2 NHF 4-7yo gd-sft			£46,509
	12/18 Navn	2m List NHF 4-7yo yield			£14,967
	12/18 Fair	2m NHF 4yo good			£5,451

Last season's outstanding novice hurdler; showed top-class form over 2m (beat subsequent Supreme runner-up Abacadabras) before stepping up in trip to win two more Grade 1 races, including a second Cheltenham Festival victory when winning the Ballymore; goes novice chasing.

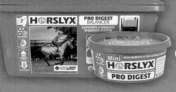

RACING POST

Epatante (Fr)

6 b m No Risk At All - Kadjara (Silver Rainbow)

Nicky Henderson   John P McManus

PLACINGS: 211/119/111-   RPR **163** +h

Starts	1st	2nd	3rd	4th	Win & Pl
9	7	1	-	-	£407,556

137	3/20	Chel	2m¹/₂f Cls1 Gd1 Hdl soft £264,610
	12/19	Kemp	2m Cls1 Gd1 Hdl soft £74,035
	11/19	Newb	2m¹/₂f Cls1 List 122-141 Hdl Hcap gd-sft.......£28,475
	2/19	Extr	2m1f Cls4 Nov Hdl gd-sft....................................£4,549
	11/18	Kemp	2m Cls4 Nov Hdl good £4,094
	11/17	StCl	1m4¹/₂f Gd1 NHF 3yo heavy.............................£21,368
	9/17	Le L	1m4f NHF 3yo v soft £7,692

Outstanding winner of the Champion Hurdle last season, putting to bed the ghosts of her sole defeat when flopping at the festival in 2019; not extended in winning three times since then, hacking up in the Christmas Hurdle before another easy victory at Cheltenham.

Eric Bloodaxe (Ire)

5 bl g Saint Des Saints - Diorissima (Sholokhov)

Joseph O'Brien (Ire)   Gigginstown House Stud

PLACINGS: 117-   RPR **131** +b

Starts	1st	2nd	3rd	4th	Win & Pl
3	2	-	-	-	£11,713

12/19	Leop	2m NHF 4-7yo yield...£6,389
12/19	Fair	2m NHF 4yo yld-sft..£5,324

Impressive winner of bumpers at Fairyhouse and Leopardstown last December, beating subsequent Cheltenham hero Ferny Hollow first time out; finished lame when well beaten in a Grade 2 at Leopardstown on final run; fine prospect for novice hurdles.

Epatante: last season's superb winner of the Champion Hurdle

Erick Le Rouge (Fr)

6 ch g Gentlewave - Imperia II (Beyssac)

Jane Williams — The Culverhill Racing Club

PLACINGS: 4452/1111P/15714-9 — RPR **146**+c

Starts	1st	2nd	3rd	4th	Win & Pl
15	6	1	-	3	£49,946

134	1/20	Kemp	2m4¹/₂f Cls3 123-141 Ch Hcap gd-sft	£8,447
	10/19	Uttx	2m4f Cls3 Ch soft	£7,018
134	2/19	Kemp	2m5f Cls3 118-134 Hdl Hcap good	£6,498
129	12/18	Kemp	2m5f Cls3 122-142 Hdl Hcap gd-sft	£12,762
119	11/18	Wwck	2m3f Cls4 101-121 Cond Hdl Hcap good	£5,198
112	10/18	Bang	2m3¹/₂f Cls4 94-120 Hdl Hcap good	£4,094

Won four of last five races over hurdles in 2018-19 and improved again when switched to fences last season; produced a career-best when winning a handicap chase at Kempton and unlucky in Grade 2 company back there next time when badly hampered by a faller.

Espoir De Guye (Fr)

6 b g Khalkevi - Penelope De Guye (Dom Alco)

Venetia Williams — Mrs J Hitchings

PLACINGS: 5172/211P- — RPR **151**+c

Starts	1st	2nd	3rd	4th	Win & Pl
8	3	2	-	-	£45,846

130	12/19	Asct	2m3f Cls2 123-145 Ch Hcap heavy	£21,896
121	12/19	Extr	2m3f Cls3 121-142 Ch Hcap soft	£10,267
	6/18	Sabl	2m3f Hdl 4yo gd-sft	£8,496

Sharply progressive novice chaser last season; got off the mark at Exeter and followed up by ten lengths in an open handicap at Ascot, going up 14lb; missed next target (had a panic attack in the horsebox) and then pulled up in the novice handicap at the Cheltenham Festival.

Esprit Du Large (Fr)

6 b g No Risk At All - Tuffslolyloly (Double Bed)

Evan Williams   Mr & Mrs William Rucker

PLACINGS: 71410/211F-   RPR **155**+c

Starts	1st	2nd	3rd	4th	Win & Pl
9	4	1	-	1	£51,063

12/19	Sand	1m7¹/₂f Cls1 Nov Gd1 Ch soft	£31,095
11/19	Extr	2m3¹/₂f Cls3 Ch soft	£7,798
3/19	Hrfd	2m3¹/₂f Cls4 Nov Hdl gd-sft	£4,094
12/18	Uttx	2m Cls4 Mdn Hdl soft	£4,094

Took really well to fences last season, winning twice including a surprise victory in a Grade 1 novice chase at Sandown (form didn't work out); subsequently kept fresh for the Racing Post Arkle but well beaten when falling two out.

Fakir (Fr)

5 b g Day Flight - Lazary (Bobinski)

Joseph O'Brien (Ire)   Gigginstown House Stud

PLACINGS: 1/5761U1-   RPR **144**+h

Starts	1st	2nd	3rd	4th	Win & Pl
7	3	-	-	-	£22,036

121	2/20	Gowr	2m4f 99-121 Hdl Hcap heavy	£8,250
	12/19	Limk	2m Nov Hdl sft-hvy	£6,655
	2/19	Fntb	1m7f NHF 4yo v soft	£6,757

Big improver when hacking up by 11 lengths on handicap debut at Gowran on final run of last season, appreciating step up to 2m4f; had been a slow learner prior to that but progressed steadily and got off the mark at Limerick; likely to go novice chasing.

Fakir D'oudairies (Fr)

5 b g Kapgarde - Niagaria Du Bois (Grand Tresor)

Joseph O'Brien (Ire)   John P McManus

PLACINGS: 4/264B1142/21122-   RPR **165**c

Starts	1st	2nd	3rd	4th	Win & Pl
14	4	5	-	3	£199,153

12/19	Fair	2m4f Nov Gd1 Ch soft	£47,838
11/19	Navn	2m1f Ch sft-hvy	£9,051
1/19	Chel	2m1f Cls1 Gd2 Hdl 4yo gd-sft	£18,006
1/19	Cork	2m Mdn Hdl 4-5yo soft	£7,492

Took really well to fences last season, winning the Drinmore over 2m4f and finishing second in two more Grade 1 races over shorter, including the Racing Post Arkle at Cheltenham; still only five and entitled to progress into a genuine Champion Chase contender.

Fanion D'Estruval (Fr)

5 b g Enrique - Urfe D'Estruval (Martaline)

Venetia Williams   David Wilson

PLACINGS: 17/11115-   RPR **151**+c

Starts	1st	2nd	3rd	4th	Win & Pl
7	5	-	-	-	£70,170

137	11/19	Newb	2m1/₂f Cls3 Nov 124-142 Ch Hcap soft	£12,449
	7/19	Autl	2m1¹/₂f Ch 4yo v soft	£22,486
	6/19	Toul	2m1¹/₂f Ch 4yo gd-sft	£9,081
	5/19	Comp	2m2f Hdl 4yo v soft	£19,459
	4/19	Angl	2m3f Hdl 4-5yo gd-sft	£5,622

Bought from France last year after winning his last three for Guillaume Macaire and immediately made a big impression when hacking up on British debut at Newbury; raised 12lb and only

Fanion D'Estruval: caught the attention with an impressive British debut at Newbury

fifth, albeit not beaten far, when favourite for a Grade 2 novice chase at Kempton behind Global Citizen.

Farclas (Fr)

6 gr g Jukebox Jury - Floriana (Seattle Dancer)

Gordon Elliott (Ire)   Gigginstown House Stud

PLACINGS: 2215/6F55P/111-   **RPR 149**h

Starts	1st	2nd	3rd	4th	Win & Pl
12	4	2	-	-	£128,502
	6/19	Rosc	2m Nov Ch good		£8,324
	5/19	Punc	2m Nov Ch good		£11,099
	5/19	DRoy	2m3¹/₂f Ch good		£6,659
	3/18	Chel	2m1f Cls1 Gd1 Hdl 4yo soft		£71,188

Won the Triumph Hurdle in 2018 but failed to make any impression in open company subsequently; got back to winning ways over fences last summer, winning three times, only to miss the rest of the season through injury.

Faugheen (Ire)

12 b g Germany - Miss Pickering (Accordion)

Willie Mullins (Ire)   Mrs S Ricci

PLACINGS: 211/1P261/2F3P/1113-   **RPR 166**c

Starts	1st	2nd	3rd	4th	Win & Pl
26	17	3	2	-	£1,116,678
	2/20	Leop	2m5f Nov Gd1 Ch yield		£75,000
	12/19	Limk	2m3¹/₂f Nov Gd1 Ch heavy		£53,153
	11/19	Punc	2m4f Ch soft		£7,720
	4/18	Punc	3m Gd1 Hdl yld-sft		£143,584
	11/17	Punc	2m Gd1 Hdl sft-hvy		£42,863
	1/16	Leop	2m Gd1 Hdl soft		£48,529
	12/15	Kemp	2m Cls1 Gd1 Hdl gd-sft		£56,950
	5/15	Punc	2m Gd1 Hdl gd-yld		£93,023
	3/15	Chel	2m1¹/₂f Cls1 Gd1 Hdl gd-sft		£227,800
	12/14	Kemp	2m Cls1 Gd1 Hdl gd-sft		£57,218
	11/14	Asct	2m3¹/₂f Cls1 Hdl soft		£50,643
	4/14	Punc	2m Nov Gd1 Hdl gd-yld		£46,500
	3/14	Chel	2m5f Cls1 Nov Gd1 Hdl good		£68,340
	12/13	Limk	3m Nov Gd3 Hdl heavy		£15,061
	12/13	Navn	2m4f Nov Hdl gd-yld		£7,293
	11/13	Punc	2m6f Mdn Hdl yield		£7,293
	5/13	Punc	2m NHF 5yo yield		£4,488

Former Champion Hurdle winner who is now very much in the veteran stage but surprised plenty of observers with a fine novice campaign over fences last season; won two Grade 1 races at around 2m4f and not beaten far when third in the Marsh at Cheltenham.

Ferny Hollow (Ire)

5 b/br g Westerner - Mirazur (Good Thyne)

Willie Mullins (Ire)   Cheveley Park Stud

PLACINGS: 1/2211-   **RPR 141+**b

Starts	1st	2nd	3rd	4th	Win & Pl
4	2	2	-	-	£50,988
	3/20	Chel	2m¹/₂f Cls1 Gd1 NHF 4-6yo soft		£42,203
	2/20	Fair	2m NHF 5-7yo heavy		£5,000

Impressive winner of last season's Champion Bumper at Cheltenham, storming home from

---

almost last to beat Appreciate It; had taken time to come good (beaten at odds-on in first two runs) before improving when applied with a hood; top hurdling prospect.

Fiddlerontheroof (Ire)

6 b g Stowaway - Inquisitive Look (Montjeu)

Colin Tizzard   Taylor, Burley & O'Dwyer

PLACINGS: 4/5321/22110-   **RPR 152+**h

Starts	1st	2nd	3rd	4th	Win & Pl
8	3	3	1	-	£52,521
	1/20	Sand	2m Cls1 Nov Gd1 Hdl soft		£28,475
	12/19	Sand	2m Cls3 Nov Hdl heavy		£6,256
	3/19	Navn	2m NHF 5-7yo soft		£5,827

Impressive winner of last season's Tolworth Hurdle at Sandown, albeit in a weak race for the grade; well below best when tailed off in the Supreme; strong stayer at 2m, with both wins over the trip coming on soft/heavy ground, and could benefit from returning to further.

First Flow (Ire)

8 b g Primary - Clonroche Wells (Pierre)

Kim Bailey   A N Solomons

PLACINGS: 4/4111P/5/22112111-   **RPR 156+**c

Starts	1st	2nd	3rd	4th	Win & Pl
15	7	4		2	£72,977
	3/20	Carl	2m Cls3 Nov Ch heavy		£9,747
	2/20	Donc	2m¹/₂f Cls4 Nov Ch heavy		£4,289
141	2/20	Leic	2m Cls3 Nov 125-141 Ch Hcap heavy		£6,498
	12/19	Hrfd	2m Cls3 Nov Ch soft		£8,769
	1/18	Hayd	1m7¹/₂f Cls1 Nov Gd2 Hdl heavy		£17,085
	12/17	Newb	2m¹/₂f Cls4 Hdl heavy		£4,549
	11/17	Ling	2m Cls4 Nov Hdl soft		£5,198

Kept busy last season and won four novice chases, albeit all in small fields (no bigger than four) at odds-on; beaten favourite in three of four other runs and well beaten by Angels Breath in toughest test; said to need soft ground and kept away from anything quicker since bumper days.

Fitzhenry (Ire)

8 b g Flemensfirth - She Took A Tree (Sri Pekan)

Paul Nolan (Ire)   John P McManus

PLACINGS: 5321212/6334/532206-   **RPR 147**c

Starts	1st	2nd	3rd	4th	Win & Pl
22	5	4	2		£133,026
123	2/18	Naas	2m4f Nov 116-137 Ch Hcap soft		£26,106
116	12/17	Thur	2m4¹/₂f 105-121 Ch Hcap heavy		£9,740

Hasn't won since February 2018 but has been knocking on the door in some top staying handicaps; particularly unlucky not to win last season's Paddy Power Chase at Leopardstown when nailed on the line (had been third in the same race in 2018).

Five O'Clock (Fr)

5 b g Cokoriko - Rodika (Kapgarde)

Willie Mullins (Ire)   Mrs S Ricci

PLACINGS: 0/32/2117-   RPR **143**+h

Starts	1st	2nd	3rd	4th	Win & Pl
7	2	2	1	-	£47,940
	2/20 Thur	2m5f Nov Gd3 Hdl soft			£25,000
	1/20 Limk	2m Mdn Hdl sft-hvy			£5,509

French recruit who won two novice hurdles last season, most impressively when stepped up to 2m5f to win a Grade 3 at Thurles by six lengths; had a troubled passage when seventh in the Martin Pipe at Cheltenham; looks a staying chaser in the making.

Forest Bihan (Fr)

9 ch g Forestier - Katell Bihan (Funny Baby)

Brian Ellison   Phil & Julie Martin

PLACINGS: 152/1P346/3F3247/31-   RPR **160**+c

Starts	1st	2nd	3rd	4th	Win & Pl
31	6	5	7	3	£200,753
149	10/19 Aint	2m4f Cls1 Gd2 149-169 Ch Hcap soft			£45,016
	3/18 Newc	2m¹/₂f Cls3 NHF stand			£6,498
154	10/17 Kels	2m1f Cls2 128-154 Ch Hcap good			£18,582
	1/17 Donc	2m²/₂f Cls3 Nov Ch good			£20,554
	1/17 Newc	2m¹/₂f Cls4 Nov Ch soft			£4,549
	11/16 Towc	2m Cls3 Nov Ch good			£7,220
	11/14 Engh	2m1¹/₂f Hdl 3yo heavy			£20,000

Produced a career-best performance to win last season's Old Roan Chase from Kalashnikov; hadn't won in more than two years over fences prior to that, though, and might have been helped by several fences being omitted; missed the rest of the season through injury.

Francin (Fr)

7 b g Air Chief Marshal - Fulgence (Cardoun)

Willie Mullins (Ire)   Mrs S Ricci

PLACINGS: 3/6311-   RPR **146**+h

Starts	1st	2nd	3rd	4th	Win & Pl
5	2	2	1	-	£19,947
	3/20 Navn	2m6¹/₂f Nov Hdl heavy			£11,000
	2/20 Navn	2m Mdn Hdl heavy			£6,500

French Flat winner who developed into a very useful novice hurdler last season; took time to find form after missing nearly two years but got off the mark over 2m and took a big step forward when following up over 2m6½f; looks an exciting young staying prospect.

Fred (Fr)

5 b/br g Cokoriko - Veribelle (Voix Du Nord)

Nicky Henderson   Simon Munir & Isaac Souede

PLACINGS: 9222/3311-   RPR **139**h

Starts	1st	2nd	3rd	4th	Win & Pl
8	2	3	2	-	£51,299
	2/20 Muss	1m7¹/₂f Cls2 Nov Hdl soft			£12,996
	12/19 Kemp	2m Cls2 Nov Hdl soft			£13,763

Useful novice hurdler last season, winning Class 2

novices at Kempton and Musselburgh at around 2m; rider subsequently felt he would improve again on a more galloping track; had looked a non-stayer when only third (beaten favourite) over 2m3½f at Ascot.

Frodon (Fr)

8 b g Nickname - Miss Country (Country Reel)

Paul Nicholls   P J Vogt

PLACINGS: 32321350/12111-3314-   RPR **167**+c

Starts	1st	2nd	3rd	4th	Win & Pl
35	14	3	7	2	£785,424
	1/20 Kemp	2m4¹/₂f Cls1 Gd2 Ch gd-sft			£34,170
	3/19 Chel	2m4¹/₂f Cls1 Gd1 Ch gd-sft			£196,945
	1/19 Chel	3m1¹/₂f Cls1 Gd2 Ch gd-sft			£56,536
164	12/18 Chel	2m4¹/₂f Cls1 Gd3 138-164 Ch Hcap good			£74,035
158	10/18 Chel	2m4f Cls1 Gd2 138-158 Ch Hcap good			£45,016
154	1/18 Chel	2m5f Cls1 Gd3 131-154 Ch Hcap heavy			£42,713
	2/17 Kemp	2m4¹/₂f Cls1 Nov Gd2 Ch good			£18,793
	2/17 Muss	2m4f Cls3 Nov Ch good			£7,798
149	12/16 Chel	2m5f Cls1 Gd3 132-158 Ch Hcap soft			£56,950
	11/16 Winc	2m4f Cls1 Nov Gd2 Ch good			£28,486
	9/16 Font	2m4f Cls4 Nov Ch good			£5,198
	9/16 NAbb	2m¹/₂f Cls3 Nov Ch good			£7,187
	2/16 Hayd	1m7¹/₂f Cls2 Hdl 4yo heavy			£9,747
	4/15 Autl	1m7f Hdl 3yo heavy			£20,465

Fairytale winner of the Ryanair Chase in 2019, extending his remarkable record at Cheltenham; never quite in the same form last season despite winning a Grade 2 chase at Kempton; beaten 15 lengths into fourth when bidding for a repeat in the Ryanair in March.

Front View (Fr)

5 gr g Konig Turf - Turnavue (Dom Alco)

Joseph O'Brien (Ire)   John P McManus

PLACINGS: 2B/12120-   RPR **139**+h

Starts	1st	2nd	3rd	4th	Win & Pl
7	2	3	-	-	£27,684
	11/19 Cork	2m Mdn Hdl 4yo soft			£6,922
	4/19 Punc	2m1¹/₂f NHF 4yo yld-sft			£8,324

Big gamble in last season's Martin Pipe Hurdle at Cheltenham when sent off 4-1 favourite but finished only in midfield (might have struggled to cope with big field); had looked a useful and progressive novice prior to that, finishing second in a 2m5f Grade 3 at Thurles.

Fujimoto Flyer (Jpn)

4 b f Admire Moon - Picture Princess (Sadler's Wells)

Emmet Mullins (Ire)   Simon Munir & Isaac Souede

PLACINGS: 112-FU   RPR **122**+h

Starts	1st	2nd	3rd	4th	Win & Pl
5	2	1	-	-	£45,765
	9/19 Autl	2m2f List Hdl 3yo v.soft			£32,432
	8/19 Klny	2m1f Hdl 3yo yld-sft			£6,922

Impressive winner of first two starts over hurdles last summer, notably when boldly placed to win a Listed hurdle at Auteuil by nine lengths; put in her place by Solo in the Adonis Hurdle after a long break when too keen in a first-time hood; could do better in a strongly run race.

Fury Road (Ire)

6 b g Stowaway - Molly Duffy (Oscar)

Gordon Elliott (Ire)   Gigginstown House Stud

PLACINGS: 4151/311143-					RPR **152**h
Starts	1st	2nd	3rd	4th	Win & Pl
8	4	-	2	1	£96,540

12/19	Limk	2m7f Nov Gd2 Hdl heavy	£39,865
11/19	Navn	2m4f Nov Gd3 Hdl soft	£22,590
11/19	DRoy	2m6f Mdn Hdl yld-sft	£7,986
2/19	Fair	2m NHF 5-7yo gd-yld	£5,550

Won first three novice hurdles last season and went on to run a huge race in the Albert Bartlett at Cheltenham; relished a much stiffer test of stamina after looking inconvenienced by a lack of pace when fourth behind Latest Exhibition at Leopardstown.

Fusil Raffles (Fr)

5 b g Saint Des Saints - Tali Des Obeaux (Panoramic I)

Nicky Henderson   Simon Munir & Isaac Souede

PLACINGS: 121/11P0-1					RPR **148**+c
Starts	1st	2nd	3rd	4th	Win & Pl
8	5	1	-	-	£119,293

9/20	Uttx	2m Cls4 Nov Ch good	£4,289
11/19	Winc	1m7'½f Cls1 Gd2 Hdl gd-sft	£34,572
5/19	Punc	2m Gd1 Hdl 4yo gd-yld	£53,153
2/19	Kemp	2m Cls1 Gd2 Hdl 4yo good	£17,085
7/18	Seno	2m2f Hdl 3yo soft	£5,947

French recruit who won both starts as a juvenile for current connections, including a Grade I at Punchestown, and completed a hat-trick in the Elite Hurdle last season; well beaten on both later starts, including when 11th in the Champion Hurdle; looks a bright novice chase prospect this season.

Galahad Quest (Fr)

4 b g American Post - Atacames (Dom Alco)

Nick Williams   Holt, Macnabb, Robinson & Jeffrey

PLACINGS: 4210-					RPR **121**+h
Starts	1st	2nd	3rd	4th	Win & Pl
4	1	1	-	1	£20,081

1/20	Chel	2m1f Cls1 Gd2 Hdl 4yo soft	£18,224

Won a Grade 2 juvenile hurdle at Cheltenham last season but probably dropped lucky in a weak race for the grade and well beaten on only subsequent run in the Fred Winter; bought as a staying chaser and should progress when stepped up in trip.

Galvin (Ire)

6 b g Gold Well - Burren Moonshine (Moonax)

Gordon Elliott (Ire)   R A Bartlett

PLACINGS: 1111162/F422-111					RPR **155**+c
Starts	1st	2nd	3rd	4th	Win & Pl
14	8	3	-	1	£79,706

10/20	Tipp	2m4f Nov Gd3 Ch good	£13,750
8/20	Klny	2m5f Nov Ch yield	£6,250
7/20	Klny	2m5f Ch yield	£6,250
2/19	Ayr	2m Cls4 Nov Hdl soft	£4,094
1/19	Navn	2m Nov Hdl yield	£8,879
8/18	Prth	2m Cls4 Mdn Hdl good	£4,549
7/18	Limk	2m NHF 4-7yo gd-yld	£5,996
7/18	Rosc	2m NHF 4-7yo good	£5,451

Useful hurdler (sixth in the Ballymore) who took time to come good over fences last season but produced a massive run when second in the novice handicap at the Cheltenham Festival (well backed); finally off the mark at Killarney in July and retains novice status.

Get In The Queue

6 b g Mount Nelson - Amarullah (Daylami)

Harry Fry   Masterson Holdings

PLACINGS: 111/					RPR **137**b
Starts	1st	2nd	3rd	4th	Win & Pl
3	3	-	-	-	£34,053

3/19	Newb	2m'½f Cls2 NHF 4-5yo gd-sft	£29,505
2/19	Extr	2m1f Cls5 NHF 4-6yo gd-sft	£2,274
12/18	Uttx	2m Cls5 NHF 4-6yo soft	£2,274

Missed last season through injury but had looked a future star when winning all three bumpers in 2018-19, most notably when hacking up by 16 lengths at Exeter under a penalty; well backed for the Champion Bumper but instead kept to calmer waters when winning a valuable sales bumper at Newbury.

Getabird (Ire)

8 b g Getaway - Fern Bird (Revoque)

Willie Mullins (Ire)   Mrs S Ricci

PLACINGS: 01/11/11017P/12/P1-					RPR **144**+c
Starts	1st	2nd	3rd	4th	Win & Pl
12	7	1	-	-	£102,183

11/19	Gowr	2m4f Ch heavy	£10,649
12/18	Punc	2m Ch yield	£7,632
4/18	Fair	2m Nov Gd2 Hdl heavy	£26,106
1/18	Punc	2m Nov Gd2 Hdl sft-hvy	£23,235
12/17	Punc	2m4f Mdn Hdl heavy	£6,844
1/17	Gowr	2m NHF 5-7yo soft	£6,833
12/16	Fair	2m NHF 4yo gd-yld	£4,070

Long held in high regard (sent off just 7-4 for the

Supreme Novices' Hurdle in 2018) but has run just twice since the end of that year, missing the rest of last season after a winning reappearance; still totally unexposed over fences; best going right-handed.

Getaway Trump (Ire)

7 b g Getaway - Acinorev (Cape Cross)

Paul Nicholls   Owners Group

PLACINGS: /146/41124411/33P-31					RPR **150**c
Starts	1st	2nd	3rd	4th	Win & Pl
15	5	1	3	4	£109,041
147	10/20 Wwck	2m Cls4 Ch good			£4,289
	4/19 Sand	2m Cls2 Nov 122-147 Hdl Hcap good			£61,900
	4/19 Ayr	2m Cls3 Nov Hdl good			£9,942
	12/18 Extr	2m1f Cls4 Nov Hdl 4-6yo heavy			£4,874
	11/18 Plum	2m4¹/₂f Cls4 Nov Hdl good			£4,094

Picked out by his trainer as a leading prospect for novice chases last season but managed only third in two runs, albeit running well both times, before being pulled up back over hurdles; had won four times as a novice hurdler two seasons ago and could yet make the grade over fences.

Give Me A Copper (Ire)

10 ch g Presenting - Copper Supreme (Supreme Leader)

Paul Nicholls   Done, Ferguson, Mason, Nicholls & Wood

PLACINGS: 11/161/U1/4F4/17-					RPR **150**+c
Starts	1st	2nd	3rd	4th	Win & Pl
11	5	-	-	2	£66,987
142	11/19 Winc	3m1f Cls1 List 130-150 Ch Hcap gd-sft			£34,170
	11/17 Kemp	3m Cls3 Nov Ch good			£8,133
	4/17 Ayr	2m4¹/₂f Cls3 Nov Hdl gd-sft			£6,498
	12/16 Extr	2m7f Cls4 Mdn Hdl soft			£3,249
	3/16 Cork	2m3f NHF 5-7yo heavy			£4,296

Very lightly raced for his age having had progress over fences hampered by injuries, missing more than a year after novice win in 2017; steady improver in big staying handicaps since returning and won last season's Badger Beers Trophy only to disappoint next time at Ascot.

Glen Rocco

9 ch g Shirocco - Adees Dancer (Danehill Dancer)

Nick Gifford   Kyle, Mason, Brooks, Ferguson & Stevens

PLACINGS: P/1/653/U13216/					RPR **143**c
Starts	1st	2nd	3rd	4th	Win & Pl
9	2	1	2	-	£26,609
124	1/19 Kemp	3m Cls2 124-148 Ch Hcap good			£11,574
109	11/18 Font	2m5¹/₂f Cls4 Nov 101-120 Ch Hcap gd-sft			£7,216

Missed last season through injury but improved massively in 2018-19 when stepped

up to 3m, running away with a handicap chase at Kempton by 23 lengths; outpaced in sixth when favourite for a valuable handicap back there next time; was bought as a Grand National horse.

Glenloe (Ire)

9 br g Kayf Tara - Mandys Native (Be My Native)

Gordon Elliott (Ire)   John P McManus

PLACINGS: 7/6515/22325/54/534-					RPR **142**+c
Starts	1st	2nd	3rd	4th	Win & Pl
15	1	3	2	2	£53,937
	12/16 Navn	2m7f Mdn Hdl sft-hvy			£5,653

Favourite for last season's Kim Muir at Cheltenham until ruled out through injury; yet to win since 2016, including in five runs over fences, but well handicapped on smart hurdles form (beaten a nose by Delta Work when favourite for Pertemps Final in 2018).

Global Citizen (Ire)

8 b g Alkaadhem - Lady Willmurt (Mandalus)

Ben Pauling   The Megsons

PLACINGS: 1/152116/21417/414-					RPR **154**c
Starts	1st	2nd	3rd	4th	Win & Pl
14	6	2	-	3	£152,349
	12/19 Kemp	2m Cls1 Nov Gd2 Ch soft			£22,780
	1/19 Hayd	1m7¹/₂f Cls1 Gd2 Hdl gd-sft			£42,713
146	12/18 Newb	2m¹/₂f Cls1 List 126-146 Hdl Hcap soft			£28,475
	2/18 Kemp	2m Cls1 Nov Gd2 Hdl good			£17,085
	2/18 Sthl	1m7¹/₂f Cls4 Nov Hdl good			£4,094
	10/17 Worc	2m Cls6 NHF 4-6yo gd-fm			£1,689

High-class novice chaser last season; made all the running to win a highly competitive Grade 2 at Kempton, adding to two wins over hurdles at that level; did well to finish fourth in the Racing Post Arkle having missed the break from a standing start and been hampered four out.

Good Boy Bobby (Ire)

7 b g Flemensfirth - Princess Gaia (King's Theatre)

Nigel Twiston-Davies   Paul & Clare Rooney

PLACINGS: 1131/1311/2125-					RPR **157**c
Starts	1st	2nd	3rd	4th	Win & Pl
12	7	2	2	-	£35,074
	11/19 Weth	1m7f Cls4 Nov Ch soft			£4,938
	4/19 Ffos	2m4f Cls4 Nov Hdl soft			£4,094
	3/19 Sthl	1m7¹/₂f Cls4 Nov Hdl good			£3,249
	10/18 Carl	2m1f Cls4 Nov Hdl gd-sft			£4,549
	3/18 Weth	2m Cls2 NHF 4-6yo heavy			£2,599
	1/18 Chep	2m Cls5 NHF 5-7yo heavy			£2,599
	11/17 Chep	2m Cls6 NHF 4-6yo soft			£1,949

Prolific in bumpers and novice hurdles, winning three of each, and improved again over fences

last season despite winning just once; just beaten by two high-class opponents in Brewin'upastorm and Mister Fisher before a below-par fifth behind Itchy Feet in the Scilly Isles.

Goshen (Fr)

4 b g Authorized - Hyde (Poliglote)

Gary Moore   Steven Packham

PLACINGS: 111U-					RPR **156+**h

Starts	1st	2nd	3rd	4th		Win & Pl
4	3	-	-	-		£23,623
	1/20	Asct	1m7¹/₂f Cls3 Hdl 4yo heavy			£7,018
	12/19	Sand	2m Cls2 Hdl 3yo soft			£12,512
	11/19	Font	2m1¹/₂f Cls4 Hdl 3yo soft			£4,094

Outstanding juvenile hurdler of last season who would have been a runaway winner of the Triumph Hurdle but for unseating his rider at the last; had won all three previous starts over hurdles; leading Champion Hurdle hope.

Grand Sancy (Fr)

6 b g Diamond Boy - La Courtille (Risk Seeker)

Paul Nicholls   Martin Broughton Racing Partners

PLACINGS: 4P/12114210/F23341-1					RPR **157+**c

Starts	1st	2nd	3rd	4th		Win & Pl
21	6	6	2	4		£143,015
	10/20	Chep	2m3¹/₂f Cls1 Nov List Ch good			£11,546
	2/20	Font	2m3¹/₂f Cls3 Ch soft			£9,068
	2/19	Winc	1m7¹/₂f Cls1 Gd2 Hdl good			£34,170
	11/18	Hayd	1m7¹/₂f Cls1 Nov List Hdl good			£14,238
	11/18	Winc	1m7¹/₂f Cls3 Nov Hdl 4-6yo good			£6,498
125	10/18	Chep	2m Cls2 121-132 Hdl 4yo Hcap good			£12,996

Dropped sharply in class to gain sole win at 1-5 at Fontwell last season having been very

highly tried prior to that; exposed as just below the best over hurdles and pitched straight into Graded company over fences, doing best when third behind Global Citizen at Kempton.

Greaneteen (Fr)

6 b g Great Pretender - Manson Teene (Mansonnien)

Paul Nicholls   Chris Giles

PLACINGS: 3/611/01114-					RPR **156**c

Starts	1st	2nd	3rd	4th		Win & Pl
9	5	-	1	1		£49,737
	2/20	Fknm	2m1¹/₂f Nov Ch soft			£8,058
138	2/20	Muss	2m Cls3 124-140 Ch Hcap gd-sft			£13,256
132	12/19	Asct	2m1f Cls3 Nov 119-132 Ch Hcap heavy			£10,007
	1/19	Font	2m1¹/₂f Cls4 Nov Hdl gd-sft			£4,094
	1/19	Extr	2m2¹/₂f Cls4 Mdn Hdl gd-sft			£4,549

Hugely progressive over the last two seasons, especially when switched to fences last season; won first three chases and coped well with sharp rise in class to finish fourth in the Grand Annual (best of British-trained runners) despite blundering two out; raised just 1lb.

Gumball (Fr)

6 gr g No Risk At All - Good Time Girl (Slickly)

Philip Hobbs   Terry Warner

PLACINGS: /1122P21/49/312600-3					RPR **154**h

Starts	1st	2nd	3rd	4th		Win & Pl
17	4	4	3	1		£112,286
139	11/19	Asct	1m7¹/₂f Cls1 List 119-145 Hdl Hcap gd-sft			£34,170
	4/18	Ludl	2m Cls4 Nov Hdl good			£4,874
	10/17	Chep	2m Cls4 Hdl 3yo good			£5,198
	10/17	Strf	2m¹/₂f Cls4 Hdl 3yo good			£3,899

Flourished in good handicap hurdles early last

Goshen: regarded by many as a likely big player in the Champion Hurdle

season, winning at Ascot and finishing a neck second in the Greatwood; raised 15lb for those runs and struggled subsequently, twice coming up short in top conditions races and failing to land a blow in the Betfair Hurdle.

Happy Diva (Ire)

9 b m King's Theatre - Megans Joy (Supreme Leader)

Kerry Lee · Will Roseff

PLACINGS: 21121/2B231U2/21242- · RPR **154**c

Starts	1st	2nd	3rd	4th	Win & Pl
33	7	15	3	2	£294,709
143	11/19	Chel	2m4f Cls1 Gd3 130-152 Ch Hcap soft		£90,032
	1/19	Hntg	2m4f Cls1 List Ch gd-sft		£42,914
	3/18	Asct	2m5f Cls3 Nov Ch soft		£10,007
	2/18	Bang	2m4¹/₂f Cls4 Nov Ch heavy		£5,458
	1/18	Ludl	2m4f Cls3 Nov Ch gd-sft		£7,722
121	1/17	Weth	3m Cls4 100-121 Hdl Hcap gd-sft		£3,899
114	12/16	Font	2m5¹/₂f Cls4 94-117 Hdl Hcap gd-sft		£3,899

Hugely popular mare who proved particularly well suited to big-field handicaps last season, winning the BetVictor Gold Cup and finishing second to Simply The Betts in the Plate; also beaten just a head by Lady Buttons in a Listed mares' chase at Doncaster.

Harambe

7 br g Malinas - Crystal Princess (Definite Article)

Alan King · Niall Farrell & Friends

PLACINGS: 123/B244112/71B- · RPR **143+**h

Starts	1st	2nd	3rd	4th	Win & Pl
13	4	3	1	2	£94,911
137	11/19	Chel	2m1¹/₂f Cls1 Gd3 123-149 Hdl Hcap soft		£56,270
	4/19	MRas	2m2¹/₂f Cls4 Nov Hdl good		£4,549
	3/19	Kemp	2m Cls4 Nov Hdl gd-sft		£4,159
	12/17	Ludl	1m6f Cls4 NHF 4-5yo soft		£3,899

Progressive hurdler who won last season's Greatwood Hurdle at Cheltenham, staying on strongly to get up close home; raised 7lb but still looked set to go close in the Betfair Hurdle on only subsequent run until brought down at the last.

Hardline (Ire)

8 b g Arcadio - Hidden Reserve (Heron Island)

Gordon Elliott (Ire) · Gigginstown House Stud

PLACINGS: 1138/121137/232F43-F · RPR **161**c

Starts	1st	2nd	3rd	4th	Win & Pl
29	8	6	7	1	£220,403
	12/18	Limk	2m3¹/₂f Nov Gd1 Ch soft		£52,212
	12/18	Navn	2m1f Nov Gd3 Ch yield		£20,409
	10/18	Fair	2m Ch good		£6,542
	2/18	Naas	2m Nov Gd2 Hdl soft		£24,279
	2/18	Navn	2m Nov List Hdl heavy		£17,688
	11/17	Clon	2m¹/₂f Hdl sft-hvy		£6,844
	10/17	Wxfd	2m Mdn Hdl heavy		£5,791
	11/16	Thur	2m NHF 4-7yo good		£4,070

Smart chaser from 2m-2m4f but hasn't won since a Grade 1 novice chase at Limerick in December 2018; came up short in top company last season and flattered to get close to Min when second in the John Durkan Chase (winner jumped badly).

Harry Senior (Ire)

6 b g Oscar - Surf Like A Lady (Presenting)

Colin Tizzard · Brocade Racing

PLACINGS: 33/42211P- · RPR **144+**h

Starts	1st	2nd	3rd	4th	Win & Pl
7	2	2	1	1	£26,753
	1/20	Chel	2m4¹/₂f Cls1 Nov Gd2 Hdl soft		£18,224
	12/19	Chep	2m3¹/₂f Cls4 Mdn Hdl heavy		£3,769

Progressed into a very useful novice hurdler last season, taking four attempts to get off the mark but then winning a strong Grade 2 at Cheltenham; bred to stay and subsequently stepped up in trip for the Albert Bartlett but soon pulled up after an early blunder.

Highest Sun (Fr)

6 b g Sunday Break - Highest Price (Highest Honor)

Colin Tizzard · Ashley Head

PLACINGS: 1/34210/3321457- · RPR **144+**c

Starts	1st	2nd	3rd	4th	Win & Pl
13	3	2	3	2	£34,069
	12/19	Plum	3m1¹/₂f Cls3 Nov Ch heavy		£7,343
131	2/19	Chep	2m Cls3 117-137 Hdl Hcap gd-sft		£5,718
	4/18	Chat	2m1f Hdl 4yo v soft		£8,496

Began well over fences last season when placed behind Champ and Pym before winning a match against Diablo De Rouhet; regressed subsequently, managing only fourth when favourite for a Grade 2 at Warwick and seventh in the novice handicap chase at the Cheltenham Festival.

Highway One O Two (Ire)

5 b/br g Shirocco - Supreme Dreamer (Supreme Leader)

Chris Gordon · Anthony Ward-Thomas

PLACINGS: 50/24111- · RPR **143+**h

Starts	1st	2nd	3rd	4th	Win & Pl
7	3	1	-	1	£27,859
	2/20	Kemp	2m Cls1 Nov Gd2 Hdl gd-sft		£17,085
	1/20	Plum	2m Cls4 Nov Hdl soft		£5,393
	12/19	Plum	2m Cls4 Nov Hdl heavy		£4,094

Unbeaten in three runs over hurdles last season, including the Grade 2 Dovecote at Kempton (form questionable with none of the field having run at that level but won comfortably); had schooled over fences last season and could go novice chasing.

Hogan's Height (Ire)

9 b g Indian River - Electre Du Berlais (Royal Charter)

Jamie Snowden · Foxtrot Racing: Hogan's Height

PLACINGS: 26/2721116/3P11/715- · RPR **151+**c

Starts	1st	2nd	3rd	4th	Win & Pl
17	6	3	1		£92,667
134	12/19	Aint	2m5f Cls2 126-152 Ch Hcap soft		£49,520
	2/19	Catt	3m1¹/₂f Cls4 Nov Hdl good		£4,926
	1/19	Catt	2m3¹/₂f Cls4 Nov Hdl good		£4,809
131	3/18	Hayd	2m4¹/₂f Cls3 Nov 118-131 Ch Hcap soft		£9,747
	1/18	Weth	2m3¹/₂f Cls4 Nov Ch soft		£4,679
	12/17	Ludl	2m4f Cls3 Nov Ch gd-sft		£11,078

Raced very sparingly over fences in recent

seasons but had been a successful novice in 2017-18 (won three times) and bolted up by 16 lengths over the Grand National fences in last season's Grand Sefton; 12lb higher mark puts him in National picture.

Hold The Note (Ire)

6 b g Jeremy - Keys Hope (Luso)

Mick Channon · T P Radford

PLACINGS: 14312/3P23-					RPR **151 + c**
Starts	1st	2nd	3rd	4th	Win & Pl
9	2	2	3	1	£25,403
	12/18 Donc	2m3¹/₂f Cls4 Nov Hdl 4-6yo good			£4,094
	10/18 NAbb	2m1f Cls5 NHF 4-6yo heavy			£2,395

Useful novice chaser last season despite failing to win; just beaten in a 3m Grade 2 at Warwick (outstayed after travelling best) and then stayed on into a fine third in the novice handicap chase at the Cheltenham Festival; could win good novice chases or handicaps.

Honeysuckle

6 b m Sulamani - First Royal (Lando)

Henry De Bromhead (Ire) · Kenneth Alexander

PLACINGS: 1/1111/1111-					RPR **160 + h**
Starts	1st	2nd	3rd	4th	Win & Pl
8	8	-	-	-	£334,427
	3/20 Chel	2m4f Cls1 Gd1 Hdl soft			£67,524
	2/20 Leop	2m Gd1 Hdl yield			£94,915
	12/19 Fair	2m4f Gd1 Hdl yld-sft			£66,441
	11/19 Fair	2m4f Hdl heavy			£9,318
	4/19 Fair	2m4f Nov Gd1 Hdl gd-yld			£53,153
	1/19 Fair	2m2f Nov Gd3 Hdl yield			£19,392
	12/18 Thur	2m Nov List Hdl good			£17,688
	11/18 Fair	2m4f Mdn Hdl good			£5,996

Magnificent unbeaten mare who made it eight out of eight under rules when claiming the scalp of Benie Des Dieux in the Mares' Hurdle at Cheltenham; also dropped to 2m to beat the boys in the Irish Champion Hurdle, though seemingly better over further; set to stay over hurdles.

I K Brunel

6 b g Midnight Legend - Somethinaboutmolly (Choisir)

Olly Murphy · McNeill Family & Prodec Networks

PLACINGS: 136/1841-2					RPR **137 + c**
Starts	1st	2nd	3rd	4th	Win & Pl
8	3	1	1	1	£21,383
	2/20 Muss	3m Cls2 Nov Hdl soft			£12,512
	10/19 Font	2m3f Cls5 Mdn Hdl soft			£2,794
	11/18 Carl	2m1f Cls5 NHF 4-6yo soft			£2,599

Long held in high regard but had twice flopped in Grade 2 novice hurdles either side of maiden win

Ibleo (Fr)

7 b g Dick Turpin - Mahendra (Next Desert)

Venetia Williams · The Bellamy Partnership

PLACINGS: 719/8/112-					RPR **141 + c**
Starts	1st	2nd	3rd	4th	Win & Pl
7	3	2	1		£26,505
118	2/20 Hntg	2m1¹/₂f Cls4 Nov 117-118 Ch Hcap heavy			£6,498
112	1/20 Winc	1m7¹/₂f Cls4 Nov 95-117 Ch Hcap soft			£7,473
	6/16 Comp	2m1f Hdl 3yo v soft			£7,765

Won first two races over fences last season following more than two years out, landing novice handicaps at Wincanton and Huntingdon; ran well in hat-trick bid when second under 12st 4lb back at Huntingdon, coping with step up to 2m4f; open to further improvement.

If The Cap Fits (Ire)

8 b g Milan - Derravaragh Sayra (Sayarshan)

Harry Fry · Simon Munir & Isaac Souede

PLACINGS: 114/111/21321/15-					RPR **164 + h**
Starts	1st	2nd	3rd	4th	Win & Pl
13	8	2	1	1	£287,211
	11/19 Asct	2m3¹/₂f Cls1 Gd2 Hdl soft			£56,950
	4/19 Aint	3m1¹/₂f Cls1 Gd1 Hdl good			£101,034
	11/18 Asct	2m3¹/₂f Cls1 Gd2 Hdl gd-sft			£56,950
	12/17 Kemp	2m Cls2 Nov Hdl gd-sft			£12,512
	11/17 Bang	2m1f Cls4 Nov Hdl soft			£3,249
	10/17 Extr	2m2¹/₂f Cls4 Nov Hdl good			£3,899
	2/17 Tntn	2m3¹/₂f Cls5 Am NHF 4-6yo good			£3,184
	11/16 Plum	2m1¹/₂f Cls6 NHF 4-5yo gd-sft			£1,625

Developed into a high-class stayer two seasons ago, winning a Grade 1 at Aintree; had rather a wasted campaign last season, winning a second successive Ascot Hurdle but skipping the Stayers' Hurdle in order to wait for Aintree again after a disappointing run in the Cleeve; bright novice chase prospect after winning start at Ffos Las.

Imperial Aura (Ire)

7 b g Kalanisi - Missindependence (Executive Perk)

Kim Bailey · Imperial Racing Partnership

PLACINGS: 31/11/31221-					RPR **160 + c**
Starts	1st	2nd	3rd	4th	Win & Pl
9	5	2	2	-	£83,594
143	3/20 Chel	2m4f Cls1 Nov List 138-145 Ch Hcap soft			£39,389
	11/19 Fknm	3m Cls3 Ch good			£13,666
	2/19 Newc	2m4¹/₂f Cls3 Nov Hdl gd-sft			£5,718
	10/18 Carl	2m3¹/₂f Cls4 Nov Hdl good			£4,874
	4/18 Ludl	2m Cls4 NHF 4-6yo soft			£3,899

Excelled in the two best novice handicap

If The Cap Fits: winning start over fences and looks a smart prospect

chases of last season at Cheltenham; second to subsequent Plate winner Simply The Betts in January before winning at the festival from big gamble Galvin (pair clear); up 14lb for that win; didn't appear to stay 3m1½f when second at Cheltenham in December.

Indefatigable (Ire)

7 b m Schiaparelli - Spin The Wheel (Kalanisi)

Paul Webber   Philip Rocher

PLACINGS: 31/712251/522311-					RPR **147**h
Starts	1st	2nd	3rd	4th	Win & Pl
14	5	4	2	-	£109,573
145	3/20	Chel	2m4¹/₂f Cls2 136-145 Cond Hdl Hcap soft £43,330
	2/20	Wwck	2m5f Cls1 List Hdl gd-sft £14,238
	4/19	Chel	2m4¹/₂f Cls1 Nov List Hdl good £14,068
	11/18	Uttx	2m Cls4 Nov Hdl gd-sft £4,094
	4/18	Sthl	1m7¹/₂f Cls5 NHF 4-6yo good £1,471

Confirmed herself a very smart mare when winning the Martin Pipe Hurdle at Cheltenham last season under top weight (form figures of 5121 there); raised 6lb but has options of mares' races as well as handicaps and had already won a Listed mares' hurdle last term.

Interconnected

6 br g Network - R De Rien Sivola (Robin Des Champs)

Dan Skelton   Darren & Annaley Yates

PLACINGS: F1/2/					RPR **135**h
Starts	1st	2nd	3rd	4th	Win & Pl
1	-	1	-	-	£1,335

Bought for a record £620,000 in May 2019, with new owner hoping he will prove a Gold Cup horse, but missed subsequent season through injury; ran subsequent Grade 1 runner-up Emitom close over hurdles on only run under rules when trained by Nicky Henderson.

Israel Champ (Ire)

5 b g Milan - La Dariska (Take Risks)

David Pipe   John White & Anne Underhill

PLACINGS: 1/6110-					RPR **133+**b
Starts	1st	2nd	3rd	4th	Win & Pl
4	2	-	-	-	£29,614
	12/19	Asct	1m7¹/₂f Cls1 List NHF 4-6yo heavy £17,085
	11/19	Chel	2m1¹/₂f Cls1 List NHF 4-6yo soft £12,529

Bitterly disappointing in the Champion Bumper at Cheltenham but had gone off the shortest price of the British runners after winning a pair of Listed bumpers; particularly impressive when defying a penalty at Ascot; big horse who looks made for jumping.

It Came To Pass (Ire)

10 b g Brian Boru - Satellite Dancer (Satco)

Eugene O'Sullivan (Ire)   Mrs Alurie O'Sullivan

PLACINGS: 4P79/2/3111/U1U17P1-					RPR **153+**c
Starts	1st	2nd	3rd	4th	Win & Pl
13	5	1	-	1	£50,709
	3/20	Chel	2m2¹/₂f Cls2 Am Hunt Ch gd-sft £26,685
	11/19	Cork	3m Hunt Ch soft £5,324
	5/19	Klny	2m7f Hunt Ch good £5,827
	4/19	Cork	2m4f Hunt Ch gd-yld £5,827
	12/15	Limk	2m6f Mdn Hunt Ch heavy £4,547

Last season's champion hunter chaser, winning

by ten lengths at Cheltenham; had looked out of form prior to that but found to be sick after festival prep run in a point-to-point; relishes a stiff test of stamina and had been unsuited by tight track when only seventh at Down Royal.

Itchy Feet (Fr)

6 b g Cima De Triomphe - Maeva Candas (Brier Creek)

Olly Murphy   Kate & Andrew Brooks

PLACINGS: 2/111234/411U-   RPR **160**+c

Starts	1st	2nd	3rd	4th	Win & Pl
11	5	2	1	2	£86,172
	2/20	Sand	2m4f Cls1 Nov Gd1 Ch soft		£31,323
	12/19	Leic	2m4f Cls3 Nov Ch soft		£8,382
	10/18	Kemp	2m Cls1 Nov List Hdl good		£11,390
	10/18	Sthl	1m7¹/₂f Cls4 Nov Hdl good		£4,094
	9/18	Strf	2m1¹/₂f Cls5 NHF 4-6yo good		£2,599

Third in the 2019 Supreme Novices' Hurdle and soon proved at least as good when switched to fences last season, winning a Grade 1 at Sandown; sent off just 7-2 for the Marsh Novices' Chase at Cheltenham only to unseat his rider at the sixth.

Janidil (Fr)

6 b g Indian Daffodil - Janidouce (Kaldounevees)

Willie Mullins (Ire)   John P McManus

PLACINGS: 5/422/1115-   RPR **150**+h

Starts	1st	2nd	3rd	4th	Win & Pl
8	3	2		1	£113,095
135	12/19	Fair	2m 118-144 Hdl Hcap yld-sft		£53,153
125	11/19	DRoy	2m1¹/₂f 116-139 Hdl Hcap soft		£26,577
	10/19	Tipp	2m Mdn Hdl yield		£5,857

French recruit who won three times for new connections last season, including a valuable 2m handicap hurdle at Fairyhouse; ran well enough when taking big step up in class and trip in the Albert Bartlett at Cheltenham, albeit left behind by principals in fifth.

Janika (Fr)

7 b g Saddler Maker - Majaka (Kapgarde)

Nicky Henderson   Simon Munir & Isaac Souede

PLACINGS: 52182111/2224/14442-   RPR **167**+c

Starts	1st	2nd	3rd	4th	Win & Pl
21	5	5	3	4	£301,861
162	11/19	Extr	2m1¹/₂f Cls1 Gd2 151-162 Ch Hcap soft		£40,411
	4/18	Autl	2m6f Ch heavy		£24,637
	3/18	Autl	2m2¹/₂f Ch 5yo heavy		£22,088
	2/18	Pau	2m3¹/₂f Ch 5yo heavy		£14,442
0	11/17	Autl	2m2f Hdl 4yo heavy		£22,564

Thoroughly deserved his victory in last season's Haldon Gold Cup having finished second in three big handicaps during the previous campaign; couldn't cope with a jump in class subsequently when well held over a variety of trips and when switched back to hurdles.

Bet through the award-winning Racing Post App

Jarveys Plate (Ire)

7 ch g Getaway - She's Got To Go (Glacial Storm)

Fergal O'Brien   The Yes No Wait Sorries & Chris Coley

PLACINGS: 231/32139/1449F-5   RPR **138**c

Starts	1st	2nd	3rd	4th	Win & Pl
12	3	1	2	2	£46,754
	10/19	Chep	2m3¹/₂f Cls1 Nov List Ch soft		£12,989
	1/19	Chel	2m4¹/₂f Cls1 Nov List Hdl gd-sft		£14,068
	4/18	Prth	2m Cls4 NHF 4-6yo soft		£3,165

Has won Listed novice races over hurdles and fences in the last two seasons but struggled in more competitive races; didn't progress after beating Reserve Tank on chasing debut last season and only ninth when making handicap debut at Cheltenham.

Jason The Militant (Ire)

6 b g Sans Frontieres - Rock Angel (Desert King)

Henry De Bromhead (Ire)   Peter Michael

PLACINGS: 3/2151-   RPR **144**h

Starts	1st	2nd	3rd	4th	Win & Pl
5	2	1	1	-	£35,678
	2/20	Naas	2m Nov Gd2 Hdl sft-hvy		£23,250
	12/19	Limk	2m Mdn Hdl heavy		£7,188

Claimed some notable scalps when winning a Grade 2 novice hurdle at Naas last season at 25-1, benefiting from return to much softer ground having flopped at Grade 1 level following maiden win; reportedly needs plenty of cut after getting jarred up in a bumper.

Jatiluwih (Fr)

6 ch g Linda's Lad - Jaune De Beaufai (Ultimately Lucky)

Philip Hobbs   David Maxwell Racing

PLACINGS: 336213/F62211/11128-   RPR **152**+h

Starts	1st	2nd	3rd	4th	Win & Pl
19	6	4	3	-	£87,593
137	11/19	Chel	2m5f Cls2 115-139 Hdl Hcap soft		£15,640
	10/19	Weth	2m3¹/₂f Cls4 Nov Hdl gd-sft		£4,224
	10/19	Sedg	2m4f Cls4 Nov Hdl soft		£4,094
	4/19	Chep	2m3¹/₂f Cls4 Nov Hdl good		£4,094
	3/19	Ludl	2m5f Cls4 Nov Hdl gd-sft		£5,198
	12/17	Pau	2m3¹/₂f Ch 3yo v soft		£14,769

Bought from France last year and won first five races for current connections, including a handicap hurdle at Cheltenham; improved again when second in a Pertemps qualifier but only eighth in the final; already a winner over fences in France.

Jerrysback (Ire)

8 b g Jeremy - Get A Few Bob Back (Bob Back)

Philip Hobbs   John P McManus

PLACINGS: 42/F111/51223/03-   RPR **150**c

Starts	1st	2nd	3rd	4th	Win & Pl
9	3	2	2	-	£51,614
	12/18	Bang	2m4¹/₂f Ch soft		£6,108
	2/17	Weth	2m3¹/₂f Cls4 Nov Hdl gd-sft		£3,574
	1/17	Plum	2m4¹/₂f Cls4 Nov Hdl heavy		£3,249

Promising novice chaser two seasons ago when

placed three times at Grade 2 level (2m4f-4m); ran just twice last term but went close when third in the Silver Cup at Ascot despite perhaps finding heavy ground against him (withdrawn on account of similar going subsequently).

Jon Snow (Fr)

5 br g Le Havre - Saroushka (Westerner)

Willie Mullins (Ire)   Mrs S Ricci

PLACINGS: 3321-11   RPR **150+h**

Starts	1st	2nd	3rd	4th	Win & Pl
6	2	1	1	-	£29,899
	8/20	Klny	2m7f Nov Hdl soft		£8,750
	7/20	Gway	2m4¹/₂f Nov Hdl yield		£10,000
	3/20	Leop	2m2f Mdn Hdl soft		£6,750

Had a big reputation throughout last season but was beaten in three maiden hurdles (twice when favourite) before finally getting off the mark at Leopardstown, stepping back up to 2m2f having also been tried over 2m4¹/₂f; has since won again at Galway and should continue to improve.

Kalashnikov (Ire)

7 br g Kalanisi - Fairy Lane (Old Vic)

Amy Murphy   Paul Murphy

PLACINGS: 1/11212/1122U1/2285-   RPR **166c**

Starts	1st	2nd	3rd	4th	Win & Pl
16	6	4	-	2	£254,489
	4/19	Aint	2m4f Cls1 Nov Gd1 Ch gd-sft		£56,394
	12/18	Plum	2m1f Cls3 Nov Ch soft		£7,343
	11/18	Wwck	2m Cls3 Nov Ch good		£9,495
141	2/18	Newb	2m¹/₂f Cls1 Gd3 129-148 Hdl Hcap soft		£88,273
	12/17	Donc	2m¹/₂f Cls4 Nov Hdl 4-6yo gd-sft		£3,899
	11/17	Weth	2m Cls3 Nov Hdl soft		£5,523
	3/17	Weth	2m Cls5 NHF 4-6yo gd-sft		£2,599

Grade 1 winner as a novice chaser two seasons ago but progress stalled last season, not helped by connections' refusal to go right-handed (twice beaten favourite going that way as a novice); broke blood vessels last time at Newbury having returned sick after his previous run.

Kalooki (Ger)

6 b g Martaline - Karuma (Surumu)

Philip Hobbs   Andrew L Cohen

PLACINGS: 0325/4112-   RPR **141h**

Starts	1st	2nd	3rd	4th	Win & Pl
8	2	2	1	1	£16,813
	2/20	Weth	2m5¹/₂f Cls4 Nov Hdl soft		£4,534
	1/20	Ludl	2m5f Cls4 Mdn Hdl soft		£4,224

Wide-margin winner of novice hurdles at Ludlow and Wetherby, making virtually all and relishing step up in trip; improved again when second to Ramses De Teillee in a Grade 2 at Haydock on final run (pair well clear); likely to go novice chasing.

Kauto Riko (Fr)

9 b g Ballingarry - Kauto Relstar (Art Bleu I)

Tom Gretton   Mr & Mrs J Dale & Partners

PLACINGS: 1123/111d5/P138/2520-   RPR **152c**

Starts	1st	2nd	3rd	4th	Win & Pl
20	5	4	2	2	£69,748
137	12/18	Hayd	1m7¹/₂f Cls3 111-137 Ch Hcap heavy		£9,747
123	1/18	Tntn	2m Cls3 119-138 Ch Hcap soft		£9,357
115	12/17	Newc	2m¹/₂f Cls4 Nov 105-118 Ch Hcap soft		£3,833
105	2/17	Catt	2m3¹/₂f Cls4 105-117 Hdl Hcap soft		£3,249
98	12/16	MRas	2m2¹/₂f Cls4 98-119 Hdl Hcap gd-sft		£3,899

Seems best in first two runs each season and extended that fine record when fresh with a 100-1 second in the Peterborough Chase first time out last term; form tailed off subsequently, including when looking a non-stayer on first run at 3m, but dropped 7lb in that time.

Keeper Hill (Ire)

9 b g Westerner - You Take Care (Definite Article)

Warren Greatrex   McNeill Family

PLACINGS: /121FFP/521003/1P23-   RPR **159c**

Starts	1st	2nd	3rd	4th	Win & Pl
24	8	4	3	-	£130,612
	11/19	Hayd	2m5¹/₂f Cls2 Ch gd-sft		£31,569
139	1/19	Wwck	3m1f Cls2 126-152 Hdl Hcap good		£15,640
	12/17	Donc	3m Cls1 Nov Gd2 Ch good		£20,554
	11/17	Strf	2m6¹/₂f Cls4 Nov Ch good		£4,431
	2/17	Hntg	2m3¹/₂f Cls1 Nov List Hdl gd-sft		£17,085
	1/17	Hrfd	2m3¹/₂f Cls4 Nov Hdl soft		£3,379
	11/16	Bang	2m Cls4 Nov Hdl soft		£3,899
	11/15	MRas	2m¹/₂f Cls6 NHF 4-6yo gd-sft		£1,643

Got back on track over fences last season (had been kept to hurdles since losing his way in 2017-18), winning at Haydock before a close second to Frodon in a Grade 2 at Kempton; had won at that level over 3m as a novice and could benefit from return to further.

Kemboy (Fr)

8 b g Voix Du Nord - Vitora (Victory Note)

Willie Mullins (Ire)   Kemboy, Brett Graham & Ken Sharp Syndicate

PLACINGS: 57/214F11/11U1/1427-   RPR **172c**

Starts	1st	2nd	3rd	4th	Win & Pl
18	8	3	-	2	£547,670
	5/19	Punc	3m¹/₂f Gd1 Ch yld-sft		£159,459
	4/19	Aint	3m1f Cls1 Gd1 Ch gd-sft		£112,260
	12/18	Leop	3m Gd1 Ch good		£91,372
	11/18	Clon	2m4f Gd2 Ch good		£26,106
147	4/18	Punc	2m5f Nov 126-147 Ch Hcap soft		£52,212
	4/18	Limk	3m Nov Gd3 Ch heavy		£22,190
	1/18	Fair	2m5¹/₂f Ch heavy		£7,632
	12/16	Limk	2m3f Mdn Hdl yield		£4,522

Three-time Grade 1 winner in 2018-19, notably beating Al Boum Photo at Punchestown, but didn't run to that level last season; still not far off his best when second behind Delta Work in the Irish Gold Cup but failed to land a blow when only seventh in the Cheltenham Gold Cup.

Kildisart (Ire)

8 b g Dubai Destination - Princess Mairead (Blueprint)

Ben Pauling | Simon Munir & Isaac Souede

PLACINGS: /212519/21141/36652- | RPR **158+c**

Starts		1st	2nd	3rd	4th	Win & Pl
17		5	5	1	1	£168,335
148	4/19	Aint	3m1f Cls1 Gd3 127-148 Ch Hcap good			£42,203
141	1/19	Chel	2m4½f Cls2 Nov 120-146 Ch Hcap gd-sft			£17,034
	12/18	Asct	2m5f Cls2 Ch soft			£31,280
135	3/18	Kemp	2m5f Cls2 122-135 Hdl Hcap soft			£21,896
	11/17	Asct	2m3½f Cls3 Mdn Hdl gd-sft			£6,498

Got closer and closer in top handicap chases last season and went down by just a neck behind The Conditional in the Ultima at Cheltenham; has a fine record from few opportunities beyond 3m, including a win at Aintree in 2019, and could be a Grand National contender.

Kimberlite Candy: winner of the Classic Chase at Warwick looks a prime contender for the Grand National in 2021

Kilfenora (Ire)

8 b g Yeats - Blazing Liss (Supreme Leader)

Edward Harty (Ire) | John P McManus

PLACINGS: /F5673P1P/55/31140-2 | RPR **152+h**

Starts		1st	2nd	3rd	4th	Win & Pl
22		4	1	2	2	£83,614
143	1/20	Navn	2m4f 115-143 Hdl Hcap sft-hvy			£25,000
134	11/19	Naas	2m4f 118-144 Hdl Hcap sft-hvy			£26,577
127	2/18	Punc	3m 111-139 Hdl Hcap sft-hvy			£14,423
	2/17	Punc	2m1½f Mdn Hdl heavy			£5,791

Big improver last winter when winning 2m4f handicap hurdles at Navan and Naas; only fourth when sent off favourite for the Boyne Hurdle next time and disappointed again in the Coral Cup; has run eight times over fences without finishing in the first two.

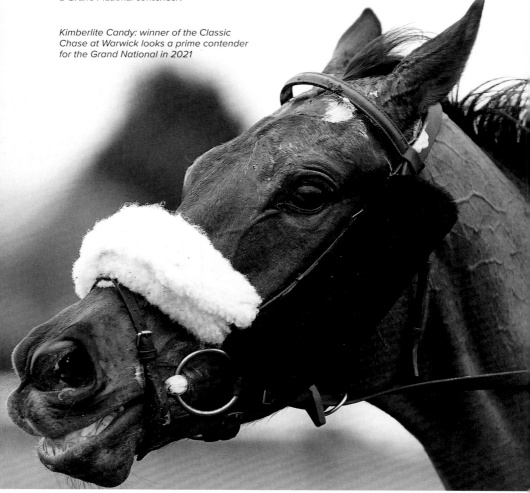

Kilfilum Cross (Ire)

9 gr g Beneficial - Singh Street (Dolphin Street)

Henry Oliver   Andy Bell & Fergus Lyons

PLACINGS: 1/7211/43124/3P422-4					RPR **147**c

Starts		1st	2nd	3rd	4th	Win & Pl
15		3	4	2	4	£55,880

132	2/19	Ludl	3m Cls3 106-132 Am Ch Hcap good	£9,109
	4/18	Kemp	3m¹/₂f Cls4 Nov Hdl soft	£4,094
	3/18	Chep	2m7¹/₂f Cls4 Nov Hdl soft	£4,194

Has finished second in the last two runnings of the Kim Muir at Cheltenham on only runs beyond 3m; largely disappointing in between but did much better on last two runs following wind surgery and addition of cheekpieces; interesting in more good staying handicaps.

Kimberlite Candy (Ire)

8 b g Flemensfirth - Mandys Native (Be My Native)

Tom Lacey   John P McManus

PLACINGS: P/5531P431/1935P/21-					RPR **160**+c

Starts		1st	2nd	3rd	4th	Win & Pl
18		6	1	3	1	£119,254

140	1/20	Wwck	3m5f Cls1 Gd3 122-148 Ch Hcap soft	£42,713
133	11/18	Ayr	3m Cls3 108-134 Ch Hcap heavy	£9,292
125	4/18	Chep	2m7¹/₂f Cls3 Nov 110-126 Ch Hcap heavy	£7,343
123	12/17	MRas	2m5¹/₂f Cls3 Nov 106-125 Ch Hcap soft	£7,798
	12/16	Newc	2m6f Cls4 Nov Hdl soft	£4,549
	11/16	Asct	2m3¹/₂f Cls3 Mdn Hdl gd-sft	£5,848

Realised long-held potential by developing into a high-class staying handicapper last season, finishing second in the Becher Chase at Aintree before winning a really strong Classic Chase at Warwick; leading contender for the Grand National before cancellation.

King Roland (Ire)

6 br g Stowaway - Kiltiernan Robin (Robin Des Champs)

Harry Fry   Masterson Holdings

PLACINGS: 1/11/212-					RPR **142**+h

Starts		1st	2nd	3rd	4th	Win & Pl
5		3	2	-	-	£18,493

1/20	Extr	2m2¹/₂f Cls4 Mdn Hdl soft	£4,549
2/19	Ffos	2m Cls5 NHF 4-6yo gd-sft	£2,924
12/18	Uttx	2m Cls5 NHF 4-6yo heavy	£2,274

Has had a big reputation ever since running under rules (sent off favourite for every run, three times at odds-on) but only backed that up once last season when a wide-margin winner at Exeter; still a decent second in a Grade 2 at Cheltenham on final run.

Latest Exhibition: could prove very useful as a novice chaser this season

Klassical Dream (Fr)

6 b g Dream Well - Klassical Way (Septieme Ciel)

Willie Mullins (Ire)   Mrs Joanne Coleman

PLACINGS: P324P/111/135-					RPR **158+**h

Starts	1st	2nd	3rd	4th	Win & Pl
11	4	1	2	1	£244,828

4/19	Punc	2m¹/₂f Nov Gd1 Hdl yield	£53,153
3/19	Chel	2m¹/₂f Cls1 Nov Gd1 Hdl soft	£70,338
2/19	Leop	2m Nov Gd1 Hdl good	£66,441
12/18	Leop	2m Mdn Hdl 4yo gd-yld	£8,177

Brilliant novice hurdler two seasons ago when winning the Supreme at Cheltenham and following up at Punchestown; well below that level in just two runs last term, notably on final run at Leopardstown; finished sore that day and subsequently missed the rest of the season.

Knight In Dubai (Ire)

7 b g Dubai Destination - Bobbies Storm (Bob Back)

Dan Skelton   Mr & Mrs Ben Houghton

PLACINGS: 21/51340/F205/112U-					RPR **149+**c

Starts	1st	2nd	3rd	4th	Win & Pl
13	3	2	1	1	£31,245

12/19	Donc	2m3f Cls4 Nov Ch gd-sft	£4,289
11/19	Bang	2m4¹/₂f Cls4 Ch heavy	£6,108
12/17	Weth	2m5¹/₂f Cls4 Nov Hdl soft	£3,899

Looked a smart chasing recruit when easily winning novice chases at Bangor and Doncaster last season; no match for Sam Brown at Haydock but had looked to be going best until getting outstayed; unseated his rider early in the novice handicap at the Cheltenham Festival.

L'Ami Serge (Ire)

10 b g King's Theatre - La Zingarella (Phardante)

Nicky Henderson   Simon Munir & Isaac Souede

PLACINGS: 33251/2122381/7/27P-					RPR **154+**h

Starts	1st	2nd	3rd	4th	Win & Pl
33	8	12	6	1	£660,325

	4/18	Aint	2m4f Cls1 Gd1 Hdl soft	£140,525
	6/17	Autl	3m1¹/₂f Gd1 Hdl v soft	£142,308
	4/17	Sand	2m5¹/₂f Cls1 Gd2 Hdl good	£28,475
	1/16	Weth	2m3¹/₂f Cls4 Nov Ch heavy	£3,899
	1/16	Plum	2m1f Cls3 Nov Ch heavy	£6,498
	1/15	Sand	2m Cls1 Nov Gd1 Hdl soft	£23,491
	12/14	Asct	1m7¹/₂f Cls1 Nov Gd2 Hdl soft	£18,690
132	11/14	Newb	2m1¹/₂f Cls1 List 129-149 Hdl Hcap soft	£22,780

Very hard to win with but had developed into a consistent staying hurdler at the top level before missing 2018-19 through injury; returned from a long layoff by finishing second in the Marsh Hurdle at Ascot last season but regressed in two subsequent runs.

Lake View Lad (Ire)

10 gr g Oscar - Missy O'Brien (Supreme Leader)

Nick Alexander   Trevor Hemmings

PLACINGS: 26/3132123/113P/533-					RPR **158**c

Starts	1st	2nd	3rd	4th	Win & Pl
24	8	3	7	1	£140,210

147	12/18	Weth	3m Cls1 Gd3 132-149 Ch Hcap gd-sft	£25,628
139	12/18	Newc	2m7¹/₂f Cls1 List 130-152 Ch Hcap soft	£39,865
136	2/18	Hayd	2m4f Cls3 Nov 124-138 Ch Hcap heavy	£10,820
132	12/17	Newc	2m7¹/₂f Cls3 Nov 115-132 Ch Hcap soft	£6,498
	4/16	Newc	2m4¹/₂f Cls4 Nov Hdl soft	£3,899
	2/16	Newc	2m3¹/₂f Cls4 Nov Hdl heavy	£3,249
	1/16	Ayr	2m4¹/₂f Cls5 Mdn Hdl heavy	£2,469
	11/15	Hexm	2m Cls6 Mdn NHF 4-6yo heavy	£1,949

Smart staying chaser who won two top prizes

in the north, the Rehearsal Chase and Rowland Meyrick, in 2018; couldn't land a blow off much higher marks in those races last term, though he stayed on eyecatchingly in the latter; switched to hurdles when third at Kelso on final run.

Lalor (Ger)

8 b g It's Gino - Laviola (Waky Nao)

Kayley Woollacott
D G Staddon

PLACINGS: 1211/23201/13P6/433-
RPR **159**c

Starts	1st	2nd	3rd	4th	Win & Pl
16	5	3	4	1	£135,848
	11/18	Chel	2m Cls1 Nov Gd2 Ch good		£19,695
	4/18	Aint	2m¹/₂f Cls1 Nov Gd1 Hdl soft		£56,130
	4/17	Aint	2m1f Cls1 Gd2 NHF 4-6yo good		£25,322
	3/17	Winc	1m7¹/₂f Cls6 Mdn NHF 4-6yo heavy		£1,949
	12/16	Winc	1m7¹/₂f Cls6 NHF 4-6yo soft		£1,625

Grade I novice hurdle winner who made a stunning chase debut at Cheltenham two seasons ago before badly losing his way; did better last season when twice going close in handicaps back at Cheltenham over 2m4½f; expected to get further by connections.

Latest Exhibition (Ire)

7 b g Oscar - Aura About You (Supreme Leader)

Paul Nolan (Ire)
Toberona Partnership

PLACINGS: 21/12112-
RPR **152**h

Starts	1st	2nd	3rd	4th	Win & Pl
7	4	3	-	-	£145,625
	2/20	Leop	2m6f Nov Gd1 Hdl yield		£75,000
	12/19	Navn	2m4f Nov Gd2 Hdl soft		£22,590
	10/19	Gway	2m¹/₂f Mdn Hdl soft		£7,454
	1/19	Naas	2m3f NHF 5-7yo yield		£5,550

Top-class staying novice hurdler last season, finishing a neck second in the Albert Bartlett; bred to stay and saw out that 3m trip but had

also shown real class over shorter, notably when quickening best off a slow pace in a 2m6f Grade I at Leopardstown; likely to go novice chasing.

Laurina (Fr)

7 b m Spanish Moon - Lamboghina (Alkalde)

Paul Nicholls
Sullivan Bloodstock

PLACINGS: F2/1111/114/1PP3-
RPR **150+**c

Starts	1st	2nd	3rd	4th	Win & Pl
13	7	1	1	1	£196,003
	11/19	Gowr	2m4f Ch heavy		£9,051
	2/19	Punc	2m4f List Hdl gd-yld		£16,622
	1/19	Sand	2m4f Cls1 List Hdl soft		£12,529
	4/18	Fair	2m4f Nov Gd1 Hdl sft-hvy		£52,212
	3/18	Chel	2m4f Cls1 Nov Gd2 Hdl soft		£51,255
	1/18	Fair	2m2f Nov Gd3 Hdl heavy		£17,688
	12/17	Tram	2m Mdn Hdl heavy		£5,791

Hugely talented but bitterly disappointing last season after a winning debut over fences, being pulled up the next twice (favourite both times) and a below-par third back over hurdles, and has since left Willie Mullins; had won her first six races for Mullins before finishing fourth in the 2019 Champion Hurdle.

Le Breuil (Fr)

8 ch g Anzillero - Slew Dancer (Fabulous Dancer)

Ben Pauling
Mrs Emma Palmer

PLACINGS: P/52015/123241/P750-
RPR **141**c

Starts	1st	2nd	3rd	4th	Win & Pl
20	6	3	3	2	£126,800
	3/19	Chel	3m7¹/₂f Cls1 Nov Gd2 Am Ch soft		£75,491
	11/18	Hntg	2m4f Cls3 Nov Ch good		£9,747
139	4/18	Fknm	2m4f Cls3 113-139 Hdl Hcap gd-sft		£7,213
	3/17	Newb	2m4¹/₂f Cls4 Nov Hdl soft		£4,549
	11/16	Sedg	2m4f Cls4 Nov Hdl gd-sft		£3,899
	5/16	Wwck	2m Cls6 NHF 4-6yo gd-sft		£1,625

Gutsy winner of a gruelling National Hunt Chase at Cheltenham in 2019, relishing step up to

Le Breuil (right): failed to score last season but a tough performer on his day

marathon trips; failed to build on that last season when no better than fifth in four runs, though campaign had all been geared towards the Grand National.

Le Patriote (Fr)

8 b g Poliglote - Sentosa (Kaldounevees)
Dr Richard Newland · Canard Vert Racing Club

PLACINGS: /589741P/811/14840-1 · RPR **146**h

Starts		1st	2nd	3rd	4th	Win & Pl
20		7		1	3	£187,372
	10/20	MRas	2m1f Cls3 Nov Ch good			£7,018
148	5/19	Hayd	1m7¹/₂f Cls1 Gd3 127-148 Hdl Hcap good			£56,950
142	4/19	Chel	2m4¹/₂f Cls2 122-146 Hdl Hcap good			£15,475
135	11/18	Ayr	2m Cls2 116-142 Hdl Hcap good			£25,992
127	2/18	Asct	2m3¹/₂f Cls2 123-149 Hdl Hcap soft			£28,152
	3/17	Comp	2m2f Hdl soft			£19,692
	11/16	Engh	2m2f Hdl 4yo heavy			£16,941

Completed a hat-trick by winning last season's Swinton Hurdle at Haydock and has shown glimpses of promise in tough races since; good fourth on chasing debut in a Grade 2 at Doncaster behind Mister Fisher and travelled strongly in the Champion Hurdle until fading late.

Le Richebourg (Fr)

7 b g Network - Fee Magic (Phantom Breeze)
Joseph O'Brien (Ire) · John P McManus

PLACINGS: 32/1116280/511211/ · RPR **165**c

Starts		1st	2nd	3rd	4th	Win & Pl
15		7	3	1	-	£205,116
	2/19	Leop	2m1f Nov Gd1 Ch good			£66,441
	12/18	Leop	2m1f Nov Gd1 Ch good			£52,212
	10/18	Tipp	2m4f Nov Gd3 Ch good			£17,688
	9/18	List	2m1f Ch yld-sft			£8,177
	7/17	Gway	2m¹/₂f Nov Hdl 4yo yield			£10,530
	7/17	Klny	2m1f Nov Hdl good			£6,844
	5/17	Klny	2m1f Mdn Hdl 4yo good			£6,055

Hasn't run since ruled out of the 2019 Racing Post Arkle through injury when ante-post favourite; had won four out of five novice chases, with sole defeat a narrow one by Delta Work in the Drinmore; looked better at 2m, twice easily beating Arkle runner-up Us And Them.

Lightly Squeeze

6 b g Poet's Voice - Zuleika Dobson (Cadeaux Genereux)
Harry Fry · J Davies, Govier & Brown

PLACINGS: 444/43/23111F- · RPR **140+**h

Starts		1st	2nd	3rd	4th	Win & Pl
11		3	1	2	4	£19,783
120	1/20	Plum	2m Cls4 96-120 Hdl Hcap soft			£5,328
117	12/19	Tntn	2m3f Cls4 84-117 Cond Hdl Hcap soft			£5,458
110	12/19	Winc	1m7¹/₂f Cls4 Nov 84-110 Hdl Hcap heavy			£4,224

Sharply progressive in handicap hurdles after Christmas, going up 27lb for three easy wins

from 2m-2m3f; improvement all came on a soft surface but running a big race back on quicker ground when falling at the last in the Betfair Hurdle.

Limited Reserve (Ire)

8 b g Court Cave - Lady Blackie (Definite Article)
Christian Williams · All Stars Sports Racing

PLACINGS: 551125/24211/403011- · RPR **132**h

Starts		1st	2nd	3rd	4th	Win & Pl
21		6	3	2	3	£157,642
127	2/20	Sand	2m7¹/₂f Cls1 Gd3 125-150 Hdl Hcap heavy			£56,270
122	1/20	Tntn	2m3f Cls2 117-136 Hdl Hcap heavy			£10,761
133	12/17	Hayd	2m3f Cls2 116-133 Hdl Hcap heavy			£12,512
125	11/17	Hayd	2m3f Cls2 123-149 Hdl Hcap heavy			£31,280
108	12/16	Ffos	2m Cls3 106-125 Hdl Hcap soft			£6,498
99	11/16	Sand	2m Cls4 Nov 95-120 Hdl Hcap gd-sft			£6,498

Slow to find best form last season after long layoff but ended up winning last two races, most notably a £100,000 handicap hurdle at Sandown when stepped up in trip (fourth win out of four on heavy ground); 6lb rise still leaves him on previous winning mark from 2017.

Liosduin Bhearna (Ire)

7 b g Beneficial - Cloth Fair (Old Vic)
Fergal O'Brien · The Fob Racing Partnership

PLACINGS: U32/232211/0F1- · RPR **143+**h

Starts		1st	2nd	3rd	4th	Win & Pl
9		3	3	1		£24,533
131	2/20	Donc	3m1¹/₂f Cls2 119-145 Hdl Hcap heavy			£12,512
120	3/19	Chep	2m3¹/₂f Cls4 101-121 Hdl Hcap gd-sft			£4,094
115	2/19	Ayr	2m4¹/₂f Cls4 98-117 Hdl Hcap gd-sft			£4,809

Progressive hurdler who won successive handicaps at the end of the 2018-19 campaign and improved again when stepped up to 3m on final run last season, winning easily at Doncaster; had missed much of the season after falling on only previous run over the trip.

Lisnagar Oscar (Ire)

7 b g Oscar - Asta Belle (Astarabad)
Rebecca Curtis · Racing For Fun

PLACINGS: 1/3221153/239F31- · RPR **162**h

Starts		1st	2nd	3rd	4th	Win & Pl
13		3	3	4		£236,750
	3/20	Chel	3m Cls1 Gd1 Hdl soft			£182,878
	2/19	Hayd	3m¹/₂f Cls1 Nov Gd2 Hdl good			£16,938
	1/19	Chep	2m3¹/₂f Cls4 Nov Hdl gd-sft			£4,094

Shock winner of last season's Stayers' Hurdle, exploiting Paisley Park's poor run to prove the best of a bad bunch; had nonetheless run well when third in the Cleeve Hurdle and relished a stiffer test of stamina; twice a beaten favourite in novice chases earlier in the season.

Lisp (Ire)

6 ch g Poet's Voice - Hora (Hernando)

Alan King   Mr & Mrs R Kelvin-Hughes

PLACINGS: 2113F/12285/43137-   RPR **149**c

Starts	1st	2nd	3rd	4th	Win & Pl
15	4	3	3	1	£80,067

12/19	Plum	2m1f Cls3 Nov Ch soft	£7,343
130	11/18	Font	2m1¹/₂f Cls3 108-134 Hdl Hcap gd-sft £7,216
	1/18	Font	2m1¹/₂f Cls4 Nov Hdl heavy £4,094
	12/17	Plum	2m Cls4 Nov Hdl soft £3,249

Useful novice chaser last season, winning well at Plumpton and finishing third in a Grade 2 at Doncaster; had done well in big-field handicaps over hurdles and was well fancied for handicap chase debut in the Grand Annual, running a fair race to finish a ten-length seventh.

Longhouse Poet (Ire)

6 b g Yeats - Moscow Madame (Moscow Society)

Martin Brassil (Ire)   Sean & Bernardine Mulryan

PLACINGS: 1/121338-   RPR **147**h

Starts	1st	2nd	3rd	4th	Win & Pl
6	2	1	2	-	£36,998

12/19	Navn	2m4f Mdn Hdl soft	£7,188
5/19	Punc	2m2f NHF 5-7yo gd-yld	£8,324

Very useful novice hurdler last season, finishing third in two Grade 1 races; well beaten by Envoi Allen at Naas but got much closer behind Latest Exhibition at Leopardstown when just outstayed over 2m6f; disappointing when dropped back in trip for the Ballymore.

Lostintranslation: big player in the top staying chases

Lord Du Mesnil (Fr)

7 b g Saint Des Saints - Ladies Choice (Turgeon)

Richard Hobson   Paul Porter & Mike & Mandy Smith

PLACINGS: U532936F3/642211122-   RPR **156**c

Starts	1st	2nd	3rd	4th	Win & Pl
28	3	6	6	3	£150,504
137	12/19	Hayd	3m4½f Cls2 132-140 Ch Hcap soft		£16,314
127	12/19	Hayd	3m1½f Cls2 127-146 Ch Hcap heavy		£31,280
122	11/19	Newc	2m7½f Cls3 Nov 118-129 Ch Hcap heavy		£7,083

Thorough stayer who went from strength to strength last season having fallen or unseated in first three runs over fences in Britain in 2018-19; came first and second in 3m4½f handicap chases at Haydock before finishing second again in the National Hunt Chase at Cheltenham.

Lord Royal (Fr)

5 gr g Lord Du Sud - Tinoroyale (Karinga Bay)

Willie Mullins (Ire)   Paul Connell & Alan McGonnell

PLACINGS: 12-   RPR **143**h

Starts	1st	2nd	3rd	4th	Win & Pl
2	1	1	-	-	£11,144
	1/20	Clon	2m4f Mdn Hdl heavy		£5,509

Bought off the Flat in France and made a big impression on hurdling and stable debut last season when trouncing a field of maidens at Clonmel by 33 lengths; fair second (pulled well clear of rest) when odds-on for a 3m Grade 3 novice hurdle at Punchestown.

Lostintranslation (Ire)

8 b g Flemensfirth - Falika (Hero's Honor)

Colin Tizzard   Taylor & O'Dwyer

PLACINGS: /221672/231221/11P3-   RPR **175+**c

Starts	1st	2nd	3rd	4th	Win & Pl
16	5	6	2		£354,318
	11/19	Hayd	3m1½f Cls1 Gd1 Ch gd-sft		£112,540
	11/19	Carl	2m4f Cls1 List Ch soft		£17,085
	4/19	Aint	3m1f Cls1 Nov Ch soft		£56,394
	1/19	Chel	2m4½f Cls1 Nov Gd2 Ch gd-sft		£19,695
	12/17	Newb	2m½f Cls3 Mdn Hdl soft		£6,498

Grand chasing type who put himself in the top tier of staying chasers last season, beating course specialist Bristol De Mai in the Betfair Chase at Haydock and finishing a close third in the Cheltenham Gold Cup; leading contender for all the top staying chases again.

Mack The Man (Ire)

6 b g Flemensfirth - Nifty Nuala (Saddlers' Hall)

Evan Williams   Mr & Mrs William Rucker

PLACINGS: 8/732P/11B-   RPR **134+**h

Starts	1st	2nd	3rd	4th	Win & Pl
8	2	1	1		£39,970
122	12/19	Sand	2m Cls1 List 124-147 Hdl Hcap heavy		£33,762
115	11/19	Wwck	2m Cls4 97-115 Hdl Hcap gd-sft		£4,549

Failed to win in first season over hurdles but much improved last season when winning two handicap hurdles, most notably a Listed race at

Sandown; might well have followed up on much quicker ground in the Betfair Hurdle but for being brought down at the last (raised just 1lb).

Magic Of Light (Ire)

9 b m Flemensfirth - Quest Of Passion (Saumarez)

Jessica Harrington (Ire)   Ann & Alan Potts Limited

PLACINGS: 220241/3112U72/3118-   RPR **150+**h

Starts	1st	2nd	3rd	4th	Win & Pl
30	8	7	5	3	£416,859
	1/20	Asct	2m7½f Gd2 Hdl heavy		£28,475
	12/19	Newb	2m7½f Cls1 List Ch soft		£17,865
	1/19	Asct	2m7½f Cls1 Gd2 Hdl gd-sft		£28,609
	12/18	Newb	2m7½f Cls1 List Ch soft		£15,846
128	4/18	Punc	2m5f 114-142 Ch Hcap soft		£39,159
	11/17	Fair	2m5f Ch soft		£6,318
107	4/17	Punc	2m5f 105-123 Hdl Hcap gd-yld		£15,769
	11/16	Navn	2m NHF 4-7yo yld-sft		£4,070

Best known for finishing second behind Tiger Roll in the 2019 Grand National; lucky to get away with some serious blunders that day and has often been found out by stiffer fences but has a big engine and won a Grade 2 mares' hurdle at Ascot last season for the second year in a row.

Magic Saint (Fr)

6 b g Saint Des Saints - Magic Poline (Trempolino)

Paul Nicholls   Mr & Mrs J D Cotton

PLACINGS: 111135/2510F2/517-   RPR **156**c

Starts	1st	2nd	3rd	4th	Win & Pl
15	6	2	1	-	£161,693
147	11/19	Newb	2m7½f Cls2 126-150 Ch Hcap gd-sft		£25,024
142	2/19	Winc	1m7½f Cls2 125-152 Ch Hcap good		£15,784
	3/18	Autl	2m2f Ch 4yo v soft		£22,088
	11/17	Autl	2m1½f Ch 3yo v soft		£21,744
	10/17	Autl	2m1½f Hdl 3yo v soft		£19,692
	9/17	Autl	2m2f Hdl 3yo heavy		£26,667

Patchy record since arriving from France two seasons ago but has excelled around the minimum trip while regularly found wanting over further; gave weight and a beating to Champion Chase third Bun Doran at Newbury last season but then failed to stay 2m4½f at Cheltenham.

Main Fact (USA)

7 b g Blame - Reflections (Sadler's Wells)

David Pipe   Munrowd's Partnership

PLACINGS: 4071P14/311111-   RPR **150+**h

Starts	1st	2nd	3rd	4th	Win & Pl
13	7	-	1		£57,746
132	3/20	Uttx	2m4f Cls2 127-144 Hdl Hcap heavy		£30,950
123	3/20	Weth	2m Cls3 123-135 Hdl Hcap heavy		£6,758
111	1/20	Ffos	2m Cls4 83-111 Hdl Hcap soft		£3,769
111	1/20	Uttx	2m Cls4 92-111 Cond Hdl Hcap heavy		£3,769
104	1/20	Wwck	2m Cls4 97-111 Hdl Hcap soft		£4,549
97	3/18	Weth	2m3½f Cls5 Nov 72-97 Hdl Hcap heavy		£3,509
89	11/17	Sedg	2m1f Cls4 80-104 Hdl Hcap soft		£3,249

One of the stories of last season, shooting up 49lb in the handicap after more than a year off the track as he won five successive handicap hurdles; particularly impressive when stepped up to 2m4f on his final run at Uttoxeter, winning by 15 lengths; raised another 15lb for that win.

Malone Road (Ire)

6 b g Kalanisi - Zaffarella (Zaffaran)

Gordon Elliott (Ire)   Cheveley Park Stud

PLACINGS: 1/11/13   RPR 135+h

Starts	1st	2nd	3rd	4th	Win & Pl
4	3	-	1	-	£20,742

8/20	Kbgn	2m Mdn Hdl soft	£5,000
11/18	Punc	2m NHF 4yo good	£6,269
11/18	DRoy	2m$\frac{1}{2}$f NHF 4-7yo gd-yld	£8,177

One-time ante-post favourite for the 2019 Champion Bumper having won both bumpers by wide margins only to suffer a knee injury; returned from more than a year out to make a winning start over hurdles this summer but let down by jumping when losing unbeaten record at Listowel.

Marie's Rock (Ire)

5 b/br m Milan - By The Hour (Flemensfirth)

Nicky Henderson   Middleham Park Racing

PLACINGS: 111-   RPR 136+h

Starts	1st	2nd	3rd	4th	Win & Pl
3	3	-	-	-	£27,788

12/19	Tntn	2m1$\frac{1}{2}$f Cls1 Nov List Hdl soft	£12,529
12/19	Hayd	1m7$\frac{1}{2}$f Cls2 Hdl soft	£12,660
5/19	Ffos	2m Cls5 NHF 4yo good	£2,599

Unbeaten in three runs under rules including two novice hurdles last season, most notably a Listed mares' race at Taunton by eight lengths; subsequently made ante-post favourite for the mares' novice hurdle at the Cheltenham Festival only to miss the meeting through injury.

Master Debonair

6 br g Yeats - Swincombe Flame (Exit To Nowhere)

Colin Tizzard   The Gosden Mob & SprayClad Uk

PLACINGS: 12105/2113-   RPR 145+h

Starts	1st	2nd	3rd	4th	Win & Pl
9	4	2	1	-	£56,618

12/19	Asct	1m7$\frac{1}{2}$f Cls1 Nov Gd2 Hdl heavy	£19,933
11/19	Asct	1m7$\frac{1}{2}$f Cls2 Hdl soft	£12,996
11/18	Chel	2m1$\frac{1}{2}$f Cls1 List NHF 4-6yo good	£12,379
5/18	Sedg	2m1f Cls5 Am Mdn NHF 4-6yo good	£2,274

Looked a smart novice hurdler last season when winning twice at Ascot, including a strong Grade 2 by eight lengths; gained that win on heavy ground but had also won a Listed bumper at Cheltenham on good; disappointing third when stepped up in trip on final run.

Master Tommytucker

9 b g Kayf Tara - No Need For Alarm (Romany Rye)

Paul Nicholls   A G Fear

PLACINGS: 11/F/1FF-2   RPR 154+c

Starts	1st	2nd	3rd	4th	Win & Pl
7	3	1	-	-	£17,738

11/19	Kemp	2m2f Cls4 Ch gd-sft	£4,809
4/18	Extr	2m5$\frac{1}{2}$f Cls4 Nov Hdl soft	£4,224
2/18	Extr	2m2$\frac{1}{2}$f Cls4 Nov Hdl soft	£4,549

Unbeaten when getting round but has fallen in three out of four runs over fences; made a winning return from more than a year out at Kempton last season but fell twice when in front in much stronger races there subsequently; still a top prospect.

McFabulous (Ire)

6 b g Milan - Rossavon (Beneficial)

Paul Nicholls   Giraffa Racing

PLACINGS: 1711/2411-1   RPR 154+h

Starts	1st	2nd	3rd	4th	Win & Pl
9	6	1	-	1	£97,908

132	10/20	Chep	2m3$\frac{1}{2}$f Cls1 Nov Gd2 Hdl good	£17,085
	3/20	Kemp	2m5f Cls1 Nov Gd3	£39,389
	2/20	MRas	2m4$\frac{1}{2}$f Cls3 Nov Hdl 4-7yo gd-sft	£6,498
	4/19	Aint	2m1f Cls1 Gd2 NHF 4-6yo soft	£25,322
	3/19	Newb	2m1$\frac{1}{2}$f Cls5 NHF 4-6yo gd-sft	£2,599
	10/18	Chep	2m Cls4 NHF 4-6yo good	£3,899

Grade 2 bumper winner who was talked up by his trainer when going hurdling last season and belatedly justified connections' faith when stepped up in trip; got off the mark at the third attempt and then ran out a brilliant winner of the EBF Final at Kempton; impressive at Chepstow on return to action this season.

Melon

8 ch g Medicean - Night Teeny (Platini)

Willie Mullins (Ire)   Mrs J Donnelly

PLACINGS: 2/1352F/442F/702142-   RPR 164+c

Starts	1st	2nd	3rd	4th	Win & Pl
18	3	6	1	3	£346,999

12/19	Leop	2m1f Ch soft	£9,318
11/17	DRoy	2m Gd2 Hdl soft	£25,214
1/17	Leop	2m Mdn Hdl good	£6,833

Agonisingly beaten by a nose in the Marsh Novices' Chase last season, meaning a fourth successive runner-up finish at the Cheltenham Festival (twice in the Champion Hurdle); generally less effective away from Cheltenham, winning just once since 2017.

Mick Pastor (Fr)

4 b g Meshaheer - Mick Oceane (Urban Ocean)

Paul Nicholls   John P McManus

PLACINGS: 1610-					RPR **132**h
Starts	1st	2nd	3rd	4th	Win & Pl
4	2	-	-	-	£24,176
1/20	Ludl	2m Cls4 Hdl 4yo soft			£4,289
5/19	Autl	2m1¹/₂f Hdl 3yo heavy			£19,459

Didn't live up to big expectations following purchase from France last season, disappointing when favourite for a Grade 2 on British debut and when well fancied even with top weight in the Fred Winter; won easily at Ludlow in between and remains a nice prospect.

Midnight Shadow

7 b g Midnight Legend - Holy Smoke (Statoblest)

Sue Smith   Mrs Aafke Clarke

PLACINGS: 222U71/20110/3F2126-					RPR **154**c
Starts	1st	2nd	3rd	4th	Win & Pl
21	6	7	1	-	£173,741
1/20	Chel	2m4¹/₂f Cls1 Nov Gd2 Ch soft			£20,026
1/19	Chel	2m4¹/₂f Cls1 Gd2 Hdl gd-sft			£28,135
141 12/18	Aint	2m4f Cls2 122-143 Hdl Hcap soft			£18,570
134 4/18	Ayr	2m Cls1 Gd2 134-154 Hdl Hcap good			£59,798
10/17	Uttx	2m Cls4 Nov Hdl 4-6yo soft			£3,899
12/16	Newc	1m6¹/₂f Cls6 NHF 3yo soft			£1,884

Ran consistently well in good 2m4f novice chases last season, albeit flattered by Grade 2 win at Cheltenham (took advantage of Champ's late exit); second to Itchy Feet in the Scilly Isles next time before sixth behind Samcro back at Cheltenham; didn't stay 3m when tried over hurdles.

Milan Native (Ire)

7 br g Milan - That's The Goose (Be My Native)

Gordon Elliott (Ire)   Gigginstown House Stud

PLACINGS: 31325/4524221-1					RPR **152**+c
Starts	1st	2nd	3rd	4th	Win & Pl
13	3	4	2	2	£73,878
10/20	Gway	2m6¹/₂f Ch soft			£7,750
141 3/20	Chel	3m2f Cls2 135-145 Am Ch Hcap soft			£41,510
2/19	Navn	2m Mdn Hdl yield			£7,492

Impressive winner of last season's Kim Muir at Cheltenham as a novice, getting off the mark over fences after showing decent form over shorter trips; relished step up in trip and open to further improvement as a stayer; could be a Grand National horse.

Min (Fr)

9 b g Walk In The Park - Phemyka (Saint Estephe)

Willie Mullins (Ire)   Mrs S Ricci

PLACINGS: 11/11d1224/1151/2121-					RPR **173**+c
Starts	1st	2nd	3rd	4th	Win & Pl
21	11	6	1	2	£916,313
3/20	Chel	2m4¹/₂f Cls1 Gd1 Ch soft			£197,115
12/19	Punc	2m4f Gd1 Ch soft			£45,180
4/19	Aint	2m4f Cls1 Gd1 Ch soft			£140,985
2/19	Leop	2m1f Gd1 Ch good			£66,441
12/18	Punc	2m4f Gd1 Ch yield			£44,381
2/18	Leop	2m1f Gd2 Ch soft			£52,212
11/17	Gowr	2m4f Ch heavy			£10,530
12/16	Leop	2m1f Nov Gd1 Ch yield			£39,044
11/16	Navn	2m1f Ch yld-sft			£7,235
1/16	Punc	2m Nov Gd2 Hdl heavy			£18,529
12/15	Punc	2m2f Mdn Hdl soft			£5,349

Vanquished Cheltenham ghosts with narrow victory in last season's Ryanair Chase, confirming preference for that longer trip after three festival

Master Tommytucker: talented chaser but does not have the best completion record

defeats over shorter; has won last four races beyond 2m2f yet beaten in his last three over shorter distances.

Minella Indo (Ire)

7 b g Beat Hollow - Carrigeen Lily (Supreme Leader)

Henry De Bromhead (Ire) — Barry Maloney

PLACINGS: 13/321/1212- — RPR **166**+c

Starts	1st	2nd	3rd	4th	Win & Pl
8	3	3	2	-	£183,379
	1/20	Navn	3m Cls1 sft-hvy		£7,262
	5/19	Punc	3m Nov Gd1 Hdl yield		£53,153
	3/19	Chel	3m Cls1 Nov Gd1 Hdl gd-sft		£73,506

Nearly became a dual Cheltenham Festival winner last season when just run down by Champ in the RSA (seemed to get racing too soon) as he attempted to follow up 2019 Albert Bartlett victory; had been very lightly raced and open to significant improvement.

Minella Melody (Ire)

6 b m Flemensfirth - Cottage Theatre (King's Theatre)

Henry De Bromhead (Ire) — Kenneth Alexander

PLACINGS: 112/31110- — RPR **139**+h

Starts	1st	2nd	3rd	4th	Win & Pl
7	4	1	1	-	£57,682
	1/20	Fair	2m2f Nov Gd3 Hdl yield		£17,000
	12/19	Punc	2m3¹/₂f Nov List Hdl soft		£14,617
	11/19	Cork	2m4f Mdn Hdl sft-hvy		£6,922
	3/19	Gowr	2m2f NHF 4-7yo soft		£5,550

Bitterly disappointing favourite in the mares' novice hurdle at last season's Cheltenham Festival but had been unbeaten over hurdles prior to that, winning three times including a 2m2f Grade 3 at Fairyhouse; has won over 2m4f and should get further.

Mister Fisher (Ire)

6 b g Jeremy - That's Amazing (Marignan)

Nicky Henderson — James & Jean Potter

PLACINGS: 10/2118/72114- — RPR **160**c

Starts	1st	2nd	3rd	4th	Win & Pl
11	5	2	-	1	£81,834
	1/20	Donc	2m¹/₂f Cls1 Nov Ch gd-sft		£19,933
	12/19	Chel	2m4¹/₂f Cls2 Nov Ch soft		£15,698
	1/19	Hayd	1m7¹/₂f Cls1 Nov Gd2 Hdl gd-sft		£17,085
	12/18	Kemp	2m Cls2 Nov Hdl gd-sft		£12,512
	3/18	Kemp	2m Cls5 Mdn NHF 4-6yo soft		£3,119

Not far off the best novice chasers in Britain last season, winning twice (at Cheltenham and then a Grade 2 at Doncaster) before a close fourth behind Samcro in the Marsh; seems equally effective at 2m and 2m4f; might be better on good ground.

Mister Malarky

7 ch g Malinas - Priscilla (Teenoso)

Colin Tizzard — Wendy & Malcolm Hezel

PLACINGS: 517320/131142/06P1P- — RPR **156**c

Starts	1st	2nd	3rd	4th	Win & Pl
21	5	2	4	1	£130,901
147	2/20	Kemp	3m Cls1 Gd3 133-159 Ch Hcap gd-sft		£56,950
	2/19	Asct	3m Cls1 Nov Gd2 Ch gd-sft		£22,780
130	1/19	Newb	2m7¹/₂f Cls3 120-130 Ch Hcap good		£7,343
126	11/18	Plum	2m3¹/₂f Cls3 Nov 126-136 Ch Hcap good		£7,522
	11/17	Kemp	2m Cls4 Nov Hdl 4-6yo gd-sft		£3,899

Smart staying chaser; relishes good ground (yet to win on worse than good to soft) and rarely got suitable conditions last season but came back in from the cold to win the Betway Handicap Chase at Kempton; likely to be aimed at the Grand National.

Mister Whitaker (Ire)

8 b g Court Cave - Benbradagh Vard (Le Bavard)

Mick Channon — T P Radford

PLACINGS: 343/31211/144P1/5P3- — RPR **157**c

Starts	1st	2nd	3rd	4th	Win & Pl
18	5	2	4	3	£148,158
149	4/19	Chel	2m4¹/₂f Cls1 Gd2 130-150 Ch Hcap good		£33,862
	11/18	Carl	2m4f Cls1 List Ch good		£17,085
137	3/18	Chel	2m4¹/₂f Cls1 Nov List 137-145 Ch Hcap soft		£39,865
129	1/18	Chel	2m5f Cls2 Nov 128-147 Ch Hcap soft		£17,204
118	11/17	Carl	2m4f Cls3 Nov 115-134 Ch Hcap gd-sft		£7,798

Has gained three of his five chase wins at Cheltenham (all in good handicaps, including at the festival in 2018) and ran another fine race at the track when finishing third in the Plate last season; had been pulled up in the Cotswold Chase (now pulled up on both runs beyond 2m5f).

Monalee (Ire)

9 b g Milan - Tempest Belle (Glacial Storm)

Henry de Bromhead (Ire) — Barry Maloney

PLACINGS: 124/1F12F/3214/P324- — RPR **173**c

Starts	1st	2nd	3rd	4th	Win & Pl
20	5	7	2	3	£315,504
	2/19	Gowr	2m4f Gd2 Ch yld-sft		£31,892
	2/18	Leop	2m5f Nov Gd1 Ch soft		£52,212
	11/17	Punc	2m4f Ch sft-hvy		£7,371
	2/17	Clon	3m Nov Gd3 Hdl heavy		£19,712
	11/16	Punc	2m6f Mdn Hdl soft		£6,331

Took form to a new level when stepped back up in trip last season, finishing second behind Delta Work in the Savills Chase and fourth (beaten less than two lengths) in the Cheltenham Gold Cup; clearly very talented but has still won just once in the last two seasons.

Monkfish (Ire)

6 ch g Stowaway - Martovic (Old Vic)

Willie Mullins (Ire)   Mrs S Ricci

PLACINGS: P/1/22111-   RPR **154+h**

Starts	1st	2nd	3rd	4th	Win & Pl
5	3	2	-	-	£91,098
	3/20	Chel	3m Cls1 Nov Gd1 Hdl soft...............................£73,506		
	1/20	Thur	2m6¹/₂f Nov Hdl yield.....................................£7,262		
	12/19	Fair	2m7f Mdn Hdl heavy.......................................£5,857		

Won a red-hot edition of the Albert Bartlett at Cheltenham last season, rallying superbly up the hill having been prominent throughout and raced keenly; had won two previous races at a much lower level by wide margins; big chasing type and a top-class prospect for staying novices.

Monsieur Lecoq (Fr)

6 b g Diamond Boy - Draga (Smadoun)

Jane Williams   Mrs Jane Williams

PLACINGS: P3/3U1120/134275-4   RPR **156h**

Starts	1st	2nd	3rd	4th	Win & Pl
15	3	2	3	2	£122,813
	138	10/19	Ffos	2m Cls2 132-152 Hdl Hcap soft...................£31,280	
	122	1/19	Sand	2m Cls2 120-136 Hdl Hcap soft...................£15,640	
		12/18	Ffos	2m Cls4 Mdn Hdl heavy............................£5,133	

Placed in three major 2m handicap hurdles during the last two seasons, including a half-length third in the Greatwood last term; forced into stronger company after that and finished a fair fourth in the International Hurdle before finding quicker ground/longer trip against him later.

Monte Cristo (Fr)

4 b g Montmartre - Rylara Des Brosses (Rapid Man)

Nicky Henderson   Simon Munir & Isaac Souede

PLACINGS: 662141-   RPR **124+h**

Starts	1st	2nd	3rd	4th	Win & Pl
6	2	1		1	£31,690
	2/20	Newb	2m¹/₂f Cls4 Hdl 4yo soft................................£3,769		
	10/19	Autl	2m2f Hdl 3yo Hcap v soft..............................£21,892		

French recruit who arrived with a big reputation last season and didn't quite deliver, finishing only fourth when odds-on in a Grade 2 at Cheltenham on British debut before scoring at 1-8 in much weaker company at Newbury; very much a future chaser.

Moon Over Germany (Ire)

9 ch g Germany - Elea Moon (Moonax)

Henry De Bromhead (Ire)   Philip J Reynolds

PLACINGS: 650/32741/413286-U40   RPR **147+c**

Starts	1st	2nd	3rd	4th	Win & Pl
23	3	3	4	3	£99,836
	8/19	Baln	2m1f Ch soft...£10,649		
	136	4/19	Aint	2m Cls3 131-149 Ch Hcap soft.................£50,517	
		12/15	Navn	2m Mdn Hdl 4yo heavy................................£6,419	

Yet to build on breakthrough win in the 2019 Red Rum Chase at Aintree but hasn't run in another

handicap chase since fourth at Punchestown the following month; placed in two Graded novice chases last season before switching to hurdles, coming sixth in the County Hurdle.

Musical Slave (Ire)

7 b g Getaway - Inghwung (Kayf Tara)

Philip Hobbs   John P McManus

PLACINGS: 6/6/6511/158132-   RPR **144+c**

Starts	1st	2nd	3rd	4th	Win & Pl
12	4	1	1	-	£48,562
	128	1/20	Extr	2m3f Cls3 Nov 125-136 Ch Hcap soft.............£10,722	
	121	5/19	Punc	2m5f 110-123 Hdl Hcap yield......................£16,622	
	117	3/19	Ludl	2m Cls3 111-129 Hdl Hcap gd-sft...................£7,538	
	110	3/19	MRas	2m¹/₂f Cls4 109-117 Hdl Hcap gd-sft................£4,159	

Won last three races over hurdles in early 2019 and resumed progress in the new year as things finally clicked over fences; good second on heavy ground when stepped up to 3m at Uttoxeter and capable of better on a sounder surface (best hurdles form on much quicker).

Native River (Ire)

10 ch g Indian River - Native Mo (Be My Native)

Colin Tizzard   Brocade Racing

PLACINGS: 321/21113/11/234/11-   RPR **174+c**

Starts	1st	2nd	3rd	4th	Win & Pl
26	13	3	6	1	£1,009,993
	2/20	Newb	2m7¹/₂f Cls1 Gd2 Ch good...............................£28,475		
	12/19	Aint	3m1f Cls1 Gd2 Ch gd-sft...............................£34,822		
	3/18	Chel	3m2¹/₂f Cls1 Gd1 Ch soft.............................£369,822		
	2/18	Newb	2m7¹/₂f Cls1 Gd2 Ch soft...............................£28,475		
	2/17	Newb	2m7¹/₂f Cls1 Gd2 Ch soft...............................£28,475		
	155	12/16	Chep	3m5¹/₂f Cls1 Gd3 139-155 Ch Hcap soft..........£85,425	
	155	11/16	Newb	3m2f Cls1 Gd3 140-166 Ch Hcap gd-sft £113,900	
		4/16	Aint	3m1f Cls1 Nov Gd1 Ch gd-sft.......................£56,319	
		11/15	Newb	2m7¹/₂f Cls1 Nov Gd2 Ch gd-sft...................£20,284	
		11/15	Extr	3m Cls2 Nov Ch soft...................................£12,974	
		2/15	Extr	2m1f Cls1 Nov List Hdl gd-sft.......................£11,390	
		11/14	Newc	2m6f Cls2 Nov Hdl soft................................£11,261	
		10/14	Strf	2m6f Cls5 Mdn Hdl good...............................£2,599	

Bold front-running chaser who enjoyed his finest hour when winning the Cheltenham Gold Cup in 2018; lightly raced since then and missed last season's Gold Cup after a setback but had looked to retain plenty of ability when winning two Grade 2 chases.

Navajo Pass

4 b g Nathaniel - Navajo Charm (Authorized)

Donald McCain   T G Leslie

PLACINGS: 1214-   RPR **140h**

Starts	1st	2nd	3rd	4th	Win & Pl
4	2	1	-	1	£42,968
	12/19	Donc	2m¹/₂f Cls1 Gd2 Hdl 3yo soft......................£28,135		
	11/19	Bang	2m¹/₂f Cls4 Mdn Hdl 3yo heavy......................£4,094		

Quickly proved a very useful juvenile hurdler last season when winning two of first three races before Christmas, including a Grade 2 at Doncaster (caught close home the time before); good fourth in the Triumph Hurdle, staying on as if likely to be suited by further.

Newtide (Ire)

7 br g Getaway - C'Est Fantastique (Hernando)

Kim Bailey   Lady Dulverton

PLACINGS: 2/41341/116-   RPR **149+**c

Starts	1st	2nd	3rd	4th	Win & Pl
8	4	-	1	2	£42,653

				Win & Pl
2/20	Weth	3m Cls1 Nov Gd2 Ch soft		£21,023
11/19	Ffos	3m Cls3 Nov Ch soft		£6,756
125 4/19	Ffos	3m Cls3 112-127 Hdl Hcap soft		£6,238
12/18	Hayd	2m7f Cls4 Mdn Hdl soft		£5,198

Won first two starts over fences last season, though fortunate to pick up a Grade 2 at Warwick after Boldmere's late fall; well beaten when sixth in the National Hunt Chase at Cheltenham; should be suited by long distances in time and seen by his trainer as a Welsh National type.

Next Destination (Ire)

8 b g Dubai Destination - Liss Alainn (Flemensfirth)

Paul Nicholls   Malcolm C Denmark

PLACINGS: 1/142/11131/   RPR **152**h

Starts	1st	2nd	3rd	4th	Win & Pl
8	5	1	1	1	£151,778

				Win & Pl
4/18	Punc	3m Nov Gd1 Hdl yield		£52,212
1/18	Naas	2m4f Nov Gd1 Hdl sft-hvy		£46,991
12/17	Navn	2m4f Nov Gd2 Hdl heavy		£21,432
11/17	Naas	2m3f Mdn Hdl sft-hvy		£6,844
1/17	Fair	2m NHF 5-7yo soft		£4,070

Has missed the last two seasons through injury but had won four out of five novice hurdles in 2017-18, including two Grade 1 races; finished fast when third in the Ballymore and relished step up to 3m when winning at Punchestown; has since left Willie Mullins; likely to go novice chasing.

Night Edition (Fr)

4 b g Authorized - Night Serenade (Golan)

David Pipe   Stuart & Simon Mercer & John Gent

PLACINGS: 4212-   RPR **132+**h

Starts	1st	2nd	3rd	4th	Win & Pl
4	1	2	-	1	£28,422

				Win & Pl
2/20	Ludl	2m Cls4 Mdn Hdl soft		£4,224

French Flat winner (on heavy ground) who progressed well in four races over hurdles last season; ran two best races at Cheltenham, finishing a length second in a Grade 2 behind Galahad Quest and again in the Fred Winter on handicap debut (pulled clear of third).

Not So Sleepy

8 ch g Beat Hollow - Papillon De Bronze (Marju)

Hughie Morrison   Lady Blyth

PLACINGS: 415/110P-   RPR **148+**h

Starts	1st	2nd	3rd	4th	Win & Pl
7	3	-	1	4	£109,067

				Win & Pl
127 12/19	Asct	1m7½f Cls1 Gd3 127-150 Hdl Hcap heavy		£85,425
122 11/19	Asct	1m7½f Cls2 122-143 Hdl Hcap soft		£18,768
2/19	Winc	1m7½f Cls4 Nov Hdl good		£4,224

Very useful Flat stayer who belatedly translated that ability to hurdles last season when winning two handicaps at Ascot, most notably by nine lengths in December; well beaten up in class for the Betfair Hurdle and Champion Hurdle but badly inconvenienced by standing starts both times.

On The Blind Side: could yet find further improvement over fences

Notebook (Ger)

7 b g Samum - Nova (Winged Love)

Henry de Bromhead (Ire)   Gigginstown House Stud

PLACINGS: F5/122120/211116-   RPR **162 + c**

Starts	1st	2nd	3rd	4th	Win & Pl
11	5	4	-	-	£185,868
	2/20	Leop	2m1f Nov Gd1 Ch yield		£75,000
	12/19	Leop	2m1f Nov Gd1 Ch yield		£53,153
	11/19	Punc	2m Nov Gd2 Ch soft		£23,653
	10/19	Punc	2m Ch gd-yld		£7,720
	1/19	Tram	2m Mdn Hdl soft		£6,659

Electrifying jumper who took a big step forward when switched to fences last season; won two Grade 1 novice chases at Leopardstown, most notably beating Fakir D'oudairies in December; only sixth when favourite for the Racing Post Arkle (second poor run at Cheltenham).

Notre Pari (Ire)

6 br g Jeremy - Glynn Approach (Zagreb)

Olly Murphy   John P McManus

PLACINGS: 23/421F1-   RPR **137 + h**

Starts	1st	2nd	3rd	4th	Win & Pl
6	2	1	1	1	£24,981
	2/20	Font	2m3f Cls4 Nov Hdl soft		£4,094
122	12/19	Aint	2m4f Cls2 122-143 Hdl Hcap gd-sft		£18,570

Progressive hurdler who flourished when sent handicapping last season, winning at Aintree and running well when favourite for Lanzarote Hurdle at Kempton (disputing second when falling at the last); easy winner back in novice company at Fontwell.

Now McGinty (Ire)

9 b g Stowaway - Western Whisper (Supreme Leader)

Stuart Edmunds   The Garratt Family

PLACINGS: /33P00112/2U2128/29-   RPR **151 c**

Starts	1st	2nd	3rd	4th	Win & Pl
23	3	5	4	3	£55,196
	1/19	Chep	2m7½f Cls3 Nov Ch gd-sft		£7,343
120	3/18	Wwck	2m5f Cls4 97-120 Hdl Hcap soft		£4,419
110	3/18	Wwck	2m5f Cls4 94-117 Hdl Hcap heavy		£4,549

Very useful novice chaser two seasons ago (second in the Reynoldstown) and looked to have improved when running Santini to a head first time out last term; subsequently well fancied for the Welsh National but finished only ninth and didn't run again.

Nube Negra (Spa)

6 br g Dink - Manly Dream (Highest Honor)

Dan Skelton   T Spraggett

PLACINGS: 12135/8B36/1122-   RPR **153 + c**

Starts	1st	2nd	3rd	4th	Win & Pl
13	4	3	2	-	£59,697
	10/19	Fknm	2m1½f Cls3 Nov Ch good		£8,058
	10/19	Wwck	2m Cls4 Ch good		£5,198
	1/18	Donc	2m1½f Cls4 Nov Hdl soft		£4,094
	11/17	MRas	2m1½f Cls4 Hdl 3yo gd-sft		£3,899

Took really well to fences last season and left

hurdling form behind, winning first two chases in fine style and twice finishing second at a higher level; seems best on flat tracks and kept back for Aintree before season's cancellation; yet to run beyond 2m1f.

Ok Corral (Ire)

10 b g Mahler - Acoola (Fiemensfirth)

Nicky Henderson   John P McManus

PLACINGS: 1/2/12125/11P/091-   RPR **157 + c**

Starts	1st	2nd	3rd	4th	Win & Pl
13	6	3	-	-	£123,013
146	1/20	Donc	3m Cls1 List 128-146 Ch Hcap gd-sft		£56,950
	1/19	Wwck	3m Cls1 Nov List Ch good		£14,238
	12/18	Plum	3m1½f Cls3 Nov Ch soft		£7,522
	2/18	Kemp	2m5f Cls4 Nov Hdl soft		£4,094
	5/17	Kemp	2m Cls4 Nov Hdl good		£3,249
	2/15	Kemp	2m Cls5 Mdn NHF 4-6yo soft		£2,274

Very lightly raced for his age, being tenderly handled since missing more than two years through injury as a youngster; took time to come right last season but won the Sky Bet Chase at Doncaster; has still run just six times over fences and open to improvement.

Oldgrangewood

9 b g Central Park - Top Of The Class (Rudimentary)

Dan Skelton   Chris Giles & Sandra Giles

PLACINGS: P3/331P4/9693/33114-   RPR **151 c**

Starts	1st	2nd	3rd	4th	Win & Pl
25	7	1	8	3	£173,252
142	1/20	Chel	2m4½f Cls1 Gd3 137-161 Ch Hcap soft		£39,389
135	11/19	Newb	2m4f Cls2 129-155 Ch Hcap gd-sft		£31,280
145	12/17	Newb	2m4f Cls2 128-152 Ch Hcap gd-sft		£31,280
134	2/17	Weth	2m3½f Cls2 124-143 Ch Hcap soft		£11,574
130	12/16	Weth	2m3½f Cls3 Nov 125-137 Ch Hcap gd-sft		£6,498
120	11/16	Kemp	2m2f Cls4 Nov 108-120 Ch Hcap good		£4,660
	2/16	Ayr	2m Cls5 Mdn Hdl soft		£2,599

Back to form last season when taking advantage of a plummeting mark to win good handicap chases at Newbury and Cheltenham (beat subsequent Ryanair runner-up Saint Calvados); ran another fine race when fourth off career-high mark in the Plate.

On The Blind Side (Ire)

8 b g Stowaway - Such A Set Up (Supreme Leader)

Nicky Henderson   A D Spence

PLACINGS: 1/1116/41P2/4P23-   RPR **152 c**

Starts	1st	2nd	3rd	4th	Win & Pl
12	4	2	1	2	£75,087
	2/20	Newc	2m1½f Cls4 NHF slow		£3,249
	1/19	Kemp	3m Cls4 Nov Ch gd-sft		£4,614
	12/17	Sand	2m4f Cls1 Nov Gd2 Hdl gd-sft		£17,085
	11/17	Chel	2m5f Cls1 Nov Gd2 Hdl gd-sft		£17,165
	10/17	Aint	2m4f Cls4 Mdn Hdl gd-sft		£5,005

Largely disappointing since winning two Grade 2 novice hurdles in 2017-18 but has slowly got the hang of fences and produced some fair efforts in defeat last season, albeit twice a beaten favourite; still quite lightly raced over fences and open to improvement.

On The Slopes

6 b g Librettist - Dalriath (Fraam)

Chris Gordon   Skill Scaffolding

PLACINGS: P/3P3212403/4233311-					RPR **148+**c

Starts	1st	2nd	3rd	4th	Win & Pl
14	3	3	5	2	£34,157
136	3/20	Kemp	2m Cls3 Nov 124-136 Ch Hcap gd-sft........£8,447
129	2/20	Kemp	2m2f Cls3 Nov 119-130 Ch Hcap gd-sft........£8,447
	12/18	Font	2m1¹/₂f Cls4 Nov Hdl soft........£4,094

Progressing really well at the end of last season when dropped in trip to win two novice handicap chases at Kempton; consistent over further earlier in the season and a fine third behind subsequent festival winners Simply The Betts and Imperial Aura at Cheltenham.

One For The Team

6 b g Shirocco - One Gulp (Hernando)

Nick Williams   Forty Winks Syndicate & Partner

PLACINGS: 1/44/2231-3					RPR **143+**h

Starts	1st	2nd	3rd	4th	Win & Pl
8	2	2	2	2	£28,300
130	2/20	Newb	3m Cls2 124-136 Hdl Hcap good........£12,512
	3/18	Winc	1m7¹/₂f Cls5 Mdn NHF 4-6yo soft........£2,274

Hugely progressive staying hurdler last season; took a big leap forward when winning a 3m handicap at Newbury on his final run by 14 lengths, relishing good ground having twice been placed in good handicaps on softer; looks a proper chasing type.

Ornua (Ire)

9 ch g Mahler - Merry Heart (Broken Hearted)

Henry De Bromhead (Ire)   John J Phelan & Syed Momin

PLACINGS: 12122F1/P28032-83332					RPR **152**c

Starts	1st	2nd	3rd	4th	Win & Pl
27	6	6	7	-	£169,401
	4/19	Aint	2m Cls1 Nov Gd1 Ch good........£56,130
	10/18	Rosc	2m¹/₂f Nov Gd3 Ch good........£20,885
	7/18	NAbb	2m¹/₂f Cls3 Nov Ch good........£11,148
	6/18	Wxfd	2m Ch good........£6,814
	5/17	Clon	2m¹/₂f Hdl good........£6,581
	5/17	DRoy	2m Mdn Hdl good........£5,791

Largely out of sorts since winning a Grade 1 novice chase at Aintree in April 2019 but did much better again when second to Castlegrace Paddy in a Grade 2 at Navan on final run last season considering unsuitably heavy ground (has form on soft but generally better on good).

Paisley Park (Ire)

8 b g Oscar - Presenting Shares (Presenting)

Emma Lavelle   Andrew Gemmell

PLACINGS: 2/1220/11111/117-					RPR **162+**h

Starts	1st	2nd	3rd	4th	Win & Pl
13	8	3	-	-	£426,282
	1/20	Chel	3m Cls1 Gd2 Hdl soft........£33,762
	11/19	Newb	3m Cls1 Gd2 Hdl gd-sft........£28,810
	3/19	Chel	3m Cls1 Gd1 Hdl gd-sft........£182,878
	1/19	Chel	3m Cls1 Gd2 Hdl gd-sft........£33,762
	12/18	Asct	3m¹/₂f Cls1 Gd1 Hdl soft........£56,950
147	11/18	Hayd	3m¹/₂f Cls1 Gd3 125-147 Hdl Hcap good........£56,950
140	10/18	Aint	2m4f Cls2 116-140 Hdl Hcap good........£17,204
	12/17	Hrfd	2m3¹/₂f Cls4 Nov Hdl soft........£4,549

Dominant staying hurdler of the last two seasons despite losing Stayers' Hurdle crown at Cheltenham in March (found to have suffered a heart fibrillation); had won his previous seven races and overcame an unsuitably steady gallop to win a second Cleeve Hurdle last season.

Palladium

4 ch g Champs Elysees - Galicuix (Galileo)

Nicky Henderson   A Meade, G Van Geest & E Kelvin-Hughes

PLACINGS: 211P-7					RPR **135+**h

Starts	1st	2nd	3rd	4th	Win & Pl
5	2	1	-	-	£14,951
	2/20	Sand	2m Cls3 Nov Hdl heavy........£6,343
	1/20	Sand	2m Cls3 Hdl 4yo soft........£6,923

Looked a smart recruit to hurdles last season, twice winning by wide margins at Sandown; reportedly unsuited by tacky surface at Cheltenham when pulled up in the Fred Winter at Cheltenham (joint-favourite).

Panic Attack (Ire)

4 b f Canford Cliffs - Toto Corde Meo (Galileo)

David Pipe   Bryan Drew

PLACINGS: 10-2					RPR **107+**h

Starts	1st	2nd	3rd	4th	Win & Pl
3	1	1	-	-	£12,496
	1/20	MRas	2m1¹/₂f Cls1 List NHF 4-6yo soft........£11,390

Exciting filly who was thrown in at Listed level on her debut at Market Rasen last season and hacked up by ten lengths; subsequently sold out of Willie Mullins' yard but disappointed on first run for David Pipe when down the field in the Champion Bumper at Cheltenham.

Petit Mouchoir (Fr)

9 gr g Al Namix - Arnette (Denham Red)

Gordon Elliott (Ire)   Gigginstown House Stud

PLACINGS: 12324/6304/442235-23					RPR **159**h

Starts	1st	2nd	3rd	4th	Win & Pl
29	5	7	7	5	£426,351
	10/17	Punc	2m Ch yld-sft........£7,634
	1/17	Leop	2m Gd1 Hdl good........£55,470
	12/16	Leop	2m Gd1 Hdl yield........£43,382
	11/15	Thur	2m Mdn Hdl 4yo soft........£5,349
	4/15	Punc	2m NHF 4-5yo gd-yld........£45,736

Lost his way after two Grade 1 wins in 2016-

Get closer to the racing.

RACE REPLAYS

Watch unlimited video race replays from all 86 British and Irish racecourses

DIGITAL NEWSPAPER

Get tomorrow's Racing Post paper digitally and in full every day at 9pm

EXPERT ANALYSIS

Study the form alongside our experts with in-running comments and post-race analysis.

Join now at racingpost.com/membersclub

For The Must-Have Racing Info

RACING POST

17 but back in his element last season in 2m hurdles, running several fine races at the top level including a fine fifth in the Champion Hurdle at Cheltenham, though still without a win since chase debut in October 2017; left Henry de Bromhead after £70,000 sale.

Phoenix Way (Ire)

7 b g Stowaway - Arcuate (Arch)

Harry Fry   John P McManus

PLACINGS: 1/521/1-   RPR **141**+h

Starts	1st	2nd	3rd	4th	Win & Pl
4	2	1	-	-	£20,858
	1/20	Hntg	3m1f Cls2 124-141 Hdl Hcap soft		£12,512
	1/19	Plum	2m4¹/₂f Cls3 Nov Hdl 4-7yo gd-sft		£6,498

Ran just once last season and did really well to overcome a year absence to land a Pertemps qualifier at Huntingdon despite racing keenly; still very lightly raced having previously run just three times in novice hurdles in 2018-19; likely to go novice chasing.

Pic D'Orhy (Fr)

5 b g Turgeon - Rose Candy (Roli Abi)

Paul Nicholls   Mrs Johnny De La Hey

PLACINGS: 11/21U220/F61-2   RPR **150**h

Starts	1st	2nd	3rd	4th	Win & Pl
12	4	4	-	-	£265,046
	2/20	Newb	2m¹/₂f Cls1 Gd3 130-153 Hdl Hcap good		£87,219
	9/18	Autl	2m2f Hdl 3yo v soft		£25,487
	4/18	Autl	1m7f Hdl 3yo v soft		£23,363
	3/18	Autl	1m7f Hdl 3yo heavy		£22,088

French Grade 1 runner-up who initially

disappointed for new connections (had been sent off just 12-1 for the Triumph Hurdle on British debut) but finally came good when a 33-1 winner of last season's Betfair Hurdle; runner-up on chase debut and seen by his trainer as a top prospect over fences.

Pileon (Ire)

6 b g Yeats - Heath Heaven (Alflora)

Philip Hobbs   Tim Syder & Martin St Quinton

PLACINGS: 421/4112-   RPR **139**h

Starts	1st	2nd	3rd	4th	Win & Pl
5	3	1		1	£24,540
	1/20	Ffos	2m4f Cls4 Nov Hdl 4-7yo heavy		£3,899
	1/20	Catt	2m3¹/₂f Cls4 Nov Hdl 4-7yo soft		£4,809
	3/19	Extr	2m1f Cls5 NHF 4-6yo gd-sft		£2,274

Easy winner of two modest novice hurdles last season and came agonisingly close in hat-trick bid in the Martin Pipe at Cheltenham, getting headed on the line by Indefatigable; should stay 3m; likely to go novice chasing.

Poker Party (Fr)

8 ch g Gentlewave - Becquarette (Nombre Premier)

Henry de Bromhead (Ire)   Robcour

PLACINGS: 11700/56U5211/3U143-   RPR **153**c

Starts	1st	2nd	3rd	4th	Win & Pl
21	5	1	2	2	£179,425
	138	9/19	List	3m 131-154 Ch Hcap yield	£106,306
	128	2/19	Naas	2m4f Nov 113-134 Ch Hcap good	£26,577
	119	1/19	Naas	2m4f Nov 104-127 Ch Hcap yld-sft	£10,267
	107	12/17	Tram	2m5f 83-107 Hdl Hcap heavy	£6,318
	100	11/17	Clon	2m3¹/₂f 82-107 Hdl Hcap sft-hvy	£6,318

Progressive handicap chaser who won last

season's Kerry National before staying on into fourth in the Paddy Power Chase and looking short of pace when third in another valuable Leopardstown handicap; should do better back at 3m and possibly further.

Politologue (Fr)

9 gr g Poliglote - Scarlet Row (Turgeon)

Paul Nicholls
J Hales

PLACINGS: 4F/111241/14422/251-
RPR **173**c

Starts	1st	2nd	3rd	4th	Win & Pl
26	11	7	-	4	£898,846
	3/20	Chel	2m Cls1 Gd1 Ch soft		£225,080
	11/18	Asct	2m5f Cls1 Gd2 Ch gd-sft		£39,865
	4/18	Aint	2m4f Cls1 Gd1 Ch soft		£140,985
	12/17	Kemp	2m Cls1 Gd2 Ch soft		£52,854
	12/17	Sand	1m7¹/₂f Cls1 Gd1 Ch gd-sft		£85,827
154	11/17	Extr	2m1¹/₂f Cls1 Gd2 142-162 Ch Hcap soft		£37,192
	2/17	Kemp	2m4¹/₂f Cls2 Ch gd-sft		£12,512
	12/16	Asct	2m5f Cls1 Nov Gd2 Ch gd-sft		£18,224
	11/16	Hayd	2m5¹/₂f Cls2 Nov Ch soft		£16,245
	2/16	Extr	2m1f Cls1 Nov List Hdl heavy		£11,524
	6/15	Autl	2m2f Hdl 4yo soft		£17,860

Smart over a variety of trips but really found his niche as a front-running two-miler last season, producing a stunning win in the Champion Chase; race fell apart overall but had also pushed Defi Du Seuil close in the Shloer Chase before breaking a blood vessel in the Tingle Creek.

Tough stayer Potters Corner takes a dip in the sea with his stablemates

Potters Corner (Ire)

10 b g Indian Danehill - Woodford Beauty (Phardante)

Christian Williams
All Stars Sports Racing & J Davies

PLACINGS: 1/2342/9P1FF1/5P011-
RPR **157**+c

Starts	1st	2nd	3rd	4th	Win & Pl
22	7	2	3	1	£214,694
145	12/19	Chep	3m6¹/₂f Cls3 Gd3 134-160 Ch Hcap heavy		£85,425
129	12/19	Chep	2m7¹/₂f Cls3 106-131 Hdl Hcap soft		£5,913
135	3/19	Uttx	4m2f Cls1 List 128-154 Ch Hcap heavy		£84,655
120	12/18	Winc	3m1f Cls3 100-124 Ch Hcap gd-sft		£12,996
	4/16	Ffos	2m4f Cls4 Nov Hdl soft		£3,249
	9/15	Chep	2m3¹/₂f Cls5 Mdn Hdl good		£2,274
	9/14	Chep	2m Cls6 NHF 4-6yo good		£1,560

Has flourished in marathon handicap chases over the last two seasons, winning the Welsh National last term to add to his Midlands National success; Chepstow form proved red-hot and should remain a big player in top staying handicaps.

Precious Cargo (Ire)

7 b g Yeats - Kilbarry Classic (Classic Cliche)

Nicky Henderson
Thomas Barr

PLACINGS: 120/116/123F-
RPR **149**+c

Starts	1st	2nd	3rd	4th	Win & Pl
10	4	2	1	-	£29,395
	12/19	Hayd	2m1¹/₂f Cls3 Nov Ch heavy		£9,405
	3/19	Sand	2m Cls4 Nov Hdl soft		£5,198
	1/19	Kemp	2m Cls4 Nov Hdl gd-sft		£4,094
	1/18	Ayr	2m Cls5 NHF 4-6yo heavy		£2,274

Has three wins and a short-head defeat in four runs at Class 3 level or below over jumps but has come up short in Graded company; still in contention for a place when falling two out in the novice handicap at the Cheltenham Festival.

Presenting Percy

9 b g Sir Percy - Hunca Munca (Presenting)

Gordon Elliott (Ire)   Philip J Reynolds

PLACINGS: 4116/131121/18/353F-   **RPR 172**c

Starts		1st	2nd	3rd	4th	Win & Pl
23		10	2	3	2	£313,835
	1/19	Gowr	3m Gd2 Hdl soft..................................£23,919			
	3/18	Chel	3m1¹/₂f Cls1 Nov Gd1 Ch soft..........£100,132			
	1/18	Gowr	3m Gd2 Hdl heavy..............................£23,496			
145	12/17	Fair	3m5f 117-145 Ch Hcap soft................£25,214			
	10/17	Gway	2m6¹/₂f Ch heavy................................£10,003			
146	3/17	Chel	3m Cls1 List 137-147 Hdl Hcap good....£54,103			
130	2/17	Fair	2m4f 108-138 Hdl Hcap heavy............£13,667			
115	11/16	Punc	2m Nov 90-121 Hdl Hcap soft..............£7,235			
	10/16	Gway	2m Mdn Hdl 4-5yo yield........................£5,879			
	4/16	Baln	2m1f NHF 4-7yo heavy..........................£4,296			

Looked to have the world at his feet when an easy winner of a red-hot RSA Chase in 2018 but has failed to win a single race over fences since then; still not far off the best last season, though, and was staying on well when falling two out in the Cheltenham Gold Cup; has since left Pat Kelly.

Put The Kettle On (Ire)

6 b m Stowaway - Name For Fame (Quest For Fame)

Henry de Bromhead (Ire)   One For Luck Racing Syndicate

PLACINGS: 52153/31111211-   **RPR 159+**c

Starts		1st	2nd	3rd	4th	Win & Pl
13		7	2	2	-	£183,708
	3/20	Chel	2m Cls1 Nov Gd1 Ch soft....................£98,764			
	11/19	Chel	2m Cls1 Nov Gd2 Ch soft....................£19,933			
	9/19	Wxfd	2m4f Nov Ch good..............................£10,649			
	7/19	Tipp	2m3¹/₂f Nov Ch good............................£8,785			
113	6/19	Dpat	2m3f 102-115 Hdl Hcap yield..............£13,851			
	5/19	Kbgn	2m4f Ch yield......................................£6,937			
	11/18	Navn	2m Mdn Auct Hdl good......................£10,903			

Massive improver last season when switched to fences, kicking off at Kilbeggan in May and making it five wins out of six over fences when back from a winter break in the Arkle at Cheltenham; proven up to 2m4f; effective on good and soft ground.

Pym (Ire)

7 b g Stowaway - Liss Rua (Bob Back)

Nicky Henderson   Mrs Patricia Pugh

PLACINGS: 1/29/12210/211PP-   **RPR 153+**c

Starts		1st	2nd	3rd	4th	Win & Pl
13		5	4	-	-	£52,603
	12/19	Chel	3m1¹/₂f Cls2 Nov Ch gd-sft................£16,218			
137	11/19	Asct	3m Cls3 Nov 123-137 Ch Hcap soft......£8,058			
	1/19	Kemp	2m5f Cls4 Nov Hdl gd-sft.....................£4,094			
	10/18	Chep	2m Cls4 Nov Hdl good..........................£4,809			
	4/17	Ayr	2m Cls3 NHF 4-6yo gd-sft.....................£6,498			

Didn't quite live up to expectations over hurdles but did much better when sent chasing last season, winning a strong novice handicap at Ascot before claiming a notable scalp in Imperial

Aura (possible non-stayer) at Cheltenham; pulled up in the Reynoldstown and RSA.

Queens Brook (Ire)

5 b m Shirocco - Awesome Miracle (Supreme Leader)

Gordon Elliott (Ire)   Noel Moran & Mrs Valerie Moran

PLACINGS: 3/113-1   **RPR 122+**h

Starts		1st	2nd	3rd	4th	Win & Pl
3		2	-	1	-	£19,957
	10/20	Fair	2m Mdn Hdl yield................................£6,500			
	2/20	Gowr	2m1f NHF 4-7yo heavy.........................£5,500			

Bought for £160,000 after winning a point-to-point last November and quickly made a big impression under rules, hacking up by 21 lengths on bumper debut and finishing third in the Champion Bumper at Cheltenham; should make a fine novice hurdler.

Quel Destin (Fr)

5 ch g Muhtathir - High Destiny (High Yield)

Paul Nicholls   Martin Broughton & Friends

PLACINGS: 54/F12111115/18512-   **RPR 157+**h

Starts		1st	2nd	3rd	4th	Win & Pl
16		8	2	-	1	£194,309
	2/20	Sand	2m Cls1 List Hdl heavy........................£17,286			
	10/19	Chel	2m Cls2 Hdl 4yo heavy........................£25,024			
	2/19	Hayd	1m7¹/₂f Cls2 Hdl 4yo gd-sft................£12,996			
	12/18	Chep	2m Cls1 Gd1 Hdl 3yo soft....................£37,018			
	12/18	Donc	2m1¹/₂f Cls1 Gd2 Hdl 3yo good..........£28,135			
	11/18	Chel	2m1¹/₂f Cls1 Gd2 Hdl 3yo good..........£18,006			
	10/18	Kemp	2m Cls3 Hdl 3yo good..........................£6,498			
	5/18	Autl	1m7f Hdl 3yo heavy............................£19,115			

High-class juvenile hurdler two seasons ago (Grade 1 winner at Chepstow) and progressed again last season, beating Call Me Lord at Sandown and unlucky not to win a Grade 2 at Fontwell (collared late having got racing too early); likely to go novice chasing.

Ramses De Teillee (Fr)

8 gr g Martaline - Princesse D'Orton (Saint Cyrien)

David Pipe   John White & Anne Underhill

PLACINGS: 121279/5122P/14110-5   **RPR 150+**h

Starts		1st	2nd	3rd	4th	Win & Pl
24		6	7	2	2	£147,770
	2/20	Hayd	3m1¹/₂f Cls1 Nov Gd2 Hdl heavy........£16,938			
	1/20	Donc	3m1¹/₂f Cls1 Nov Gd2 Hdl gd-sft........£17,085			
	10/19	Chel	3m Cls2 Nov Hdl heavy.........................£9,384			
140	12/18	Chep	2m7¹/₂f Cls2 127-142 Ch Hcap heavy....£12,660			
	1/18	Chep	2m7¹/₂f Cls3 Nov Ch heavy...................£7,343			
122	11/17	Chep	2m7¹/₂f Cls4 Nov 103-122 Ch Hcap heavy....£3,899			

Best known as a smart staying chaser but spent most of last season exploiting novice status over hurdles, winning three times including two Grade 2 contests; progressive in last full season over fences, finishing second in the Welsh National and Grand National Trial at Haydock.

Put The Kettle On: last season's Arkle winner also has winning form over fences at 2m4f

Rathhill (Ire)

7 b g Getaway - Bella Venezia (Milan)

Nicky Henderson   John P McManus

PLACINGS: 2/14/00-   RPR **119**h

Starts	1st	2nd	3rd	4th	Win & Pl
4	1	-	-	1	£7,473
12/18	Newb	2m1/2f Cls4 Mdn Hdl soft.................................£4,809			

Long held in high regard at home but reputation has taken a hit since sent off favourite for the Tolworth Hurdle in 2019 after impressive hurdling debut; only fourth at Sandown and fared even worse in two runs in handicaps last season, most recently in the County Hurdle.

Ravenhill (Ire)

10 b g Winged Love - Rhythm Hill (Orchestra)

Gordon Elliott (Ire)   Try Ravenhill Syndicate

PLACINGS: 4P/21121/312152F1-U6   RPR **157**+c

Starts	1st	2nd	3rd	4th	Win & Pl
17	6	4	1	1	£164,382
	3/20	Chel	3m6f Cls1 Nov Gd2 Am Ch soft....................£74,306		
128	7/19	Limk	2m6f 109-132 Ch Hcap good........................£15,946		
	5/19	Limk	2m3½f Ch good £8,047		
	8/18	Sedg	2m4f Cls4 Nov Hdl gd-fm £4,094		
	6/18	Kbgn	3m1f Nov Hdl good £7,359		
	6/18	Dpat	2m5½f Mdn Hdl good £5,996		

Produced a fine staying performance to win the National Hunt Chase at Cheltenham last season; had quickly established himself in top handicaps

after starting chasing in the summer, notably when a head second in the Kerry National; could improve again back on quicker ground.

Real Steel (Fr)

7 b g Loup Breton - Kalimina (Monsun)

Paul Nicholls | Sullivan Bloodstock

PLACINGS: 1F50P4/F1162/1141P6-   RPR **168c**

Starts	1st	2nd	3rd	4th	Win & Pl
18	6	2	-	2	£170,390
	1/20	Thur	2m4½f Gd2 Ch yield		£22,500
	11/19	DRoy	2m3½f Gd2 Ch soft		£26,577
151	5/19	Punc	2m5f Nov 130-151 Ch Hcap gd-yld		£53,153
	2/19	Thur	2m2f Ch good		£14,405
	1/19	Fair	2m5½f Ch yield		£7,769
	11/17	Thur	2m Mdn Hdl 4yo soft		£5,791

Highly tried throughout his career and justified connections' faith with some fine performances last season despite going 0-8 at Grade 1 level overall; won two Grade 2 races by wide margins and finished sixth in the Cheltenham Gold Cup on first run beyond 2m5f over fences; has since left Willie Mullins.

Red Risk (Fr)

5 b g No Risk At All - Rolie De Vindecy (Roli Abi)

Paul Nicholls | Middleham Park Racing & A&J Ryan

PLACINGS: 7/P17524/9131-3   RPR **147c**

Starts	1st	2nd	3rd	4th	Win & Pl
12	3	1	2	1	£82,997
135	2/20	Ludl	2m4f Cls3 Nov 124-135 Ch Hcap soft		£7,863
	9/19	Autl	2m1½f Ch 4yo v soft		£22,486
	10/18	Autl	2m1½f Hdl 3yo v soft		£19,115

French chase winner who proved himself a smart recruit when winning easily on his second start for new connections in a novice handicap chase at Ludlow; might well have benefited from step up to 2m4f; 9lb higher mark unlikely to be limit of his ability.

Redford Road

6 b g Trans Island - Maryscross (Presenting)

Nigel Twiston-Davies | Options O Syndicate

PLACINGS: 2/112150-3   RPR **142+h**

Starts	1st	2nd	3rd	4th	Win & Pl
8	3	2			£31,261
	12/19	Chel	3m Cls1 Nov Gd2 Hdl soft		£18,224
	11/19	Weth	2m3½f Cls4 Nov Hdl soft		£4,224
	9/19	Wwck	2m Cls5 NHF 4-6yo gd-sft		£2,599

Won three of first four races over hurdles last season, most notably a 3m Grade 2 novice at Cheltenham when relishing the step up in trip; failed to build on that, managing only fifth in a Listed hurdle at the same track and tailed off in the Albert Bartlett; likely to go novice chasing.

Relegate (Ire)

7 b m Flemensfirth - Last Of The Bunch (Silver Patriarch)

Colm Murphy (Ire) | Paul McKeon

PLACINGS: 1117/215/45-   RPR **139+h**

Starts	1st	2nd	3rd	4th	Win & Pl
9	3	1	-	1	£104,971
	12/18	Naas	2m Mdn Hdl yield		£7,359
	3/18	Chel	2m1½f Cls1 Gd1 NHF 4-6yo soft		£42,713
	2/18	Leop	2m Gd2 NHF 4-7yo soft		£39,159
	1/18	Punc	2m NHF 5-7yo sft-hvy		£6,550

Yet to build on Champion Bumper win at Cheltenham in 2018 but continued to shape with promise over hurdles after more than a year out last season; given too much to do when joint-favourite for the Pertemps Final but stayed on really well into fifth.

Reserve Tank (Ire)

6 b g Jeremy - Lady Bellamy (Black Sam Bellamy)

Colin Tizzard | The Reserve Tankers

PLACINGS: 37111/1212P-   RPR **152+c**

Starts	1st	2nd	3rd	4th	Win & Pl
10	5	2	1	-	£151,892
	11/19	Winc	2m4f Cls1 Nov Gd2 Ch gd-sft		£19,021
	5/19	Punc	2m4f Nov Gd1 Hdl gd-yld		£53,153
	4/19	Aint	2m4f Cls1 Nov Gd1 Hdl good		£56,130
	3/19	Kemp	2m5f Cls4 Nov Hdl gd-sft		£4,260
	2/19	Sand	2m Cls4 Nov Hdl soft		£5,198

Failed to build on promising start over fences last season and pulled up in the Marsh Novices' Chase at Cheltenham; had been given a break after 1-2 defeat at Newbury as felt to be best in spring (big improver at that time of year in 2019 when winning two Grade 1 novice hurdles).

Ribble Valley (Ire)

7 b g Westerner - Miss Greinton (Greinton)

Nicky Richards   David Wesley Yates

PLACINGS: 161/112-   RPR **140+**h

Starts	1st	2nd	3rd	4th	Win & Pl
6	4	1	-	-	£21,084
11/19	Weth	2m Cls4 Nov Hdl soft			£4,224
11/19	Hexm	2m Cls4 Nov Hdl heavy			£4,419
1/19	Ayr	2m Cls5 NHF 4-6yo gd-sft			£2,274
11/18	Ayr	2m Cls5 Am Mdn NHF 4-6yo good			£2,395

Has won four out of six races under rules, adding

to two bumper wins in 2018-19 with two more victories in novice hurdles last season, hacking up at Hexham and Wetherby; disappointing second when odds-on for a Grade 2 at Ascot on final run.

Riders Onthe Storm (Ire)

7 br g Scorpion - Endless Moments (Saddlers' Hall)

Nigel Twiston-Davies   Carl Hinchy And Mark Scott

PLACINGS: 5/521260/431FP/111F-   RPR **167+**c

Starts	1st	2nd	3rd	4th	Win & Pl
17	5	2	1	2	£214,463
	2/20	Asct	2m5f Cls1 Gd1 Ch soft		£97,448
	12/19	Asct	2m5f Cls2 Ch heavy		£31,280
140	11/19	Aint	2m4f Cls2 131-147 Ch Hcap soft		£49,520
	2/19	Punc	2m Nov Ch gd-yld		£10,267
	1/18	Navn	2m Nov Hdl heavy		£8,722

Went from strength to strength last season and

Reserve Tank: disappointing in final two starts last season

won all three completed races, though perhaps fortunate to win the Ascot Chase after Cyrname flopped and Traffic Fluide fell at the last; still well in contention when falling three out in the Ryanair Chase at Cheltenham.

Road To Respect (Ire)

9 ch g Gamut - Lora Lady (Lord America)

Noel Meade (Ire)   Gigginstown House Stud

PLACINGS: 2211/12143/13235/13-   RPR **170**c

Starts		1st	2nd	3rd	4th	Win & Pl
26		8	6	7	2	£584,114
	11/19	DRoy	3m Gd1 Ch soft			£79,730
	11/18	DRoy	3m Gd1 Ch gd-yld			£73,097
	12/17	Leop	3m Gd1 Ch yield			£75,641
	10/17	Punc	3m1f Gd3 Ch soft			£20,171
	4/17	Fair	2m4f Nov Gd1 Ch gd-yld			£50,427
145	3/17	Chel	2m5f Cls1 Gd3 133-158 Ch Hcap good			£59,798
	11/16	Naas	2m3f Ch yld-sft			£6,105
	2/16	Thur	2m6½f Mdn Hdl heavy			£4,522

Three-time Grade 1 winner in Ireland, including

Robin De Carlow

7 br m Robin Des Champs - La Reine De Riogh (Presenting)

Willie Mullins (Ire)   Catchherifucan Racing Syndicate

PLACINGS: 11311541F/11P21-   RPR **146**c

Starts		1st	2nd	3rd	4th	Win & Pl
14		8	1	1	1	£117,589
	10/19	Tipp	2m4f Nov Gd3 Ch gd-yld			£23,919
	7/19	Klny	2m7f Nov Ch good			£9,584
	6/19	Kbgn	2m4f Ch gd-yld			£6,659
	3/19	Limk	2m6f Nov Gd3 Hdl heavy			£19,669
	11/18	Cork	3m Nov List Hdl gd-yld			£20,885
	10/18	Limk	2m6½f List Hdl good			£19,049
	7/18	Kbgn	2m4f Mdn Hdl good			£5,996
	5/18	Baln	2m½f NHF 4-7yo good			£5,996

Four-time hurdles winner who proved even

better when switched to fences last summer, with three wins including a half-length defeat of Arkle heroine Put The Kettle On in a Grade 3 at Tipperary; missed the rest of the season but set to return.

Roksana (Ire)

8 b m Dubai Destination - Talktothetail (Flemensfirth)

Dan Skelton   Mrs Sarah Faulks

PLACINGS: 4/31112/312/2524-					RPR **151**h
Starts	1st	2nd	3rd	4th	Win & Pl
13	4	4	2	2	£191,210

	3/19	Chel	2m4f Cls1 Gd1 Hdl soft.................................£70,563
130	3/18	Newb	2m4¹/₂f Cls1 Nov Gd2 115-135 Hdl Hcap soft..£22,780
	12/17	Font	2m3f Cls4 Nov Hdl heavy...............................£3,249
	11/17	Plum	2m4¹/₂f Cls4 Nov Hdl good £3,249

Fortuitous winner of the Mares' Hurdle at

Ronald Pump

7 ch g Schiaparelli - Fruit Yoghurt (Hernando)

Matthew Smith (Ire)   Laois Limerick Syndicate

PLACINGS: 4R/4404911411/12242-					RPR **161**h
Starts	1st	2nd	3rd	4th	Win & Pl
21	5	3	1	6	£154,011

	11/19	Fair	2m5f Ch heavy...£6,389
136	4/19	Fair	3m Nov 112-136 Hdl Hcap gd-yld.................£29,234
123	3/19	Cork	3m 108-130 Hdl Hcap soft..............................£9,989
108	1/19	Fair	3m 81-108 Hdl Hcap good...............................£6,659
102	12/18	Cork	2m4f Nov 80-102 Hdl Hcap sft-hvy.................£5,996

Cheltenham in 2019 but only fourth in the same race last season; had run better when second to Summerville Boy in the Relkeel Hurdle; best form at 3m, finishing second in Grade 1 races at Aintree on only two previous runs at the trip.

Failed to build on impressive chasing debut last season in two more runs over fences (jumping fell apart) but thrived back over hurdles, finishing second in the Stayers' Hurdle at Cheltenham; had been progressive in that sphere previously and still open to improvement.

Rouge Vif (Fr)

6 b g Sageburg - Rouge Amour (Cadoudal)

Harry Whittington   Kate & Andrew Brooks

PLACINGS: 1/5212113/14213-					RPR **158+**c
Starts	1st	2nd	3rd	4th	Win & Pl
13	6	3	2	1	£117,360

	2/20	Wwck	2m Cls1 Nov Gd2 Ch gd-sft £22,780
	10/19	MRas	2m1f Cls3 Nov Ch gd-sft..................................£7,988
	3/19	Kels	2m2f Cls1 Nov Gd2 Hdl gd-sft.......................£28,475
	1/19	Newc	2m Cls4 Nov Hdl soft......................................£4,094
	12/18	Sthl	1m7¹/₂f Cls4 Mdn Hdl gd-sft £4,094
	3/18	Ludl	2m Cls4 NHF 4-6yo soft..................................£4,809

Very smart novice chaser last season, relishing the sharp circuits of Warwick (won the Kingmaker) and Kempton (second in the Wayward Lad); fair third in the Racing Post Arkle given it might not be his track (last of four there in November); open to improvement and could develop into Champion Chase contender,

Road To Respect: a loving hug from Sean Flanagan after their victory at Down Royal last November

Royal Rendezvous (Ire)
8 b g King's Theatre - Novacella (Beyssac)

Willie Mullins (Ire)   Dr S P Fitzgerald

PLACINGS: 4F1/5111/P1351-2   RPR **153**+c

Starts	1st	2nd	3rd	4th	Win & Pl
10	5	1	1	-	£85,903

	3/20	Naas	2m4f Nov Gd3 Ch soft £16,250
	11/19	Thur	2m2f Ch soft £6,389
	10/18	Gway	2m¹/₂f Mdn Hdl yield £7,632
	10/18	Tipp	2m NHF 4-7yo good £7,087
	8/18	Dpat	2m3f NHF 4-7yo gd-yld £5,451

Very lightly raced gelding who ran a cracker on handicap debut in July when a close second in the Galway Plate; had been slow to build on victory on chasing debut last season but was highly tried (twice beaten in Grade I races behind Notebook); open to further improvement.

Saint Calvados (Fr)
7 b g Saint Des Saints - Lamorrese (Pistolet Bleu)

Harry Whittington   Kate & Andrew Brooks

PLACINGS: 1116/1114/1337/1422-   RPR **172**+c

Starts	1st	2nd	3rd	4th	Win & Pl
16	8	2	2	2	£282,786

155	10/19	Chel	2m Cls2 129-155 Ch Hcap heavy £37,164
	11/18	Naas	2m Gd3 Ch yield £17,688
	2/18	Wwck	2m Cls1 Nov Gd2 Ch soft £22,780
147	1/18	Newb	2m¹/₂f Cls3 Nov 135-147 Ch Hcap soft £7,343
143	12/17	Newb	2m¹/₂f Cls3 Nov 127-143 Ch Hcap heavy £8,656
	3/17	Autl	2m2f Hdl 4yo v soft £28,718
	12/16	Cagn	2m1¹/₂f Hdl 3yo soft £15,882
	11/16	Fntb	2m2f Hdl 3yo heavy £8,118

Finally fulfilled early potential last season following switch to hold-up tactics and step up in trip; twice went close over 2m4½f at Cheltenham, notably behind Min in the Ryanair Chase; last of four behind Defi Du Seuil in the Shloer Chase had exposed limitations over 2m.

Saint Roi (Fr)
5 br g Coastal Path - Sainte Vigne (Saint Des Saints)

Willie Mullins (Ire)   John P McManus

PLACINGS: 3/511-1   RPR **151**+h

Starts	1st	2nd	3rd	4th	Win & Pl
5	3	-	1	-	£87,171

	10/20	Tipp	2m Gd3 Hdl good £17,500
137	3/20	Chel	2m1f Cls1 Gd3 133-150 Hdl Hcap soft £56,270
	1/20	Tram	2m Mdn Hdl soft £5,760

Hugely impressive winner of last season's County Hurdle at Cheltenham on handicap debut, hacking up by four and a half lengths from subsequent Galway Hurdle winner Aramon; likely to have Grade I pretensions.

Saint Sonnet (Fr)
5 b g Saint Des Saints - Leprechaun Lady (Irish Wells)

Paul Nicholls   Colm Donlon

PLACINGS: 311/1156317-   RPR **150**c

Starts	1st	2nd	3rd	4th	Win & Pl
10	5		2	-	£114,084

	2/20	Catt	2m3f Cls4 Nov Ch heavy £5,458
	9/19	Autl	2m2f List Ch 4yo v soft £32,432
	8/19	Lign	2m Ch 4yo gd-sft £7,351
	11/18	Autl	2m1¹/₂f Hdl 3yo heavy £27,611
	10/18	Autl	2m1¹/₂f Hdl 3yo v soft £19,115

Won four times in France, including sole run over fences, and shaped with real promise for one so inexperienced in two runs in Britain last season; travelled well for a long way when seventh in the Marsh Novices' Chase at Cheltenham; open to significant improvement.

Saldier (Fr)
6 b g Soldier Hollow - Salve Evita (Monsun)

Willie Mullins (Ire)   Mrs S Ricci

PLACINGS: 1531/F/1-   RPR **161**+h

Starts	1st	2nd	3rd	4th	Win & Pl
6	3	-	1	-	£119,459

	11/19	Punc	2m¹/₂f Gd1 Hdl soft £53,153
	4/18	Punc	2m Gd1 Hdl 4yo yld-sft £52,212
	2/18	Gowr	2m Mdn Hdl 4yo heavy £7,359

Has run just twice since his juvenile campaign three seasons ago but has shaped with huge promise, notably when easily beating solid yardstick Petit Mouchoir in last season's Morgiana Hurdle; prominent in Champion Hurdle market until ruled out with latest setback.

Salsaretta (Fr)
7 b m Kingsalsa - Kendoretta (Kendor)

Willie Mullins (Ire)   Mrs S Ricci

PLACINGS: 392/F5/11U79/P1111-   RPR **150**+c

Starts	1st	2nd	3rd	4th	Win & Pl
15	6	1	1	-	£99,519

	3/20	Limk	2m6¹/₂f Nov Gd2 Ch heavy £25,000
	2/20	Thur	2m6¹/₂f Nov Ch soft £10,750
	12/19	Punc	2m4f Ch yield £10,649
	11/19	Punc	2m3¹/₂f Nov Ch soft £14,351
	12/18	Limk	2m4f Hdl sft-hvy £8,450
	5/18	Slig	2m Mdn Hdl yield £5,996

Unbeaten in four races over fences last season, although kept to a much lower level after failing to finish better than fifth in five Grade I runs over hurdles; last three wins came at odds-on in mares' company and fortunate to win on final run (leader fell two out).

Saint Calvados: high-class performer chases home Min in last season's Ryanair Chase

Sam Brown

8 b g Black Sam Bellamy - Cream Cracker (Sir Harry Lewis)

Anthony Honeyball   T C Frost

Starts	1st	2nd	3rd	4th	Win & Pl
7	5	-	-	1	£31,165

1/20	Hayd	2m4f Cls1 Nov Gd2 Ch heavy	£18,793
1/20	Ling	2m7½f Cls4 Nov Ch heavy	£4,289
12/17	Plum	2m4½f Cls4 Nov Hdl soft	£3,249
3/17	Newb	2m1½f Cls5 NHF 4-6yo soft	£2,599
2/17	Winc	1m7½f Cls6 NHF 4-6yo heavy	£1,949

RPR **157**+c

Fragile but hugely talented stayer who returned in fine form last season having missed more than two years since winning three times in 2017; hacked up in first two novice chases on heavy ground, including a Grade 2 at Haydock; pulled up when favourite for the Reynoldstown.

Sam Spinner

8 b g Black Sam Bellamy - Dawn Spinner (Arctic Lord)

Jedd O'Keeffe   Caron & Paul Chapman

PLACINGS: 211/21153/UU428/111-   RPR **157**+c

Starts	1st	2nd	3rd	4th	Win & Pl
19	9	4	1		£277,544

12/19	Donc	3m Cls1 Nov Gd2 Ch soft	£24,920
11/19	Weth	3m Cls4 Nov Ch soft	£4,809
10/19	Weth	2m3½f Cls4 Nov Ch gd-sft	£4,504
12/17	Asct	3m1½f Cls1 Gd1 Hdl gd-sft	£56,950
139	11/17	Hayd	2m7f Cls1 Gd3 130-156 Hdl Hcap heavy	£56,950
2/17	Catt	2m3½f Cls4 Nov Hdl 4-7yo soft	£3,899
1/17	Catt	2m3½f Cls4 Nov Hdl gd-sft	£3,899
11/16	Newc	2m Cls4 Nov Hdl gd-sft	£6,498
2/16	Catt	1m7½f Cls6 Mdn NHF 4-6yo soft	£1,949

Top-class staying hurdler who took to fences with aplomb last season, winning three out of three until struck down by injury; had become

increasingly inconsistent over hurdles but was classy enough to win the Long Walk in 2017 and finish second in the Stayers' Hurdle in 2019.

Sam's Adventure

8 b g Black Sam Bellamy - My Adventure (Strong Gale)

Brian Ellison   Julie & Phil Martin

PLACINGS: 11/21/302415/42271-   RPR **142**+c

Starts	1st	2nd	3rd	4th	Win & Pl
15	5	4	1	2	£81,170

129	3/20	Uttx	3m Cls2 Nov 129-138 Ch Hcap heavy	£25,024
118	3/19	Newc	2m6f Cls2 Nov 110-126 Hdl Hcap heavy	£12,512
	1/17	Ayr	2m Cls6 NHF 4-6yo heavy	£1,949
	3/16	Newb	2m¹/₂f Cls2 NHF 4-5yo soft	£29,505
	2/16	Weth	2m Cls6 NHF 4-6yo heavy	£1,949

Taking an age to fulfil bumper potential (won three times in that sphere) but again looked a good staying prospect when sent chasing last season; had three runs at around 3m, twice finishing second to subsequent winners before getting his head in front and landing a good novice handicap at Uttoxeter.

Samcro (Ire)

8 ch g Germany - Dun Dun (Saddlers' Hall)

Gordon Elliott (Ire)   Gigginstown House Stud

PLACINGS: /111/1111F/225/1F21-   RPR **165**+c

Starts	1st	2nd	3rd	4th	Win & Pl
15	9	3	-	-	£321,237

	3/20	Chel	2m4f Cls1 Nov Gd1 Ch soft	£84,405
	11/19	DRoy	2m3¹/₂f Ch soft	£7,986
	3/18	Chel	2m5f Cls1 Nov Gd1 Hdl soft	£71,188
	2/18	Leop	2m Nov Gd1 Hdl soft	£52,212
	11/17	Navn	2m4f Nov Gd3 Hdl sft-hvy	£21,432
	10/17	Punc	2m Mdn Hdl yld-sft	£6,844
	4/17	Fair	2m NHF 4-7yo gd-yld	£8,424
	12/16	Navn	2m List NHF 4-7yo sft-hvy	£12,436
	11/16	Punc	2m NHF 4yo soft	£4,522

Emerged from two years in the doldrums with a thrilling win in last season's Marsh Novices' Chase at Cheltenham, pipping Melon having seemingly been helped by a wind operation after latest disappointment at Limerick; long seen as a stayer but yet to run beyond 2m5f; could yet prove a force over further.

Sams Profile

6 b g Black Sam Bellamy - Lucylou I (Bob Back)

Mouse Morris (Ire)   Michael O'Flynn & John F O'Flynn

PLACINGS: 13/1225/2-   RPR **150**h

Starts	1st	2nd	3rd	4th	Win & Pl
6	1	3	1	-	£50,027

	11/18	Cork	2m Mdn Hdl 4yo yield	£7,359

Missed last season through injury but had been a smart novice hurdler in 2018-19; finished second behind Battleoverdoyen and Reserve Tank in 2m4f Grade 1 races, though beaten 15 lengths when fifth in the Ballymore at Cheltenham; point-to-point winner and likely to go novice chasing.

Santini

8 b g Milan - Tinagoodnight (Sleeping Car)

Nicky Henderson   Mr & Mrs R Kelvin-Hughes

PLACINGS: 1/1131/132/112-   RPR **175**+c

Starts	1st	2nd	3rd	4th	Win & Pl
10	6	2	2	-	£372,958

	1/20	Chel	3m1¹/₂f Cls1 Gd2 Ch soft	£57,268
	11/19	Sand	3m Cls1 List Ch soft	£17,085
	12/18	Newb	2m7¹/₂f Cls1 Nov Gd2 Ch soft	£22,780
	4/18	Aint	3m¹/₂f Cls1 Nov Gd1 Hdl soft	£56,224
	1/18	Chel	2m4¹/₂f Cls1 Nov Gd2 Hdl heavy	£18,224
	12/17	Newb	2m4³/₄f Cls3 Nov Hdl soft	£6,498

Came of age last season when winning the Cotswold Chase and finishing second in the Cheltenham Gold Cup, despite a moderate gallop not playing to his strengths; still very lightly raced after just six runs over fences and open to further improvement.

Scaramanga (Ire)

5 b g Mastercraftsman - Herboriste (Hernando)

Paul Nicholls   Malcolm C Denmark

PLACINGS: 3212/8170-   RPR **145**+h

Starts	1st	2nd	3rd	4th	Win & Pl
8	2	2	1	4	£24,829

132	12/19	Winc	1m7¹/₂f Cls3 107-132 Hdl Hcap gd-sft	£10,072
	3/19	Tntn	2m¹/₂f Cls4 Mdn Hdl gd-sft	£5,133

Useful and progressive hurdler granted a sound surface; has form figures of 870 on soft ground or worse but has a good record otherwise, finishing juvenile campaign with an unlucky second in a good handicap at Ascot and winning well at Wincanton last season.

Sceau Royal (Fr)

8 b g Doctor Dino - Sandside (Marchand De Sable)

Alan King   Simon Munir & Isaac Souede

PLACINGS: 69/12111/14232/6325-   RPR **168**c

Starts	1st	2nd	3rd	4th	Win & Pl
29	11	6	3	2	£359,894

	11/18	Chel	2m Cls1 Gd2 Ch good	£42,203
	1/18	Donc	2m1¹/₂f Cls1 Nov Gd2 Ch soft	£19,933
	12/17	Sand	1m7¹/₂f Cls1 Nov Gd1 Ch gd-sft	£29,810
	11/17	Wwck	2m Cls3 Nov Ch 4-5yo gd-sft	£9,384
	10/17	Wwck	2m Cls4 Nov Ch good	£5,198
	11/16	Winc	1m7¹/₂f Cls1 Gd2 133-149 Hdl Hcap good	£35,772
149	1/16	Chel	2m¹/₂f Cls2 Hdl 4yo good	£21,977
	12/15	Hntg	2m Cls2 Hdl 4yo good	£12,512
	12/15	Chel	2m1f Cls2 Hdl 3yo soft	£12,628
	11/15	Wwck	2m Cls4 Hdl 3yo gd-sft	£3,249
	3/15	Bord	2m¹/₂f Hdl 3yo v soft	£7,814

Has failed to win since the 2018 Shloer Chase but has run some fine races in defeat in that time, notably when third in the Champion Chase that season; prefers good ground and ran best race last term (second to Altior at Newbury) when getting good ground for only time.

Samcro: back in the top spot after his scintillating victory in last season's Marsh Chase under Davy Russell

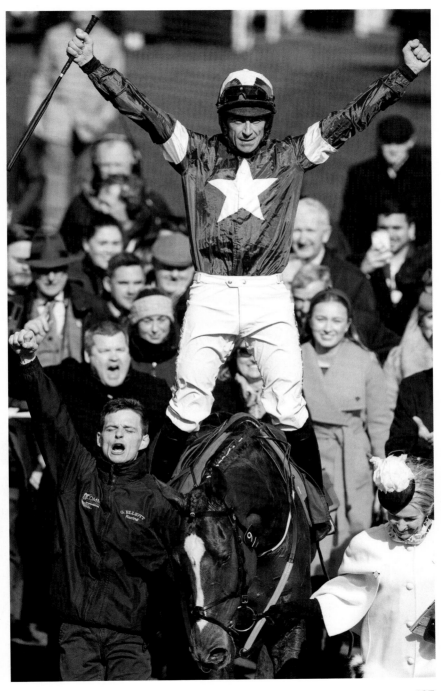

Sebastopol (Ire)

6 b g Fame And Glory - Knockcroghery (Pelder)

Tom Lacey   C Boultbee-Brooks

| PLACINGS: 11/43/141- | | | | | RPR **141**+h |

Starts	1st	2nd	3rd	4th	Win & Pl
6	3	-			£42,544
136	2/20	Muss	1m7¹/₂f Cls2 116-139 Hdl Hcap gd-sft		£21,896
127	10/19	Winc	1m7¹/₂f Cls3 107-132 Hdl Hcap good		£11,696
	4/18	Ayr	2m Cls3 NHF 4-6yo good		£6,498

Progressed into a useful handicap hurdler last season, winning twice including the Scottish County Hurdle at Musselburgh; handled good to soft ground that day but trainer believes he needs it quicker (beaten at 2-5 in only run on soft); likely to go novice chasing.

Secret Investor

8 b g Kayf Tara - Silver Charmer (Charmer)

Paul Nicholls   Hills Of Ledbury

| PLACINGS: /22721/1122411/202-1 | | | | | RPR **165**+c |

Starts	1st	2nd	3rd	4th	Win & Pl
17	6	8	-	1	£120,050
153	10/20	Chep	2m7¹/₂f Cls2 137-156 Ch Hcap good		£15,825
	4/19	Ayr	2m4¹/₂f Cls1 Nov Gd2 Ch good		£25,979
	3/19	Winc	2m4f Cls4 Nov Ch good		£5,523
	10/18	Chep	2m3¹/₂f Cls1 Nov Gd2 Hdl gd-sft		£22,780
	5/18	Kemp	3m¹/₂f Cls4 Nov Hdl good		£4,194
	4/18	Strf	2m6f Cls4 Nov Hdl gd-sft		£6,758

Won Grade 2 novice races over hurdles and fences two seasons ago; couldn't make a similar impact in open company last season but did better when getting preferred good ground for only time in the Denman Chase at Newbury, chasing home Native River on first run over 3m.

Sempo (Ire)

6 b g Oscar - Miss Cozzene (Solid Illusion)

Joseph O'Brien (Ire)   Martin O'Sullivan

| PLACINGS: 4316/3216- | | | | | RPR **145**+h |

Starts	1st	2nd	3rd	4th	Win & Pl
8	2	1	2	1	£18,833
	2/20	Thur	2m6¹/₂f Mdn Hdl gd-yld		£5,500
	2/19	Thur	2m NHF 5-7yo good		£5,550

Improved when stepping up in trip last season, easily breaking his hurdles duck over 2m6½f and running well when sixth in the Albert Bartlett (matched his 2019 Cheltenham sixth in the Champion Bumper); expected to improve when chasing.

Sharjah (Fr)

7 b g Doctor Dino - Saaryeh (Royal Academy)

Willie Mullins (Ire)   Mrs S Ricci

| PLACINGS: 11F7846/31311B/4162- | | | | | RPR **166**+h |

Starts	1st	2nd	3rd	4th	Win & Pl
17	6	1	2	2	£472,168
	12/19	Leop	2m Gd1 Hdl yield		£66,441
	12/18	Leop	2m Gd1 Hdl gd-yld		£65,265
	11/18	Punc	2m Gd1 Hdl good		£52,212
146	8/18	Gway	2m 135-146 Hdl Hcap soft		£156,637
	11/17	Gowr	2m Nov Hdl 4yo heavy		£8,161
	9/17	Gowr	2m Mdn Hdl 4yo heavy		£6,844

Three-time Grade 1 winner during the last two

seasons and produced probably the best display in a 2m hurdle in Ireland all season when winning the Matheson Hurdle; disappointed in the Irish Champion but bounced back with a fine second in the Champion Hurdle at Cheltenham.

Shishkin (Ire)

6 b g Sholokhov - Labarynth (Exit To Nowhere)
Nicky Henderson   Mrs J Donnelly

PLACINGS: 3/11/F111-					RPR **162**+h
Starts	1st	2nd	3rd	4th	Win & Pl
5	4	-	-	-	£95,291
3/20	Chel	2m¹/₂f Cls1 Nov Gd1 Hdl soft			£70,338
2/20	Hntg	2m3¹/₂f Cls1 Nov List Hdl gd-sft			£17,286
1/20	Newb	2m¹/₂f Cls4 Nov Hdl heavy			£4,549
3/19	Kemp	2m Cls5 Mdn NHF 4-6yo gd-sft			£3,119

Brilliant winner of last season's Supreme Novices' Hurdle, getting up close home having been shuffled much further back than ideal as proven stamina (had previously won over 2m3½f) was decisive; point-to-point winner and likely to go novice chasing.

Shishkin: the Supreme Novices' Hurdle winner schools over fences at Seven Barrows

Silver Forever (Ire)

6 gr m Jeremy - Silver Prayer (Roselier)
Paul Nicholls   Colm Donlon

PLACINGS: 11312/1131-					RPR **145**+h
Starts	1st	2nd	3rd	4th	Win & Pl
8	5	1	2	-	£46,982
1/20	Sand	2m4f Cls1 List Hdl soft			£12,529
11/19	Newb	2m¹/₂f Cls2 Nov Hdl gd-sft			£12,996
10/19	Chep	2m3¹/₂f Cls4 Nov Hdl soft			£4,159
2/19	Asct	1m7¹/₂f Cls4 NHF 4-6yo gd-sft			£4,549
11/18	Chep	2m Cls5 NHF 4-6yo soft			£2,274

Exciting mare who won three out of four over hurdles last season; put sole defeat behind her with an impressive win in a Listed hurdle at Sandown, relishing step up in trip and beating more experienced mares; should stay further again.

Silver Streak (Ire)

7 gr g Dark Angel - Happy Talk (Hamas)
Evan Williams   L Fell

PLACINGS: 4/12U6/1122235/1326-					RPR **158**h
Starts		1st	2nd	3rd	4th	Win & Pl
21		6	6	3	2	£334,243
	10/19	Kemp	2m Cls1 List Hdl good			£23,048
139	10/18	Ffos	2m Cls2 139-159 Hdl Hcap gd-sft			£28,152
132	5/18	Hayd	1m7¹/₂f Cls1 Gd3 130-156 Hdl Hcap good			£56,950
122	10/17	Chep	2m Cls2 120-135 Hdl 4yo Hcap gd-sft			£12,996
116	3/17	Muss	1m7¹/₂f Cls4 100-122 Hdl Hcap good			£4,549
96	12/16	Tntn	2m¹/₂f Cls5 74-102 Hdl Hcap good			£3,899

Has won only a Listed hurdle at Kempton since progressing out of handicaps in 2018 but has

run well in a string of top races during that time, notably when third in the Champion Hurdle in 2019; only sixth in that race last term after finishing second in the Christmas Hurdle.

Simply The Betts (Ire)

7 b g Arcadio - Crimson Flower (Soviet Lad)

Harry Whittington   Kate & Andrew Brooks

PLACINGS: 13420/1184/11211-   RPR **159+c**

Starts					Win & Pl
14		7	2	1	£113,254

149	3/20	Chel	2m4¹/₂f Cls1 Gd3 140-157 Ch Hcap soft	£61,897
140	1/20	Chel	2m4¹/₂f Cls2 Nov 121-147 Ch Hcap soft	£17,204
132	11/19	Newc	2m¹/₂f Cls3 Nov 125-132 Ch Hcap heavy	£7,018
125	11/19	Chep	2m Cls3 Nov 109-127 Ch Hcap soft	£7,018
	10/18	Hexm	2m Cls4 Nov Hdl soft	£4,159
	5/18	Wwck	2m Cls5 Mdn Hdl good	£3,249
	9/17	MRas	2m¹/₂f Cls6 NHF 4-6yo good	£1,560

Went from strength to strength when switched to fences last season, winning four out of five; beat more experienced handicappers in the Plate at Cheltenham having seen off another subsequent festival winner Imperial Aura at the track in January; has more to come.

Sir Psycho (Ire)

4 b g Zoffany - Open Book (Mark Of Esteem)

Paul Nicholls   Martin Broughton & Friends

PLACINGS: 414115-5   RPR **141h**

Starts					Win & Pl
7		3	-	-	2	£27,728

	2/20	Hayd	1m7¹/₂f Cls2 Hdl 4yo heavy	£12,996
	1/20	Extr	2m1f Cls4 Nov Hdl soft	£4,549
	10/19	Winc	1m7¹/₂f Cls4 Hdl 3yo good	£4,874

Won three juvenile hurdles last season, most notably when running away with the Victor Ludorum at Haydock to earn official mark of 147; didn't quite live up to that assessment when a well-beaten fifth in the Triumph Hurdle at Cheltenham.

Sire Du Berlais (Fr)

8 b g Poliglote - Royale Athenia (Garde Royale)

Gordon Elliott (Ire)   John P McManus

PLACINGS: 3130/248/8618/4941-   RPR **164+h**

Starts					Win & Pl
15		3	1	2	1	£136,799

152	3/20	Chel	3m Cls1 Gd3 131-152 Hdl Hcap soft	£56,270
145	3/19	Chel	3m Cls1 Gd3 134-148 Hdl Hcap gd-sft	£56,270
	5/16	Comp	2m1f Hdl 4yo v soft	£7,765

Dual winner of the Pertemps Final at Cheltenham, doing particularly well to defy a mark of 152 last season (performance rated better than Stayers' Hurdle winner Lisnagar Oscar on Racing Post Ratings); likely to step up into Grade 1 company now.

Siruh Du Lac (Fr)

7 b g Turgeon - Margerie (Le Balafre)

David Pipe   John White & Anne Underhill

PLACINGS: 324/P113/1111/PF-   RPR **154c**

Starts					Win & Pl
13		6	1	2	1	£145,397

141	3/19	Chel	2m4¹/₂f Cls1 Gd3 135-156 Ch Hcap gd-sft	£61,897
134	1/19	Chel	2m4¹/₂f Cls1 Gd3 131-151 Ch Hcap gd-sft	£42,203
129	12/18	Extr	2m3f Cls3 124-137 Ch Hcap soft	£16,245
123	11/18	Newb	2m4f Cls3 116-137 Ch Hcap good	£8,058
118	12/17	Extr	2m3f Cls4 100-120 Ch Hcap soft	£7,148
112	11/17	Bang	2m4¹/₂f Cls4 93-122 Ch Hcap soft	£3,899

Failed to complete in both runs last season

Simply The Betts: leading past the stands at Cheltenham, where he won the Plate last March

but had been hugely progressive during the previous two campaigns, completing a four-timer when winning the Plate at Cheltenham in 2019; back on song in that race last term but fell two out when still in front; has since left Nick Williams.

Sizing Pottsie (Fr)

6 b/br g Kapgarde - Line Salsa (Kingsalsa)

Jessica Harrington (Ire) — Ann & Alan Potts Limited

PLACINGS: 14/53/33U11F- — RPR **154+c**

Starts	1st	2nd	3rd	4th	Win & Pl
10	3	-	3	1	£43,713

	3/20	Navn	2m Nov Gd3 Ch heavy	£21,250
	2/20	Fair	2m1½f Ch heavy	£8,500
	3/18	Leop	2m NHF 4yo soft	£6,269

Long seen as a top chasing prospect and switched to fences midway through last season, storming to two wide-margin wins including a Grade 3 at Navan; generally a fine jumper but lost confidence and coming off worst against Zero Ten when fell two out at Thurles on final run.

Skandiburg (Fr)

6 b g Sageburg - Skandia (Robin Des Champs)

Olly Murphy — Kate & Andrew Brooks

PLACINGS: 4/131281/2110-4 — RPR **138+h**

Starts	1st	2nd	3rd	4th	Win & Pl
12	5	2	1	2	£48,036

134	1/20	Chel	3m Cls2 134-160 Hdl Hcap soft	£15,640
128	11/19	Aint	3m½f Cls2 115-140 Hdl Hcap soft	£12,512
	4/19	Hntg	2m3½f Cls4 Nov Hdl good	£4,159
	12/18	Fknm	2m4f Cls4 Nov Hdl gd-sft	£5,393
	10/18	Fknm	2m Cls5 Am NHF 4-6yo good	£2,274

Hugely progressive hurdler over the last two seasons; thrived when stepped up in trip in staying handicaps last season, winning a Pertemps qualifier at Aintree and following up at Cheltenham before disappointing back there for the Pertemps Final; likely to go novice chasing.

Slate House (Ire)

8 b g Presenting - Bay Pearl (Broadway Flyer)

Colin Tizzard — Eric Jones, Geoff Nicholas & John Romans

PLACINGS: /1145F8/4528/1F11P6- — RPR **159+c**

Starts	1st	2nd	3rd	4th	Win & Pl
16	5	1	-	2	£117,014

	12/19	Kemp	3m Cls1 Nov Gd1 Ch soft	£57,955
	12/19	Hntg	2m7½f Cls3 Nov Ch gd-sft	£9,986
	10/19	Chel	2m4f Cls2 Nov Ch heavy	£15,857
	11/17	Chel	2m½f Cls1 Nov Gd2 Hdl soft	£17,085
	10/17	Chel	2m½f Cls3 Mdn Hdl good	£6,256

Bounced back from a poor first season over fences when winning three times during his second campaign as a novice last season; made up for a late fall in the BetVictor Gold Cup to win a Grade 1 novice chase at Kempton; twice flopped when facing tougher tests at Cheltenham.

Solo (Fr)

4 b g Kapgarde - Flameche (Balko)

Paul Nicholls — Mrs Johnny De La Hey

PLACINGS: 2118- — RPR **145+h**

Starts	1st	2nd	3rd	4th	Win & Pl
4	2	1	-	-	£48,231

	2/20	Kemp	2m Cls1 Gd2 Hdl 4yo gd-sft	£17,085
	11/19	Autl	2m1½f Hdl 3yo heavy	£19,459

Exciting French recruit who hacked up by 13 lengths in the Adonis Hurdle at Kempton on British debut last season, earning an eye-watering opening mark of 157 (since reduced to 149); poor eighth in the Triumph Hurdle at Cheltenham; has since been gelded.

Song For Someone (Ger)

5 ch g Medicean - Sweni Hill (Danehill Dancer)

Tom Symonds — Sir Peter & Lady Gibbings

PLACINGS: 3122116/1321- — RPR **154h**

Starts	1st	2nd	3rd	4th	Win & Pl
11	5	3	2	-	£75,752

	2/20	Kemp	2m Cls1 Gd2 Hdl gd-sft	£25,748
136	11/19	Font	2m1½f Cls3 108-136 Hdl Hcap soft	£7,216
	2/19	Wwck	2m Cls4 Hdl 4yo good	£4,419
	12/18	Newb	2m½f Cls3 Hdl 3yo gd-sft	£6,238
	7/18	Le L	2m1½f Hdl 3yo gd-sft	£8,496

Massive improver last season; won by 12 lengths at Fontwell and was then placed under big weights in two much stronger handicaps before landing the Kingwell Hurdle, rallying strongly having been outpaced over Kempton's sharp 2m; should prove even better back up in trip.

Southfield Stone

7 gr g Fair Mix - Laureldean Belle (Supreme Leader)

Paul Nicholls — Mrs Angela Hart & Mrs Angela Yeoman

PLACINGS: 3/1113217/22312- — RPR **152c**

Starts	1st	2nd	3rd	4th	Win & Pl
13	5	4	3	-	£60,725

	2/20	Muss	2m4½f Cls3 Nov Ch gd-sft	£7,538
	2/19	Kemp	2m Cls1 Nov Gd2 Hdl good	£17,085
	12/18	Tntn	2m½f Cls4 Nov Hdl good	£5,133
	11/18	Tntn	2m½f Cls4 Nov Hdl good	£5,133
	11/18	Tntn	2m½f Cls4 Mdn NHF 4-6yo gd-fm	£3,249

Grade 2 winner as a novice hurdler in 2019 and proved just as good over fences last season despite just being beaten in that grade in the Pendil at Kempton; jumped left on several occasions and open to improvement on left-handed tracks.

Speak Easy

7 b g Beneficial - For Bill (Presenting)

Joseph O'Brien (Ire) — John P McManus

PLACINGS: 1/1532/3F3- — RPR **148+c**

Starts	1st	2nd	3rd	4th	Win & Pl
7	1	1	3	-	£25,614

	12/17	Navn	2m Mdn Hdl 4yo soft	£6,844

Very useful novice hurdler in 2017-18 but missed the following season and ran just three times over fences last season; set to improve on reappearance third until falling at the last behind Carefully Selected at Punchestown but disappointed when favourite for a Grade 2 at Navan.

Spiritofthegames (Ire)

8 b g Darsi - Lucy Walters (King's Ride)

Dan Skelton   N W Lake

PLACINGS: 1/12357/14335/P0226-   RPR **154**c

Starts	1st	2nd	3rd	4th	Win & Pl
19	4	4	3	2	£127,568
129	10/18 Chep	2m3¹/₂f Cls1 Nov List Ch good			£16,465
	11/17 Ling	2m3¹/₂f Cls3 112-132 Hdl Hcap soft			£7,596
	3/17 Tntn	2m3f Cls4 Nov Hdl good			£4,549
	10/16 Ayr	2m4¹/₂f Cls5 Nov Mdn Hdl gd-sft			£2,729

Without a win since chasing debut in October 2018 but has run well in several good handicaps, especially at Cheltenham; beaten a head in last season's Caspian Caviar Gold Cup and again went close at the track in January; solid sixth in the Plate on final run.

Sporting John (Ire)

5 b/br g Getaway - Wild Spell (Oscar)

Philip Hobbs   John P McManus

PLACINGS: 1/1117-   RPR **150+**h

Starts	1st	2nd	3rd	4th	Win & Pl
4	3	-	-	-	£26,926
	2/20 Asct	2m3¹/₂f Cls2 Nov Hdl soft			£15,640
	12/19 Extr	2m1f Cls4 Nov Hdl 4-6yo soft			£4,224
	11/19 Extr	2m1f Cls3 Nov Hdl soft			£6,238

Won first three races over hurdles last season, most notably when stepped up in trip at Ascot (Master Debonair a below-par third); finished distressed after coming home only seventh in the Ballymore; expected to be better over fences and likely to go novice chasing.

Springfield Fox

7 gr g Sagamix - Marlbrook Fox (Bob Back)

Tom George   O'Donohoe, Cavanagh, Robinson & Nelson

PLACINGS: 111/F2211U-   RPR **149+**c

Starts	1st	2nd	3rd	4th	Win & Pl
6	2	2	-	-	£16,990
127	2/20 Extr	3m Cls3 Nov 123-135 Ch Hcap heavy			£10,397
117	1/20 Chep	2m7¹/₂f Cls4 Nov 97-122 Ch Hcap heavy			£4,289

Three-time point-to-point winner who was sent chasing as soon as he had a handicap mark last season and immediately won by wide margins at Chepstow and Exeter, shooting up 25lb in the weights; starting to struggle when unseating his rider in the National Hunt Chase.

Stolen Silver (Fr)

5 gr g Lord Du Sud - Change Partner (Turtle Island)

Nigel Twiston-Davies   Walters Plant Hire & Potter Group

PLACINGS: 52/U1218P-3   RPR **143**h

Starts	1st	2nd	3rd	4th	Win & Pl
9	2	2	1	-	£26,003
	1/20 Hayd	1m7¹/₂f Cls1 Nov Gd2 Hdl heavy			£17,085
	11/19 Ffos	2m Cls4 Nov Hdl soft			£3,769

Won two novice hurdles last season, including a Grade 2 at Haydock; subsequently switched to handicaps and shaped with real promise in the Betfair Hurdle, staying on into a close eighth after being left at the standing start, but pulled up in the County Hurdle.

Stoney Mountain (Ire)

7 ch g Mountain High - Cherry Pie (Dolpour)

Jamie Snowden   Trevor Hemmings

PLACINGS: 5101/12123P/11U59-   RPR **145+**h

Starts	1st	2nd	3rd	4th	Win & Pl
15	6	2	1	-	£103,384
138	11/19 Hayd	3m¹/₂f Cls1 Gd3 128-147 Hdl Hcap gd-sft			£56,950
134	10/19 Aint	2m4f Cls2 115-135 Hdl Hcap soft			£17,204
	12/18 Sthl	2m4¹/₂f Cls1 Nov Hdl 4-6yo soft			£4,094
	10/18 Aint	2m4f Cls4 Mdn Hdl good			£5,198
	4/18 Bang	2m¹/₂f Cls5 Am NHF 4-6yo gd-sft			£2,274
	1/18 Wwck	2m Cls5 NHF 4-6yo heavy			£2,599

Useful novice hurdler in 2018-19 and progressed again early last season, winning two handicaps including a valuable contest at Haydock; just found out off higher marks back over hurdles after a difficult chasing debut (unseated rider four out after lacking fluency); since left Henry Daly after £140,000 sale.

Stormy Ireland (Fr)

6 b m Motivator - Like A Storm (Ultimately Lucky)

Paul Nicholls   Sullivan Bloodstock

PLACINGS: 21FU/131222/261115-2   RPR **150+**h

Starts	1st	2nd	3rd	4th	Win & Pl
18	6	7	1	-	£194,150
	1/20 Naas	2m Gd3 Hdl yld-sft			£17,000
	12/19 Leop	2m4¹/₂f Gd3 Hdl yield			£21,261
	11/19 Punc	2m2f List Hdl soft			£15,946
	11/18 Punc	2m2f List Hdl good			£16,327
	5/18 Klny	2m1f List Hdl yield			£16,327
	12/17 Fair	2m Mdn Hdl 3yo heavy			£6,055

Prolific in mares' races in Ireland last season, winning a pair of Grade 3 hurdles to go with Listed victory at Punchestown (odds-on every time); effective from 2m-2m4f but didn't seem to get the longer trip on soft ground when fifth in the Mares' Hurdle at Cheltenham; has since left Willie Mullins.

Terrefort: missed last season but is a dual Grade 1 winner over fences and would be a force if recapturing his best form

Summerville Boy (Ire)

8 b g Sandmason - Suny House (Carroll House)

Tom George   R S Brookhouse

PLACINGS: 122311/474/61F125-   RPR **154+**c

Starts		1st	2nd	3rd	4th	Win & Pl
15		5	3	1	2	£195,107
	1/20	Chel	2m4¹/₂f Cls1 Gd2 Hdl soft			£28,475
	11/19	Uttx	2m Cls3 Ch soft			£7,018
	3/18	Chel	2m¹/₂f Cls1 Nov Gd1 Hdl heavy			£71,188
	1/18	Sand	2m Cls1 Nov Gd1 Hdl heavy			£28,475
	5/17	Klny	2m1f NHF 5-7yo soft			£5,265

Finally built on promise of 2018 Supreme Novices' Hurdle win when stepped up in trip and switched back to hurdles last season, winning the Relkeel Hurdle and chasing home Paisley Park in the Cleeve; not quite as effective off a stronger gallop in the Stayers' Hurdle.

Supasundae

10 b g Galileo - Distinctive Look (Danehill)

Jessica Harrington (Ire)   Ann & Alan Potts Limited

PLACINGS: 12/321221/22271/247-   RPR **155**h

Starts		1st	2nd	3rd	4th	Win & Pl
28		8	9	2	3	£766,525
	4/19	Aint	2m4f Cls1 Gd1 Hdl soft			£141,325
	4/18	Punc	2m Gd1 Hdl soft			£143,584
	2/18	Leop	2m Gd1 Hdl soft			£75,000
148	3/17	Chel	2m5f Cls1 Gd3 136-156 Hdl Hcap gd-sft			£54,103
	12/16	Punc	2m4f Hdl soft			£9,044
	12/15	Leop	2m Mdn Hdl heavy			£7,488
	12/14	Asct	1m7¹/₂f Cls1 List NHF 4-6yo soft			£11,390
	3/14	Weth	2m Cls6 NHF 4-6yo good			£1,711

Classy and versatile hurdler who has won three Grade 1 hurdles and finished second in eight more; most often seen at 2m recently, finishing seventh in last season's Champion Hurdle, but ideally suited by 2m4f and even stays 3m (second in the 2018 Stayers' Hurdle).

Tarada

7 br g Kayf Tara - Kerada (Astarabad)

Oliver Sherwood   Trevor Hemmings

PLACINGS: 221/21-   RPR **136**c

Starts		1st	2nd	3rd	4th	Win & Pl
5		2	3		-	£13,656
	12/19	Weth	3m Cls4 Nov Ch soft			£4,952
	2/19	Font	2m3f Cls4 Nov Hdl gd-sft			£3,639

Restricted to just two runs last season but had already proved himself a very useful novice chaser, pushing subsequent Grade 1 winner Slate House to half a length first time out before winning easily at Wetherby; could make a high-class staying chaser.

Terrefort (Fr)

7 gr g Martaline - Vie De Reine (Mansonnien)

Nicky Henderson   Simon Munir & Isaac Souede

PLACINGS: /5226/13131121/432P/   RPR **164**c

Starts		1st	2nd	3rd	4th	Win & Pl
18		5	5	3	1	£215,692
	4/18	Aint	3m1f Cls1 Nov Gd1 Ch soft			£56,337
	2/18	Sand	2m4f Cls1 Nov Gd1 Ch soft			£31,323
137	1/18	Hntg	2m4f Cls3 Nov 120-137 Ch Hcap soft			£7,798
	9/17	Claf	2m2f Hdl 4yo heavy			£9,436
	8/17	Claf	2m3¹/₂f Ch 4yo heavy			£14,769

Smart staying chaser who hasn't run since pulled

up in the 2019 Ryanair Chase; had just come up short in open company that season but was still a close third in the Cotswold Chase and had been a dual Grade 1 winner as a novice in 2018.

The Big Breakaway (Ire)

5 ch g Getaway - Princess Mairead (Blueprint)

Colin Tizzard   Eric Jones, Geoff Nicholas & John Romans

PLACINGS: 1/114-					RPR **145**h
Starts	1st	2nd	3rd	4th	Win & Pl
3	2	-	-	1	£13,902
12/19	Newb	2m4^1/$_2$f Cls4 Nov Hdl 4-6yo soft			£4,484
11/19	Chep	2m3^1/$_2$f Cls5 Mdn Hdl soft			£2,794

Tall, imposing gelding who looked a terrific recruit when easily winning his first two races over hurdles last season, albeit at a modest level; struggling a long way out when stepped sharply up in grade for the Ballymore but stuck on for a fair fourth; likely to go novice chasing.

The Big Getaway (Ire)

6 b g Getaway - Saddlers Dawn (Saddlers' Hall)

Willie Mullins (Ire)   Mrs J Donnelly

PLACINGS: 1/2/21413-					RPR **152**h
Starts	1st	2nd	3rd	4th	Win & Pl
6	2	2	1	1	£32,504
1/20	Naas	2m3f Mdn Hdl yld-sft			£8,014
11/19	Punc	2m^1/$_2$f NHF 4-7yo soft			£5,857

Big, tall gelding who took to hurdling really well last season; would have won first two starts over hurdles but for final-flight blunder on debut and then finished third in the Ballymore behind Envoi Allen; won his point-to-point by a distance in 2018 and set to go novice chasing.

The Conditional (Ire)

8 b g Kalanisi - Gorrie Vale (Saddlers' Hall)

David Bridgwater   P J Cave

PLACINGS: 52140/24F4654/31241-					RPR **148+**c
Starts	1st	2nd	3rd	4th	Win & Pl
17	3	3	1	5	£175,829
139	3/20	Chel	3m1f Cls1 Gd3 133-159 Ch Hcap soft		£61,897
131	10/19	Chel	3m1f Cls2 127-147 Ch Hcap soft		£37,164
	3/18	Thur	2m7f Mdn Hdl heavy		£7,632

Developed into a smart handicap chaser last

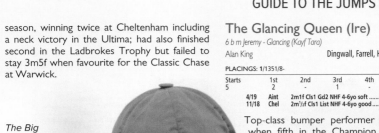

season, winning twice at Cheltenham including a neck victory in the Ultima; had also finished second in the Ladbrokes Trophy but failed to stay 3m5f when favourite for the Classic Chase at Warwick.

The Big Breakaway: could prove a potent force in novice chases this season

The Glancing Queen (Ire)

6 b m Jeremy - Glancing (Kayf Tara)

Alan King — Dingwall, Farrell, Hornsey & Murray

PLACINGS: 1/1351/8-					RPR **111**b
Starts	1st	2nd	3rd	4th	Win & Pl
5	2	-	1	-	£43,160

4/19	Aint	2m1f Cls1 Gd2 NHF 4-6yo soft	£25,322
11/18	Chel	2m¹/₂f Cls1 List NHF 4-6yo good	£12,379

Top-class bumper performer in 2018-19 when fifth in the Champion Bumper at Cheltenham before winning the Grade 2 mares' bumper at Aintree; held up by a splint problem last term and below-par after long layoff back in the Champion Bumper; set to go novice hurdling at last.

The Jam Man (Ire)

7 br g Papal Bull - Kathy Jet (Singspiel)

Ronan McNally (Ire)   Ronan M P McNally

PLACINGS: 16702F9P/071111429-P					RPR **153**h

Starts		1st	2nd	3rd	4th	Win & Pl
31		9	3	1	1	£104,945
128	12/19	Navn	3m¹/₂f 122-150 Hdl Hcap soft			£42,523
122	7/19	NAbb	3m2¹/₂f Cls3 103-129 Hdl Hcap gd-fm			£6,583
121	6/19	Ctml	3m1¹/₂f Cls4 96-122 Ch Hcap good			£5,289
114	6/19	Sthl	3m4 Nov 93-122 Ch Hcap good			£4,614
115	9/18	Sthl	2m4¹/₂f Cls4 100-115 Hdl Hcap good			£4,094
109	6/18	Hexm	2m7¹/₂f Cls3 92-117 Hdl Hcap good			£7,083
94	3/18	Sedg	2m4f Cls4 79-105 Hdl Hcap heavy			£4,094
87	3/18	Ayr	2m1¹/₂f Cls5 73-101 Hdl Hcap soft			£3,184
80	3/18	Catt	3m1¹/₂f Cls5 75-98 Hdl Hcap soft			£3,509

Hugely progressive over the last 12-18 months, completing a four-timer at the end of 2019 with two wins apiece over hurdles and fences; competitive off a much higher mark when second at Leopardstown but only ninth in the Stayers' Hurdle; could exploit much lower chase mark.

The King Of May (Fr)

6 b g High Rock - Waltzingi (Cadeaux Genereux)

Brian Ellison   Phil & Julie Martin

PLACINGS: 5/611302/131-					RPR **137**c

Starts		1st	2nd	3rd	4th	Win & Pl
10		4	1	2		£37,716
131	1/20	Sedg	2m¹/₂f Cls3 Nov 123-135 Ch Hcap soft			£7,018
125	10/19	Carl	2m Cls3 Nov 123-135 Ch Hcap gd-sft			£8,123
	8/17	Stma	2m Hdl 3yo gd-sft			£9,026
	6/17	Stma	2m Hdl 3yo gd-sft			£7,385

Did well to win two novice handicap chases last season, with sole defeat when flopping on heavy ground at Newcastle; had beaten subsequent Grade 1 winner Esprit Du Large first time out and got back to winning ways in good style at Sedgefield; should have more to come.

The Very Man (Ire)

6 b g Jeremy - Mill Meadow (Kalanisi)

Gordon Elliott (Ire)   Gigginstown House Stud

PLACINGS: F/117/F34211-114					RPR **138+**h

Starts		1st	2nd	3rd	4th	Win & Pl
11		5	1	1	2	£46,705
	7/20	Gway	2m¹/₂f Nov List Hdl good			£15,000
	7/20	Rosc	1m7¹/₂f Hdl good			£5,750
	3/20	Dpat	2m3f Hdl yield			£9,000
	3/20	Naas	2m3f Mdn Hdl yld-sft			£6,750
	12/18	Navn	2m NHF 4-7yo yield			£5,724

Progressive novice hurdler last season; broke his maiden at the fifth attempt when stepped up to 2m3f for the first time at Naas and followed up by eight lengths over the same trip at Downpatrick; should appreciate going further again; likely to go novice chasing.

The Worlds End (Ire)

9 b g Stowaway - Bright Sprite (Beneficial)

Tom George   McNeill Family

PLACINGS: /84474/1316P9/131P-P					RPR **156**h

Starts		1st	2nd	3rd	4th	Win & Pl
23		9		3	3	£219,172
	12/19	Asct	3m1¹/₂f Cls1 Gd1 Hdl heavy			£56,950
	11/19	Weth	3m Cls1 Gd2 Hdl soft			£25,748
	12/18	Chel	3m1¹/₂f Cls2 Nov Ch good			£15,857
	10/18	Chep	2m7¹/₂f Cls3 Ch good			£7,408
	4/17	Aint	3m1¹/₂f Cls1 Nov Gd1 Hdl good			£56,141
	2/17	Hayd	2m7f Cls1 Nov Gd2 Hdl gd-sft			£16,972
	1/17	Chep	2m3¹/₂f Cls4 Nov Hdl soft			£3,249
	12/16	Chep	2m3¹/₂f Cls3 Mdn Hdl gd-sft			£6,498
	4/16	Chep	2m Cls6 NHF 4-6yo soft			£1,949

Justified the decision to switch back to hurdles last season by winning the Grade 1 Marsh Hurdle at Ascot, albeit in a desperately weak race for the grade; rated 7lb lower over fences but has been let down by his jumping in stronger company.

Thebannerkingrebel (Ire)

7 b g Arakan - One Love (Bravefoot)

Jamie Snowden   Sir Chips Keswick

PLACINGS: 11P/2/11F130-					RPR **148+**h

Starts		1st	2nd	3rd	4th	Win & Pl
10		5	1	1	-	£40,893
	11/19	Hayd	1m7¹/₂f Cls1 Nov List Hdl gd-sft			£14,238
	6/19	NAbb	2m1f Cls4 Nov Hdl good			£4,484
	5/19	Wwck	2m Cls4 Mdn Hdl good			£4,549
	2/18	Bang	2m1¹/₂f Cls5 NHF 4-6yo heavy			£2,274
	1/18	Wwck	2m Cls5 NHF 4-6yo soft			£2,599

Three-time winner in novice hurdles last season and unlucky not to win more, falling at the last when in front at Wetherby and going close after another late blunder under a 5lb penalty in a Grade 2 at Haydock; disappointing on handicap debut in the Betfair Hurdle.

Third Time Lucki (Ire)

5 br g Arcadio - Definite Valley (Definite Article)

Dan Skelton   Mike And Eileen Newbould

PLACINGS: 2/3114-1					RPR **128+**h

Starts		1st	2nd	3rd	4th	Win & Pl
5		3	-	1	1	£12,960
	10/20	Uttx	2m Cls4 Nov Hdl 4-6yo gd-sft			£3,769
	1/20	Hntg	2m Cls5 NHF 4-6yo soft			£2,274
	12/19	MRas	2m1¹/₂f Cls5 Mdn NHF 4-6yo soft			£2,274

Comfortably best of the British-trained runners when fourth in the Champion Bumper at Cheltenham last season; had won previous two races on flat tracks at Market Rasen and Huntingdon but shapes as if possessing plenty of stamina.

Third Wind

6 b/br g Shirocco - Act Three (Beat Hollow)

Hughie Morrison · Mouse Hamilton-Fairley

PLACINGS: 30/1211/714- · RPR **144**h

Starts		1st	2nd	3rd	4th	Win & Pl
9		4	1	1	1	£71,010
137	12/19	Winc	2m5¹/₂f Cls2 120-146 Hdl Hcap heavy			£11,574
131	3/19	Sand	2m4f Cls1 Nov Gd3 123-138 Hdl 4-7yo Hcap soft			£42,203
	2/19	Tntn	2m3f Cls4 Nov Hdl soft			£5,133
	12/18	Plum	2m4¹/₂f Cls4 Mdn Hdl soft			£4,094

Progressive staying hurdler who has won four of his last six in that sphere, including the EBF Final in 2019 and a Pertemps qualifier at Wincanton before finishing fourth in the final at Cheltenham; well below best on only run over fences last season.

Thistlecrack

12 b g Kayf Tara - Ardstown (Ardross)

Colin Tizzard · John & Heather Snook

PLACINGS: 1111/11112/54/32P/2- · RPR **154**c

Starts		1st	2nd	3rd	4th	Win & Pl
25		13	4	2	1	£743,650
	12/16	Kemp	3m Cls1 Gd1 Ch good			£119,026
	11/16	Newb	2m7¹/₂f Cls1 Nov Gd2 Ch gd-sft			£20,167
	11/16	Chel	3m¹/₂f Cls2 Nov Ch gd-sft			£16,025
	10/16	Chep	2m7¹/₂f Cls3 Nov Ch gd-sft			£7,798
	4/16	Aint	3m¹/₂f Cls1 Gd1 Hdl soft			£84,405
	3/16	Chel	3m Cls1 Gd1 Hdl good			£170,850
	1/16	Chel	3m Cls1 Gd2 Hdl heavy			£34,170
	12/15	Asct	3m Cls1 Gd1 Hdl gd-sft			£56,950
	11/15	Newb	3m Cls1 Gd2 Hdl soft			£25,628
	4/15	Aint	3m Cls1 Nov Gd1 Hdl gd-sft			£56,437
	2/15	Asct	1m7¹/₂f Cls2 Nov Hdl soft			£9,384
	1/15	Winc	1m7¹/₂f Cls4 Nov Hdl heavy			£3,899
	4/14	Winc	1m7¹/₂f Cls6 NHF 4-6yo good			£1,625

Hasn't won since landing the 2016 King George as a novice but bounced back to somewhere close to that form two seasons ago, finishing second in the same race; ran Paisley Park to a length when reverting to hurdles last season only to miss the spring through injury.

Thomas Darby (Ire)

7 b g Beneficial - Silaoce (Nikos)

Olly Murphy · Mrs Diana L Whateley

PLACINGS: 112312/2313- · RPR **157**h

Starts		1st	2nd	3rd	4th	Win & Pl
10		4	3	3	-	£89,490
151	1/20	Asct	2m3¹/₂f Cls1 Gd3 125-151 Hdl Hcap heavy			£28,475
	1/19	Tntn	2m3f Cls4 Nov Hdl gd-sft			£5,133
	10/18	Chel	2m¹/₂f Cls3 Mdn Hdl good			£9,285
	5/18	Hntg	2m Cls5 Am Mdn NHF 4-6yo good			£2,274

High-class hurdler who finished second in the 2019 Supreme Novices' Hurdle and won a hot handicap at Ascot last season before a fair third in a Grade 2 at Fontwell; had flopped over fences

earlier in the campaign but likely to go novice chasing again.

Thyme Hill

6 b g Kayf Tara - Rosita Bay (Hernando)

Philip Hobbs · The Englands & Heywoods

PLACINGS: 123/1114- · RPR **152+**h

Starts		1st	2nd	3rd	4th	Win & Pl
7		4	1	1	1	£85,687
	12/19	Newb	2m4¹/₂f Cls1 Nov Gd1 Hdl soft			£25,929
	11/19	Chel	2m5f Cls1 Nov Gd2 Hdl soft			£18,006
	10/19	Chep	2m3¹/₂f Cls1 Nov Gd1 Hdl gd-sft			£19,933
	10/18	Worc	2m Cls5 NHF 4-6yo good			£2,274

Top-class novice hurdler last season; won first three races, all at Graded level, including the Challow Hurdle at Newbury; perhaps unlucky not to add the Albert Bartlett at Cheltenham, finishing a length fourth after struggling to get a run and proving stamina over 3m.

Thyme White (Fr)

4 b g Anodin - Jane (Samum)

Paul Nicholls · The Stewart Family

PLACINGS: 2210-1 · RPR **137+**h

Starts		1st	2nd	3rd	4th	Win & Pl
5		2	2	-	-	£37,721
130	10/20	Chep	2m Cls2 119-136 Hdl 4yo Hcap good			£10,397
	2/20	Muss	1m7¹/₂f Cls1 List Hdl 4yo soft			£19,933

Generally progressive in juvenile hurdles last season and built on two runner-up efforts when winning the Listed Scottish Triumph Hurdle at Musselburgh; disappointing on handicap debut in the Fred Winter; big horse who should continue to improve.

Tidal Flow

7 b g Black Sam Bellamy - Mrs Philip (Puissance)

Philip Hobbs · Brocade Racing

PLACINGS: 14/11642/3121-3 · RPR **152+**c

Starts		1st	2nd	3rd	4th	Win & Pl
12		5	2	2	2	£31,691
	3/20	Strf	2m5f Cls4 Nov Ch soft			£5,458
	12/19	Uttx	2m4f Cls3 Ch heavy			£7,190
	12/18	Newb	2m4¹/₂f Cls4 Nov Hdl 4-6yo soft			£4,809
	11/18	Kemp	2m5f Cls4 Nov Hdl good			£4,094
	11/17	Newb	2m¹/₂f Cls5 NHF 4-6yo gd-sft			£2,599

Has looked impressive in winning two novice hurdles and two novice chases over the last two seasons, albeit at a relatively low level; had become disappointing over hurdles, though, and well beaten into second on handicap debut over fences last season.

Tiger Roll (Ire)
10 b g Authorized - Swiss Roll (Entrepreneur)

Gordon Elliott (Ire)   Gigginstown House Stud

PLACINGS: 1331P/2P511/4111/52-   RPR **155c**

Starts		1st	2nd	3rd	4th	Win & Pl
36		12	6	3	4	£1,378,454
159	4/19	Aint	4m2¹/₂f Cls1 Gd3 142-164 Ch Hcap gd-sft			£500,000
	3/19	Chel	3m6f Cls2 Ch soft			£40,235
	2/19	Navn	2m5f Gd2 Hdl yield			£23,919
150	4/18	Aint	4m2¹/₂f Cls1 Gd3 142-161 Ch Hcap heavy			£500,000
	3/18	Chel	3m6f Cls2 Ch soft			£40,261
	3/17	Chel	4m Cls1 Nov Gd2 Am Ch gd-sft			£71,952
138	10/16	Limk	3m 131-144 Ch Hcap yield			£43,382
	6/16	Kbgn	2m4f Nov Ch good			£6,331
	5/16	Baln	2m1f Ch good			£5,200
	10/14	Chel	2m1¹/₂f Cls2 Hdl 4yo gd-sft			£18,768
	3/14	Chel	2m1f Cls1 Gd1 Hdl 4yo soft			£68,340
	11/13	MRas	2m1¹/₂f Cls4 Hdl 3yo soft			£3,899

Went into folklore when becoming the first horse since Red Rum to win back-to-back Grand Nationals in 2019; had already won the Boyne Hurdle and Cross Country Chase at Cheltenham that season but finished fifth and a distant second in the same races last term.

Tobefair
10 b/br g Central Park - Nan (Buckley)

Debra Hamer   Down The Quay Club

PLACINGS: 10/493/849P221/1346-   RPR **154h**

Starts		1st	2nd	3rd	4th	Win & Pl
28		9	3	2	4	£114,932
149	10/19	Chel	3m Cls2 128-149 Hdl Hcap heavy			£15,485
142	4/19	Chel	3m Cls2 120-144 Hdl Hcap good			£12,380
134	2/17	Newb	3m Cls2 115-139 Hdl Hcap soft			£12,512
126	1/17	Wwck	3m2f Cls2 115-138 Hdl Hcap soft			£12,512
120	12/16	Chep	2m7¹/₂f Cls3 110-129 Hdl Hcap good			£6,498
116	11/16	Ffos	3m Cls3 115-132 Hdl Hcap good			£6,498
109	9/15	Chep	2m7f Cls4 93-120 Hdl Hcap good			£3,249
95	7/15	Worc	2m7f Cls5 Nov 74-100 Hdl Hcap gd-fm			£2,599
81	6/15	Worc	2m7f Cls5 Nov 73-99 Hdl Hcap gd-fm			£2,599

Progressive over the last 18 months; won two handicap hurdles at Cheltenham after near miss in the 2019 Pertemps Final and then ran two fine races when stepped up in class, finishing fourth in the Cleeve Hurdle and sixth in the Stayers' Hurdle.

Top Notch (Fr)
9 b g Poliglote - Topira (Pistolet Bleu)

Nicky Henderson   Simon Munir & Isaac Souede

PLACINGS: 1123/31141/310P/113-   RPR **159c**

Starts		1st	2nd	3rd	4th	Win & Pl
30		16	4	5	1	£470,634
	12/19	Hntg	2m4f Cls1 Gd2 Ch gd-sft			£37,192
	11/19	Aint	2m4f Cls1 Gd2 Ch soft			£28,152
	1/19	Kemp	2m4¹/₂f Cls1 List Ch good			£23,048
	4/18	Sand	2m6¹/₂f Cls1 Gd2 Ch gd-sft			£31,470
	12/17	Tntn	2m5¹/₂f Cls1 Gd2 Ch good			£28,475
	11/17	Asct	2m5f Cls1 Gd2 Ch gd-sft			£39,865
	2/17	Sand	2m4f Cls1 Nov Gd1 Ch soft			£28,475
	12/16	Asct	2m5f Cls2 Ch gd-sft			£15,640
	11/16	Plum	2m1f Cls3 Nov Ch gd-sft			£6,498
	11/16	Wwck	2m Cls3 Nov Ch 4-5yo soft			£9,384
	2/16	Kels	2m2f Cls2 Hdl heavy			£16,245
	2/15	Hayd	1m7¹/₂f Cls2 Hdl 4yo soft			£9,747
	1/15	Asct	1m7¹/₂f Cls3 Hdl 4yo soft			£6,498
	12/14	Newb	2m1¹/₂f Cls3 Hdl 3yo gd-sft			£6,498
	4/14	Engh	2m¹/₂f Hdl 3yo v soft			£19,200
	3/14	Bord	2m1¹/₂f Hdl 3yo heavy			£8,400

Prolific winner when pitched in at the right level, making it six wins in a row below Grade 1 when winning last season's Peterborough Chase; below his best last term, though, struggling to see off a 100-1 runner-up that day before disappointing at Kempton behind Frodon.

Top Ville Ben (Ire)
8 b g Beneficial - Great Decision (Simply Great)

Philip Kirby   Harbour Rose Partnership

PLACINGS: 321PF8F/115F13/5313-   RPR **166+c**

Starts		1st	2nd	3rd	4th	Win & Pl
24		8	2	4	1	£105,236
154	12/19	Weth	3m Cls1 Gd3 132-155 Ch Hcap soft			£25,628
	3/19	Weth	3m Cls3 Nov Ch soft			£8,151
	12/18	Weth	3m Cls4 Nov Ch gd-sft			£5,059
	11/18	Hexm	3m Cls4 Nov Ch soft			£6,108
130	2/17	Hayd	2m7f Cls3 115-132 Hdl Hcap heavy			£6,498
	2/17	Towc	1m7¹/₂f Cls4 Nov Hdl heavy			£3,899
	1/17	Leic	1m7¹/₂f Cls4 Nov Hdl gd-sft			£5,198
	12/16	Ludl	1m6f Cls4 NHF 4-5yo gd-sft			£3,899

Impressive winner of last season's Rowland Meyrick Chase at Wetherby, making up for a luckless defeat in the Rehearsal Chase when headed close home; yet to run to form in five runs at a higher level, most recently finishing a distant third behind Santini in the Cotswold Chase.

Topofthegame (Ire)
8 ch g Flemensfirth - Derry Vale (Mister Lord)

Paul Nicholls   Chris Giles & Mr&mrs P K Barber

PLACINGS: 1/142/F412/2212/   RPR **167c**

Starts		1st	2nd	3rd	4th	Win & Pl
11		3	5	2		£240,041
	3/19	Chel	3m1¹/₂f Cls1 Nov Gd1 Ch soft			£98,473
142	2/18	Sand	2m7¹/₂f Cls1 Gd3 123-147 Hdl Hcap soft			£56,270
	12/16	Asct	2m5¹/₂f Cls3 Mdn Hdl gd-sft			£7,798

Was a work in progress for some time (novice chase campaign even aborted three seasons ago) but got it right when it mattered by winning the RSA Chase at Cheltenham in 2019; missed last season through injury but back on the Gold Cup trail.

Tornado Flyer (Ire)

7 b g Flemensfirth - Mucho Macabi (Exceed And Excel)

Willie Mullins (Ire)   T F P Partnership

PLACINGS: 131/1P/411P35-   RPR **155**c

Starts	1st	2nd	3rd	4th	Win & Pl
11	5		2	1	£119,462
	12/19	Navn	2m1f Nov Gd3 Ch soft £19,932
	11/19	Naas	2m3f Ch sft-hvy £7,720
	12/18	Punc	2m4f Mdn Hdl good £7,087
	4/18	Punc	2m¹/²f Gd1 NHF 4-7yo yield £52,212
	1/18	Fair	2m NHF 5-7yo soft £5,451

Grade 1 bumper winner who came up short at that level when sent novice chasing last season; suffering from a respiratory infection when pulled up in pursuit of a hat-trick at Naas but managed only third behind Faugheen and fifth behind Samcro after that.

Torpillo (Fr)

5 ch g Alanadi - Astherate (Balko)

Nigel Twiston-Davies   Simon Munir & Isaac Souede

PLACINGS: 1/1140/131450-   RPR **146+**c

Starts	1st	2nd	3rd	4th	Win & Pl
11	5	-	1	2	£61,891
	11/19	Wwck	2m Cls3 Nov Ch soft £12,606
137	10/19	Chep	2m Cls2 117-137 Hdl 4yo Hcap soft £12,996
	1/19	Sand	2m Cls3 Hdl 4yo soft £6,498
	12/18	Sand	2m Cls2 Hdl 3yo heavy £12,512
	4/18	Nanc	2m1f Hdl 3yo soft £8,496

Useful hurdler (rated 148 after winning at Chepstow first time out last season) and made a promising start to chasing career when winning well at Warwick; found out in stronger races subsequently (second time form has petered out later in the season).

Total Recall (Ire)

11 b g Westerner - Augest Weekend (Dr Massini)

Willie Mullins (Ire)   Slaneyville Syndicate

PLACINGS: 105/111FPP/23P/8631-   RPR **164+**c

Starts	1st	2nd	3rd	4th	Win & Pl
29	7	1	4	3	£330,054
149	1/20	Gowr	3m1f 134-152 Ch Hcap sft-hvy £50,000
125	2/18	Leop	3m 117-145 Hdl Hcap soft £39,159
147	12/17	Newb	3m2f Cls1 Gd3 139-165 Ch Hcap gd-sft £142,375
129	10/17	Limk	3m 128-145 Ch Hcap soft £50,427
	12/16	Navn	2m4f Nov Ch sft-hvy £7,235
123	3/16	Naas	2m3f 115-135 Hdl Hcap sft-hvy £11,305
	2/15	Punc	2m4f Mdn Hdl soft £6,419

Brilliantly coaxed back to form last season, winning the Thyestes Chase in January in impressive fashion; had endured a long barren spell since a fine campaign in 2017-18, winning the Ladbrokes Trophy and going well until falling three out in the Cheltenham Gold Cup.

Traffic Fluide (Fr)

10 b g Astarabad - Petale Rouge (Bonnet Rouge)

Gary Moore   Galloping On The South Downs Partnership

PLACINGS: 46632/4575011/21/F0-   RPR **162+**c

Starts	1st	2nd	3rd	4th	Win & Pl
26	6	4	3	3	£213,108
149	11/18	Asct	3m Cls1 Gd3 134-149 Ch Hcap good £56,950
140	4/18	Chel	2m5f Cls1 Gd2 135-160 Ch Hcap good £34,170
	4/18	Plum	2m4¹/²f Cls4 Nov Hdl heavy £5,003
135	3/15	Sand	1m7¹/²f Cls3 Nov 122-140 Ch Hcap good £6,498
129	2/15	Plum	2m1f Cls3 Nov 129-145 Ch Hcap gd-sft £7,988
	10/14	Stra	2m4f Ch 4yo heavy £8,800

Has run only twice since landing the Silver Cup at Ascot in late 2018 but still looked on an upward curve last season, very nearly overcoming his long layoff to win the Ascot Chase (fell at the last when looking a likely winner); now beaten on all eight runs at Grade 1 level.

Truckers Lodge (Ire)

8 b g Westerner - Galeacord (Accordion)

Paul Nicholls   Gordon & Su Hall

PLACINGS: 11/42/1441221/24121-   RPR **158+**c

Starts	1st	2nd	3rd	4th	Win & Pl
15	6	5	-	4	£158,752
141	3/20	Uttx	4m2f Cls1 List 131-157 Ch Hcap heavy £84,478
	10/19	Chep	2m7¹/²f Cls3 Ch gd-sft £7,018
	3/19	Extr	2m7f Cls4 Nov Hdl gd-sft £4,224
123	12/18	Chep	2m7¹/²f Cls3 110-129 Hdl Hcap heavy £6,758
	5/18	Sthl	2m4¹/²f Cls5 Mdn Hdl good £3,444
	4/17	Chep	2m Cls6 NHF 4-6yo good £1,949

Did extraordinarily well for one so inexperienced in top staying handicaps last season, easily winning the Midlands National in just his fifth chase having finished second in the Welsh National; raised 14lb for that win but has time on his side.

Two For Gold (Ire)

7 b g Gold Well - Two Of Each (Shernazar)

Kim Bailey   May We Never Be Found Out Partnership 2

PLACINGS: 161/4114/1112-   RPR **152+**c

Starts	1st	2nd	3rd	4th	Win & Pl
11	7	1	-	2	£66,272
	1/20	Wwck	3m Cls1 Nov Gd2 Ch soft £19,933
	12/19	Kels	2m7¹/²f Cls3 Nov Ch soft £12,116
132	11/19	Carl	2m4f Cls3 Nov 117-135 Ch Hcap soft £8,123
	1/19	Bang	2m7f Cls4 Nov Hdl gd-sft £4,094
	12/18	Weth	2m5¹/²f Cls4 Nov Hdl soft £4,224
	2/18	Donc	2m¹/²f Cls5 NHF 4-6yo gd-sft £2,599
	12/17	Sthl	1m7¹/²f Cls5 Am NHF 4-6yo good £2,599

Progressive novice chaser last season, winning his first three chases including a 3m Grade 2 at Warwick when outstaying some useful rivals; no match for Copperhead when second in the Reynoldstown; expected to stay further and could even be a Grand National horse.

Uhtred (Ire)

5 b g Fame And Glory - Ingred Hans (Beneficial)

Joseph O'Brien (Ire)   Gigginstown House Stud

PLACINGS: 1/21-					RPR **131+**h
Starts	1st	2nd	3rd	4th	Win & Pl
3	2	1	-	-	£70,007
12/19	Navn	2m List NHF 4-7yo soft			£14,617
4/19	Fair	2m NHF 4-5yo gd-yld			£53,153

Hugely impressive winner of a Listed bumper at Navan last season to maintain unbeaten record in that discipline; had previously run a fine race on hurdling debut when second behind subsequent Fred Winter favourite Front View; could be a top novice.

Us And Them (Ire)

7 b g Stowaway - Manorville (Flemensfirth)

Joseph O'Brien (Ire)   Burnham Plastering & Dry Lining

PLACINGS: 20/4122222/U37883-08					RPR **154**c
Starts	1st	2nd	3rd	4th	Win & Pl
22	3	7	3	2	£157,503
11/18	Navn	2m1f Ch good			£9,267
12/17	Punc	2m Nov Hdl heavy			£9,477
11/17	Cork	2m Mdn Hdl 4yo sft-hvy			£6,844

Badly out of sorts for much of last season but bounced back to form with a fine third in the Grand Annual at Cheltenham (well backed); had finished fourth in four Grade 1 novice chases in 2018-19, including the Racing Post Arkle; yet to prove he stays 2m4f (tried three times).

Vegas Blue (Ire)

5 b m Getaway - Bella Venezia (Milan)

Nicky Henderson   Crimbourne Bloodstock

PLACINGS: 115-1					RPR **120+**h
Starts	1st	2nd	3rd	4th	Win & Pl
4	3	-	-	-	£17,941
10/20	Hntg	2m3¹/₂f Cls4 Mdn Hdl good			£3,769
12/19	Hntg	2m Cls1 List NHF 4-6yo gd-sft			£11,390
5/19	Bang	2m1¹/₂f Cls5 NHF 4-6yo good			£2,274

Bitterly disappointing on only run over hurdles at Kempton last season (reportedly unsuited by soft ground) but had looked a potential star when winning both bumpers, including a Listed race at Huntingdon; should do well in mares' novice hurdles.

Verdana Blue (Ire)

8 b m Getaway - Blue Gallery (Bluebird)

Nicky Henderson   Mrs Doreen Tabor

PLACINGS: 1143/51300/114151/4-					RPR **146**h
Starts	1st	2nd	3rd	4th	Win & Pl
22	8	1	2	4	£274,840
154	4/19	Ayr	2m Cls1 Gd2 134-154 Hdl Hcap good		£59,798
	12/18	Kemp	2m Cls1 Gd1 Hdl gd-sft		£74,035
	11/18	Winc	1m7¹/₂f Cls1 Gd2 Hdl good		£34,170
	10/18	Asct	2m Cls1 List Hdl good		£22,780
136	11/17	Asct	1m7¹/₂f Cls2 117-137 Hdl Hcap gd-sft		£18,768
	2/17	Tntn	2m3f Cls4 Nov Hdl good		£6,330
	1/17	Hrfd	2m Cls4 Nov Hdl gd-sft		£3,379
	7/16	Klny	2m1f NHF 4-7yo good		£4,748

Developed into a top-class hurdler two seasons ago, memorably getting up to beat Buveur D'Air in the Christmas Hurdle at Kempton; fourth in that race on unsuitably soft ground on only run over hurdles last term but back on song on the Flat this summer.

Vinndication (Ire)

7 b g Vinnie Roe - Pawnee Trail (Taipan)

Kim Bailey   Moremoneythan

PLACINGS: 1111/1135/14-					RPR **165**c
Starts	1st	2nd	3rd	4th	Win & Pl
10	7	-	1	1	£134,198
151	11/19	Asct	3m Cls1 Gd3 137-163 Ch Hcap gd-sft	£56,950
	12/18	Asct	2m5f Cls1 Nov Gd2 Ch soft	£19,933
	11/18	Carl	2m4f Cls3 Nov Ch soft	£7,473
	2/18	Hntg	2m3¹/₂f Cls1 Nov List Hdl soft	£17,085
	1/18	Asct	2m5¹/₂f Cls3 Nov Hdl 4-7yo soft	£6,758
	12/17	Leic	2m4¹/₂f Cls3 Nov Hdl soft	£6,498
	11/17	Ludl	2m Cls4 NHF 4-6yo good	£3,249

Produced a tremendous performance to win the Sodexo Gold Cup at Ascot first time out last season; fine fourth in the Ultima at Cheltenham on only subsequent run; had been felt to need a right-handed track earlier in his career and could still be better going that way around.

Vintage Clouds (Ire)

10 gr g Cloudings - Rare Vintage (Germany)

Sue Smith   Trevor Hemmings

PLACINGS: 124233/1P2F6/5P3158-					RPR **159+**c
Starts	1st	2nd	3rd	4th	Win & Pl
34	5	11	5	1	£213,882
143	1/20	Hayd	3m1¹/₂f Cls1 Gd2 136-156 Ch Hcap heavy	£42,713
143	11/18	Hayd	3m1¹/₂f Cls2 130-144 Ch Hcap good	£31,714
132	10/17	Aint	3m1f Cls3 Nov 120-133 Ch Hcap gd-sft	£9,097
	11/15	Hayd	2m3f Cls3 Nov Hdl 4-7yo soft	£6,498
	1/15	Weth	2m Cls6 NHF 4-6yo soft	£1,643

Consistent staying chaser who landed his biggest victory in last season's Peter Marsh Chase at Haydock having been placed in a string of top handicaps in recent years; raised 11lb and starts the season still 6lb above highest winning mark even after two subsequent flops.

Vision Des Flos (Fr)

7 b g Balko - Marie Royale (Turgeon)

Colin Tizzard   Ann & Alan Potts Limited

PLACINGS: 622/U2352310/635160-					RPR **146+**c
Starts	1st	2nd	3rd	4th	Win & Pl
22	4	5	4	1	£209,921
	1/20	Chep	2m7¹/₂f Cls3 Nov Ch heavy	£7,018
	2/19	Font	2m3f Cls1 Gd2 Hdl gd-sft	£45,560
	2/18	Extr	2m1f Cls1 Nov List Hdl heavy	£14,238
	4/17	Punc	2m NHF 4-5yo gd-yld	£50,427

Very smart hurdler (placed twice at Grade 1 level as a novice in 2018 and won a Grade 2 the following year) but failed to match that level over fences last season; won only a two-runner race at Chepstow and well beaten on all three runs in more competitive races.

Waiting Patiently (Ire)
9 b g Flemensfirth - Rossavon (Beneficial)

Ruth Jefferson   Richard Collins

PLACINGS: 221/111/111/U23-3-   RPR **169+**c

Starts		1st	2nd	3rd	4th	Win & Pl
13		7	3	2	-	£238,079
	2/18	Asct	2m5f Cls1 Gd1 Ch soft			£85,827
	1/18	Kemp	2m4¹/₂f Cls1 List Ch gd-sft			£22,780
	11/17	Carl	2m4f Cls1 List Ch gd-sft			£17,085
	1/17	Hayd	2m4f Cls1 Nov Gd2 Ch soft			£18,546
	12/16	Newc	2m¹/₂f Cls3 Nov Ch soft			£6,498
123	11/16	Sedg	2m¹/₂f Cls3 Nov 115-130 Ch Hcap soft			£6,498
	1/16	Sedg	2m4f Cls4 Nov Hdl gd-sft			£3,798

Talented but fragile chaser who has raced just four times since winning the Ascot Chase in 2018; disappointed the following season but bounced back with a tremendous staying-on third in last season's Tingle Creek only to miss the rest of the campaign through injury.

Walk In The Mill (Fr)
10 b g Walk In The Park - Libre Amour (Lost World)

Robert Walford   Baroness Harding

PLACINGS: 1197/513P/31334/P12-   RPR **154+**c

Starts		1st	2nd	3rd	4th	Win & Pl
27		6	5	6	1	£307,416
141	12/19	Aint	3m2f Cls1 Gd3 133-159 Ch Hcap soft			£84,195
137	12/18	Aint	3m2f Cls1 Gd3 134-160 Ch Hcap soft			£84,195
131	11/17	Asct	3m Cls3 122-135 Ch Hcap gd-sft			£16,245
126	1/17	Winc	2m4f Cls2 126-144 Ch Hcap soft			£12,558
121	11/16	Extr	2m3f Cls3 111-123 Ch Hcap soft			£9,583
	4/15	Fntb	2m3f Ch v soft			£8,558

Aintree specialist who has won the last two runnings of the Becher Chase; finished fourth in the 2019 Grand National in between and looked to have improved again when landing last season's Becher from subsequent big-race winner Kimberlite Candy; National surely the aim again.

Weakfield (Ire)
7 b g Court Cave - Thats The Lot (Flemensfirth)

Brian Ellison   Phil & Julie Martin

PLACINGS: 1/6441/1-   RPR **135**c

Starts		1st	2nd	3rd	4th	Win & Pl
5		2	-	-	2	£12,256
120	10/19	Hexm	2m4f Cls4 Nov 94-122 Ch Hcap soft			£6,433
109	1/19	MRas	2m7f Cls4 102-116 Hdl Hcap good			£5,198

Missed nearly all of last season but had announced himself as a smart prospect over fences when hacking up by 12 lengths on chasing debut at Hexham; had also been progressive over hurdles, making a successful handicap debut on final run in January 2019.

Welsh Saint (Fr)
6 b g Saint Des Saints - Minirose (Mansonnien)

Nicky Henderson   Walters Plant Hire & Potter Group

PLACINGS: 421/F21310-   RPR **139+**h

Starts		1st	2nd	3rd	4th	Win & Pl
9		3	2	1	1	£25,596
134	2/20	Hayd	3m¹/₂f Cls2 128-153 Hdl Hcap heavy			£12,996
	12/19	Wwck	2m5f Cls4 Mdn Hdl heavy			£4,660
	3/19	Wwck	2m Cls5 Mdn NHF 4-6yo good			£2,599

Useful novice hurdler last season despite disappointing when 6-1 for the Pertemps Final at Cheltenham; had won a qualifier at Haydock on handicap debut after finishing third in a good Listed novice at Cheltenham; both hurdles wins on heavy ground but won a bumper on good.

West Approach
10 b g Westerner - Ardstown (Ardross)

Colin Tizzard   John And Heather Snook

PLACINGS: 6P/3P522966/21U3P4P-   RPR **156**c

Starts		1st	2nd	3rd	4th	Win & Pl
37		5	5	7	2	£175,031
142	11/19	Chel	3m3¹/₂f Cls1 Gd3 132-153 Ch Hcap soft			£33,828
	12/17	Extr	2m3f Cls2 Nov Ch soft			£16,025
	10/17	Ffos	2m5f Cls3 Ch soft			£9,097
	5/16	NAbb	2m1f Cls2 Nov Hdl good			£9,495
	1/15	Newb	2m¹/₂f Cls5 NHF 4-6yo heavy			£2,053

Smart staying hurdler who has hinted at greater potential over fences but struggled to put together any consistency; hacked up in a handicap chase at Cheltenham last term but departed early when favourite for the Ladbrokes Trophy; out of form when switched back to hurdles.

Whatmore
8 b g Schiaparelli - Polymiss (Poliglote)

Henry Daly   Strachan, Lewis, Gabb, Graham & Inkin

PLACINGS: 114681/31772/134344-   RPR **144+**c

Starts		1st	2nd	3rd	4th	Win & Pl
21		5	2	3	5	£57,312
	5/19	MRas	2m5¹/₂f Cls4 Nov Ch good			£4,952
135	11/18	Bang	2m3¹/₂f Cls2 121-144 Hdl Hcap gd-sft			£14,076
	3/18	Wwck	2m Cls4 Nov Hdl soft			£4,419
	10/17	Bang	2m¹/₂f Cls4 Nov Hdl good			£3,249
	5/17	Aint	2m1f Cls4 Nov Hdl good			£3,899

Developed into a useful novice chaser last season despite failing to add to debut win at Market Rasen; ran well in two top handicaps, notably a close fourth behind Mister Malarky at Kempton before filling the same spot in the novice handicap at the Cheltenham Festival.

Follow us
@RacingPost

Who Dares Wins (Ire)

8 b g Jeremy - Savignano (Polish Precedent)

Alan King   Hp Racing Who Dares Wins

PLACINGS: 140/4U1033/353/2210-   RPR **153**c

Starts		1st	2nd	3rd	4th	Win & Pl
17		4	2	4	2	£97,963
	2/20	Kemp	2m4¹/₂f Cls1 Nov Gd2 Ch gd-sft			£18,310
140	11/16	Newb	2m¹/₂f Cls1 List 120-140 Hdl Hcap gd-sft			£25,628
	12/15	Donc	2m¹/₂f Cls1 Gd2 Hdl 3yo heavy			£17,165
	11/15	Ludl	2m Cls4 Hdl 3yo gd-sft			£3,899

Wonderfully versatile horse who had shown smart form on the Flat and over hurdles before turning his hand to fences last season, winning a Grade 2 novice chase at Kempton; well fancied on handicap chase debut at Cheltenham but might have found 3m too far.

Windsor Avenue (Ire)

8 b g Winged Love - Zaffarella (Zaffaran)

Brian Ellison   Phil & Julie Martin

PLACINGS: P/111/21412/112F-   RPR **153+**c

Starts		1st	2nd	3rd	4th	Win & Pl
11		6	3	-	1	£48,548
	11/19	Carl	2m4f Cls3 Nov Ch soft			£7,473
	10/19	Sedg	2m3¹/₂f Cls4 Ch soft			£4,614
	1/19	Sedg	2m4f Cls4 Nov Hdl 4-7yo gd-sft			£4,094
	11/18	Hexm	2m4f Cls4 Mdn Hdl good			£4,094
	2/18	Carl	2m1f Cls5 NHF 4-6yo heavy			£2,599
	1/18	Sedg	2m1f Cls5 NHF 4-6yo soft			£2,274

Held in very high regard at home and justified connections' faith last season with wide-margin wins on first two runs over fences; scoped dirty after a thumping defeat by Sam Spinner next time and still in contention when falling two out in a Grade 2 behind Sam Brown on final run.

Form figures in this season's key horses include runs up to October 18, 2020

Yala Enki (Fr)

10 b/br g Nickname - Cadiane (Cadoudal)

Paul Nicholls   Hills Of Ledbury

PLACINGS: /P364F166/1357/0313-   RPR **164**c

Starts		1st	2nd	3rd	4th	Win & Pl
40		10	5	7	5	£342,083
	1/20	Tntn	3m4¹/₂f Cls2 Ch heavy			£31,714
150	11/18	Bang	3m Cls2 126-150 Ch Hcap gd-sft			£16,266
146	2/18	Hayd	3m4¹/₂f Cls1 Gd3 138-161 Ch Hcap heavy			£60,067
146	3/17	Kels	3m2f Cls2 125-147 Ch Hcap heavy			£17,545
139	12/16	Hayd	2m7f Cls2 120-139 Ch Hcap soft			£15,640
	2/16	Asct	2m3¹/₂f Cls2 Nov Hdl soft			£15,640
130	1/16	Kemp	2m5f Cls1 List 127-153 Hdl Hcap soft			£22,780
	11/15	Extr	2m5¹/₂f Cls3 Nov Hdl gd-sft			£5,523
	2/14	Fntb	2m2f Ch 4yo v soft			£9,600
	10/13	Pari	2m1f Ch 3yo gd-sft			£7,415

Very smart handicap chaser who has run well in a string of gruelling tests of stamina in recent seasons; gained his biggest win in the Grand National Trial at Haydock in 2018 and has since finished third in the last two editions of the Welsh Grand National.

Younevercall (Ire)

9 b g Yeats - Afarka (Kahyasi)

Kim Bailey   Youneverknow Partnership

PLACINGS: 31/1F61/17/2181/   RPR **158**h

Starts		1st	2nd	3rd	4th	Win & Pl
12		6	1	1	-	£66,577
	4/19	Sand	2m5¹/₂f Cls1 Gd2 Hdl good			£31,323
144	11/18	Kemp	2m5f Cls2 122-145 Hdl Hcap good			£11,886
135	11/16	Kemp	2m5f Cls2 128-135 Hdl Hcap good			£11,886
	4/16	Hntg	2m4¹/₂f Cls4 Nov Hdl gd-sft			£3,899
	10/15	Uttx	2m Cls5 Mdn Hdl good			£2,599
	4/15	Sthl	1m7¹/₂f Cls6 NHF 4-6yo good			£1,949

Fragile gelding who has been very lightly raced through injury but has won five of last eight races over jumps going back to 2016; stepped up again when winning a Grade 2 at Sandown on last run over hurdles in April 2019; could go novice chasing.

KEY HORSES LISTED BY TRAINER

Nick Alexander
Elvis Mail (Fr)
Lake View Lad (Ire)

Caroline Bailey
Boldmere

Kim Bailey
First Flow (Ire)
Imperial Aura (Ire)
Newtide (Ire)
Two For Gold (Ire)
Vinndication (Ire)
Younevercall (Ire)

Martin Brassil
City Island (Ire)
Longhouse Poet (Ire)

David Bridgwater
The Conditional (Ire)

Mick Channon
Hold The Note (Ire)
Mister Whitaker (Ire)

David Cottin
Easysland (Fr)

Gavin Cromwell
Alfa Mix
Darver Star (Ire)

Sean Curran
Domaine De L'Isle (Fr)

Rebecca Curtis
Lisnagar Oscar (Ire)

Henry Daly
Stoney Mountain (Ire)
Whatmore

Henry de Bromhead
A Plus Tard (Fr)
Aspire Tower (Ire)
Captain Guinness (Ire)
Chris's Dream (Ire)
Cobbler's Way (Ire)
Honeysuckle
Jason The Militant (Ire)
Minella Indo (Ire)
Minella Melody (Ire)
Monalee (Ire)
Moon Over Germany (Ire)
Notebook (Ger)
Ornua (Ire)
Petit Mouchoir (Fr)
Poker Party (Fr)
Put The Kettle On (Ire)

Stuart Edmunds
1275 Now McGinty (Ire)

Gordon Elliott
Abacadabras (Fr)
1010 Andy Dufresne (Ire)
Aramax (Ger)
Battleoverdoyen (Ire)
Black Tears
Chosen Mate (Ire)
Column Of Fire (Ire)
Commander Of Fleet (Ire)
Cracking Smart (Ire)
Dallas Des Pictons (Fr)
Daylight Katie (Ire)
Defi Bleu (Fr)
Delta Work (Fr)

Easywork (Fr)
Eclair De Beaufeu (Fr)
Envoi Allen (Fr)
Farclas (Fr)
Fury Road (Ire)
Galvin (Ire)
Glenloe (Ire)
Hardline (Ire)
Malone Road (Ire)
Milan Native (Ire)
Presenting Percy
Queens Brook (Ire)
Ravenhill (Ire)
Samcro (Ire)
Sire Du Berlais (Fr)
The Very Man (Ire)
Tiger Roll (Ire)

Brian Ellison
Definitly Red (Ire)
Forest Bihan (Fr)
Sam's Adventure
The King Of May (Fr)
Weakfield (Ire)
Windsor Avenue (Ire)

Pat Fahy
Castlegrace Paddy (Ire)

Harry Fry
Captain Drake (Ire)
Get In The Queue
If The Cap Fits (Ire)
King Roland (Ire)
Lightly Squeeze
Phoenix Way (Ire)

Tom George
Black Op (Ire)
Bun Doran (Ire)
Clondaw Castle (Ire)
Springfield Fox
Summerville Boy (Ire)
The Worlds End (Ire)

Nick Gifford
Glen Rocco

Chris Gordon
Baddesley Knight (Ire)
Commanche Red (Ire)
Highway One O Two (Ire)
On The Slopes

Warren Greatrex
Bob Mahler (Ire)
Emitom (Ire)
Keeper Hill (Ire)

Tom Gretton
Kauto Riko (Fr)

Debra Hamer
Tobefair

Micky Hammond
Cornerstone Lad

Jessica Harrington
Magic Of Light (Ire)
Sizing Pottsie (Fr)
Supasundae

Eddie Harty
Kilfenora (Ire)

Nicky Henderson
Allart (Ire)

Altior (Ire)
Apple's Shakira (Fr)
Beware The Bear (Ire)
Birchdale (Ire)
Burrows Edge (Fr)
Buveur D'Air (Fr)
Buzz (Fr)
Call Me Lord (Fr)
Caribean Boy (Fr)
Champ (Fr)
Champagne Platinum (Ire)
Chantry House (Ire)
Claimantakinforgan (Fr)
Dame De Compagnie (Fr)
Dickie Diver (Ire)
Dragon D'Estruval (Fr)
Epatante (Fr)
Fred (Fr)
Fusil Raffles (Fr)
Janika (Fr)
L'Ami Serge (Ire)
Marie's Rock (Ire)
Mister Fisher (Ire)
Monte Cristo (Fr)
Ok Corral (Ire)
On The Blind Side (Ire)
Palladium
Precious Cargo (Ire)
Pym (Ire)
Rathhill (Ire)
Santini
Shishkin (Ire)
Terrefort (Fr)
Top Notch (Fr)
Vegas Blue (Ire)
Verdana Blue (Ire)
Welsh Saint (Fr)

Philip Hobbs
Defi Du Seuil (Fr)
Gumball (Fr)
Jatiluwih (Fr)
Jerrysback (Ire)
Kalooki (Ger)
Musical Slave (Ire)
Pileon (Ire)
Sporting John (Ire)
Thyme Hill
Tidal Flow

Richard Hobson
Lord Du Mesnil (Fr)

Anthony Honeyball
Sam Brown

Ruth Jefferson
Clondaw Caitlin (Ire)
Waiting Patiently (Ire)

Alan King
Blacko (Fr)
Deyrann De Carjac (Fr)
Edwardstone
Harambe
Lisp (Fr)
Sceau Royal (Fr)
The Glancing Queen (Ire)
Who Dares Wins (Ire)

Philip Kirby
Top Ville Ben (Ire)

Tom Lacey
Kimberlite Candy (Ire)
Sebastopol (Ire)

Emma Lavelle
De Rasher Counter
Paisley Park (Ire)

Kerry Lee
Happy Diva (Ire)

Donald McCain
Cloudy Dream (Ire)
Navajo Pass

Dermot McLoughlin
Captain Cj (Ire)

Ronan McNally
The Jam Man (Ire)

Graeme McPherson
Ask Ben (Ire)

Noel Meade
Beacon Edge (Ire)
Road To Respect (Ire)

Gary Moore
Baron Alco (Fr)
Botox Has (Fr)
Goshen (Fr)
Traffic Fluide (Fr)

Mouse Morris
Sams Profile

Hughie Morrison
Not So Sleepy
Third Wind

Emmet Mullins
Fujimoto Flyer (Jpn)

Willie Mullins
Acapella Bourgeois (Fr)
Al Boum Photo (Fr)
Allaho (Fr)
Annamix (Fr)
Appreciate It (Ire)
Asterion Forlonge (Fr)
Bacardys (Fr)
Bachasson (Fr)
Bapaume (Fr)
Benie Des Dieux (Fr)
Blackbow (Ire)
Blue Sari (Fr)
Breaken (Fr)
Burning Victory (Fr)
Burrows Saint (Fr)
Cabaret Queen
Cadmium (Fr)
Carefully Selected (Ire)
Cash Back (Fr)
Castlebawn West (Fr)
Chacun Pour Soi (Fr)
Ciel De Neige (Fr)
Cilaos Emery (Fr)
Concertista (Fr)
Dolcita (Fr)
Douvan (Fr)
Duc Des Genievres (Fr)
Easy Game (Fr)
Eglantine Du Seuil (Fr)
Elfile (Fr)
Elimay (Fr)
Elixir D'Ainay (Fr)

Faugheen (Ire)
Ferny Hollow (Ire)
Five O'Clock (Fr)
Francin (Fr)
Getabird (Ire)
Janidil (Fr)
Jon Snow (Fr)
Kemboy (Fr)
Klassical Dream (Fr)
Lord Royal (Fr)
Melon
Min (Fr)
Monkfish (Ire)
Robin De Carlow
Royal Rendezvous (Ire)
Saint Roi (Fr)
Saldier (Fr)
Salsaretta (Fr)
Sharjah (Fr)
The Big Getaway (Ire)
Tornado Flyer (Ire)
Total Recall (Ire)

Amy Murphy
Kalashnikov (Ire)

Colm Murphy
Relegate (Fr)

Olly Murphy
Brewin'upastorm (Ire)
I K Brunel
Itchy Feet (Fr)
Notre Pari (Ire)
Skandiburg (Fr)
Thomas Darby (Ire)

Richard Newland
Caid Du Lin (Fr)
Le Patriote (Fr)

Paul Nicholls
Ask For Glory (Ire)
Black Corton (Fr)
Brelan D'As (Fr)
Capeland (Fr)
Cat Tiger (Fr)
Christopher Wood (Ire)
Clan Des Obeaux (Fr)
Cyrname (Fr)
Danny Kirwan (Ire)
Danny Whizzbang (Ire)
Diego Du Charmil (Fr)
Dolos (Fr)
Enrilo (Fr)
Frodon (Fr)
Getaway Trump (Ire)
Give Me A Copper (Ire)
Grand Sancy (Fr)
Greaneteen (Fr)
Laurina (Fr)
Magic Saint (Fr)
Master Tommytucker
McFabulous (Fr)
Mick Pastor (Fr)
Next Destination (Ire)
Pic D'Orhy (Fr)
Politologue (Fr)
Quel Destin (Fr)
Real Steel (Fr)
Red Risk (Fr)
Saint Sonnet (Fr)
Scaramanga (Ire)

203

KEY HORSES LISTED BY TRAINER

Secret Investor
Silver Forever (Ire)
Sir Psycho (Ire)
Solo (Fr)
Southfield Stone
Stormy Ireland (Fr)
Thyme White (Fr)
Topofthegame (Ire)
Truckers Lodge (Ire)
Yala Enki (Fr)

Paul Nolan
Discorama (Fr)
Fitzhenry (Ire)
Latest Exhibition (Ire)

Fergal O'Brien
Champagne Well (Ire)
Jarveys Plate (Ire)
Liosduin Bhearna (Ire)

Joseph O'Brien
A Wave Of The Sea (Ire)
Assemble
Band Of Outlaws (Ire)
Cerberus
Darasso (Fr)
Early Doors (Fr)
Embittered (Fr)
Eric Bloodaxe (Ire)
Fakir (Fr)
Fakir D'oudairies (Fr)
Front View (Fr)
Le Richebourg (Fr)
Sempo (Ire)

Speak Easy
Uhtred (Ire)
Us And Them (Ire)

Jedd O'Keeffe
Sam Spinner

Jonjo O'Neill
Annie Mc (Ire)

Eugene O'Sullivan
It Came To Pass (Ire)

Henry Oliver
Kilfilum Cross (Ire)

Ben Pauling
Bright Forecast (Ire)
Delire D'Estruval (Fr)
Global Citizen (Ire)
Kildisart (Ire)
Le Breuil (Fr)

David Pipe
Israel Champ (Ire)
Main Fact (USA)
Night Edition (Fr)
Panic Attack (Ire)
Ramses De Teillee (Fr)

Alastair Ralph
Billingsley (Ire)

Nicky Richards
Ribble Valley (Ire)

Jeremy Scott
Dashel Drasher

Oliver Sherwood
Tarada

Dan Skelton
Allmankind
Beakstown (Ire)
Bennys King (Ire)
Boss Man Fred (Ire)
Captain Chaos (Ire)
Ch'tibello (Fr)
Clondaw Anchor (Ire)
Interconnected
Knight In Dubai (Ire)
Nube Negra (Spa)
Oldgrangewood
Roksana (Ire)
Spiritofthegames (Ire)
Third Time Lucki (Ire)

Matthew Smith
Ronald Pump

Sue Smith
Midnight Shadow
Vintage Clouds (Ire)

Jamie Snowden
Hogan's Height (Ire)
Thebannerkingrebel (Ire)

Tom Symonds
Song For Someone (Ger)

Colin Tizzard
Christmas In April (Fr)
Copperhead
Eldorado Allen (Fr)

Elegant Escape (Ire)
Elixir De Nutz (Fr)
Fiddlerontheroof (Ire)
Harry Senior (Ire)
Highest Sun (Fr)
Lostintranslation (Ire)
Master Debonair
Mister Malarky
Native River (Ire)
Reserve Tank (Ire)
Slate House (Ire)
The Big Breakaway (Ire)
Thistlecrack
Vision Des Flos (Fr)
West Approach

Nigel Twiston-Davies
Ballyandy
Ballyoptic (Ire)
Bristol De Mai (Fr)
Count Meribel
Crievehill (Ire)
Earlofthecotswolds (Fr)
Good Boy Bobby (Ire)
Redford Road
Riders Onthe Storm (Ire)
Stolen Silver (Fr)
Torpillo (Fr)

Robert Walford
Walk In The Mill (Fr)

Ted Walsh
Any Second Now (Ire)

Paul Webber
Indefatigable (Ire)

Harry Whittington
Rouge Vif (Fr)
Saint Calvados (Fr)
Simply The Betts (Ire)

Christian Williams
Limited Reserve (Ire)
Potters Corner (Ire)

Evan Williams
Esprit Du Large (Fr)
Mack The Man (Ire)
Silver Streak (Ire)

Mrs Jane Williams
Erick Le Rouge (Fr)
Monsieur Lecoq (Fr)

Nick Williams
Galahad Quest (Fr)
One For The Team
Siruh Du Lac (Fr)

Noel Williams
Another Crick

Venetia Williams
Aso (Fr)
Cepage (Fr)
Espoir De Guye (Fr)
Fanion D'Estruval (Fr)
Ibleo (Fr)

Kayley Woollacott
Lalor (Ger)

Splashing through the new water walk at Nicky Henderson's Seven Barrows stables

INDEX OF HORSES

RACING POST

INDEX OF HORSES

INDEX OF HORSES

INDEX OF HORSES